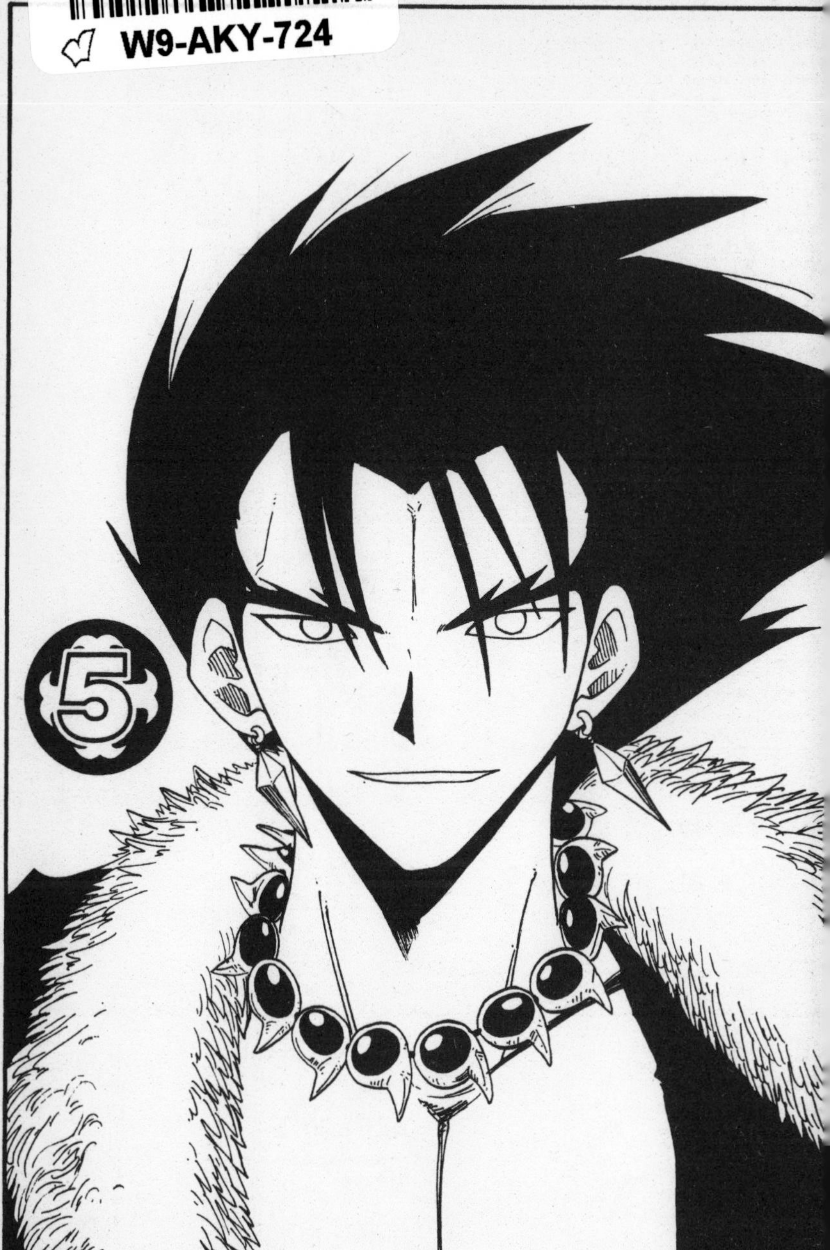
5

ALSO AVAILABLE FROM TOKYOPOP.

VOLUME 5

Story and Art by
HIRO MASHIMA

TOKYOPOP

Los Angeles · Tokyo · London

Translator - Amy Forsyth
English Adaptation - James Lucas Jones
Copy Editor - Tim Beedle
Retouch and Lettering - Marnie Echols
Cover Colors - Pauline Sim
Cover Layout - Raymond Makowski

Editor - Jake Forbes
Managing Editor - Jill Freshney
Production Coordinator - Antonio DePietro
Production Manager - Jennifer Miller
Art Director - Matt Alford
Editorial Director - Jeremy Ross
VP of Production - Ron Klamert
President & C.O.O. - John Parker
Publisher & C.E.O. - Stuart Levy

Email: editor@TOKYOPOP.com
Come visit us online at www.TOKYOPOP.com

A  Manga

TOKYOPOP Inc.
5900 Wilshire Blvd. Suite 2000
Los Angeles, CA 90036

ISBN: 1-59182-212-2

First TOKYOPOP® printing: October 2003

10 9 8 7 6 5

CONTENTS

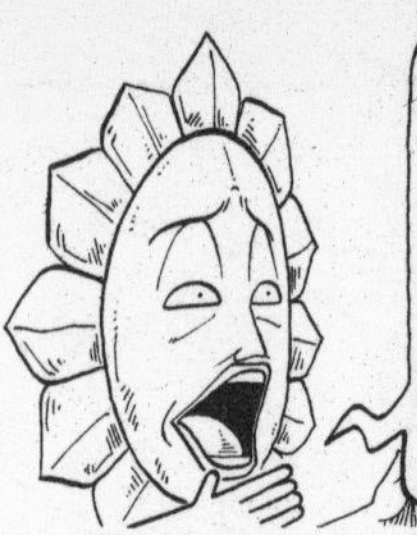

The Story So Far...

HARU GLORY is the RAVE MASTER, the only one capable of wielding RAVE and stopping the evil society DEMON CARD. His Guide is PLUE, a strange creature who can track down the four missing Raves. They are joined by ELIE, a girl in search of her memories. Our heroes have traveled to Tremolo Mountain in search of one of the missing Raves. Deep inside the caverns of Akumu Hall they are attacked by the Demon Card assassin, Dr. Schneider, but are saved when MUSICA comes to their aid. At the heart of the mountain they find DEERHOUND, guardian of the Rave of Knowledge. But as soon as he hands the Rave to Haru, evil strikes again...

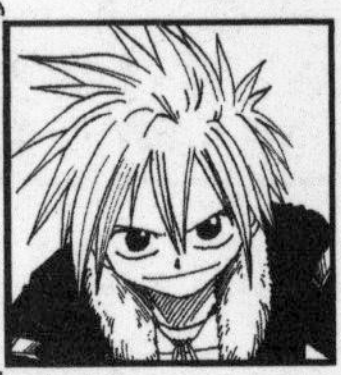

HARU GLORY: The Rave Master. Haru is the heir to Rave, the only one capable of wielding it and destroying Dark Bring. Impulsive and headstrong, he's not afraid to put himself in danger to do what is right. His father disappeared in search of Rave when he was very young.

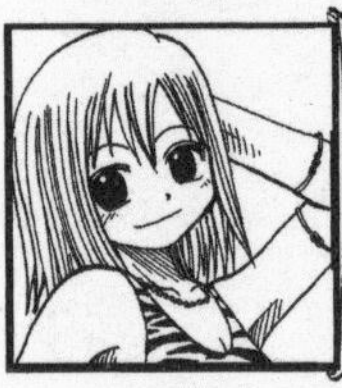

ELIE: A Girl with no past. Elie travels the world in search of the key to her forgotten memories. Outwardly cheerful, she hides a great sadness from her past. She's hot-headed, so when she pulls out her explosive Tonfa Blasters, bad guys watch out!

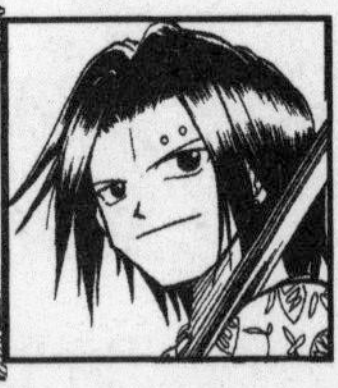

MUSICA: Leader of the Silver Rhythm Gang. An orphan whose family was slaughtered when he was a baby, Musica became a street-fighting petty thief, but he has a good heart.

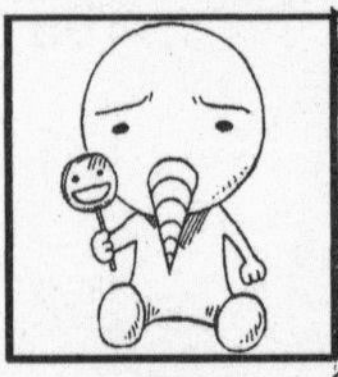

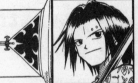

PLUE: The Rave Bearer. Plue is supposed to be Haru's guide in finding the Rave Stones, but so far he's just gotten him in and out of trouble. No one knows exactly what Plue is, but he seems to have healing abilities and is smarter than your average...whatever he is.

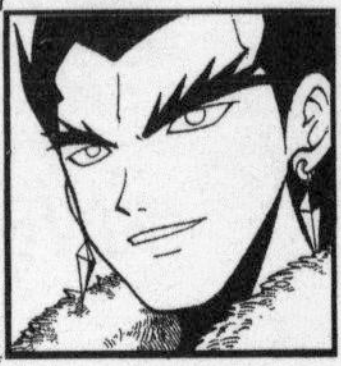

SHUDA: One of Demon Card's top-ranking officers, Shuda led the attack on Garage Island that destroyed Haru's home. He now leads the excavation at Tremolo Mountain. He sent the assassin Dr. Schneider to take out Haru and company.

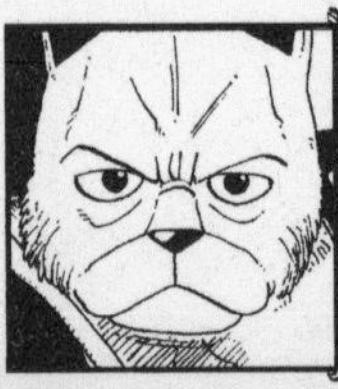

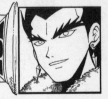

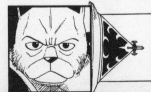

DEERHOUND: One of the Knights of the Blue Sky who fought beside the former Rave Master, Shiba, 50 years ago. He died, but his spirit was reborn in the body of a bear. He now guards the Rave of Knowledge within Tremolo mountain.

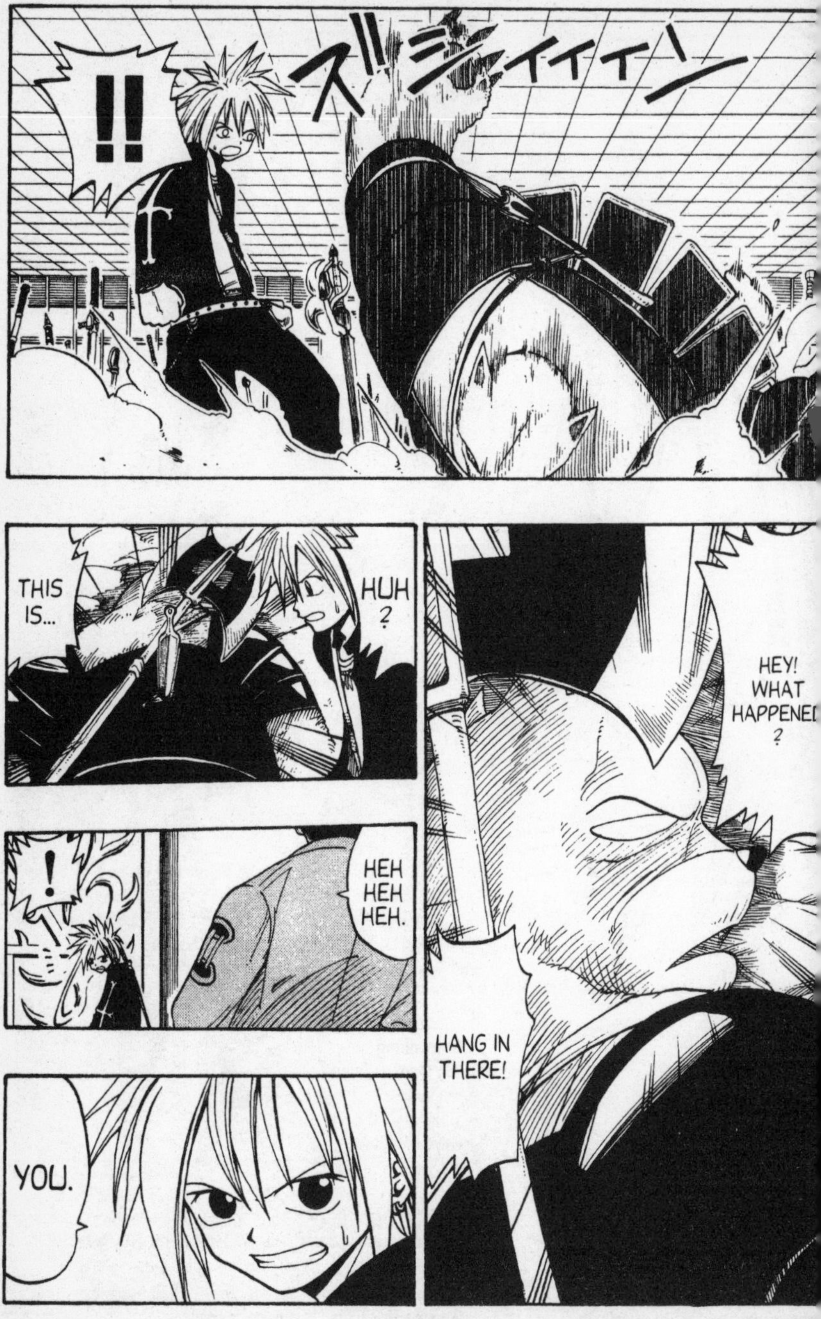

!!
HEY! WHAT HAPPENE ?
HANG IN THERE!
HUH ?
THIS IS...
!
HEH HEH HEH.
YOU.

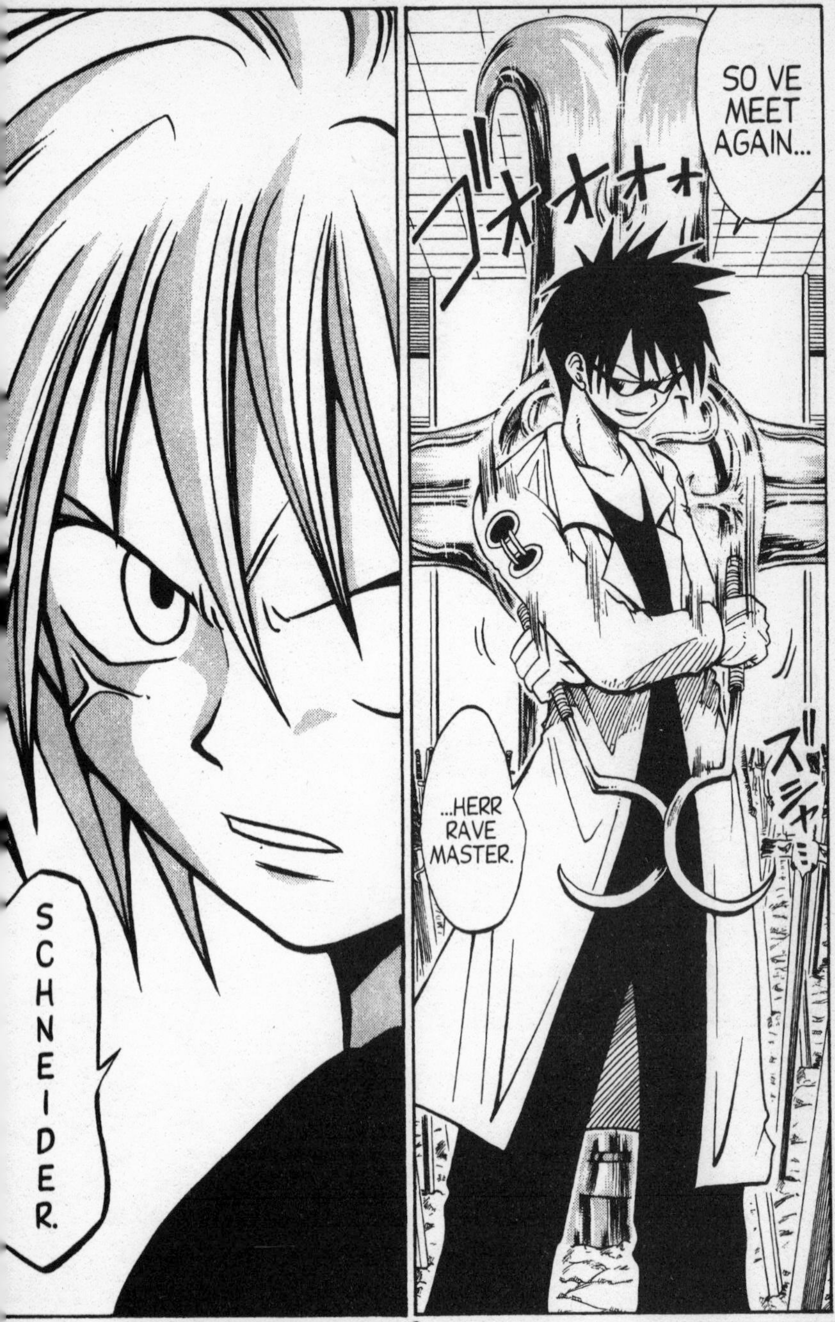
SO VE MEET AGAIN...
...HERR RAVE MASTER.
SCHNEIDER.

RAVE MASTER™

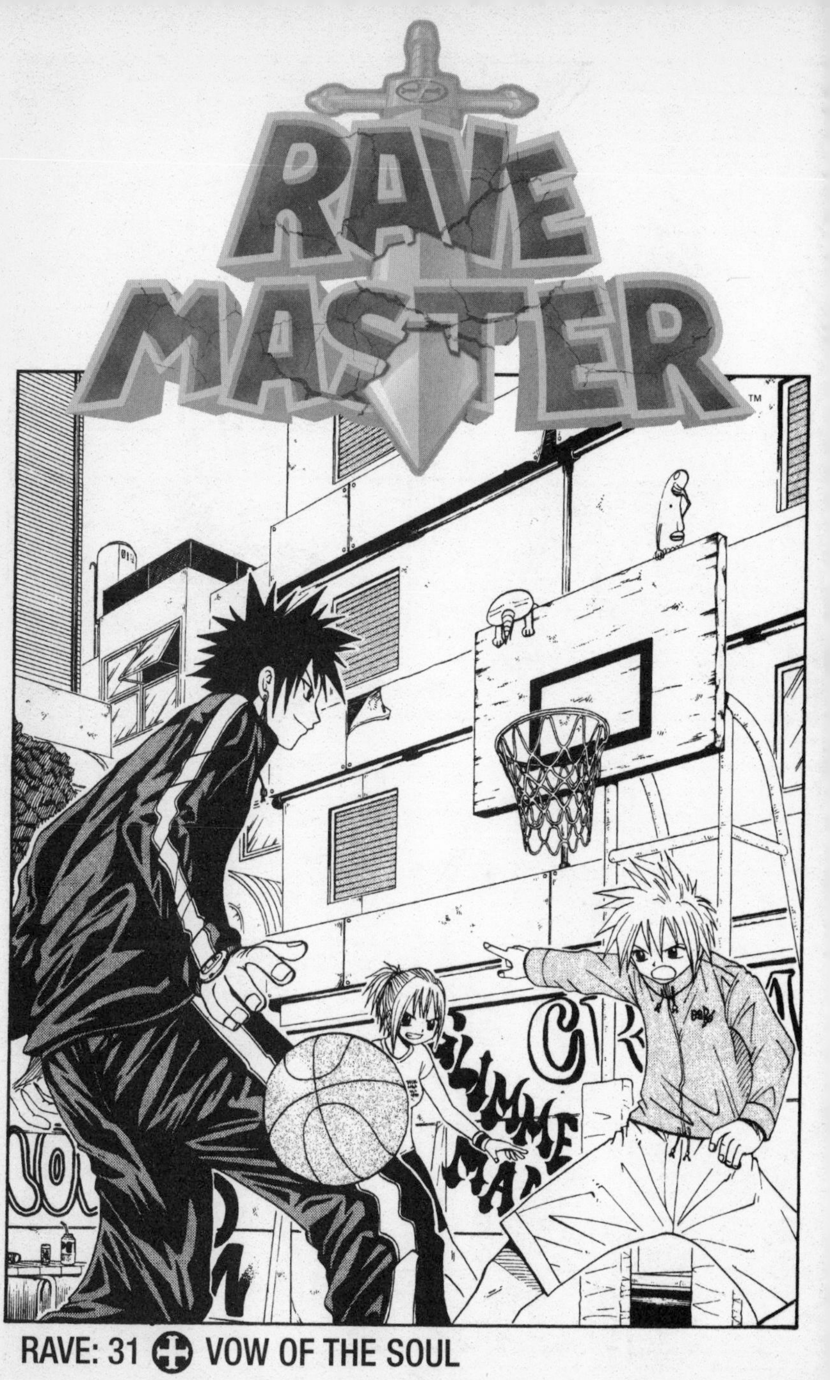

RAVE: 31 ✣ VOW OF THE SOUL

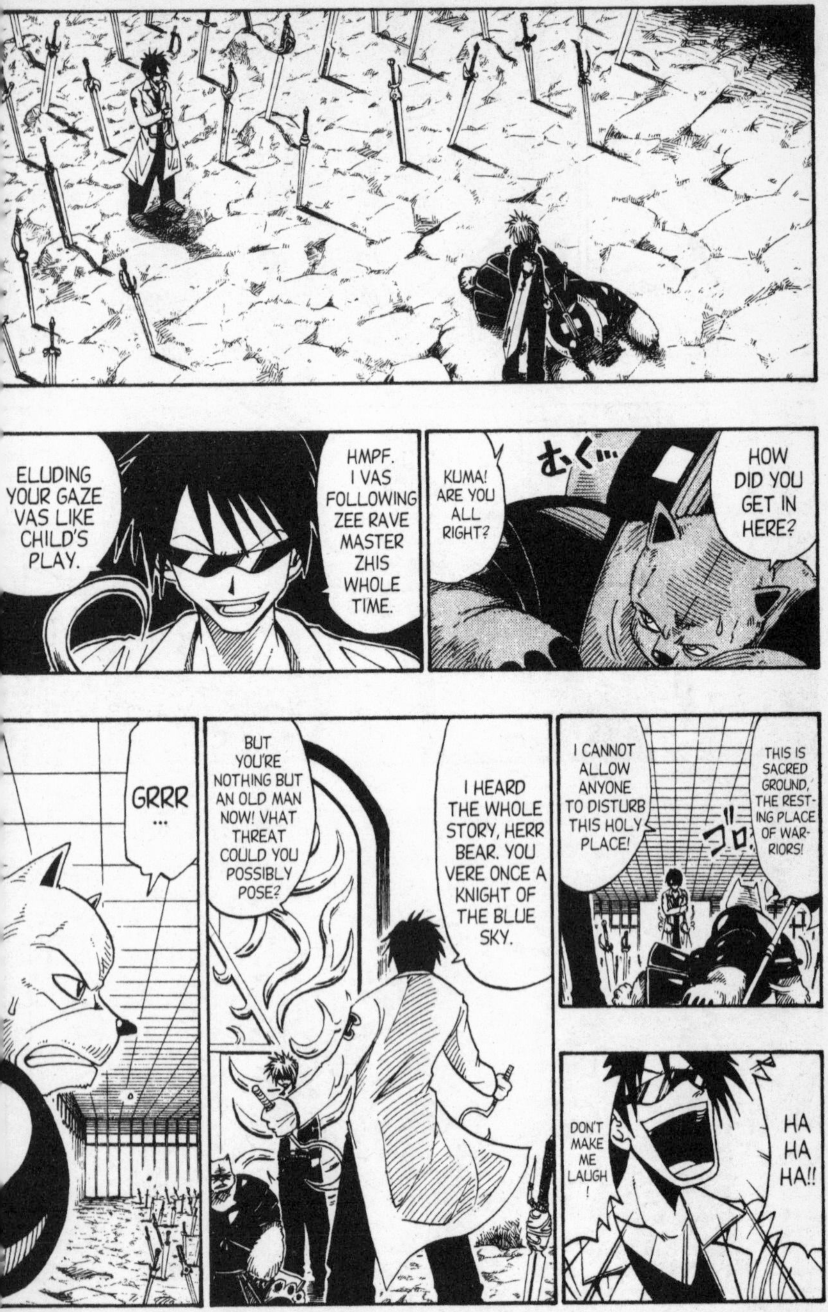
HOW DID YOU GET IN HERE?
KUMA! ARE YOU ALL RIGHT?
むくッ
HMPF. I VAS FOLLOWING ZEE RAVE MASTER ZHIS WHOLE TIME.
ELUDING YOUR GAZE VAS LIKE CHILD'S PLAY.
THIS IS SACRED GROUND, THE RESTING PLACE OF WARRIORS!
ゴロ
I CANNOT ALLOW ANYONE TO DISTURB THIS HOLY PLACE!
HA HA HA!!
DON'T MAKE ME LAUGH!
I HEARD THE WHOLE STORY, HERR BEAR. YOU VERE ONCE A KNIGHT OF THE BLUE SKY.
BUT YOU'RE NOTHING BUT AN OLD MAN NOW! VHAT THREAT COULD YOU POSSIBLY POSE?
GRRR ...

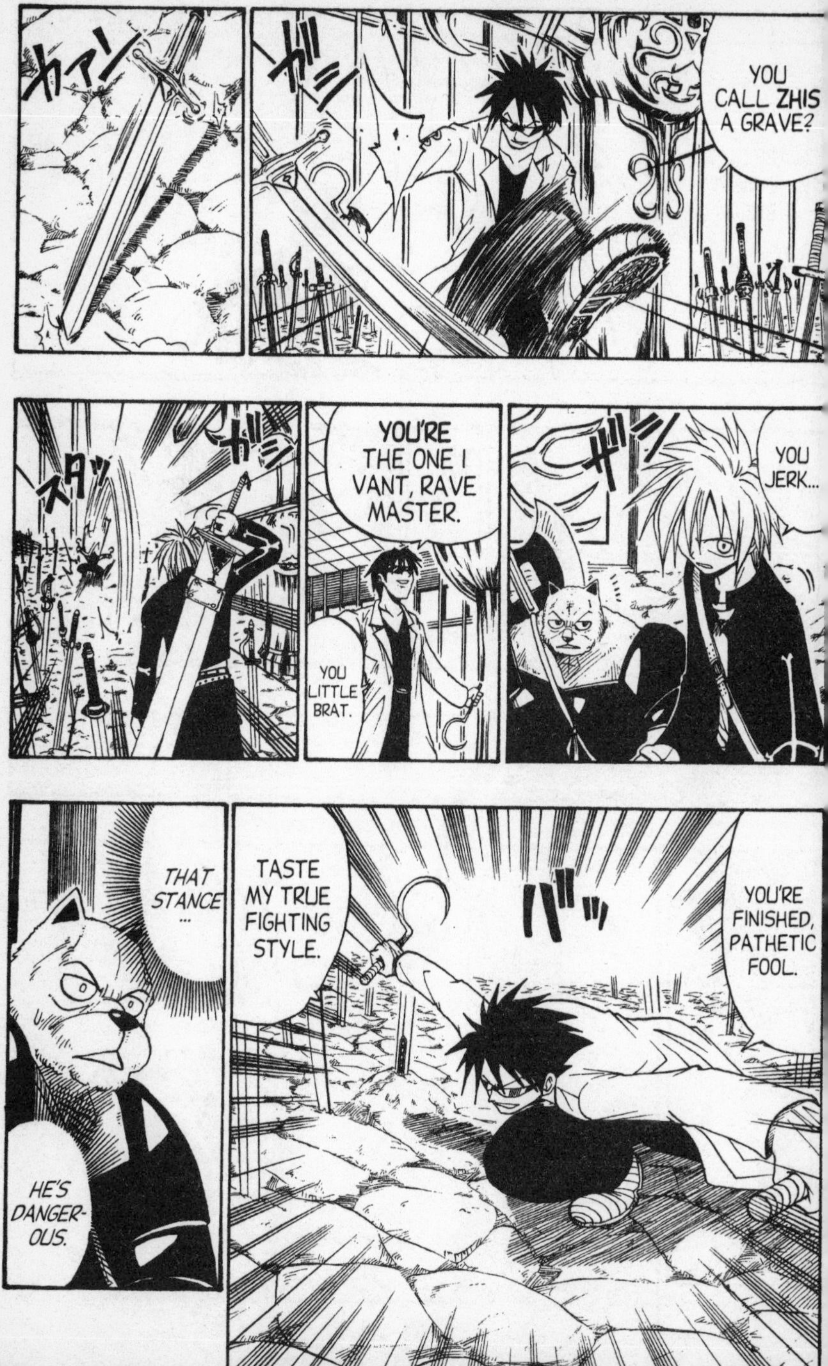
YOU CALL ZHIS A GRAVE?
YOU JERK...
YOU'RE THE ONE I VANT, RAVE MASTER.
YOU LITTLE BRAT.
YOU'RE FINISHED, PATHETIC FOOL.
TASTE MY TRUE FIGHTING STYLE.
THAT STANCE ...
HE'S DANGER-OUS.

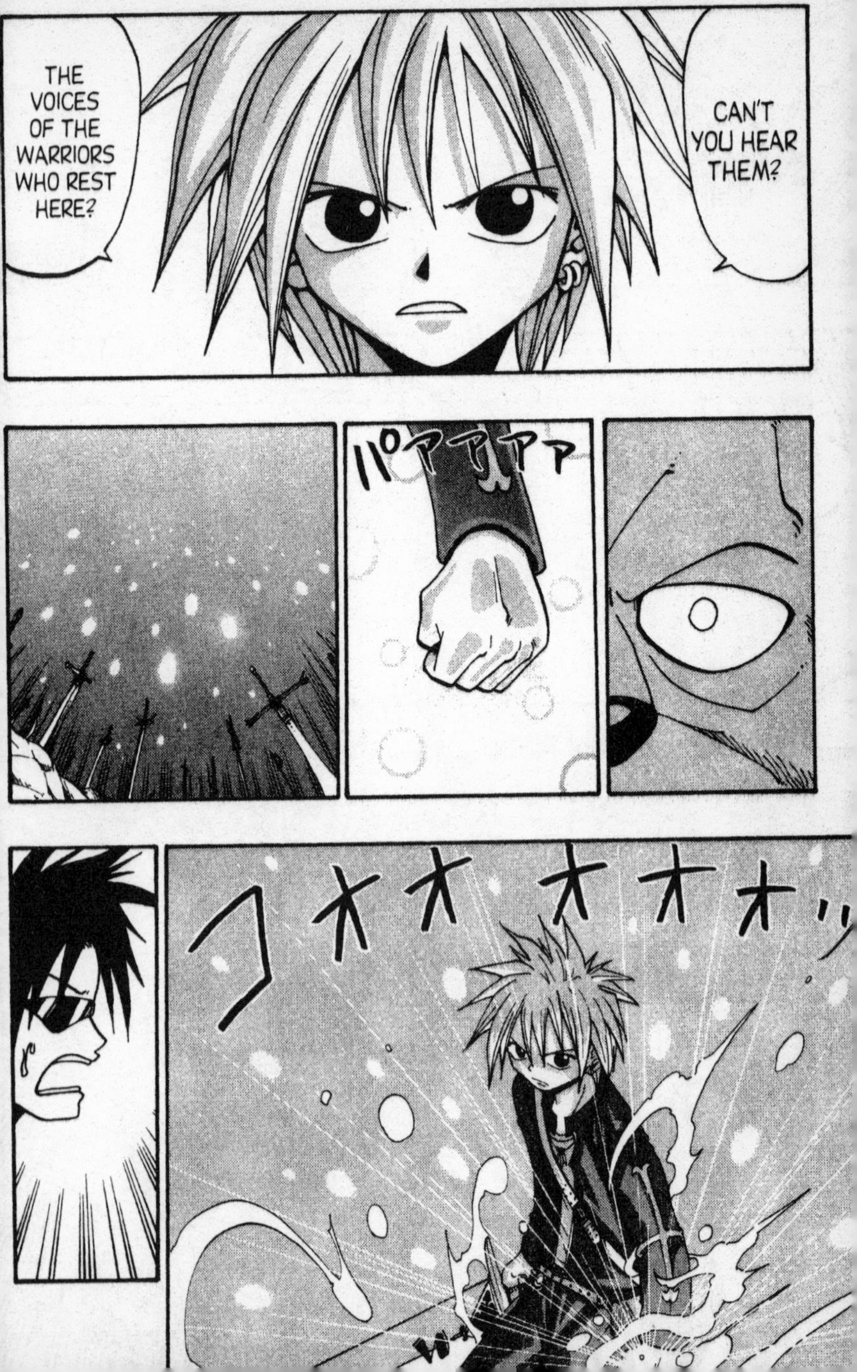
CAN'T YOU HEAR THEM?
THE VOICES OF THE WARRIORS WHO REST HERE?
パアアアア
コオオオオオッ

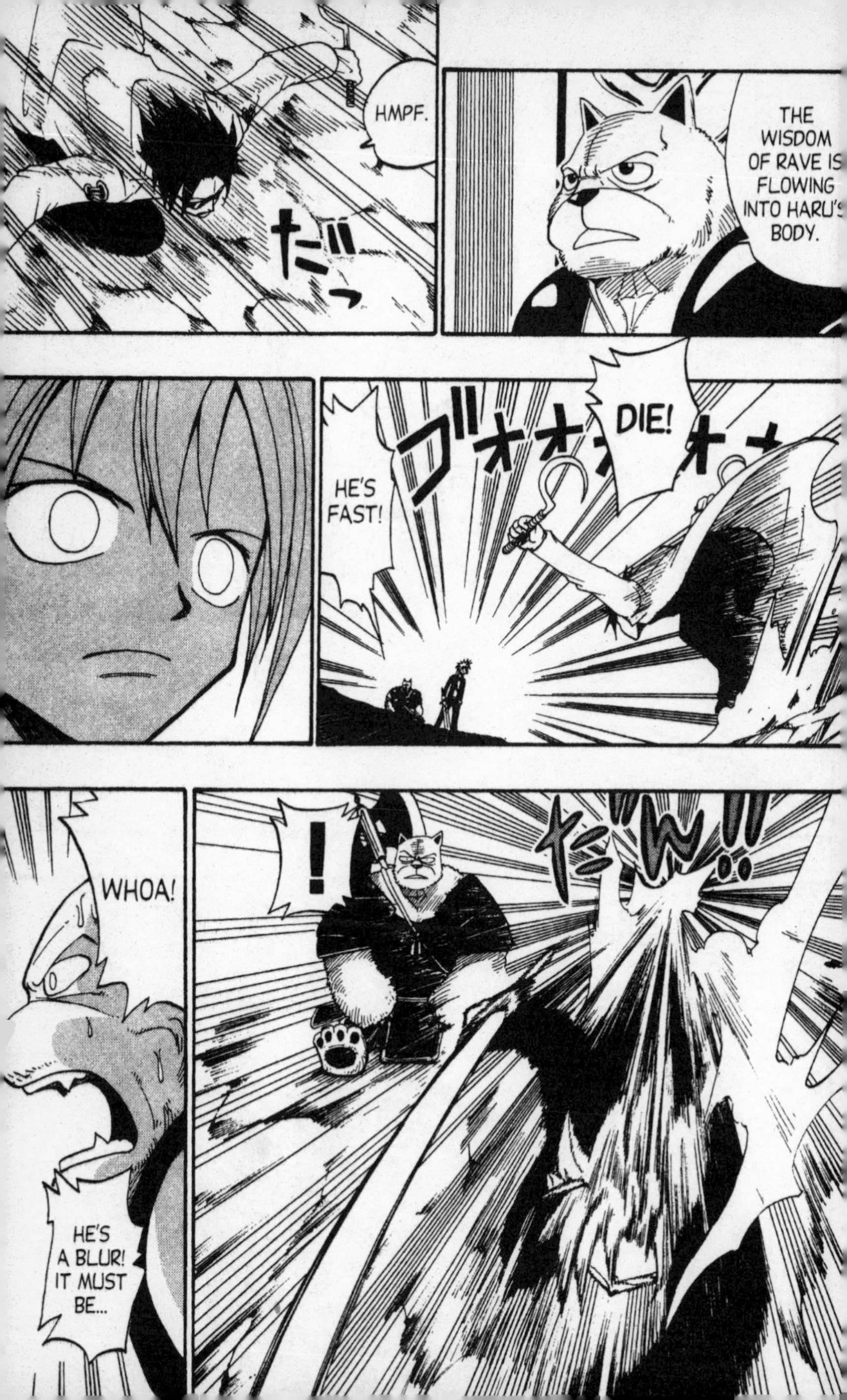
THE WISDOM OF RAVE IS FLOWING INTO HARU'S BODY.
HMPF.
DIE!
HE'S FAST!
!
WHOA!
HE'S A BLUR! IT MUST BE...

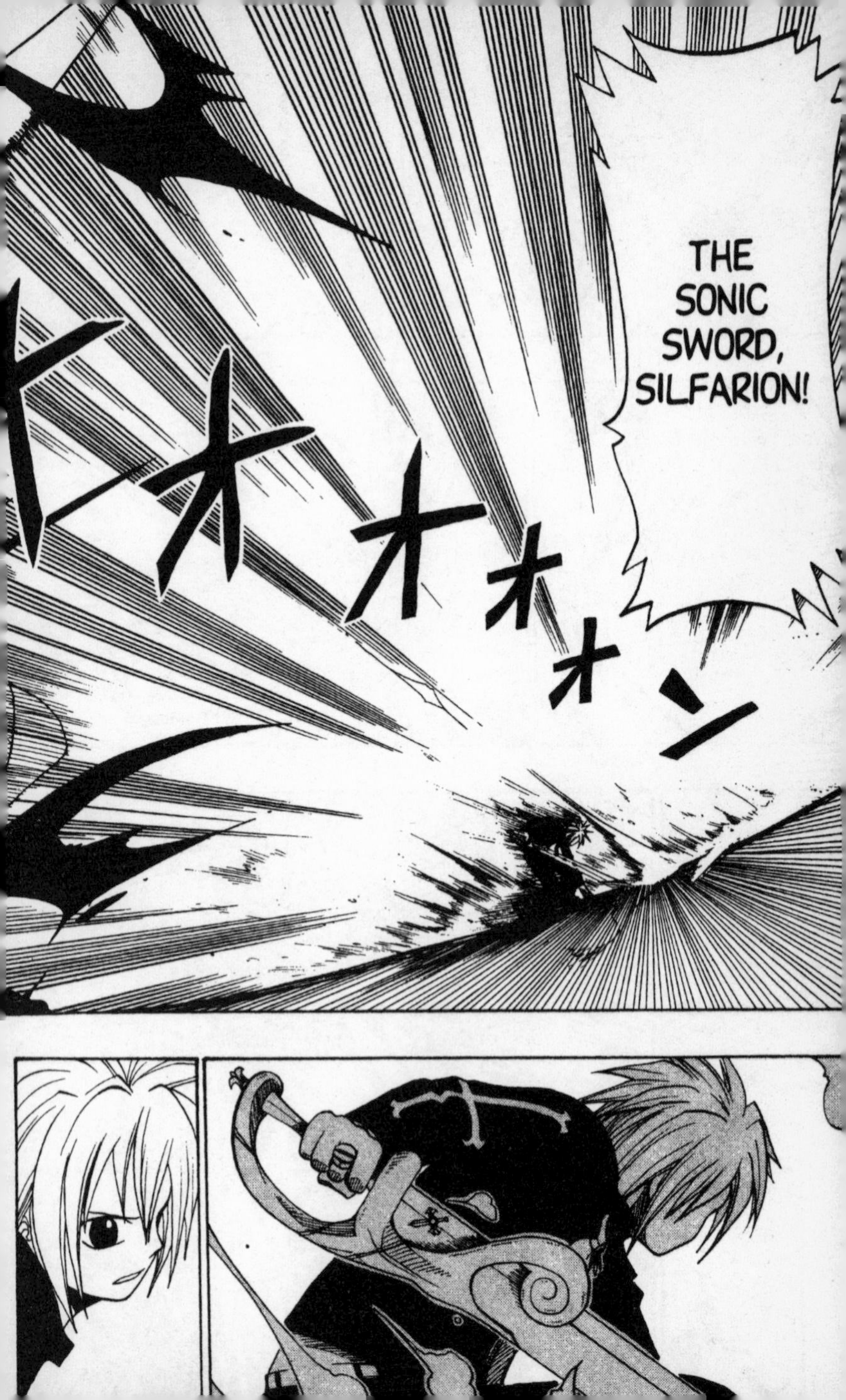
THE SONIC SWORD, SILFARION!

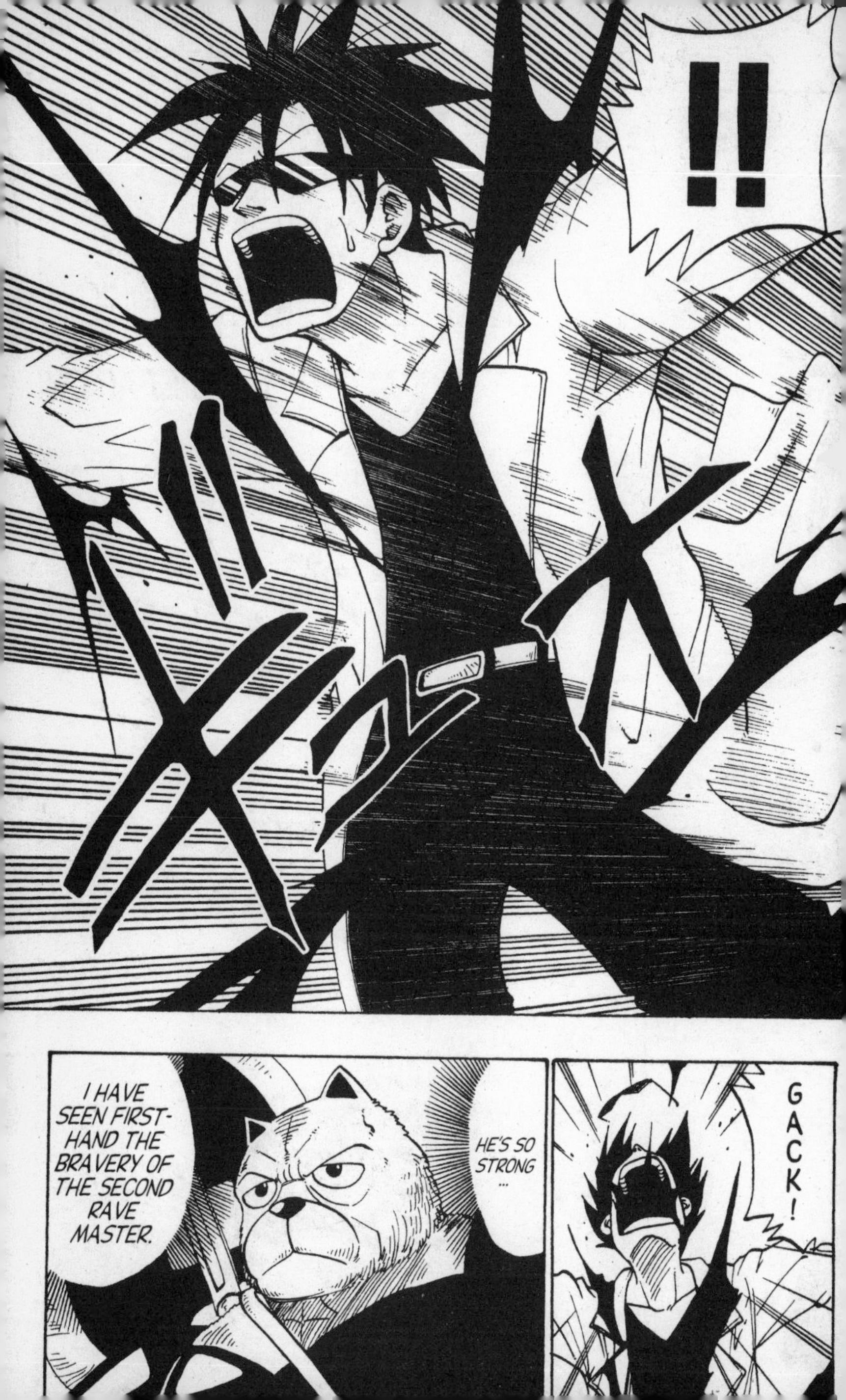
!!
GACK!
HE'S SO STRONG ...
I HAVE SEEN FIRST-HAND THE BRAVERY OF THE SECOND RAVE MASTER.

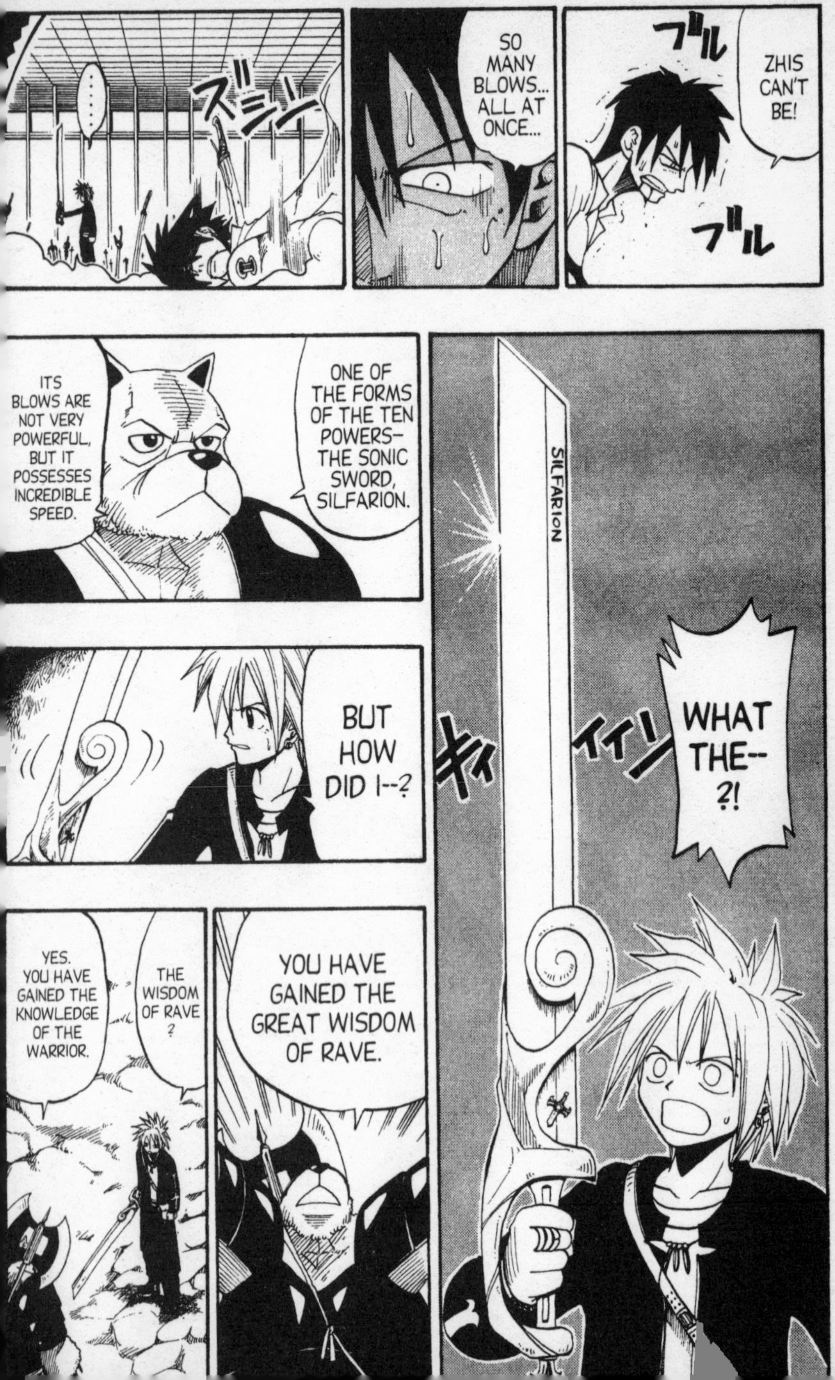
ブル
ZHIS CAN'T BE!
ブル
SO MANY BLOWS... ALL AT ONCE...
......
ズシーン
SILFARION
キィイイン
WHAT THE--?!
ONE OF THE FORMS OF THE TEN POWERS– THE SONIC SWORD, SILFARION.
ITS BLOWS ARE NOT VERY POWERFUL, BUT IT POSSESSES INCREDIBLE SPEED.
BUT HOW DID I--?
YOU HAVE GAINED THE GREAT WISDOM OF RAVE.
THE WISDOM OF RAVE?
YES. YOU HAVE GAINED THE KNOWLEDGE OF THE WARRIOR.

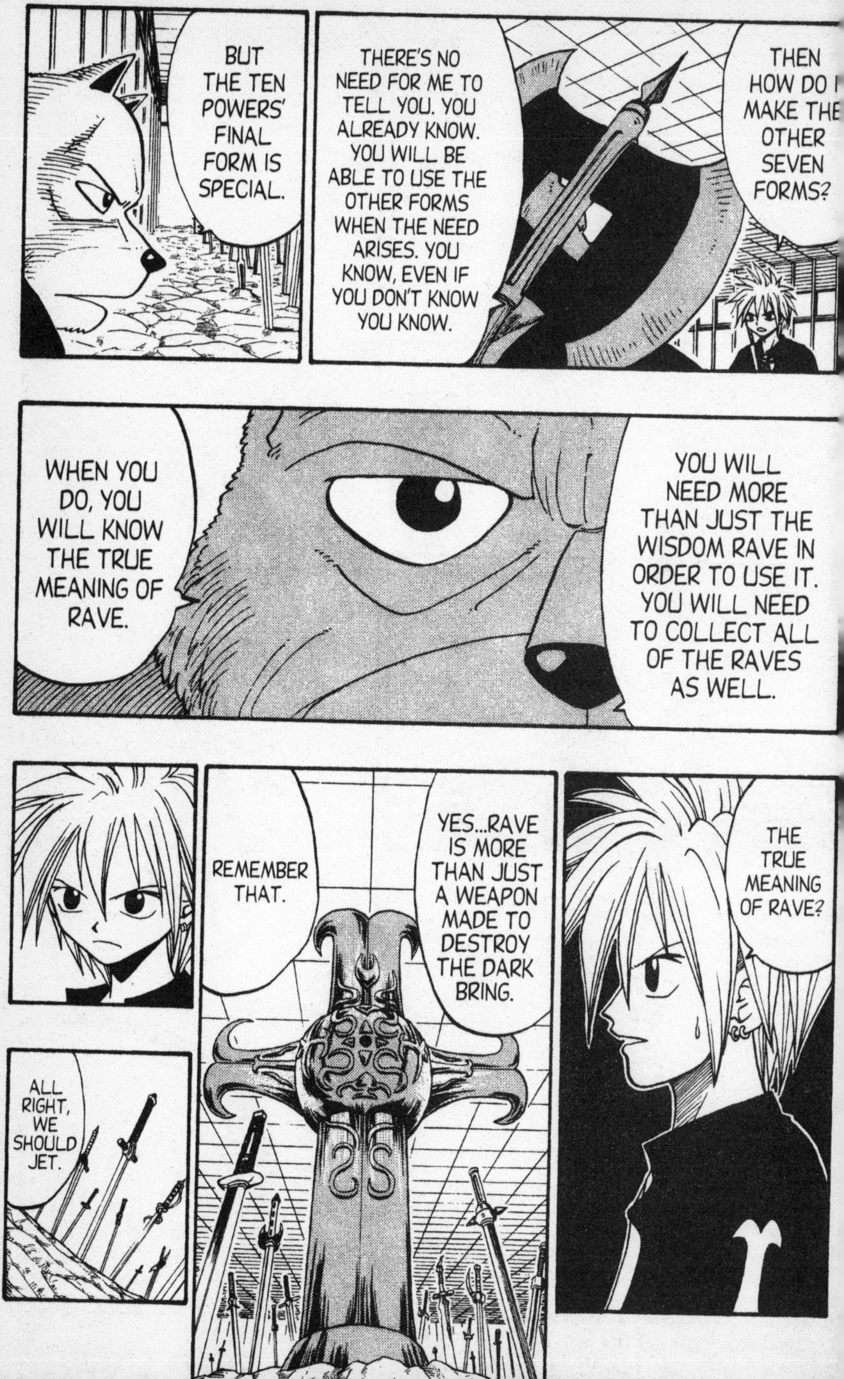
THEN HOW DO I MAKE THE OTHER SEVEN FORMS?
THERE'S NO NEED FOR ME TO TELL YOU. YOU ALREADY KNOW. YOU WILL BE ABLE TO USE THE OTHER FORMS WHEN THE NEED ARISES. YOU KNOW, EVEN IF YOU DON'T KNOW YOU KNOW.
BUT THE TEN POWERS' FINAL FORM IS SPECIAL.
YOU WILL NEED MORE THAN JUST THE WISDOM RAVE IN ORDER TO USE IT. YOU WILL NEED TO COLLECT ALL OF THE RAVES AS WELL.
WHEN YOU DO, YOU WILL KNOW THE TRUE MEANING OF RAVE.
THE TRUE MEANING OF RAVE?
YES...RAVE IS MORE THAN JUST A WEAPON MADE TO DESTROY THE DARK BRING.
REMEMBER THAT.
ALL RIGHT, WE SHOULD JET.

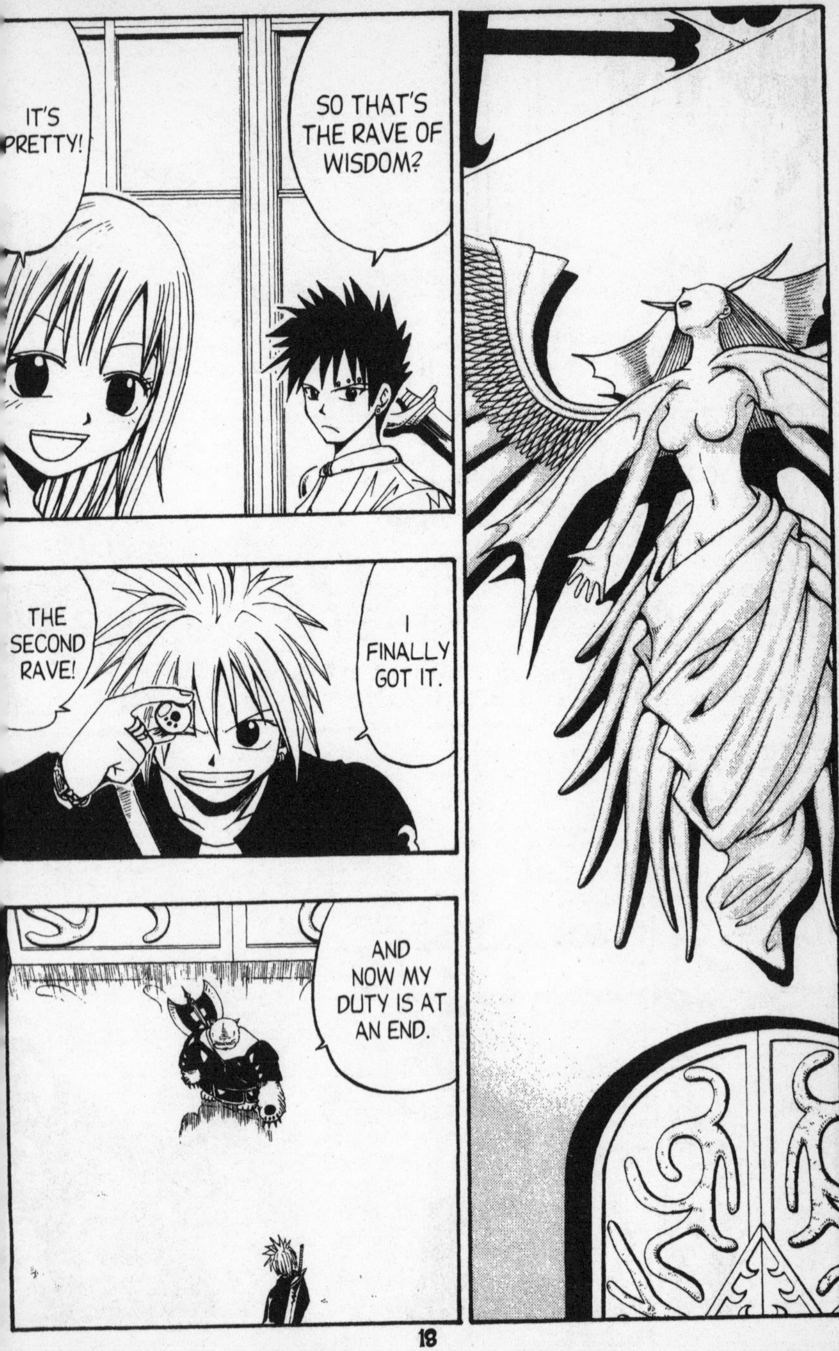
SO THAT'S THE RAVE OF WISDOM?
IT'S PRETTY!
I FINALLY GOT IT.
THE SECOND RAVE!
AND NOW MY DUTY IS AT AN END.

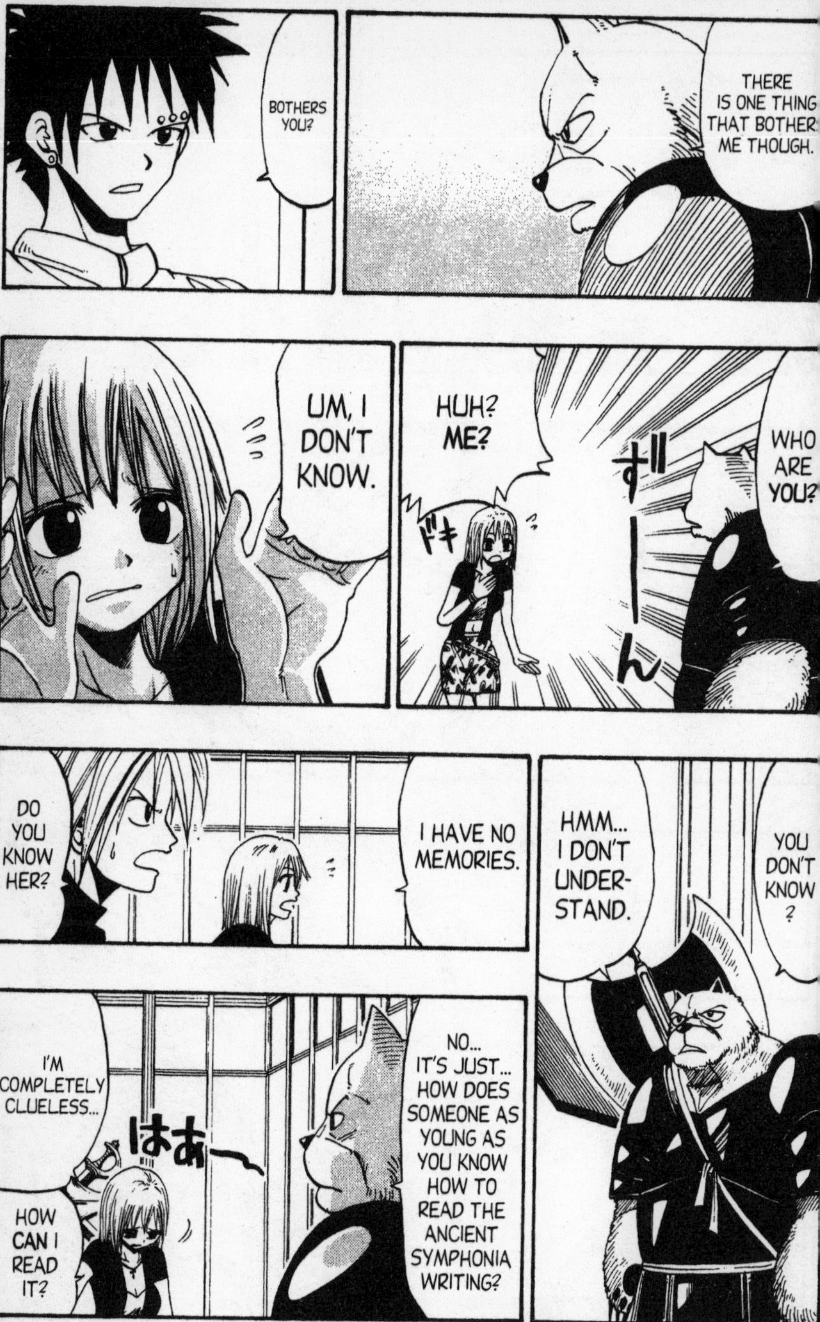

THERE IS ONE THING THAT BOTHERS ME THOUGH.
BOTHERS YOU?
WHO ARE YOU?
ずーーん
HUH? ME?
ドキ
UM, I DON'T KNOW.
YOU DON'T KNOW?
HMM... I DON'T UNDERSTAND.
I HAVE NO MEMORIES.
DO YOU KNOW HER?
NO... IT'S JUST... HOW DOES SOMEONE AS YOUNG AS YOU KNOW HOW TO READ THE ANCIENT SYMPHONIA WRITING?
I'M COMPLETELY CLUELESS...
はあ~
HOW CAN I READ IT?

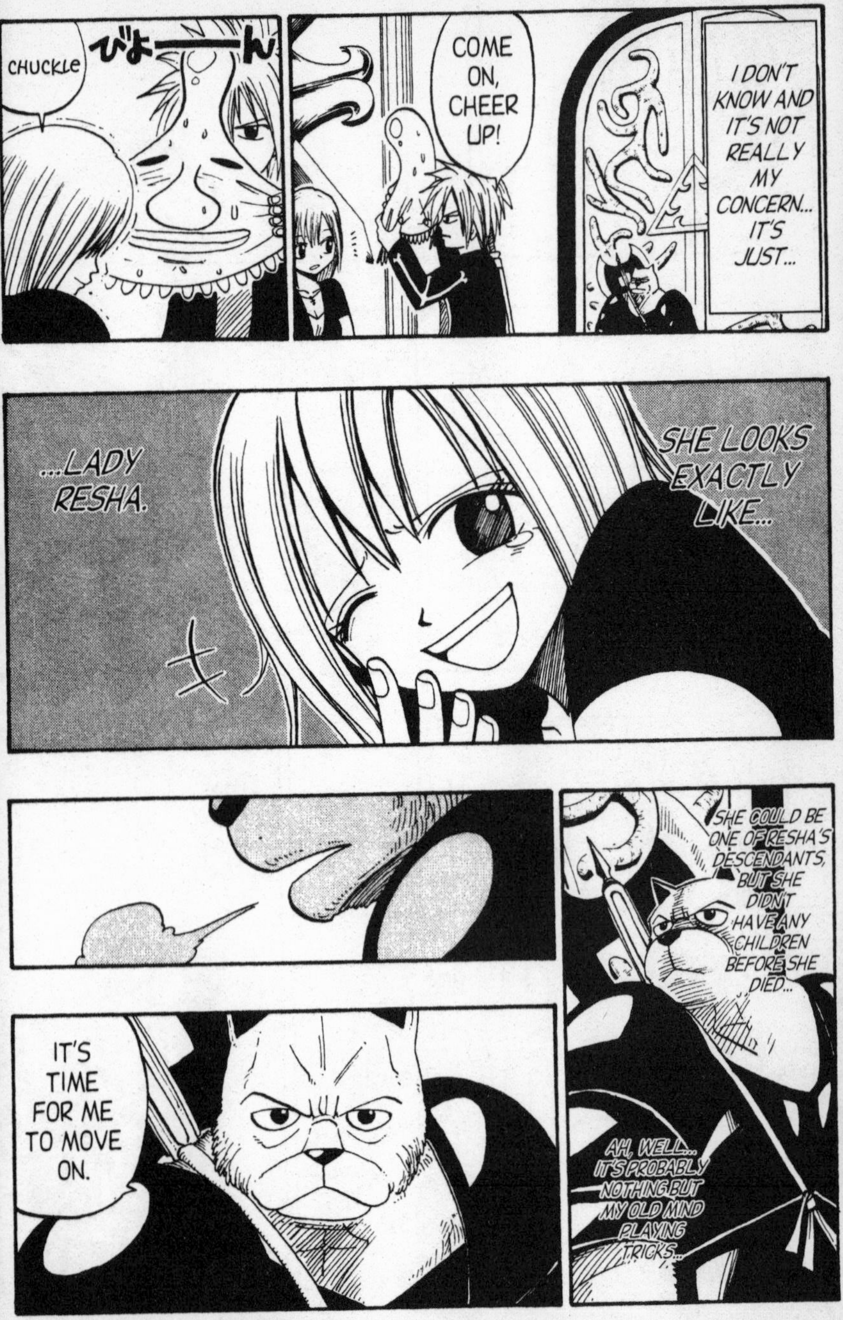
I DON'T KNOW AND IT'S NOT REALLY MY CONCERN... IT'S JUST...
COME ON, CHEER UP!
びよーーん
CHUCKLE
SHE LOOKS EXACTLY LIKE...
...LADY RESHA.
SHE COULD BE ONE OF RESHA'S DESCENDANTS, BUT SHE DIDN'T HAVE ANY CHILDREN BEFORE SHE DIED...
AH, WELL... IT'S PROBABLY NOTHING BUT MY OLD MIND PLAYING TRICKS...
IT'S TIME FOR ME TO MOVE ON.

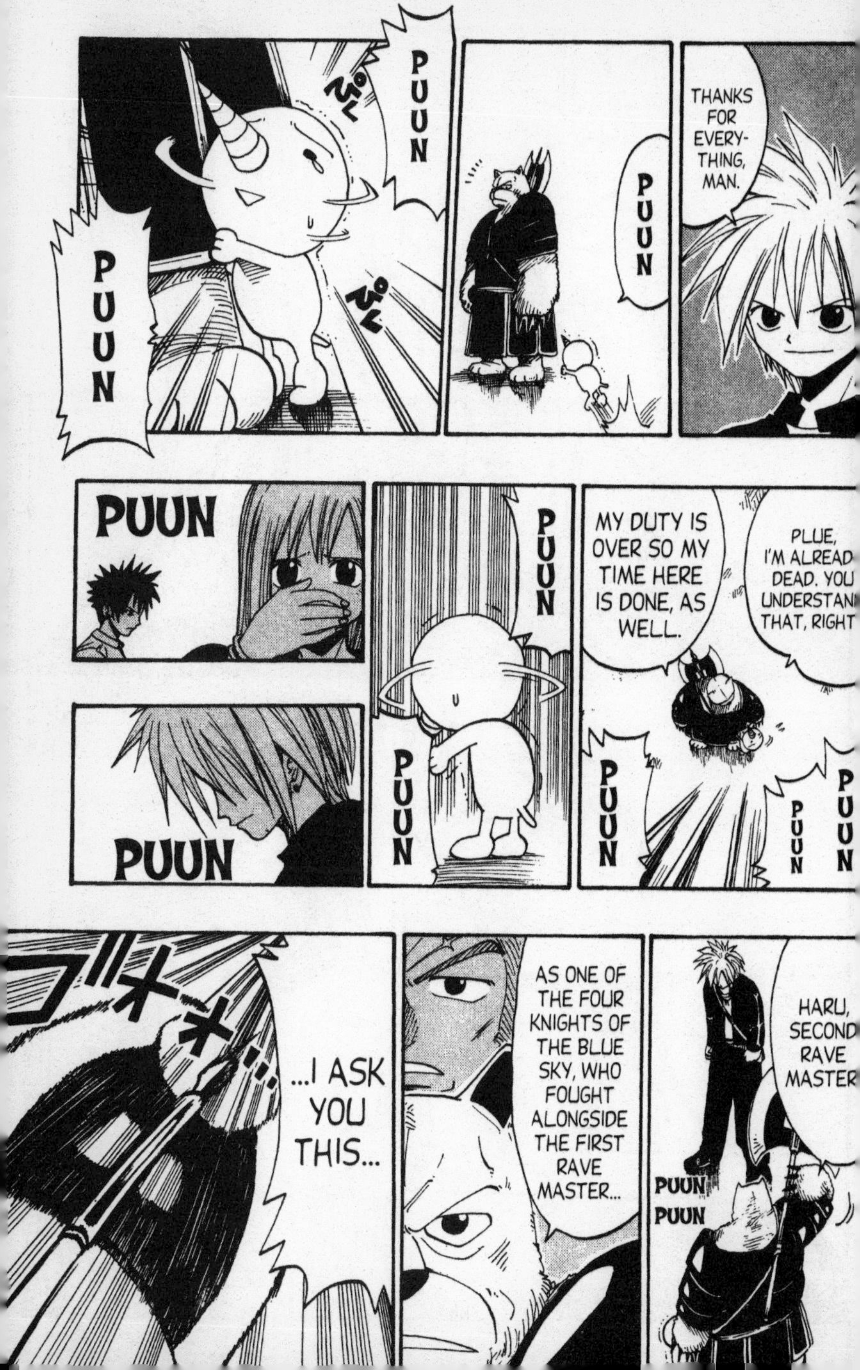
THANKS FOR EVERY-THING, MAN.
PUUN
PUUN
PUUN
PLUE, I'M ALREAD DEAD. YOU UNDERSTAN THAT, RIGHT
MY DUTY IS OVER SO MY TIME HERE IS DONE, AS WELL.
PUUN
PUUN
PUUN
PUUN
PUUN
PUUN
PUUN
HARU, SECOND RAVE MASTER
PUUN
PUUN
AS ONE OF THE FOUR KNIGHTS OF THE BLUE SKY, WHO FOUGHT ALONGSIDE THE FIRST RAVE MASTER...
...I ASK YOU THIS...

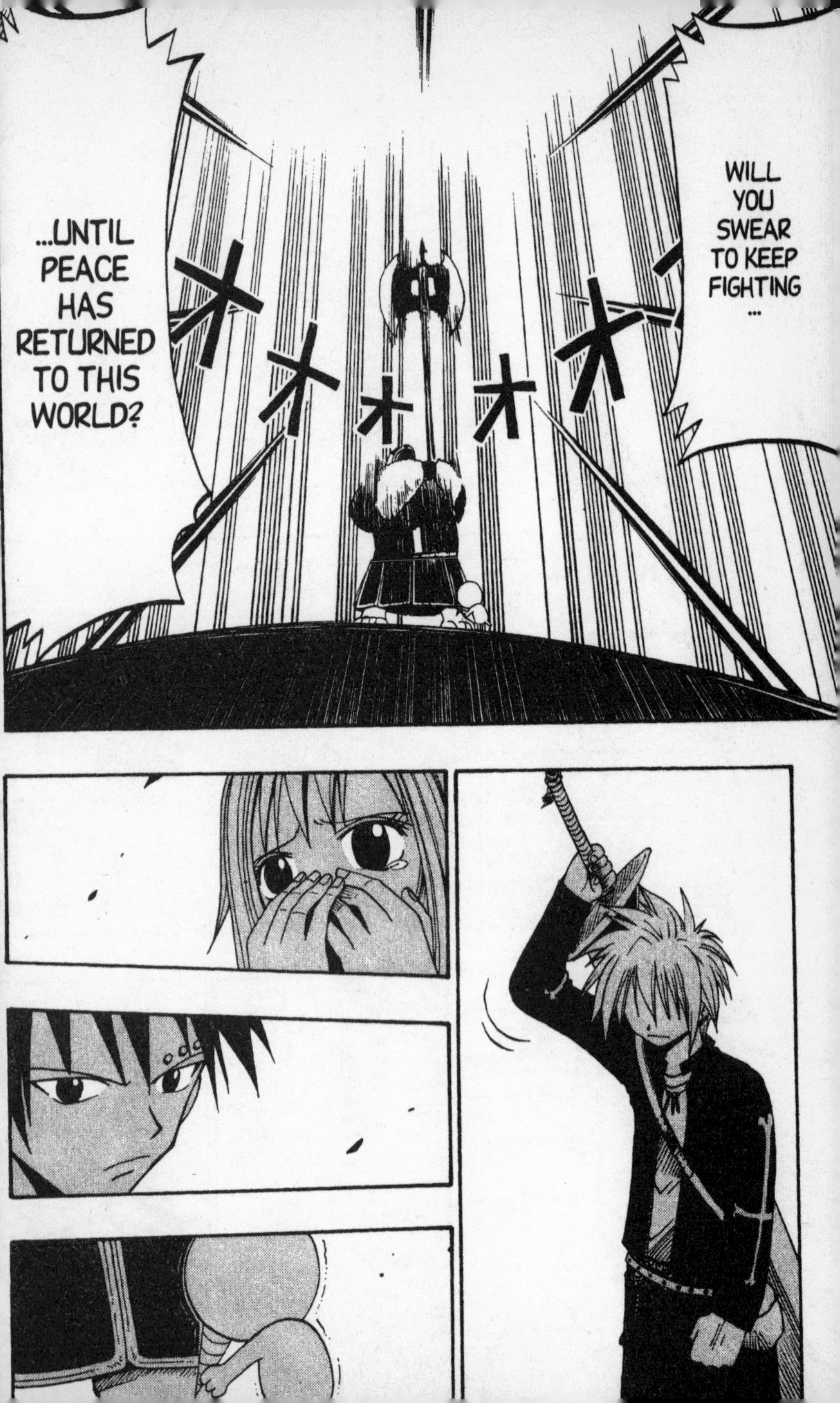
WILL YOU SWEAR TO KEEP FIGHTING...
...UNTIL PEACE HAS RETURNED TO THIS WORLD?
オオオオオ

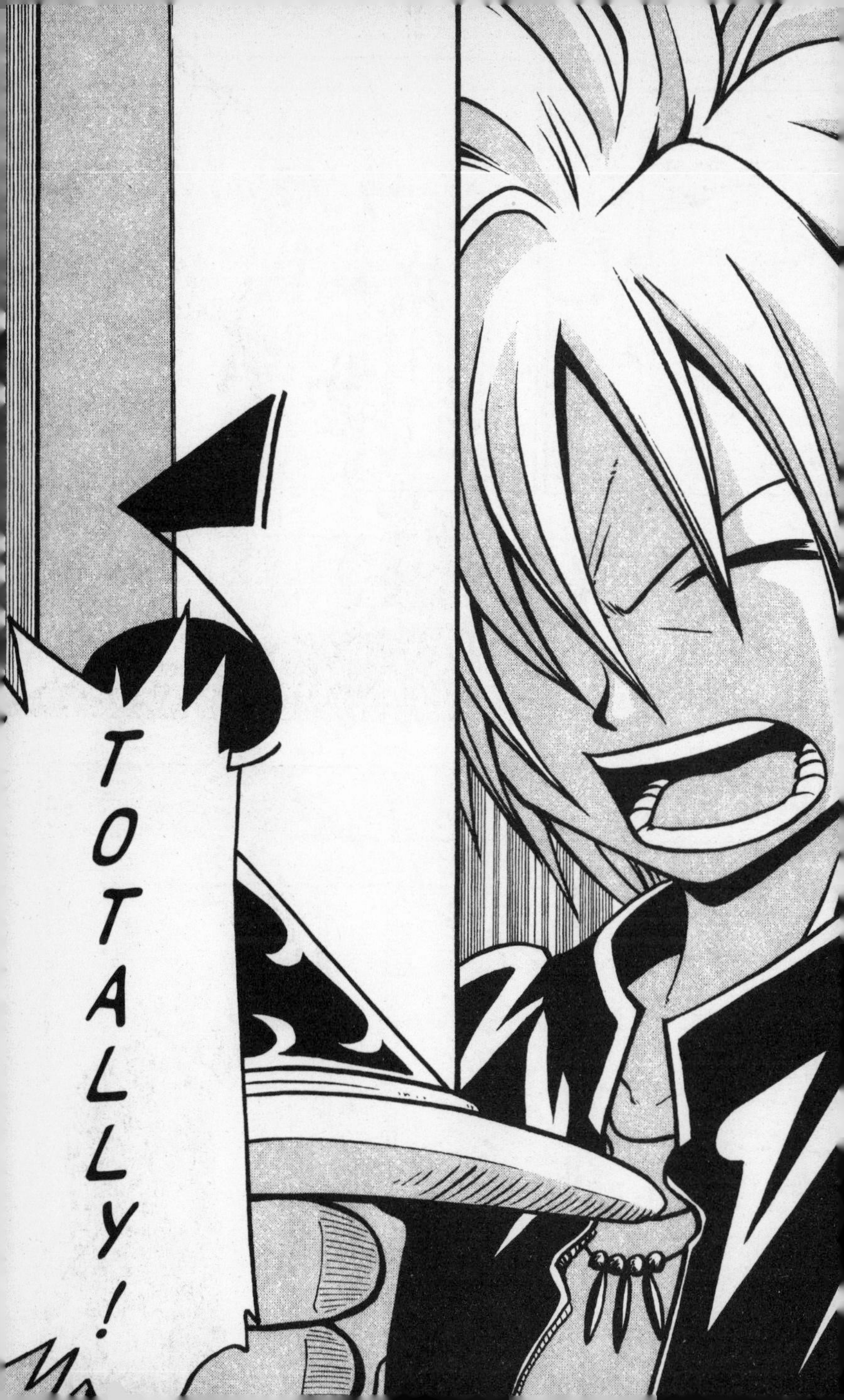
TOTALLY!

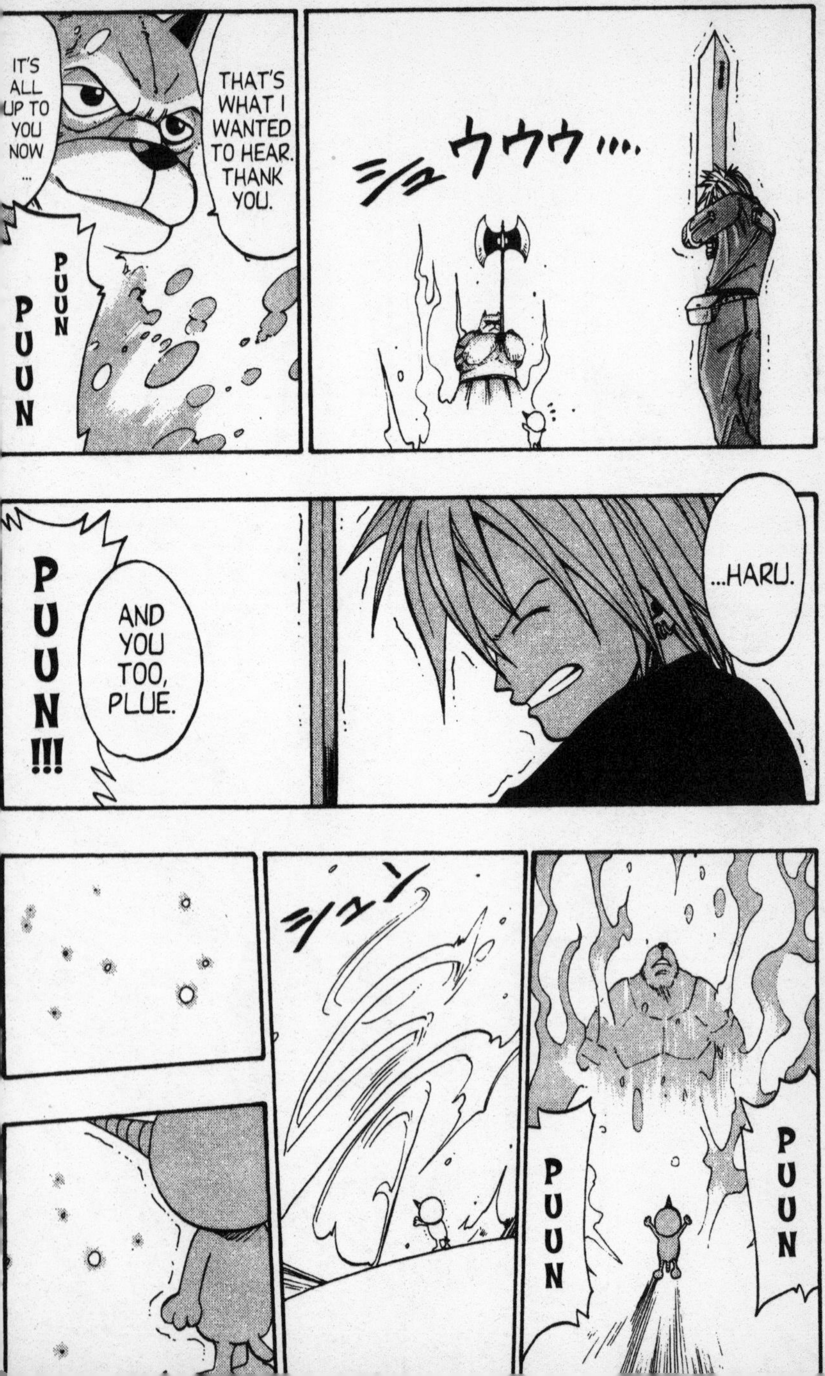
シュウウウ…
THAT'S WHAT I WANTED TO HEAR. THANK YOU.
IT'S ALL UP TO YOU NOW ...
PUUN
PUUN
...HARU.
AND YOU TOO, PLUE.
PUUUN!!!
PUUN
PUUN
シュン

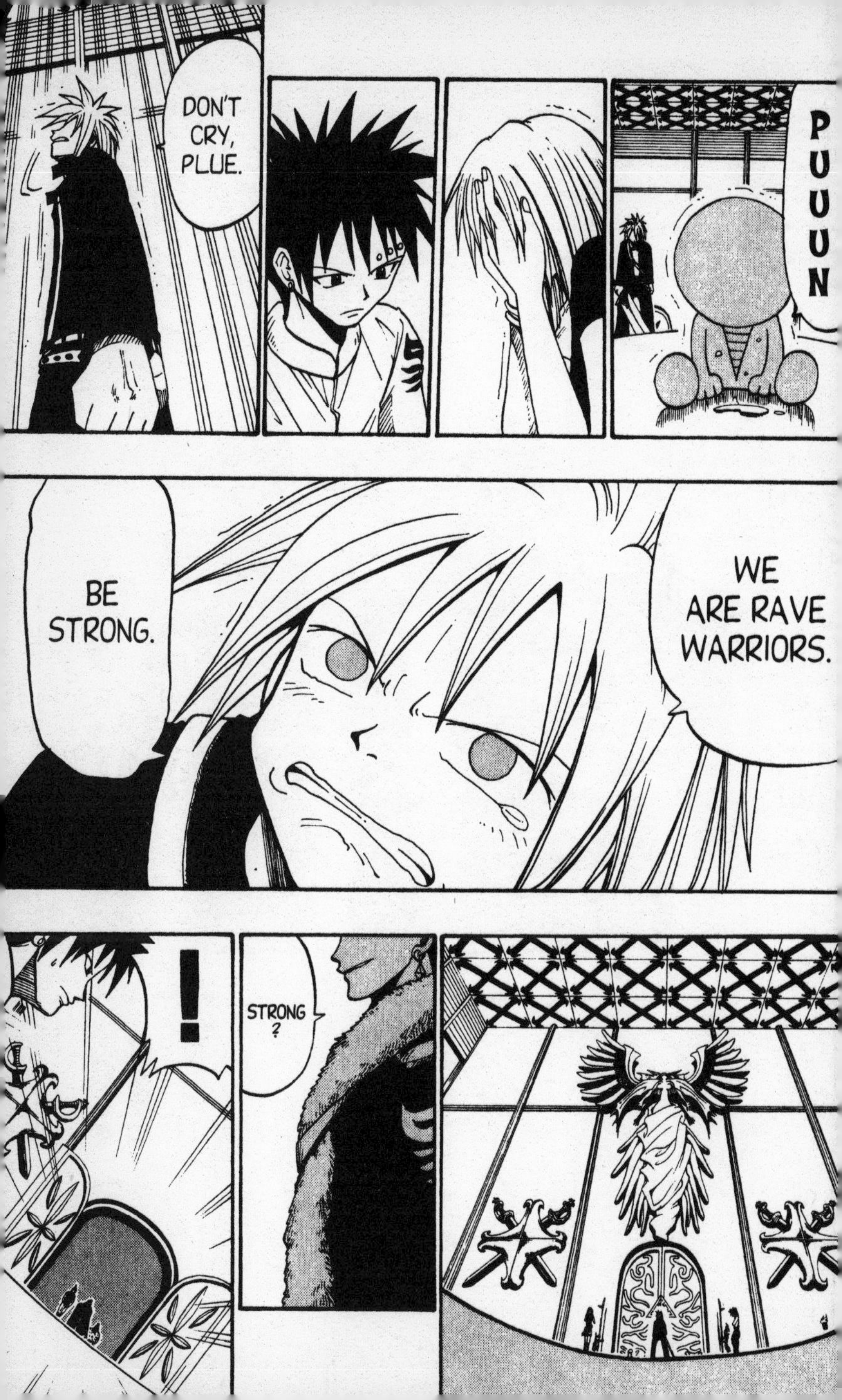
PUUUN
DON'T CRY, PLUE.
WE ARE RAVE WARRIORS.
BE STRONG.
STRONG?
!

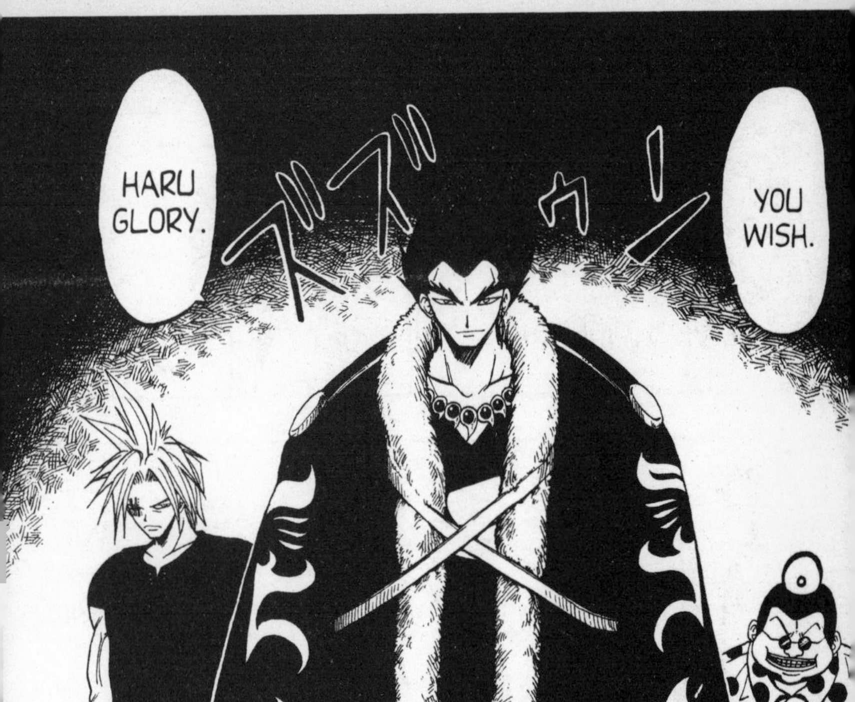
YOU WISH.
ズズゥーン
HARU GLORY.
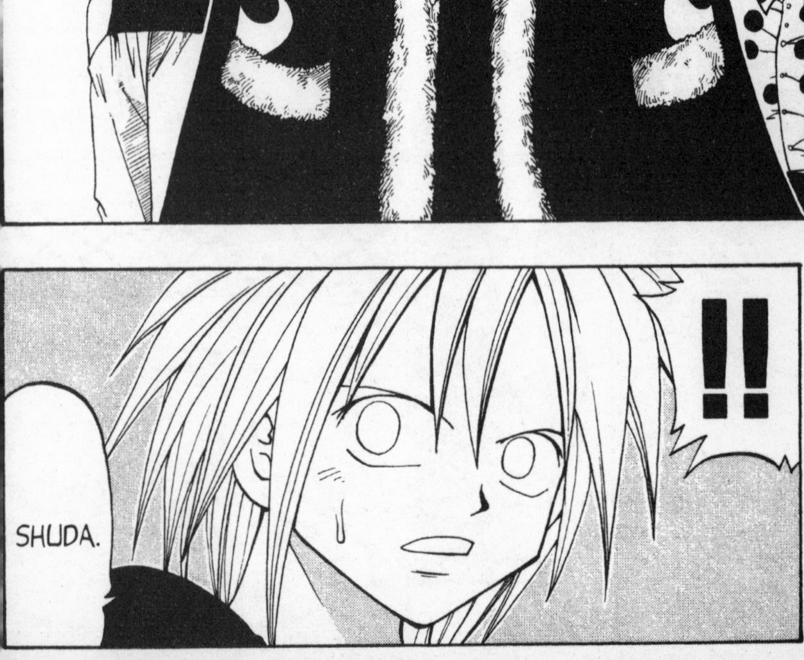
!!
SHUDA.

RAVE MASTER™

RAVE: 32 ✠ BREAK THESE CHAINS

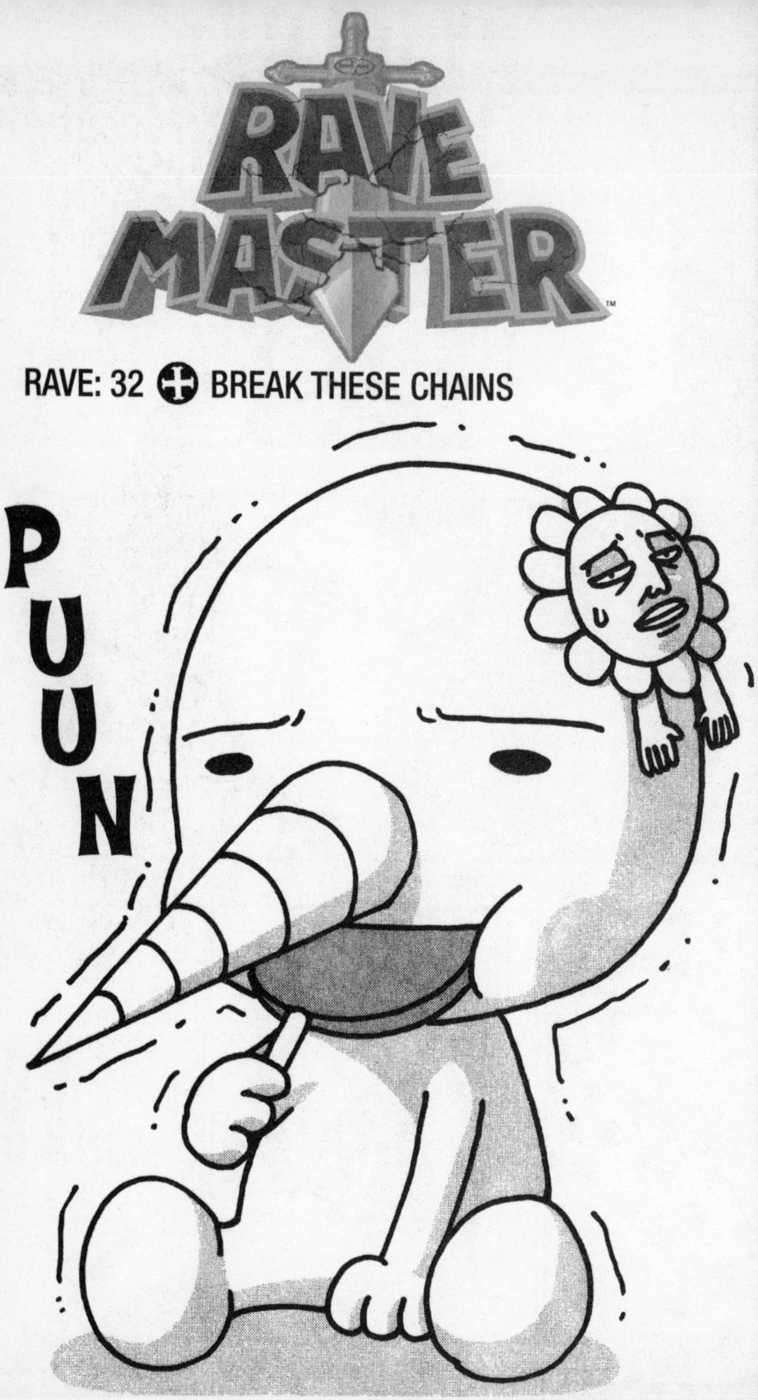
PUUN

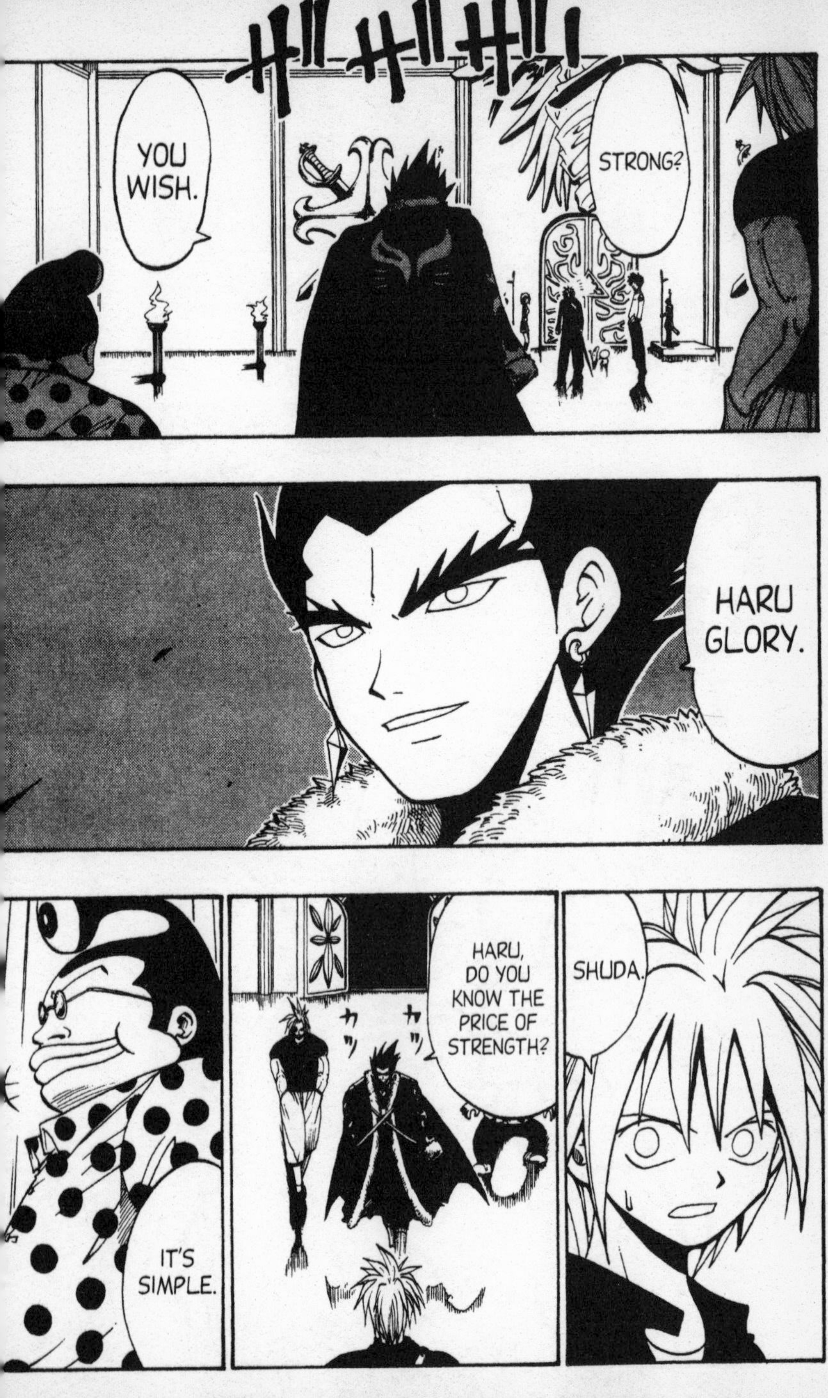

STRONG?
YOU WISH.
HARU GLORY.
SHUDA.
カッ
カッ
HARU, DO YOU KNOW THE PRICE OF STRENGTH?
IT'S SIMPLE.

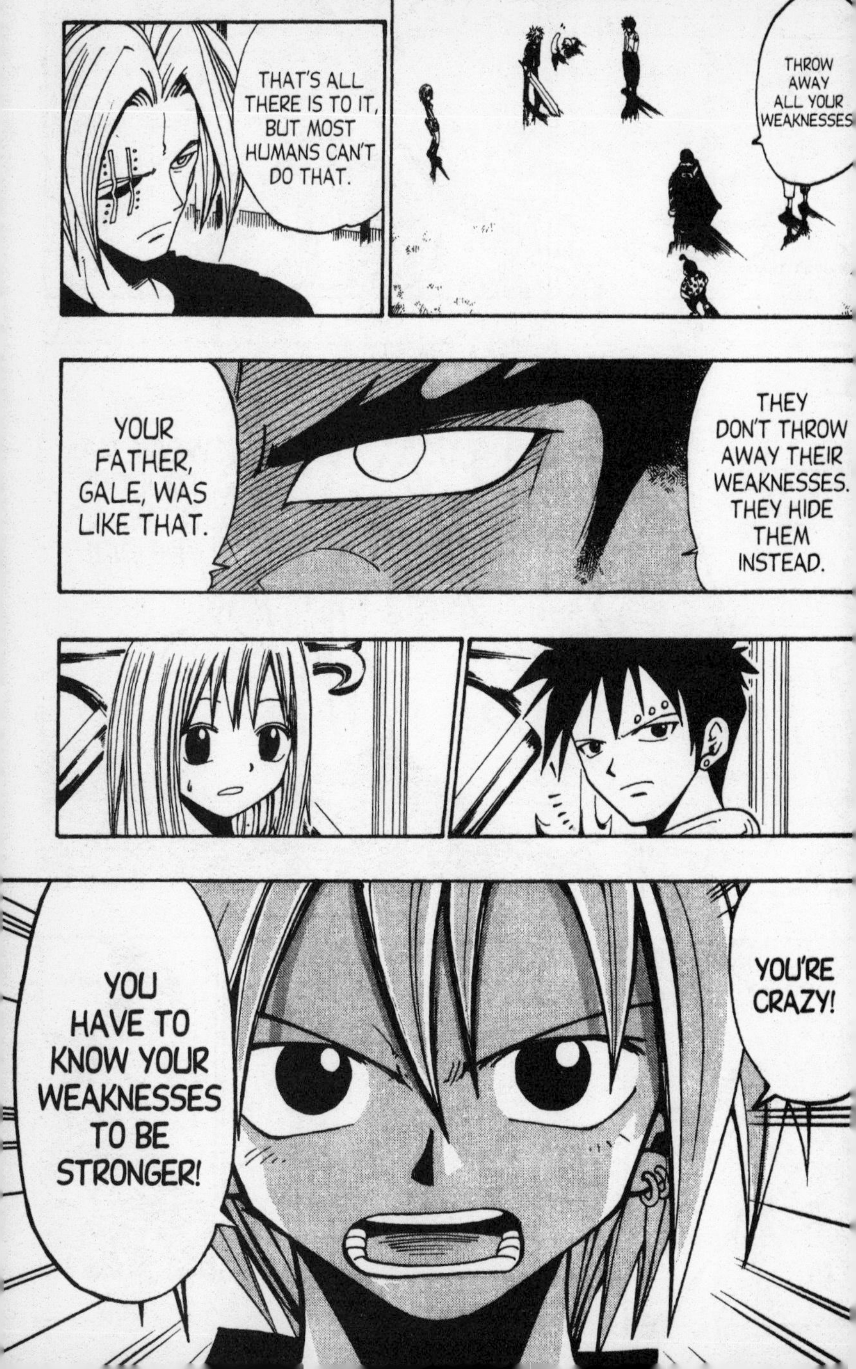
THROW AWAY ALL YOUR WEAKNESSES
THAT'S ALL THERE IS TO IT, BUT MOST HUMANS CAN'T DO THAT.
THEY DON'T THROW AWAY THEIR WEAKNESSES. THEY HIDE THEM INSTEAD.
YOUR FATHER, GALE, WAS LIKE THAT.
YOU'RE CRAZY!
YOU HAVE TO KNOW YOUR WEAKNESSES TO BE STRONGER!

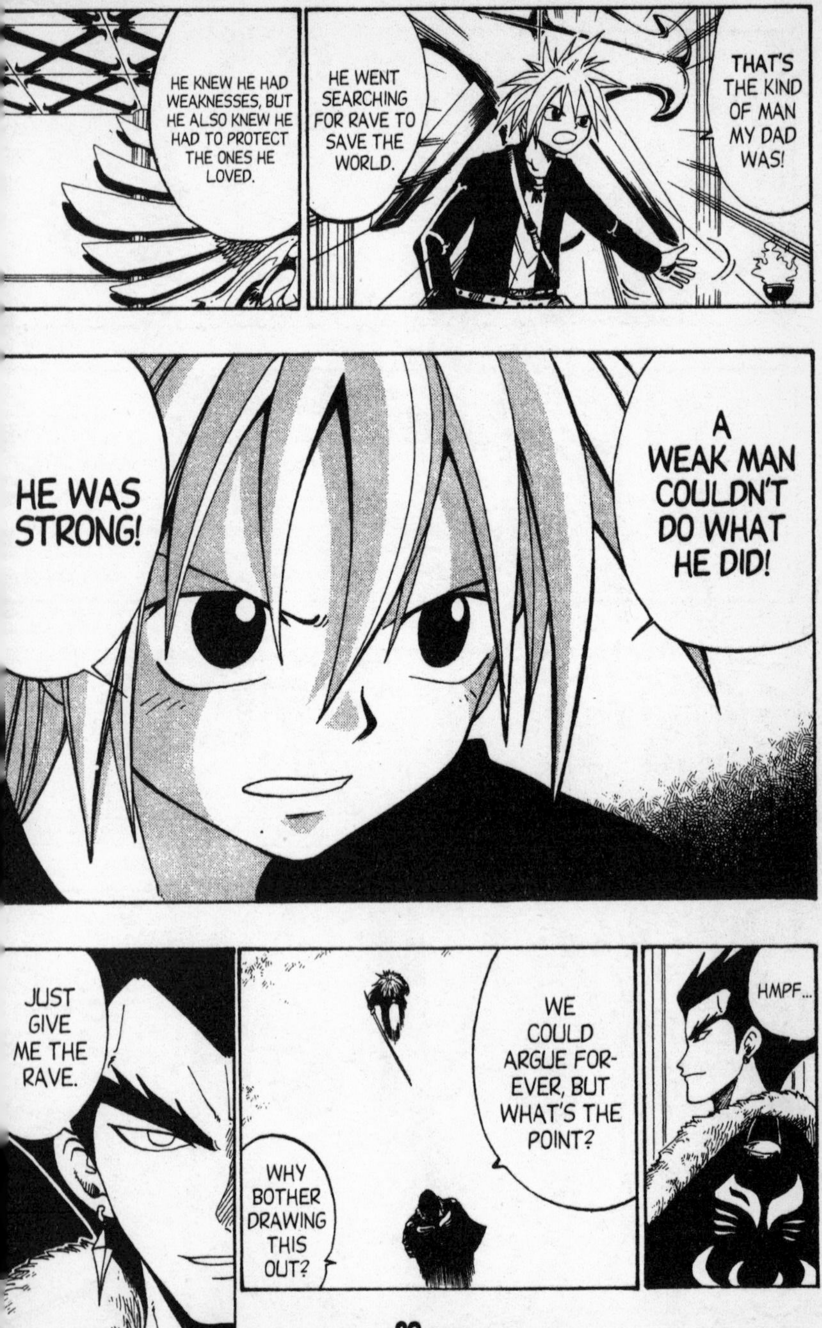
THAT'S THE KIND OF MAN MY DAD WAS!
HE WENT SEARCHING FOR RAVE TO SAVE THE WORLD.
HE KNEW HE HAD WEAKNESSES, BUT HE ALSO KNEW HE HAD TO PROTECT THE ONES HE LOVED.
A WEAK MAN COULDN'T DO WHAT HE DID!
HE WAS STRONG!
HMPF...
WE COULD ARGUE FOR-EVER, BUT WHAT'S THE POINT?
WHY BOTHER DRAWING THIS OUT?
JUST GIVE ME THE RAVE.

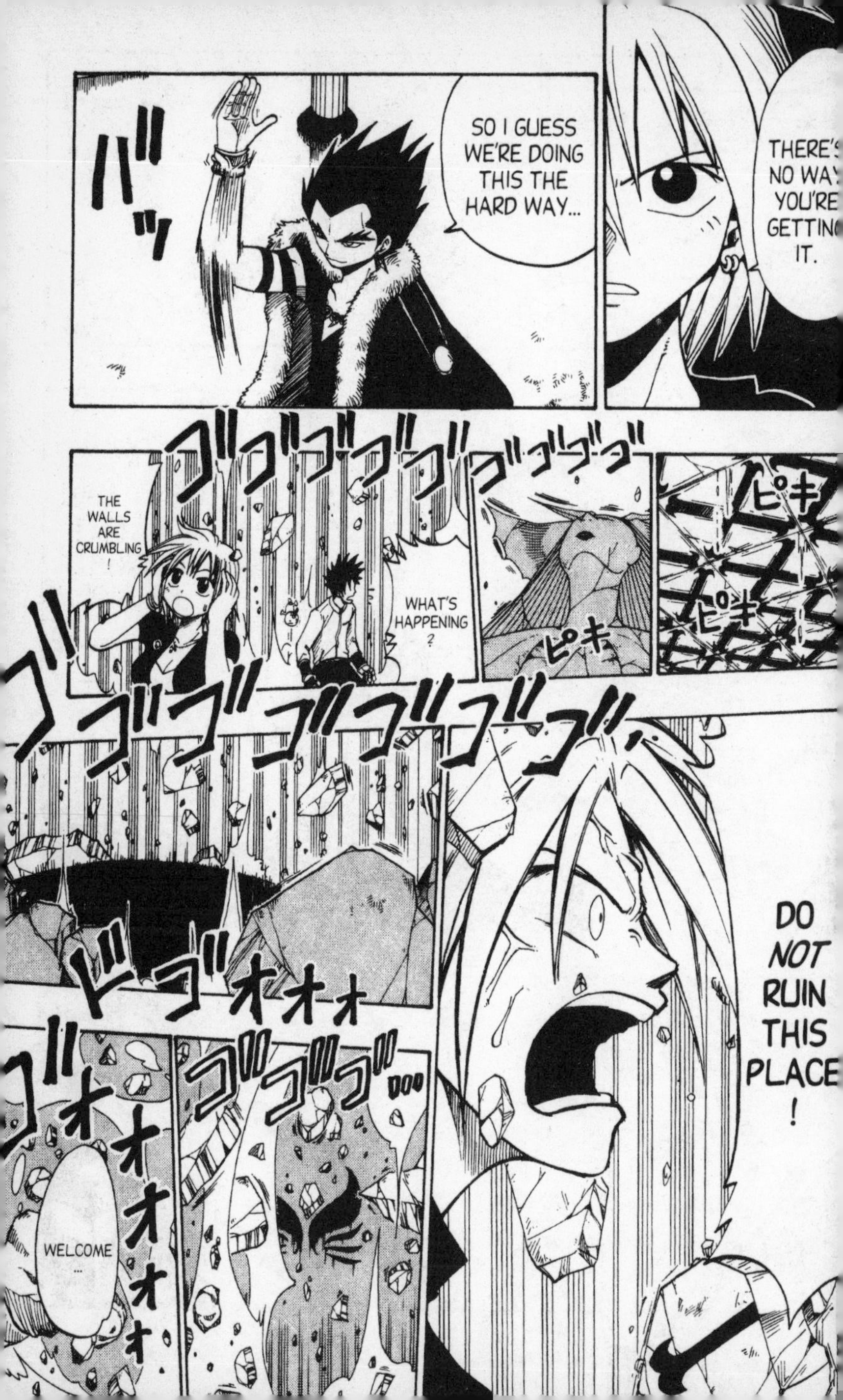
THERE'S NO WAY YOU'RE GETTIN IT.
SO I GUESS WE'RE DOING THIS THE HARD WAY...
バッ
ピキ
ピキ
ゴゴゴゴ
ピキ
WHAT'S HAPPENING?
THE WALLS ARE CRUMBLING!
ゴゴゴゴゴ
DO NOT RUIN THIS PLACE!
ゴゴゴゴゴゴゴ
ドゴオオオ
ゴゴゴ...
ゴオオオオオ
WELCOME...

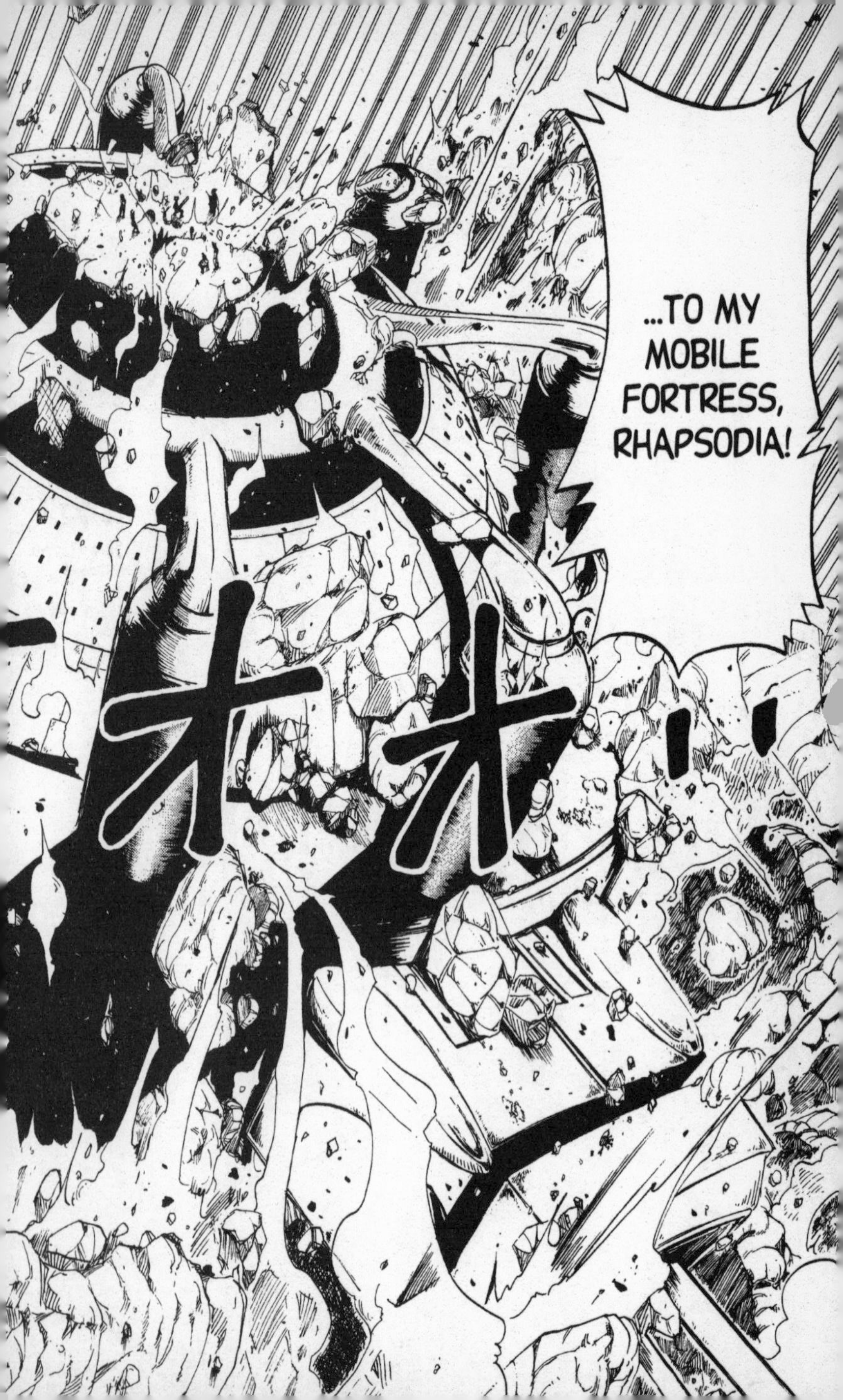
...TO MY MOBILE FORTRESS, RHAPSODIA!
オオ

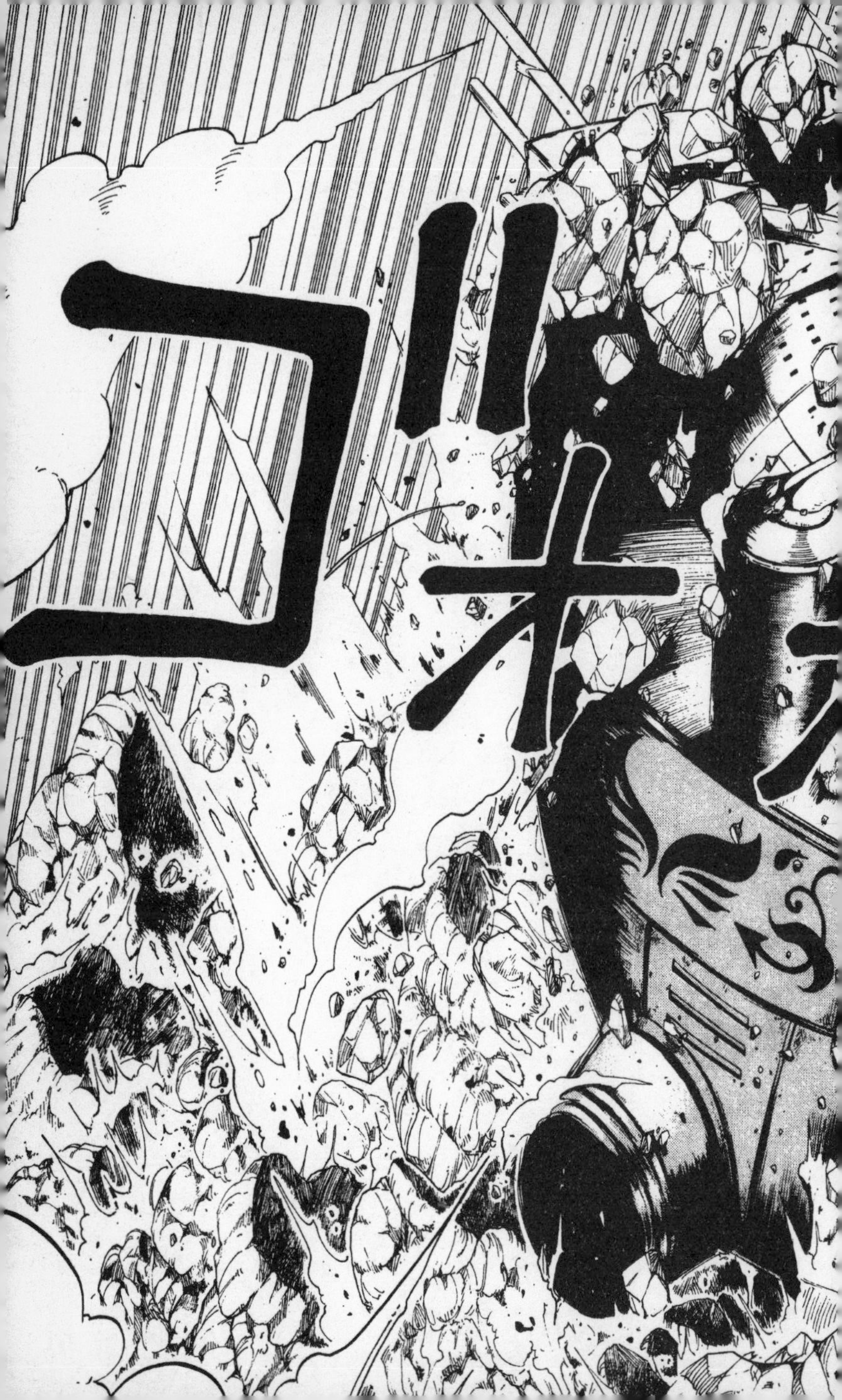
ゴオ

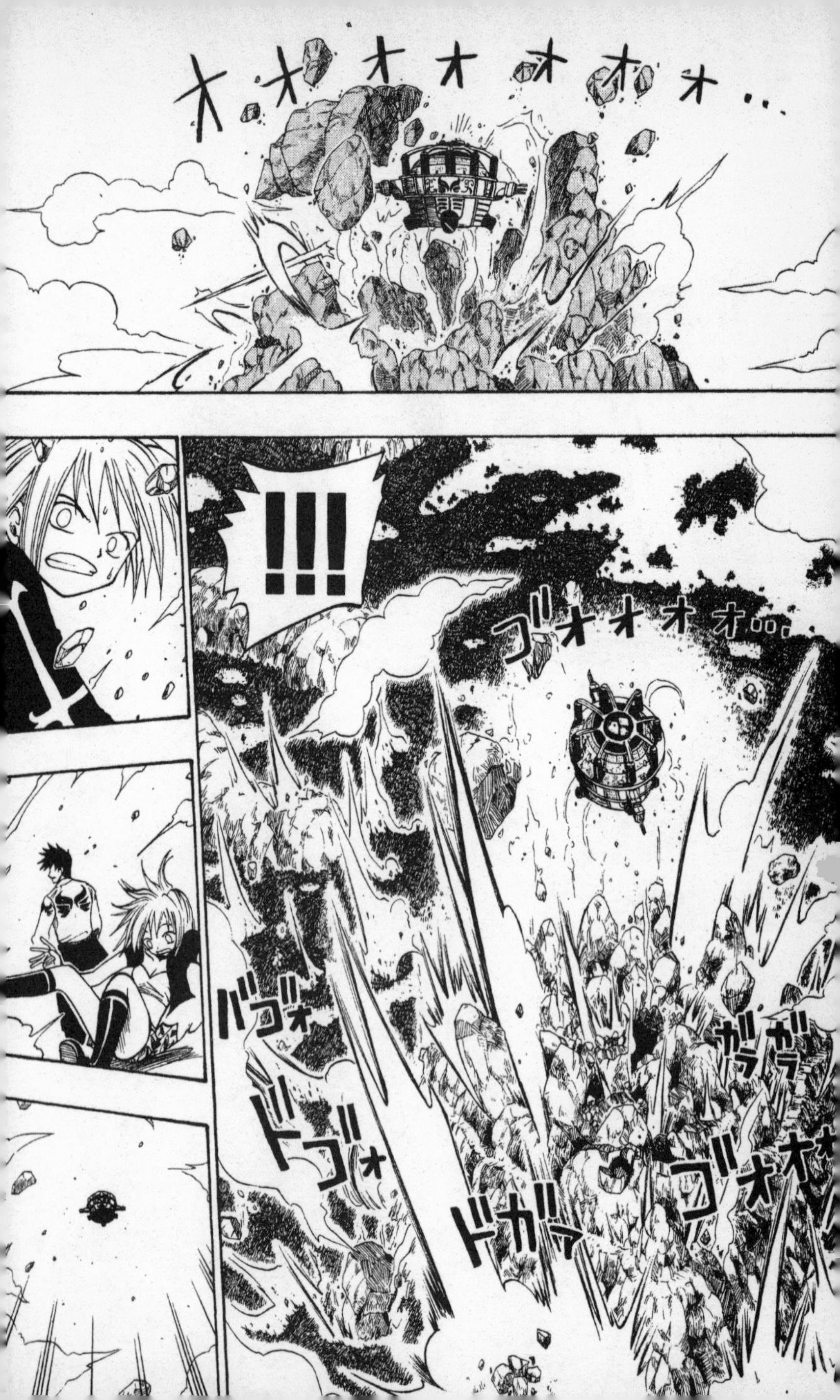
オオオオオオオ…
!!!
ゴォオオオ…
ガラガラ
ゴオオ
バゴォ
ドゴォ
ドガァ

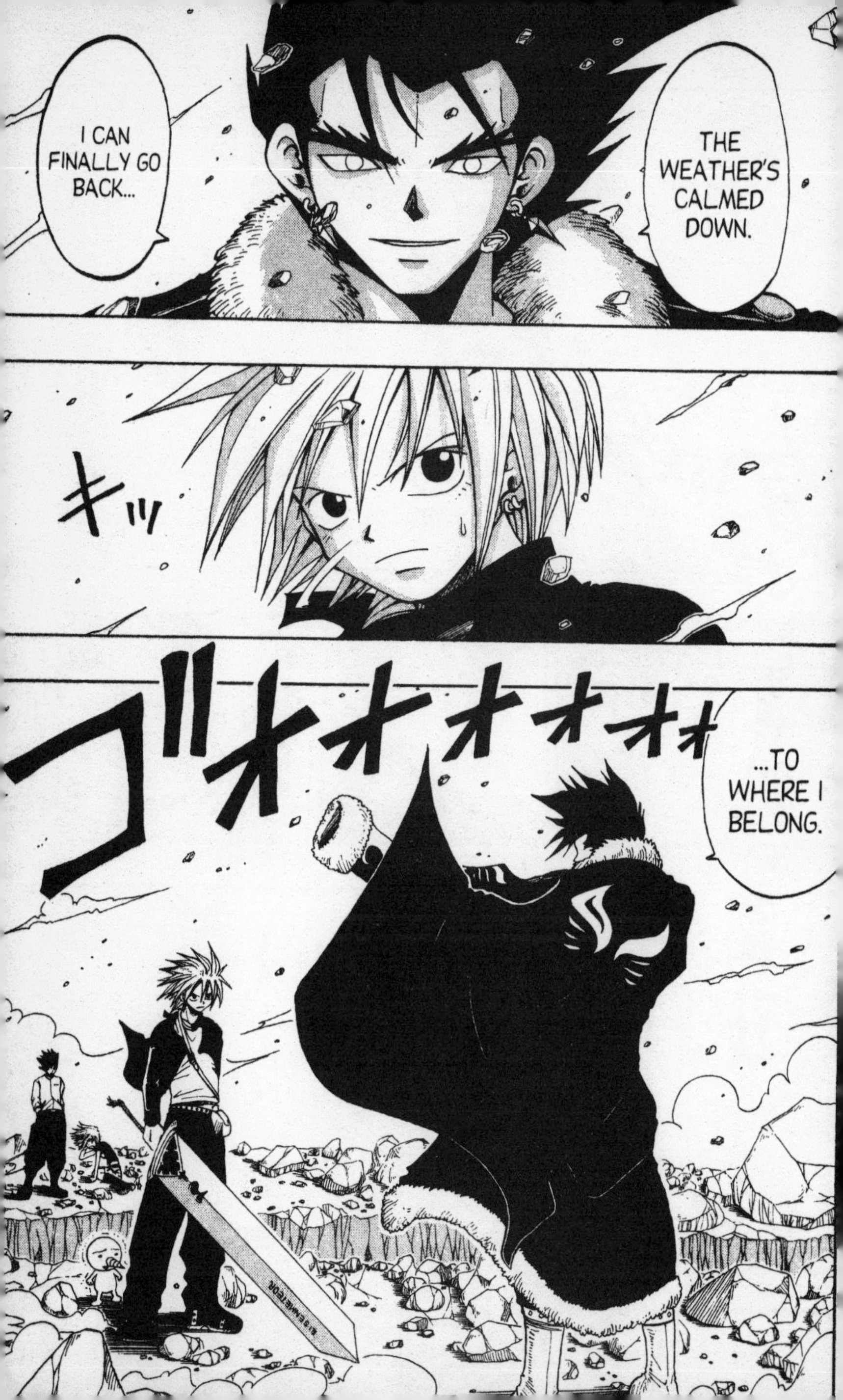
THE WEATHER'S CALMED DOWN.
I CAN FINALLY GO BACK...
キッ
ゴオオオオオオ
...TO WHERE I BELONG.

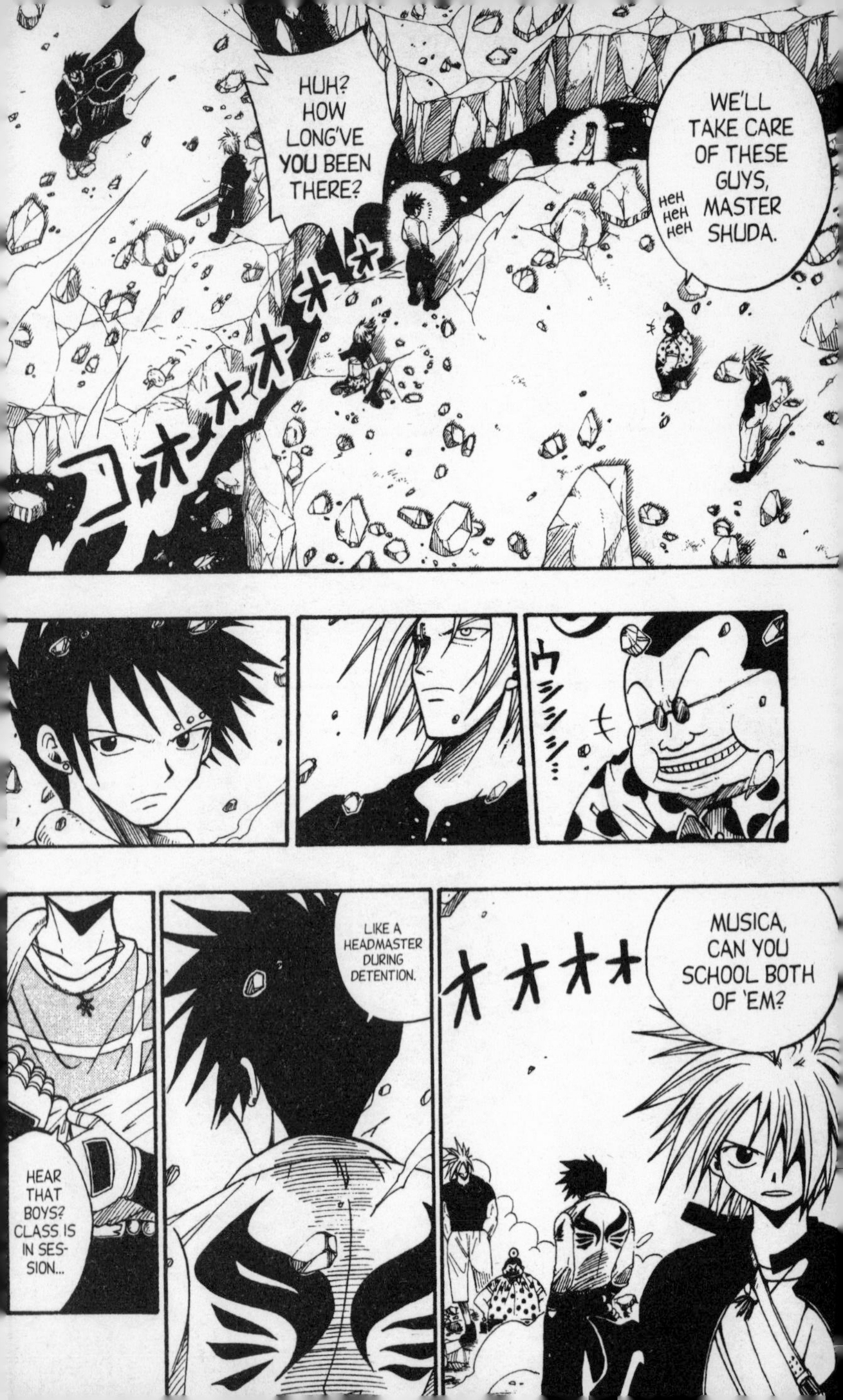
WE'LL TAKE CARE OF THESE GUYS, MASTER SHUDA.
HEH HEH HEH
HUH? HOW LONG'VE YOU BEEN THERE?
MUSICA, CAN YOU SCHOOL BOTH OF 'EM?
LIKE A HEADMASTER DURING DETENTION.
HEAR THAT BOYS? CLASS IS IN SES-SION...

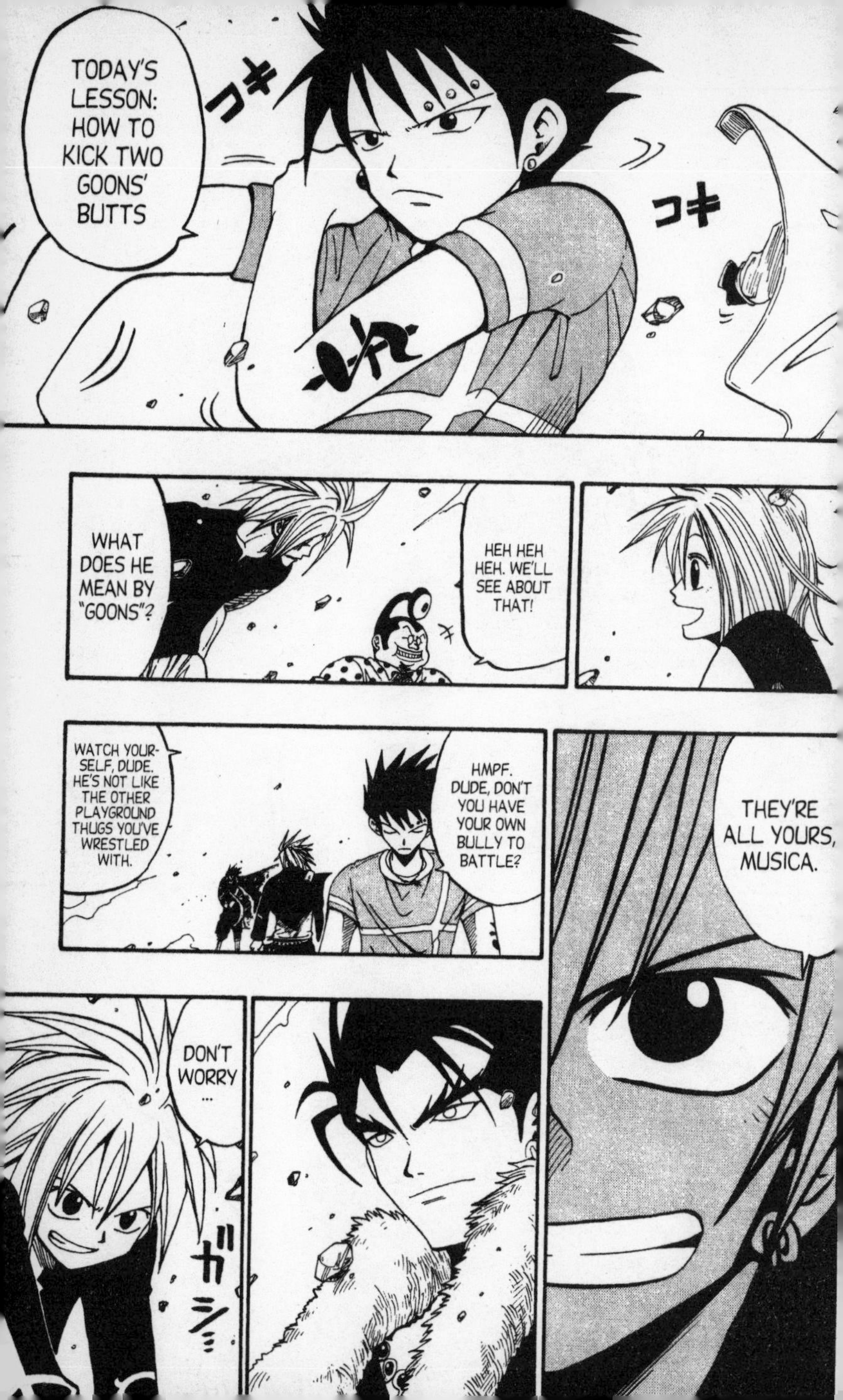
TODAY'S LESSON: HOW TO KICK TWO GOONS' BUTTS
コキ
コキ
HEH HEH HEH. WE'LL SEE ABOUT THAT!
WHAT DOES HE MEAN BY "GOONS"?
THEY'RE ALL YOURS, MUSICA.
HMPF. DUDE, DON'T YOU HAVE YOUR OWN BULLY TO BATTLE?
WATCH YOUR-SELF, DUDE. HE'S NOT LIKE THE OTHER PLAYGROUND THUGS YOU'VE WRESTLED WITH.
ガシ
DON'T WORRY ...

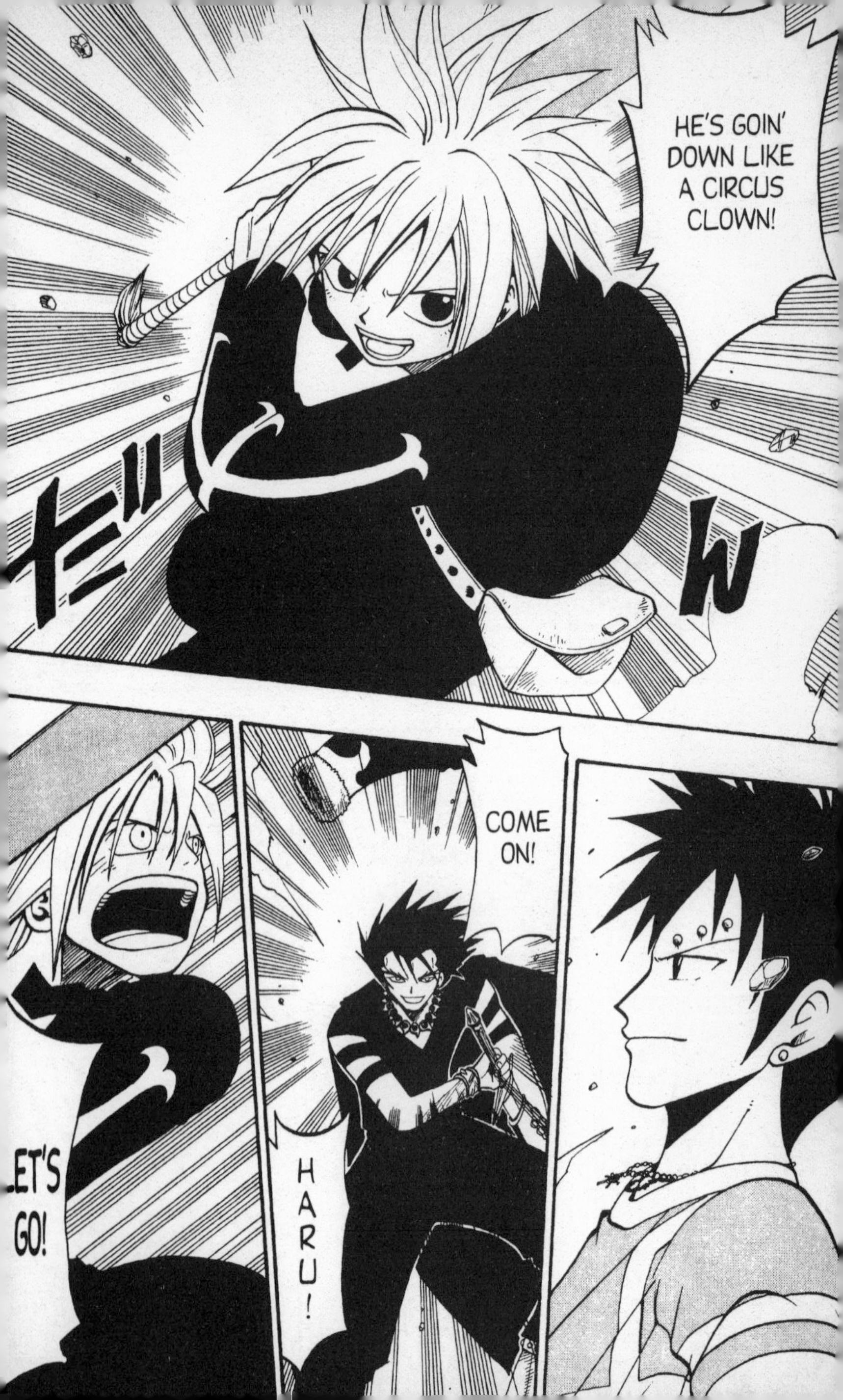

HE'S GOIN' DOWN LIKE A CIRCUS CLOWN!
W
COME ON!
HARU!
LET'S GO!

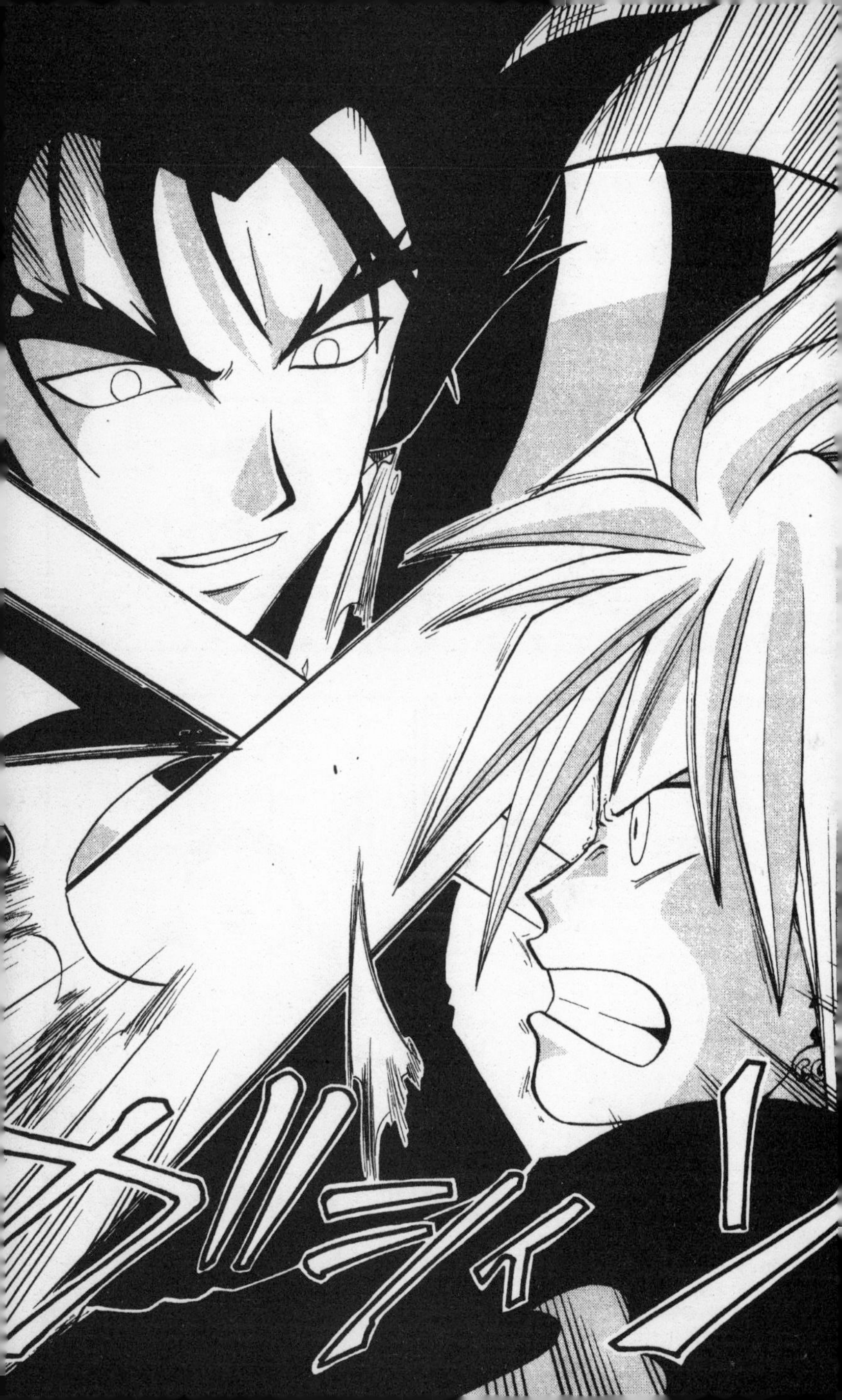

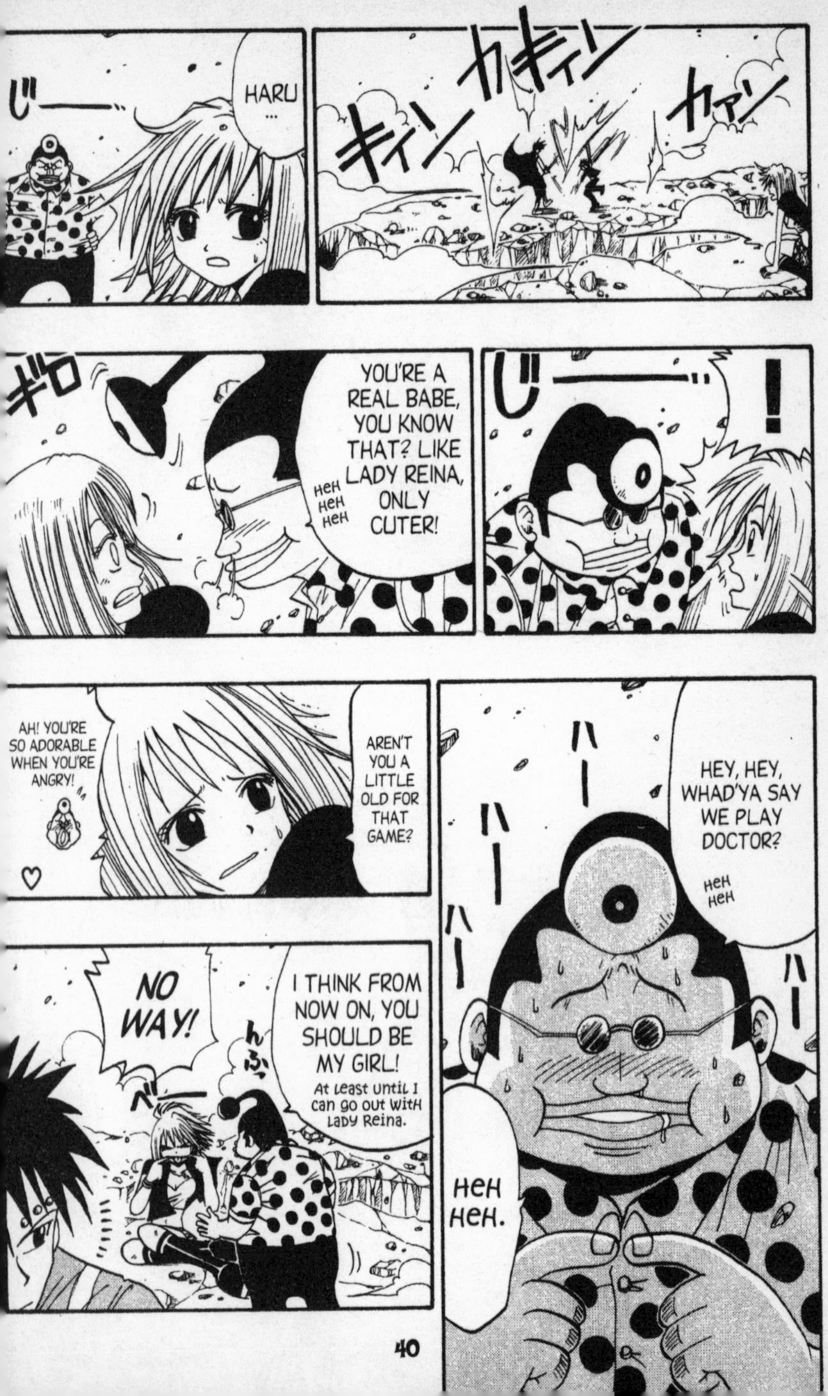
カァン
カキィン
キィン
HARU ...
じーー
!
じーー
YOU'RE A REAL BABE, YOU KNOW THAT? LIKE LADY REINA, ONLY CUTER!
HEH HEH HEH
ギロ
ハー
ハー
ハー
ハー
HEY, HEY, WHAD'YA SAY WE PLAY DOCTOR?
HEH HEH
HEH HEH.
AREN'T YOU A LITTLE OLD FOR THAT GAME?
AH! YOU'RE SO ADORABLE WHEN YOU'RE ANGRY!
♡
I THINK FROM NOW ON, YOU SHOULD BE MY GIRL!
At least until I can go out with Lady Reina.
んふ
NO WAY!
べー

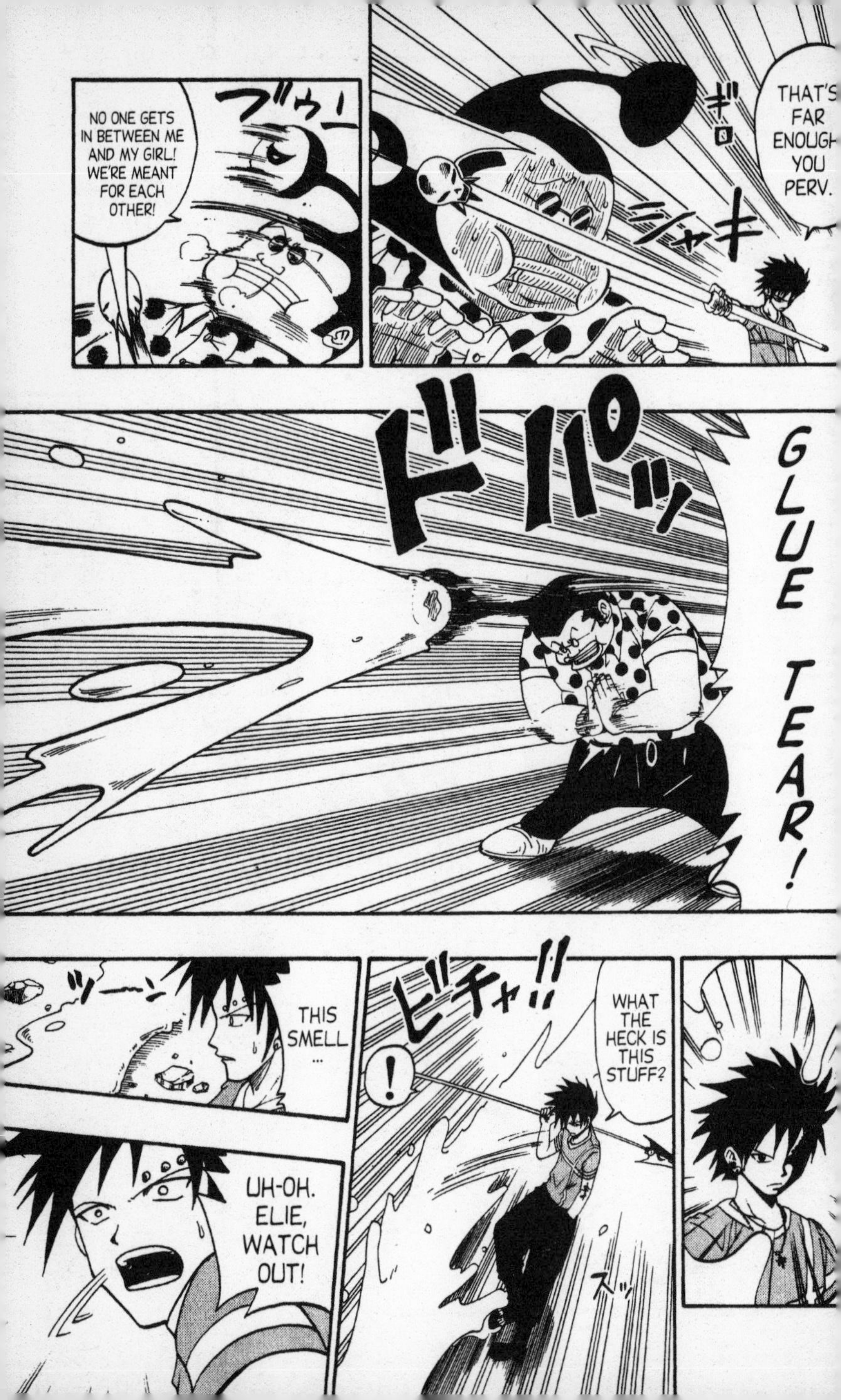

THAT'S FAR ENOUGH YOU PERV.
シャキ
NO ONE GETS IN BETWEEN ME AND MY GIRL! WE'RE MEANT FOR EACH OTHER!
ドパッ
GLUE TEAR!
ビチャ!!
!
WHAT THE HECK IS THIS STUFF?
THIS SMELL ...
UH-OH. ELIE, WATCH OUT!

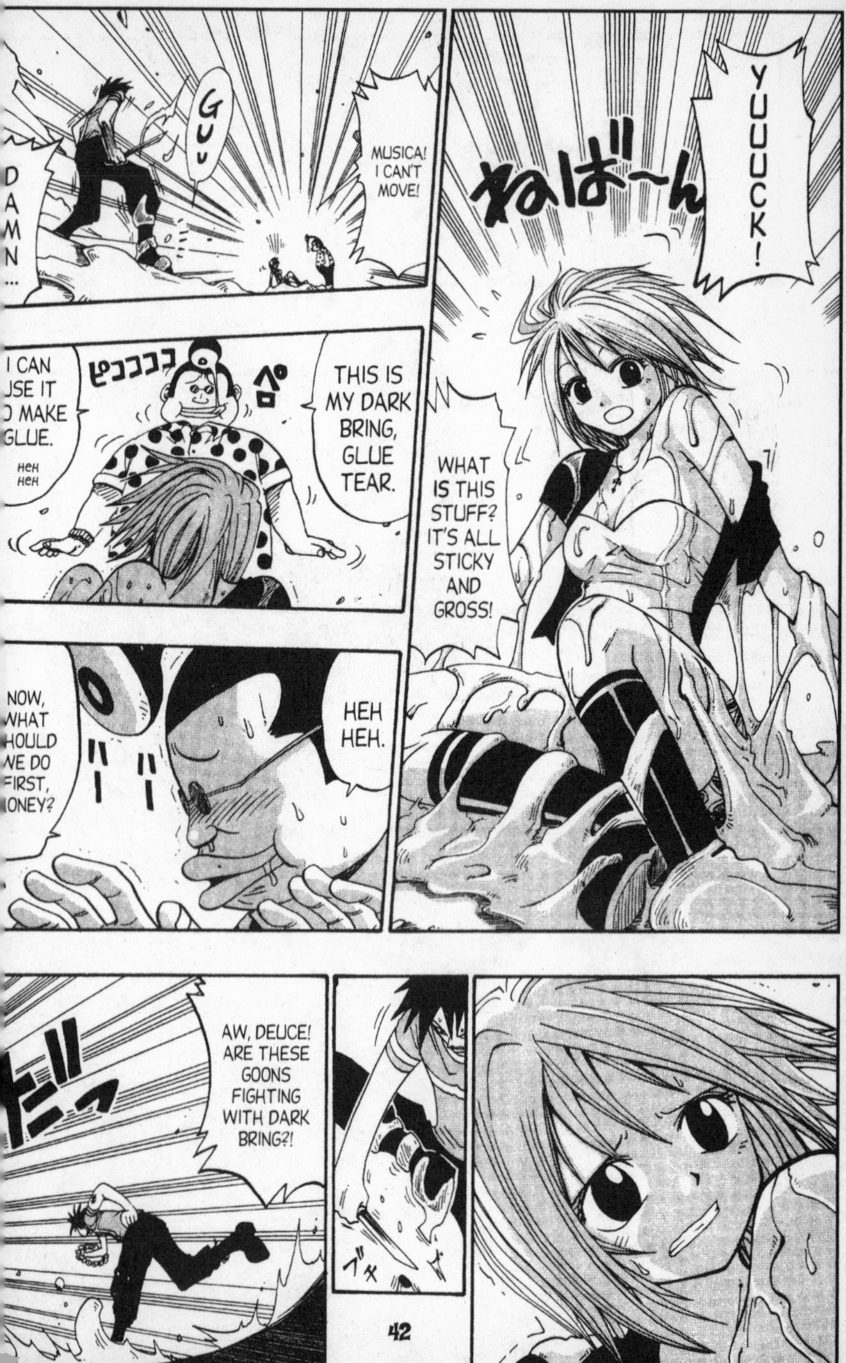
YUUUCK!
ねばーん
WHAT IS THIS STUFF? IT'S ALL STICKY AND GROSS!
MUSICA! I CAN'T MOVE!
GUU
DAMN...
THIS IS MY DARK BRING, GLUE TEAR.
ぺ
ぴこここここ
I CAN JSE IT O MAKE GLUE.
HEH HEH
HEH HEH.
ハー ハー
NOW, WHAT HOULD WE DO FIRST, ONEY?
ブタ
AW, DEUCE! ARE THESE GOONS FIGHTING WITH DARK BRING?!
だーっ

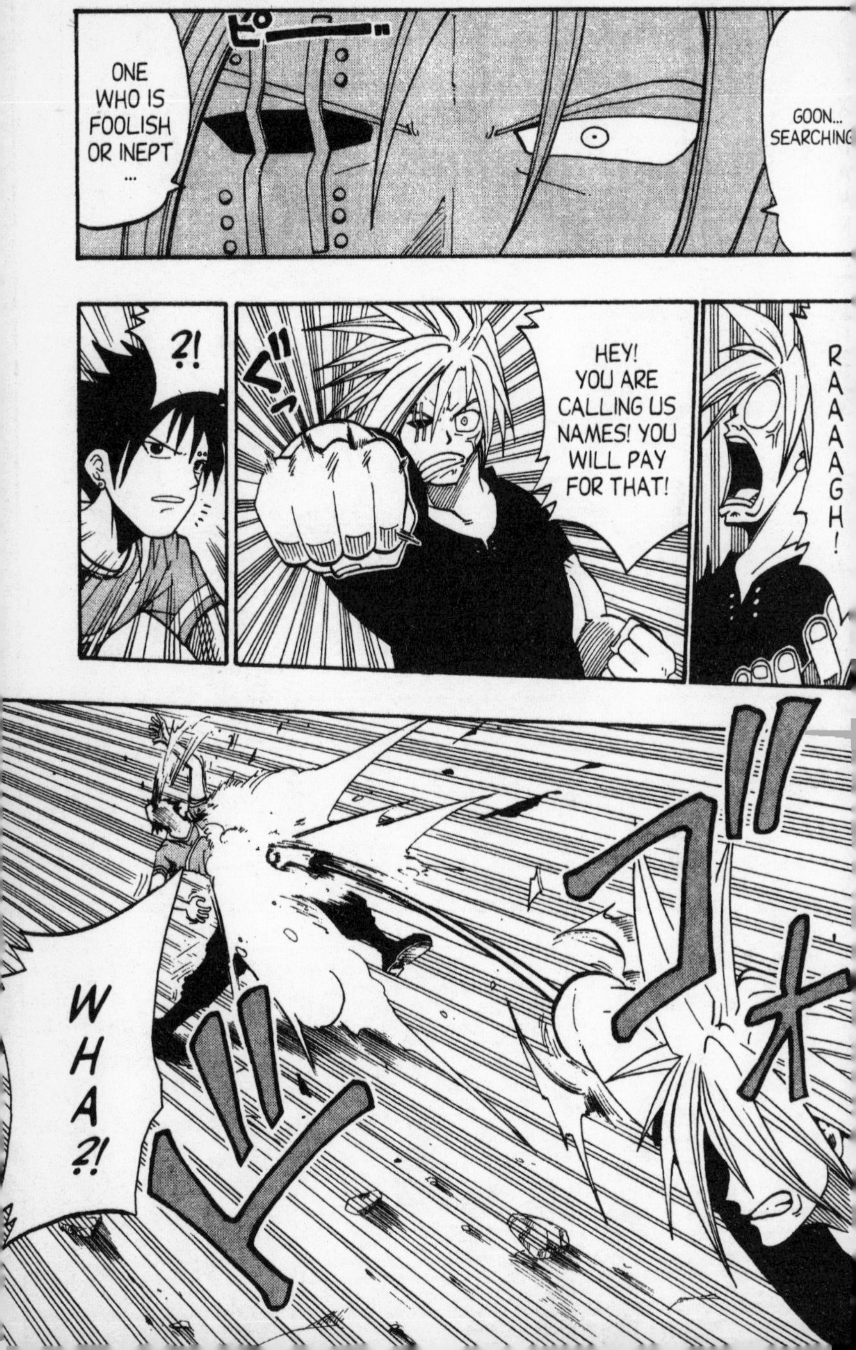
GOON... SEARCHING
ONE WHO IS FOOLISH OR INEPT ...
RAAAAGH!
HEY! YOU ARE CALLING US NAMES! YOU WILL PAY FOR THAT!
?!
WHA?!

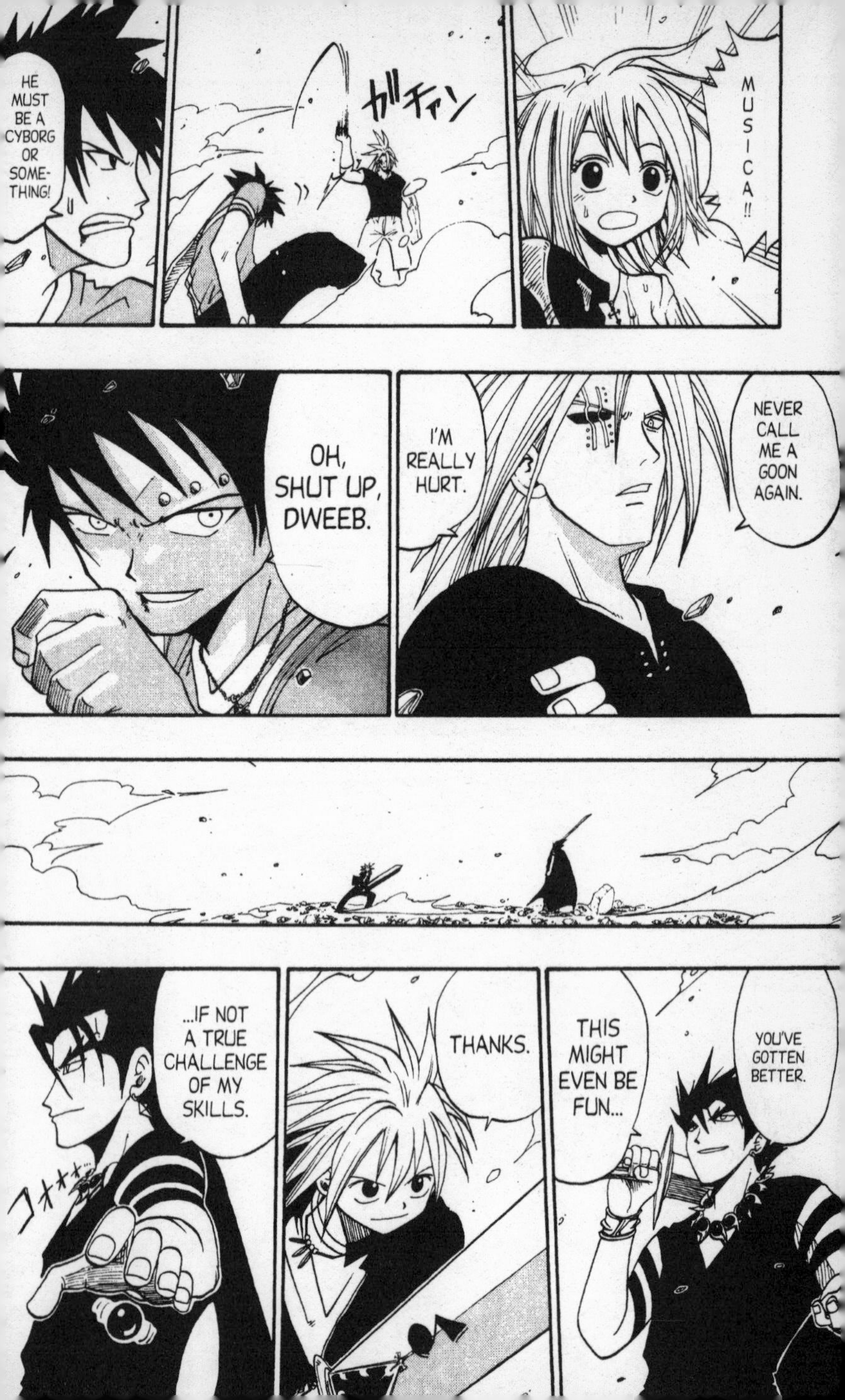
MUSICA!!
ガチャン
HE MUST BE A CYBORG OR SOME-THING!
NEVER CALL ME A GOON AGAIN.
I'M REALLY HURT.
OH, SHUT UP, DWEEB.
YOU'VE GOTTEN BETTER.
THIS MIGHT EVEN BE FUN...
THANKS.
...IF NOT A TRUE CHALLENGE OF MY SKILLS.

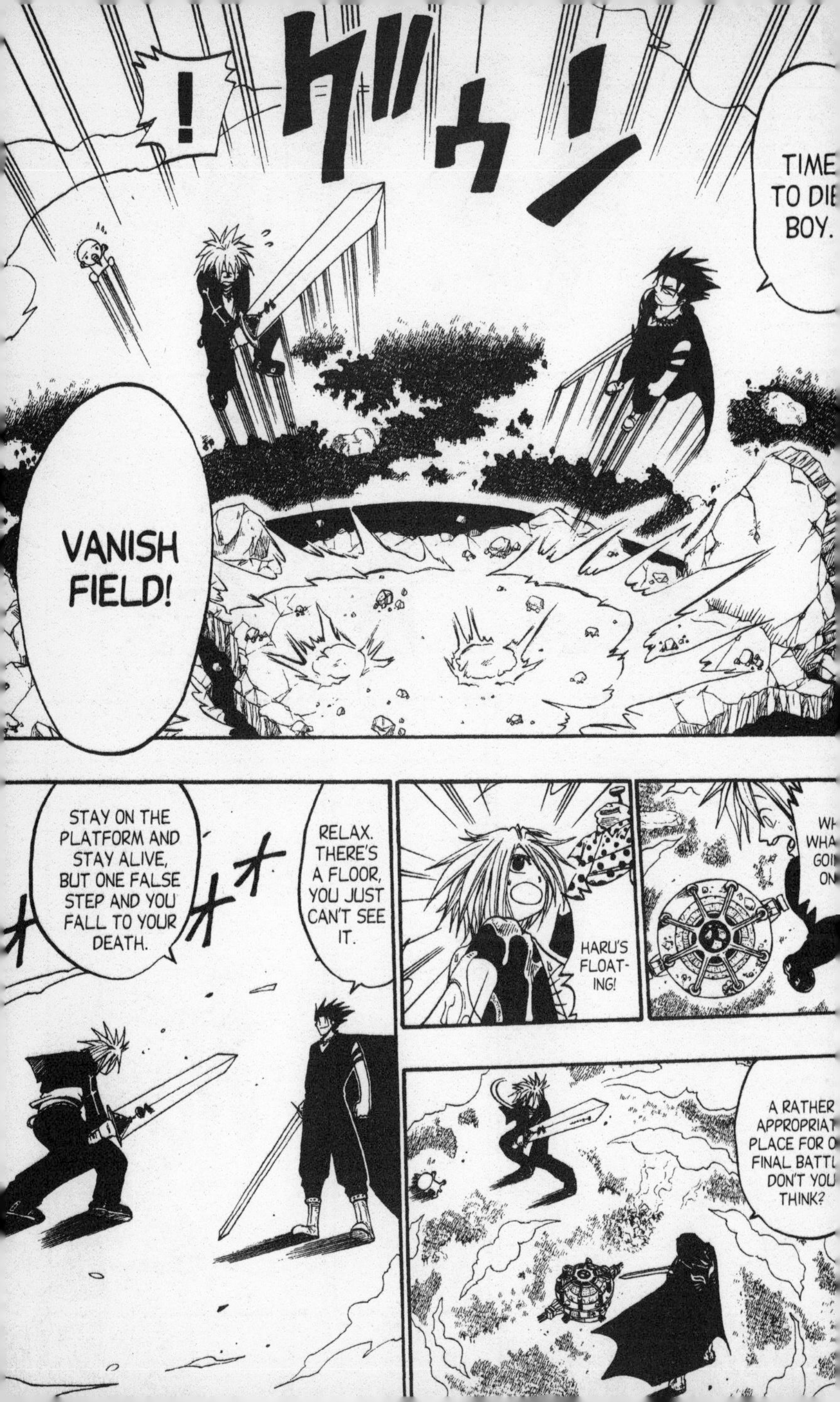

TIME TO DIE BOY.
グゥン
!
VANISH FIELD!
WH WHA GOI ON
HARU'S FLOAT-ING!
A RATHER APPROPRIAT PLACE FOR O FINAL BATTL DON'T YOU THINK?
RELAX. THERE'S A FLOOR, YOU JUST CAN'T SEE IT.
STAY ON THE PLATFORM AND STAY ALIVE, BUT ONE FALSE STEP AND YOU FALL TO YOUR DEATH.

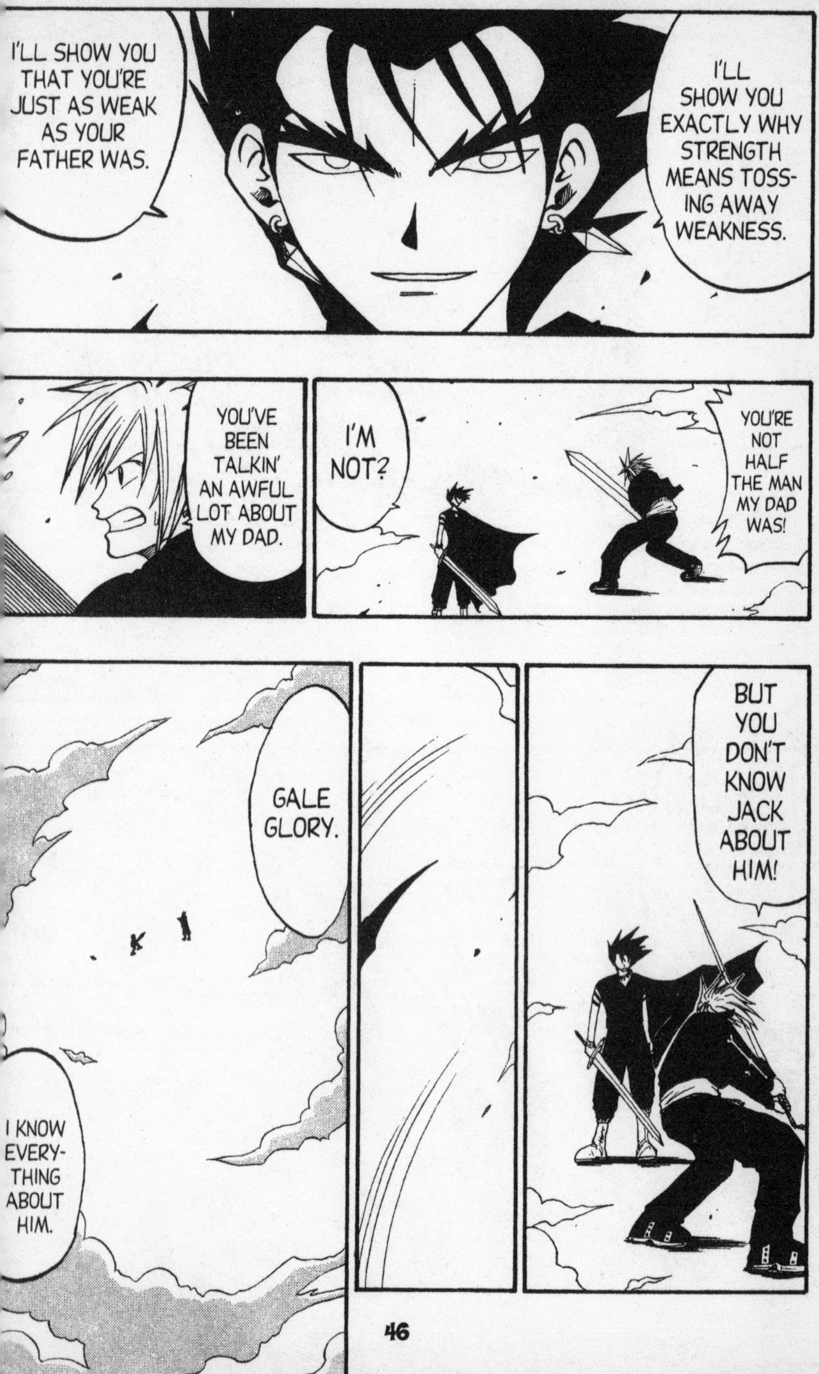
I'LL SHOW YOU EXACTLY WHY STRENGTH MEANS TOSS-ING AWAY WEAKNESS.
I'LL SHOW YOU THAT YOU'RE JUST AS WEAK AS YOUR FATHER WAS.
YOU'RE NOT HALF THE MAN MY DAD WAS!
I'M NOT?
YOU'VE BEEN TALKIN' AN AWFUL LOT ABOUT MY DAD.
BUT YOU DON'T KNOW JACK ABOUT HIM!
GALE GLORY.
I KNOW EVERY-THING ABOUT HIM.

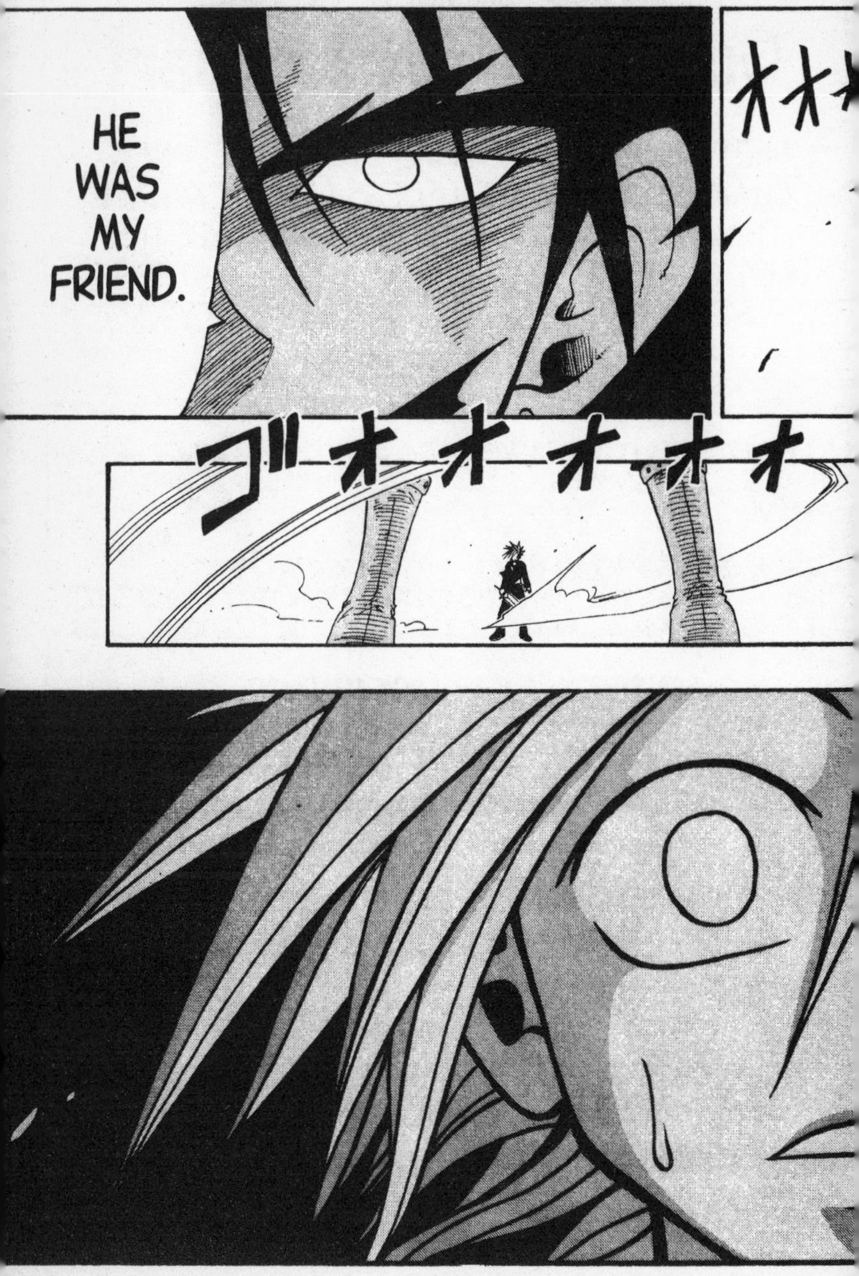
オオオ
HE WAS MY FRIEND.
ゴオオオオオ

Question and Answer!

I GET A LOT OF QUESTIONS EVERY TIME A NEW CHAPTER COMES OUT. I GUESS I DON'T EXPLAIN THINGS AS MUCH AS I SHOULD! OR MAYBE IT'S JUST BECAUSE THERE ARE A LOT OF MYSTERIES. LET'S SEE IF I CAN'T ANSWER SOME OF YOUR QUESTIONS!

Q. WAS THE TEN POWERS MADE BY THE OLD MUSICA A LONG TIME AGO?
HIRO: YES. THE OLD MUSICA MADE IT TO FIT SHIBA'S RAVE WHEN HE WAS 20.

Q. HOW DOES THE YOUNG MUSICA PUT HIS EYEBROW PIERCINGS IN?
HIRO: HE PINCHES THE SKIN OF HIS EYEBROW! NOW THAT I THINK ABOUT IT, IT SEEMS PAINFUL. MAYBE HE JUST USES GLUE TO STICK THEM ON.

Q. COULD LEVIN'S (FROM RAVE 0077) MOM AND DAD BE...?
HIRO: BE WHO? (LAUGHS) THEY'RE PROBABLY NOT WHO YOU EXPECT.

Q: IS PLUE REALLY A DOG?
HIRO: NO MATTER HOW MANY TIMES I TELL YOU HE'S A DOG, YOU STILL DON'T BELIEVE ME! POOR PLUE. PLEASE FORGIVE THEM.

Q: DO YOU READ FAN LETTERS WITHOUT A RETURN ADDRESS OR NAME?
HIRO: I'M BUSY, BUT I READ ALL OF THE FAN LETTERS THAT I GET, EVEN IF THERE'S NO RETURN ADDRESS OR NAME. I KEEP THEM ALL IN A SAFE PLACE. THEY'RE MY TREASURES.

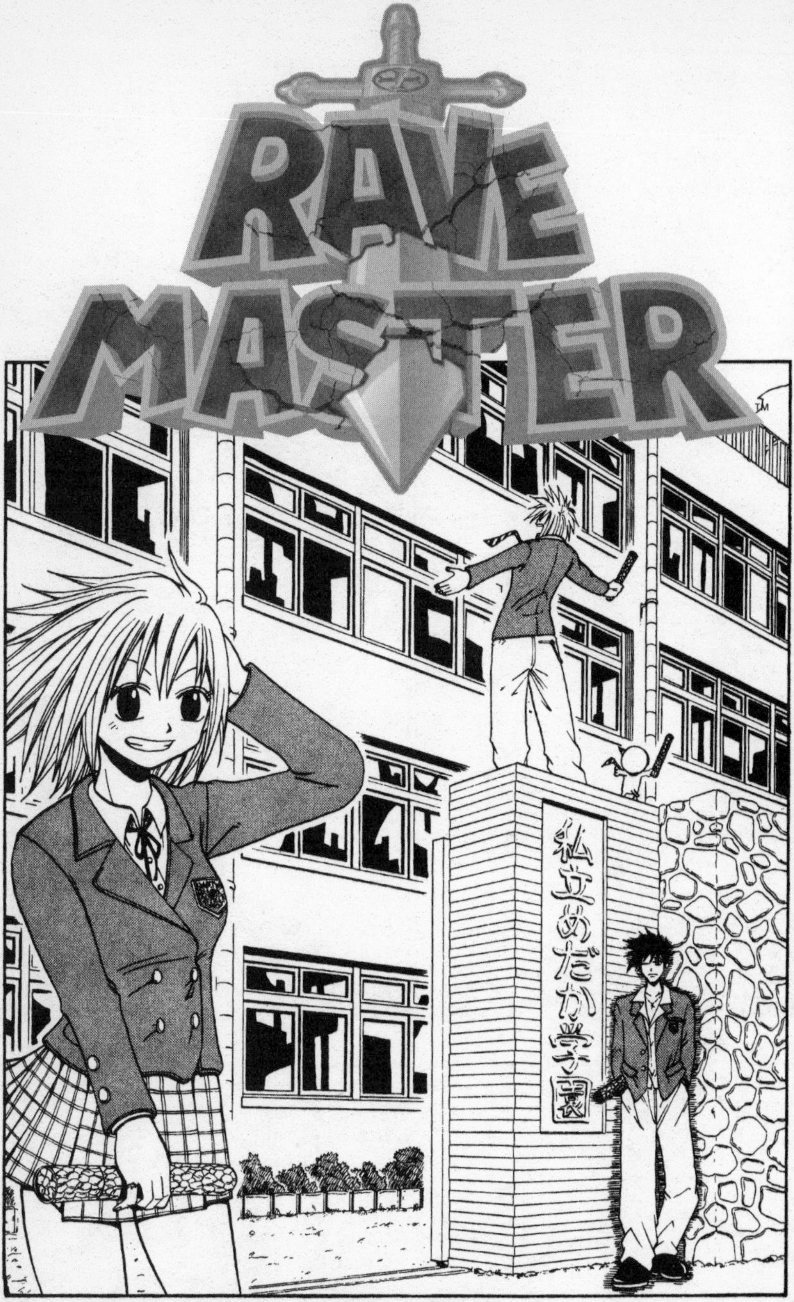
RAVE MASTER
私立めだか学園

RAVE: 33 ✠ DISTANT PROMISE

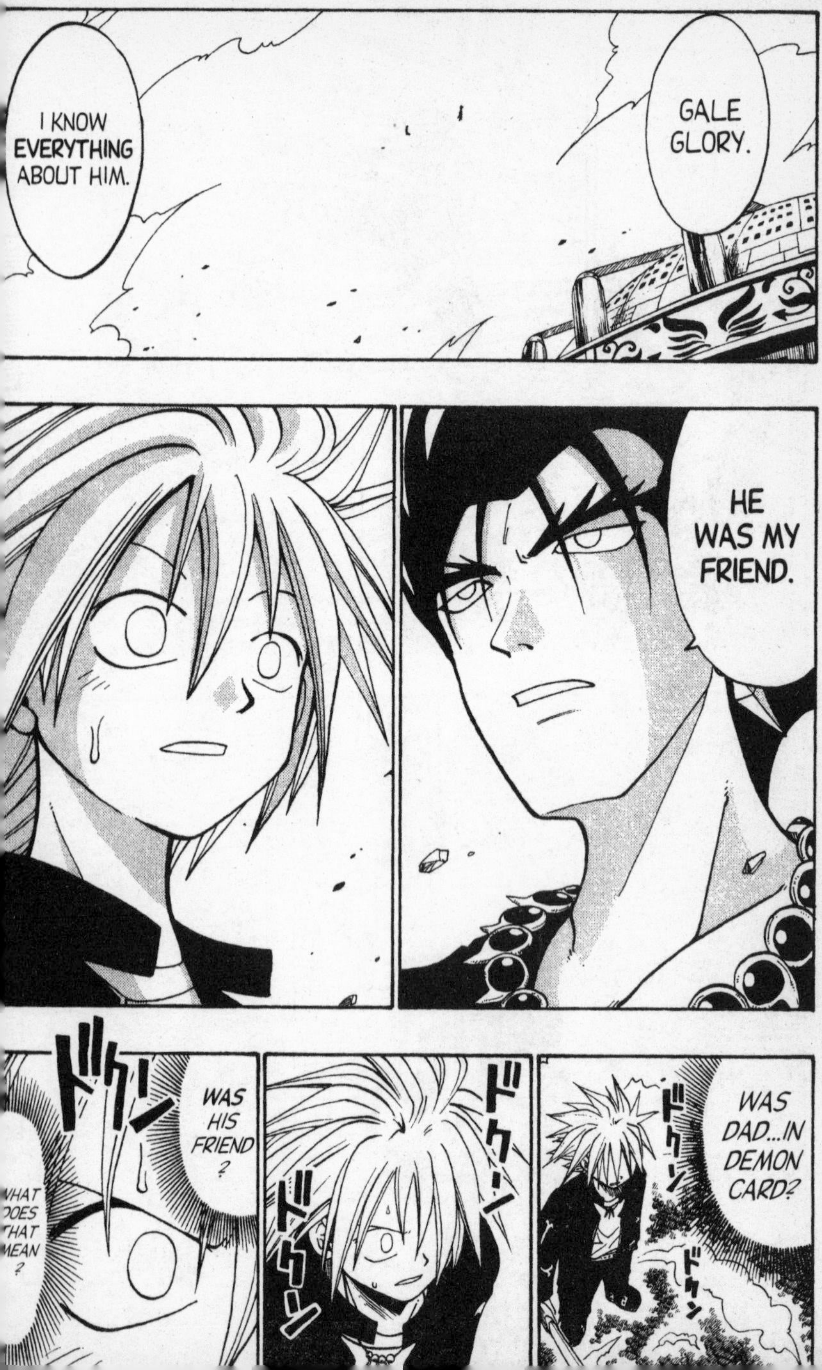
GALE GLORY.
I KNOW EVERYTHING ABOUT HIM.
HE WAS MY FRIEND.
WAS DAD...IN DEMON CARD?
ドクン
ドクン
ドクン
ドクン
ドクン
WAS HIS FRIEND?
WHAT DOES THAT MEAN?

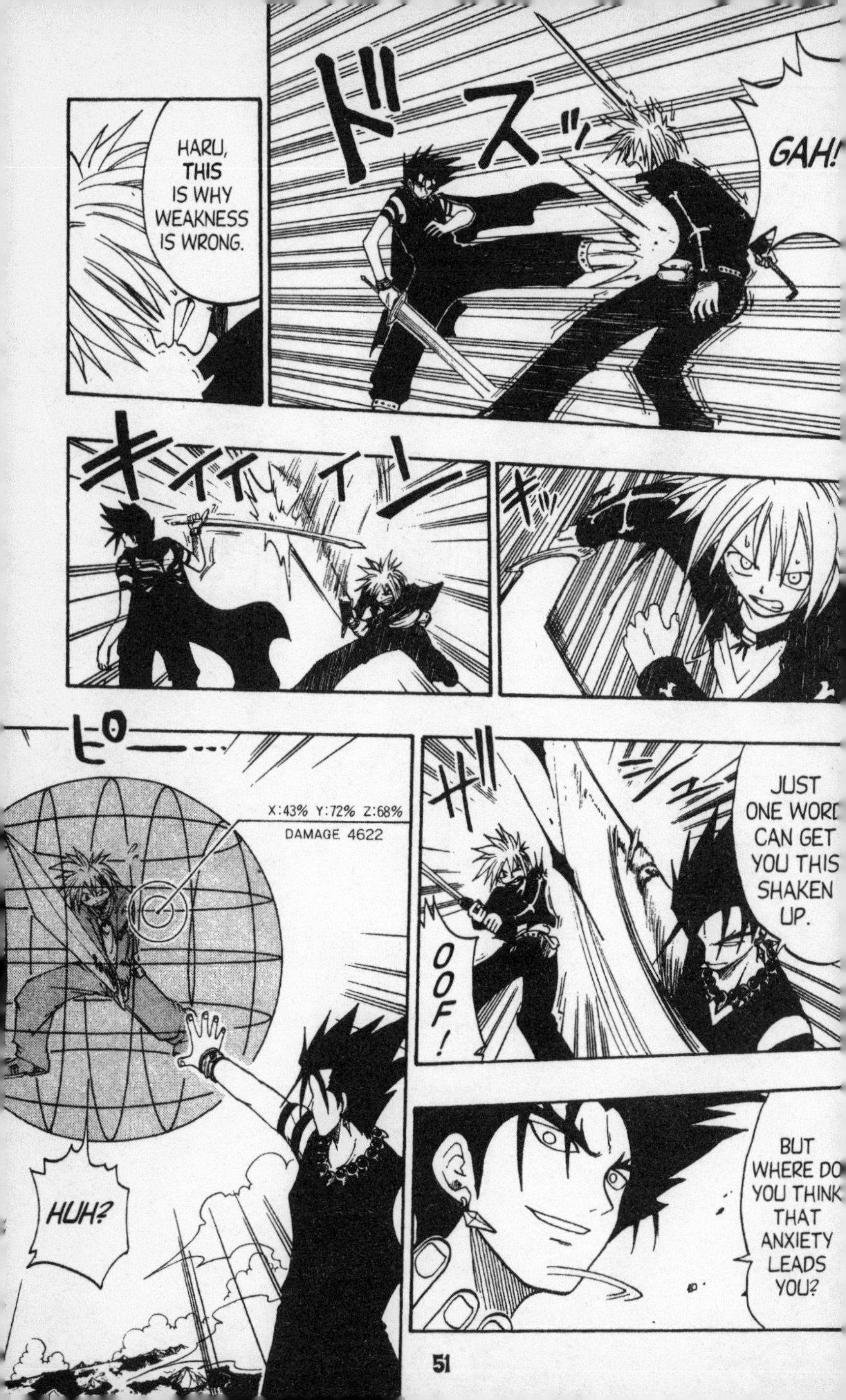
GAH!
HARU, THIS IS WHY WEAKNESS IS WRONG.
JUST ONE WORD CAN GET YOU THIS SHAKEN UP.
OOF!
BUT WHERE DO YOU THINK THAT ANXIETY LEADS YOU?
X:43% Y:72% Z:68%
DAMAGE 4622
HUH?

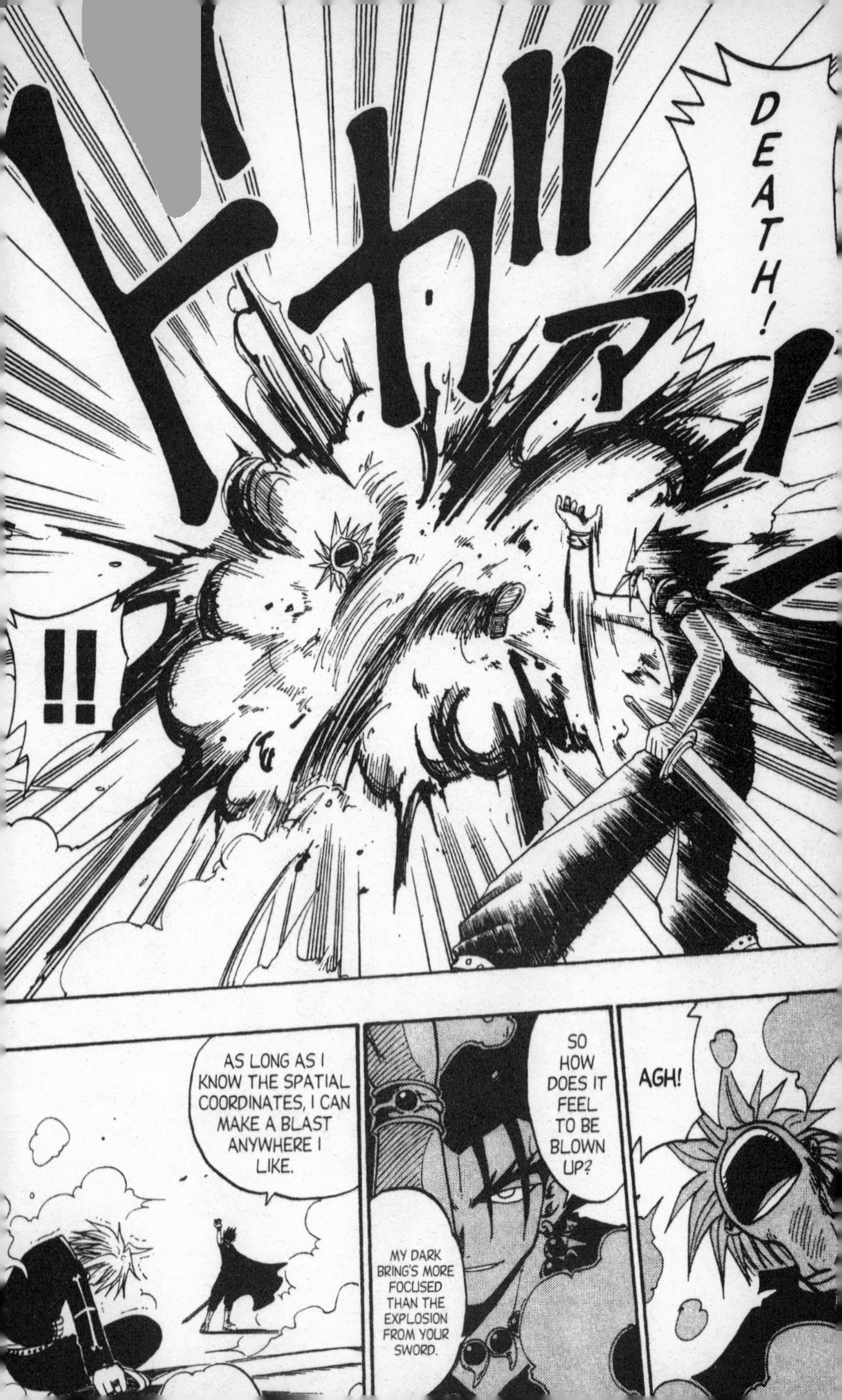
DEATH!
!!
AGH!
SO HOW DOES IT FEEL TO BE BLOWN UP?
MY DARK BRING'S MORE FOCUSED THAN THE EXPLOSION FROM YOUR SWORD.
AS LONG AS I KNOW THE SPATIAL COORDINATES, I CAN MAKE A BLAST ANYWHERE I LIKE.

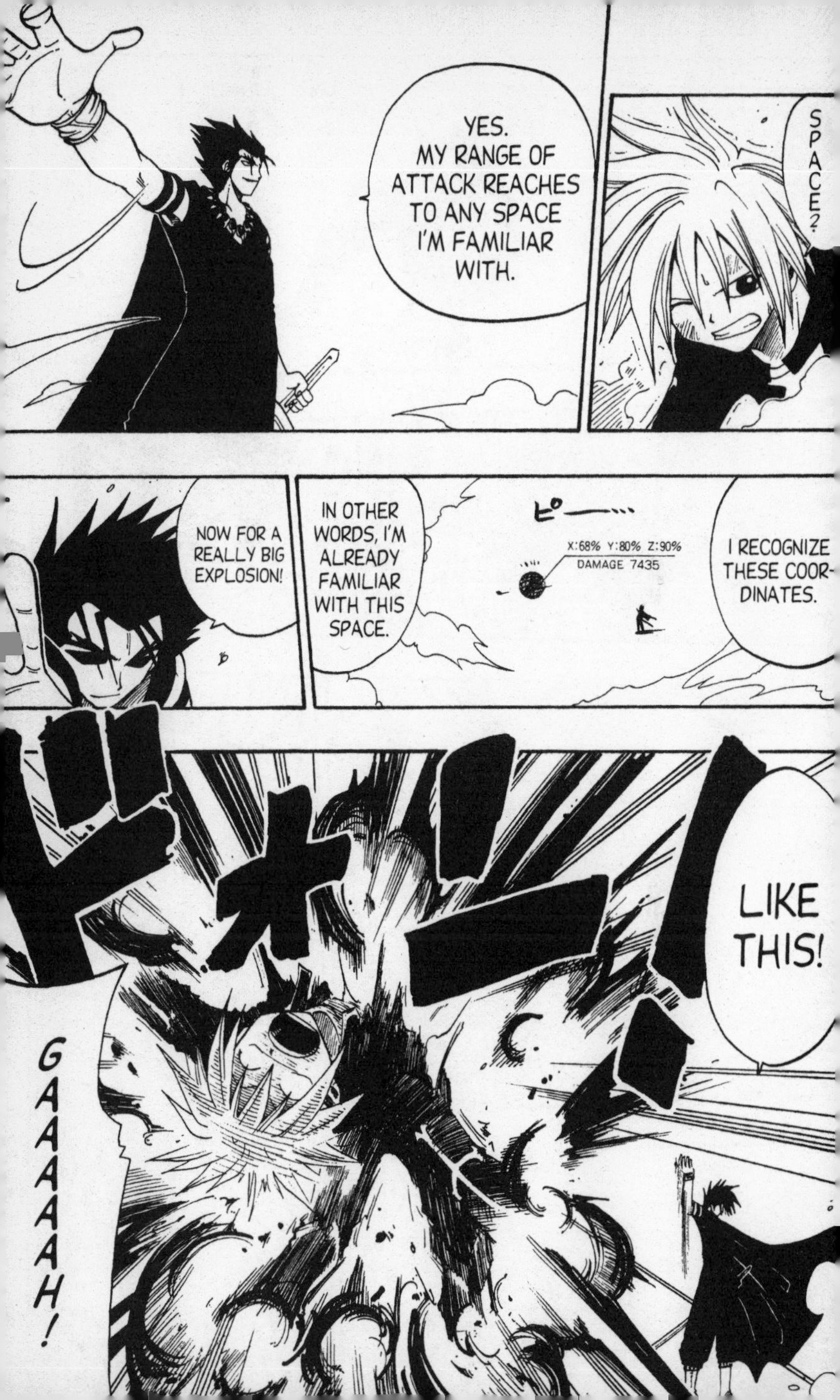
SPACE?
YES.
MY RANGE OF ATTACK REACHES TO ANY SPACE I'M FAMILIAR WITH.
I RECOGNIZE THESE COORDINATES.
ピー…
X:68% Y:80% Z:90%
DAMAGE 7435
IN OTHER WORDS, I'M ALREADY FAMILIAR WITH THIS SPACE.
NOW FOR A REALLY BIG EXPLOSION!
LIKE THIS!
GAAAAAH!

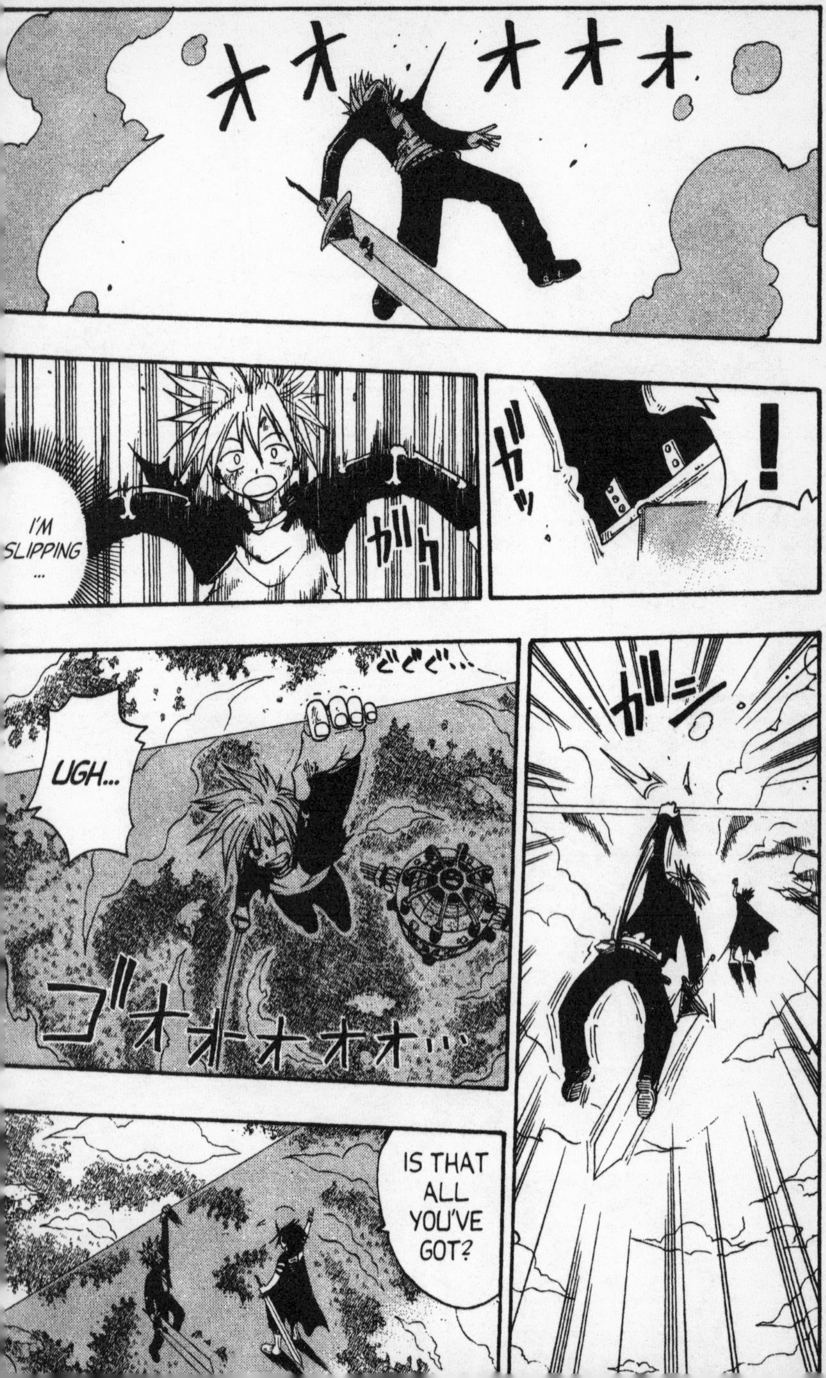
オオオ
オオオ
ガッ
!
I'M SLIPPING ...
UGH...
ゴオオーオオオ
IS THAT ALL YOU'VE GOT?

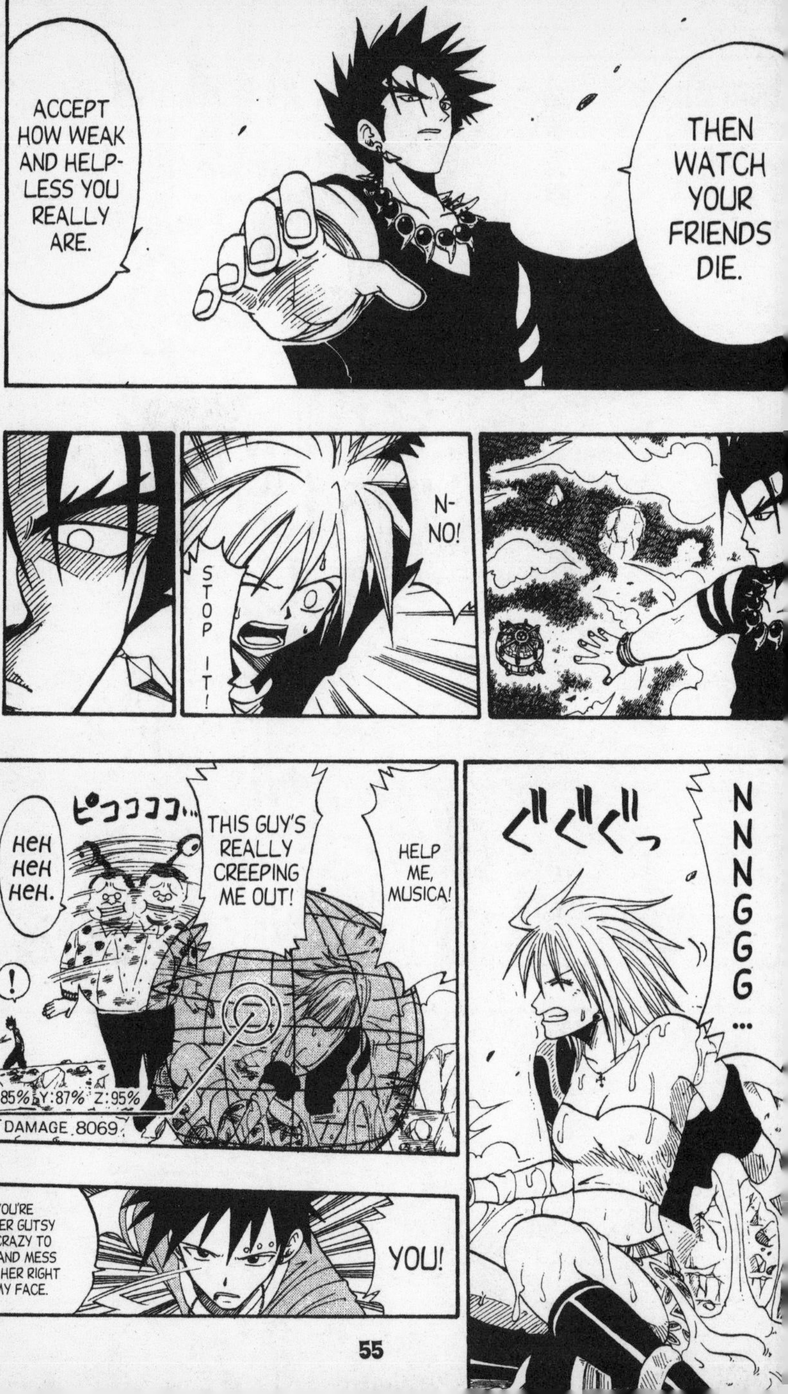
ACCEPT HOW WEAK AND HELP-LESS YOU REALLY ARE.
THEN WATCH YOUR FRIENDS DIE.
N-NO!
STOP IT!
NNNGGG...
ぐぐぐっ
HELP ME, MUSICA!
THIS GUY'S REALLY CREEPING ME OUT!
ピコココココ…
HEH HEH HEH.
!
X:85% Y:87% Z:95%
DAMAGE 8069
YOU!
YOU'RE EITHER GUTSY OR CRAZY TO TRY AND MESS WITH HER RIGHT IN MY FACE.

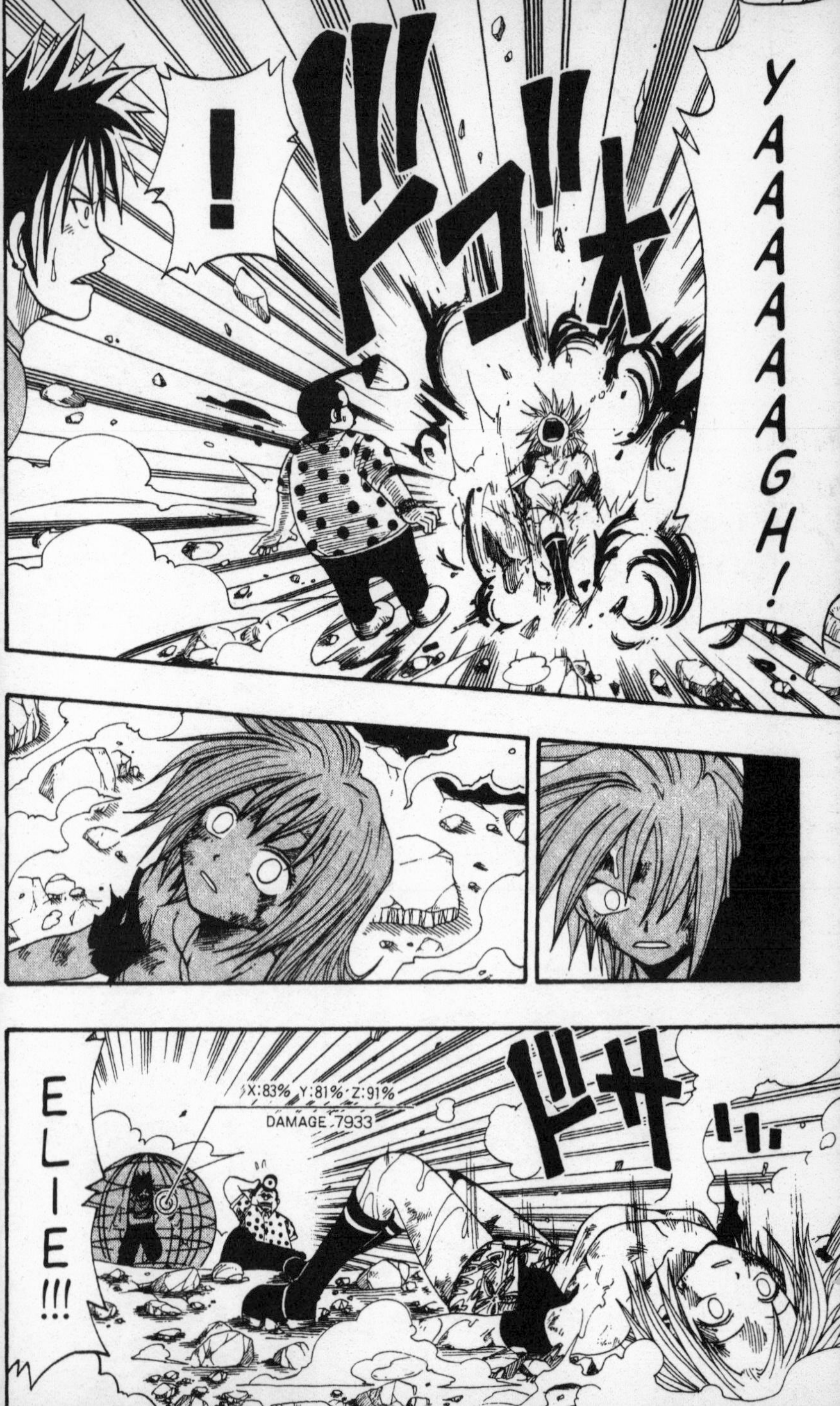
YAAAAAAGH!
ドゴォ
!
ドサッ
X:83% Y:81% Z:91%
DAMAGE 7933
ELIE!!!

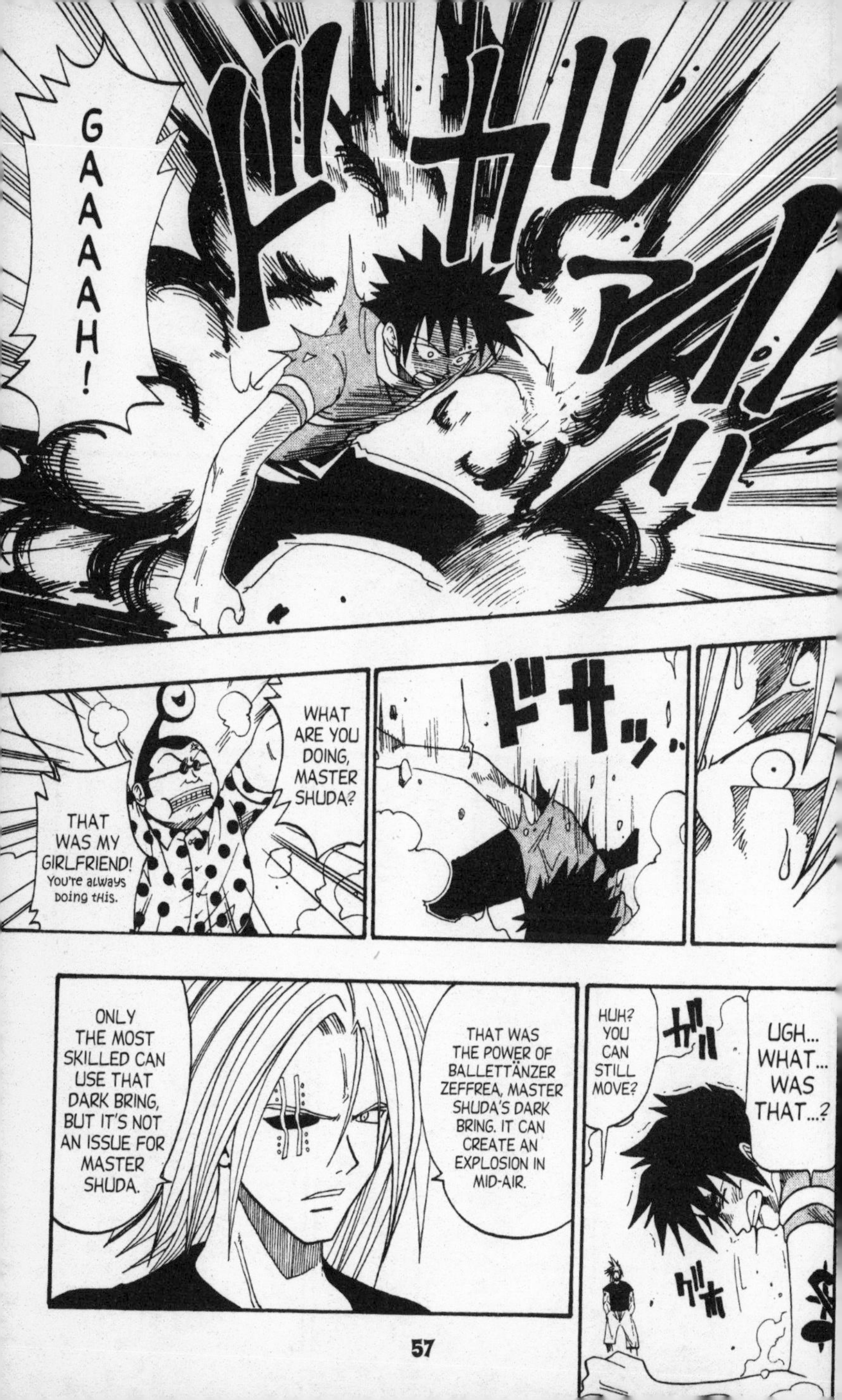
GAAAAAH!
ドサッ
WHAT ARE YOU DOING, MASTER SHUDA?
THAT WAS MY GIRLFRIEND! You're always doing this.
UGH... WHAT... WAS THAT...?
HUH? YOU CAN STILL MOVE?
THAT WAS THE POWER OF BALLETTÄNZER ZEFFREA, MASTER SHUDA'S DARK BRING. IT CAN CREATE AN EXPLOSION IN MID-AIR.
ONLY THE MOST SKILLED CAN USE THAT DARK BRING, BUT IT'S NOT AN ISSUE FOR MASTER SHUDA.

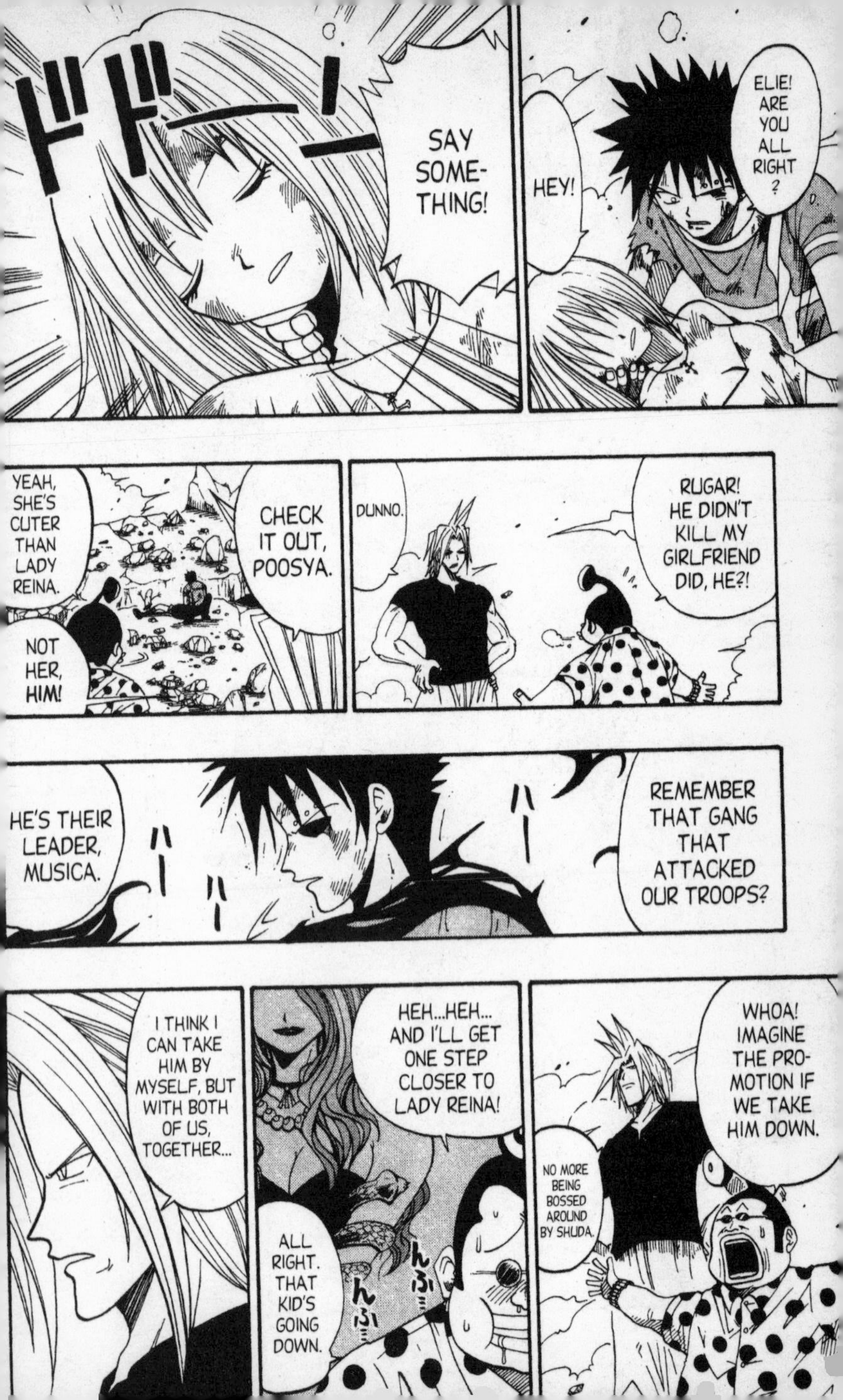
ELIE! ARE YOU ALL RIGHT?
HEY!
SAY SOME-THING!
ドドーー
RUGAR! HE DIDN'T KILL MY GIRLFRIEND DID, HE?!
DUNNO.
CHECK IT OUT, POOSYA.
YEAH, SHE'S CUTER THAN LADY REINA.
NOT HER, HIM!
REMEMBER THAT GANG THAT ATTACKED OUR TROOPS?
ハー
ハー
ハー
HE'S THEIR LEADER, MUSICA.
WHOA! IMAGINE THE PRO-MOTION IF WE TAKE HIM DOWN.
NO MORE BEING BOSSED AROUND BY SHUDA.
HEH...HEH... AND I'LL GET ONE STEP CLOSER TO LADY REINA!
んふ
んふ
ALL RIGHT. THAT KID'S GOING DOWN.
I THINK I CAN TAKE HIM BY MYSELF, BUT WITH BOTH OF US, TOGETHER...

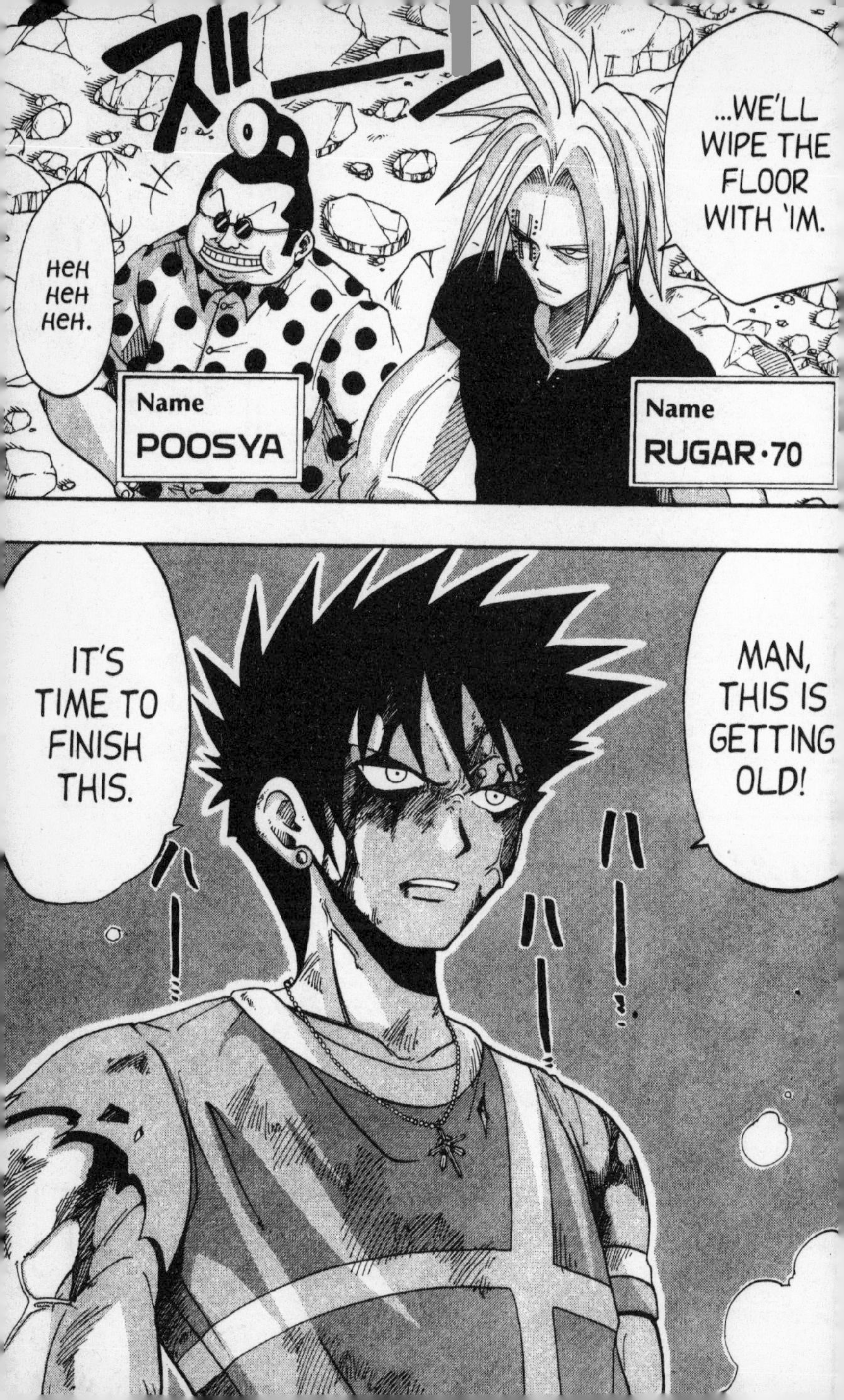
...WE'LL WIPE THE FLOOR WITH 'IM.
Name
RUGAR·70
HEH HEH HEH.
Name
POOSYA
MAN, THIS IS GETTING OLD!
IT'S TIME TO FINISH THIS.

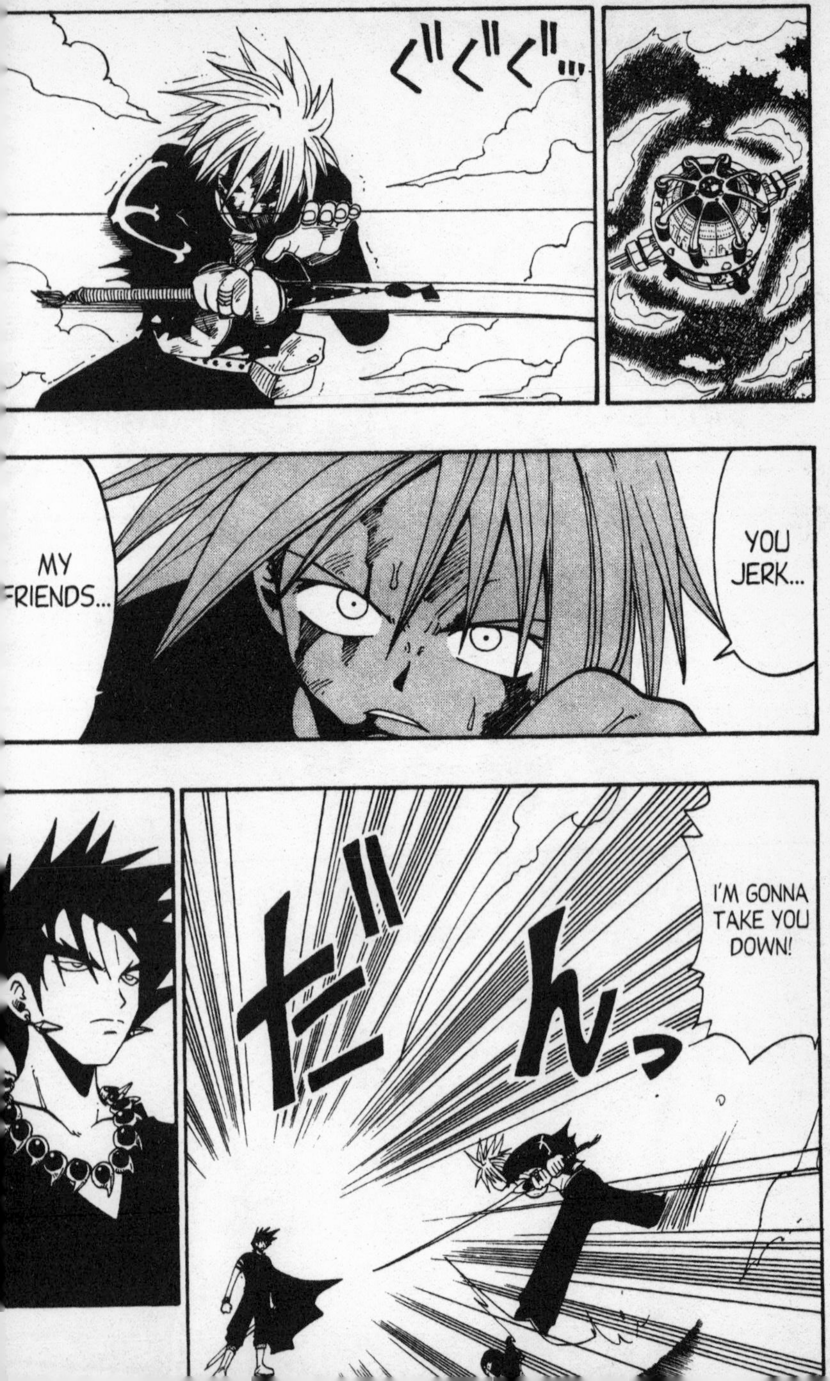
ぐぐぐ…
YOU JERK...
MY FRIENDS...
I'M GONNA TAKE YOU DOWN!
だんっ

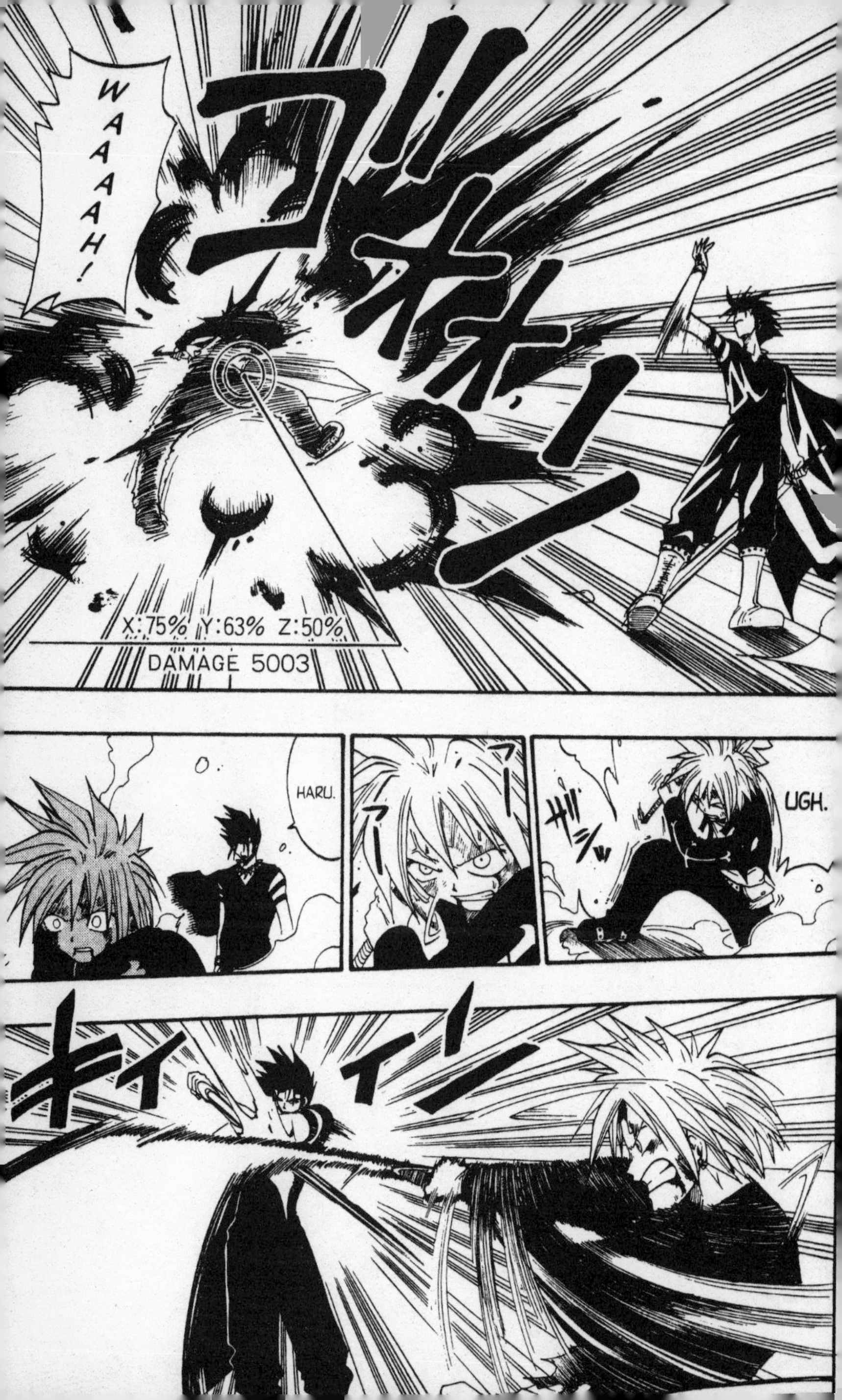
WAAAAAH!
X:75% Y:63% Z:50%
DAMAGE 5003
UGH.
HARU.

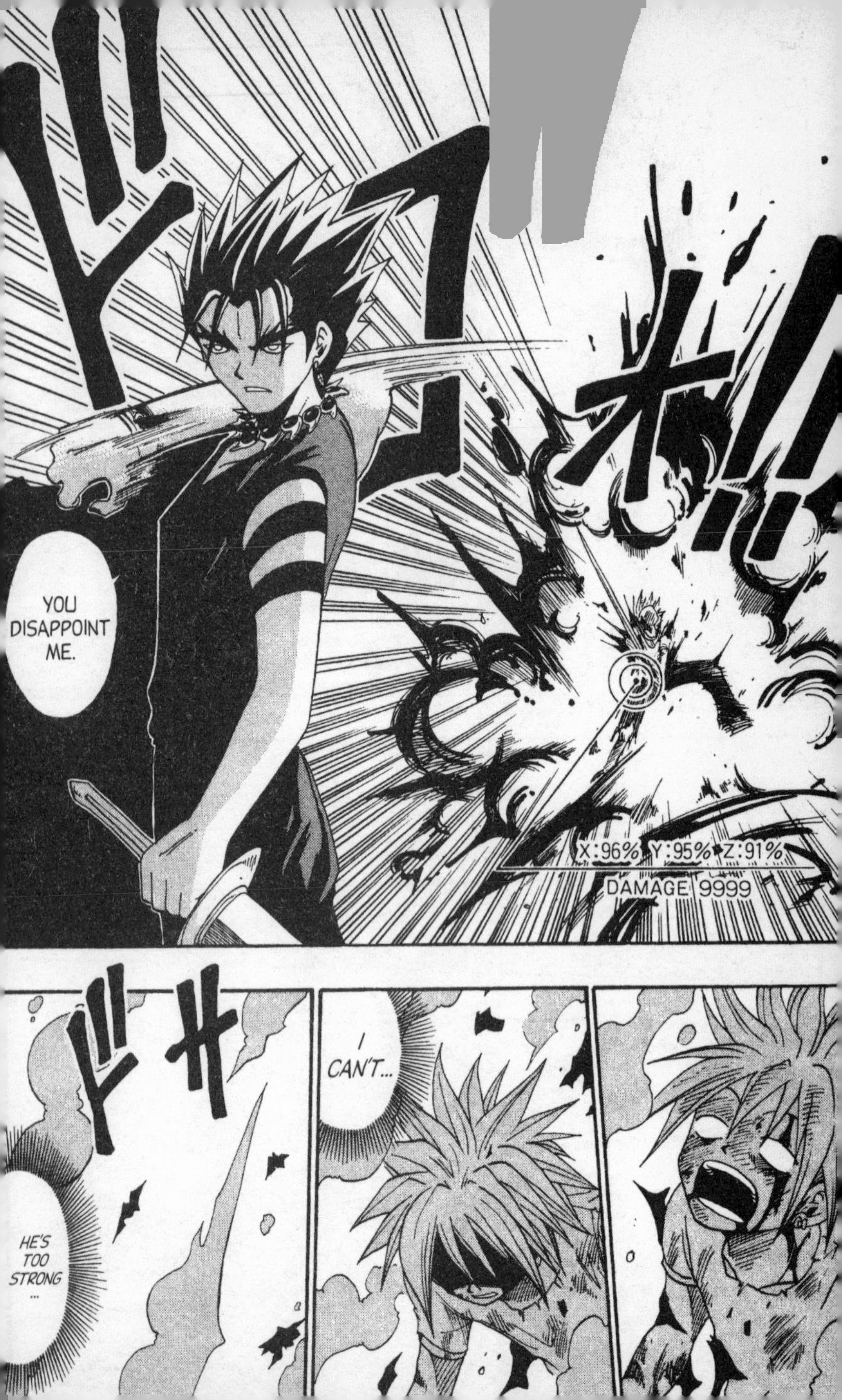
X:96% Y:95% Z:91%
DAMAGE 9999
YOU DISAPPOINT ME.
I CAN'T...
HE'S TOO STRONG ...

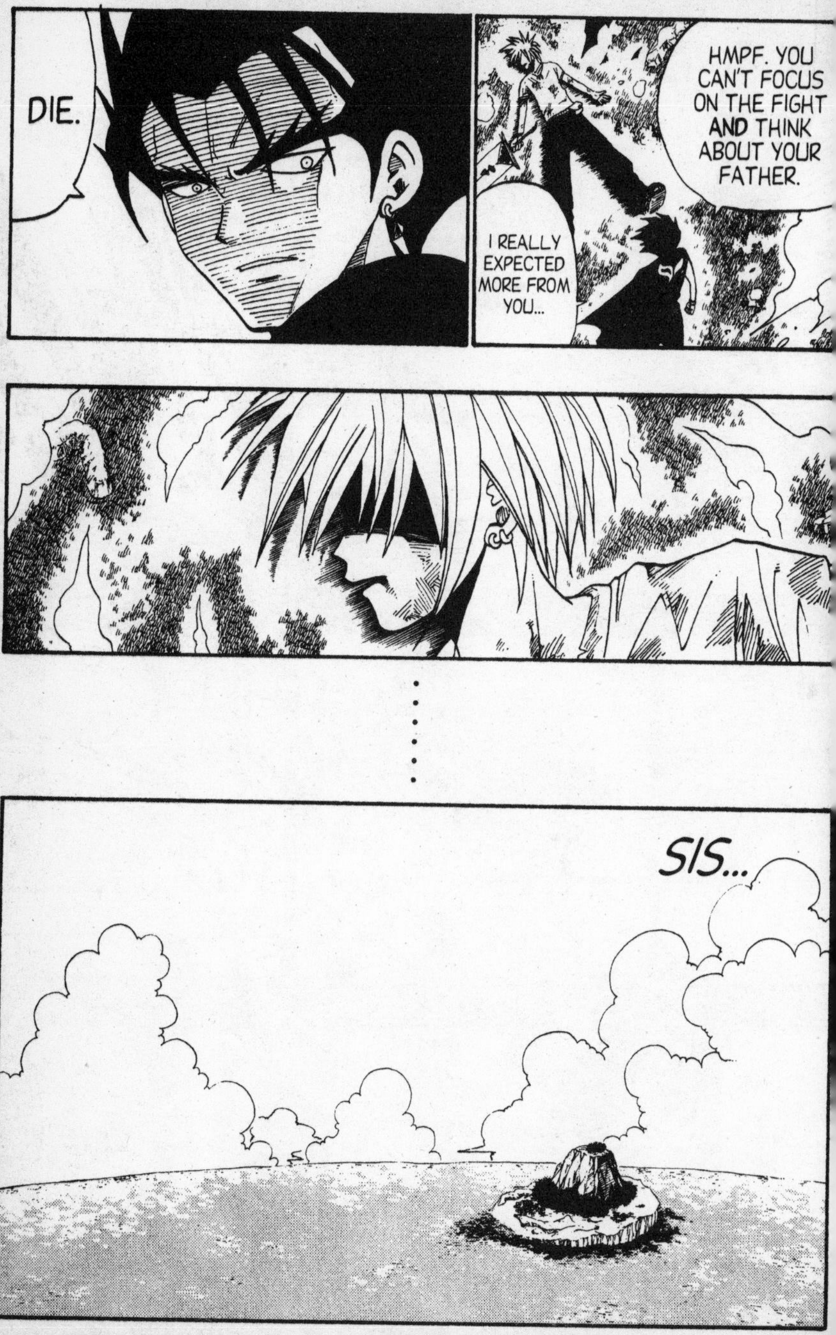
HMPF. YOU CAN'T FOCUS ON THE FIGHT AND THINK ABOUT YOUR FATHER.
I REALLY EXPECTED MORE FROM YOU...
DIE.
......
SIS...

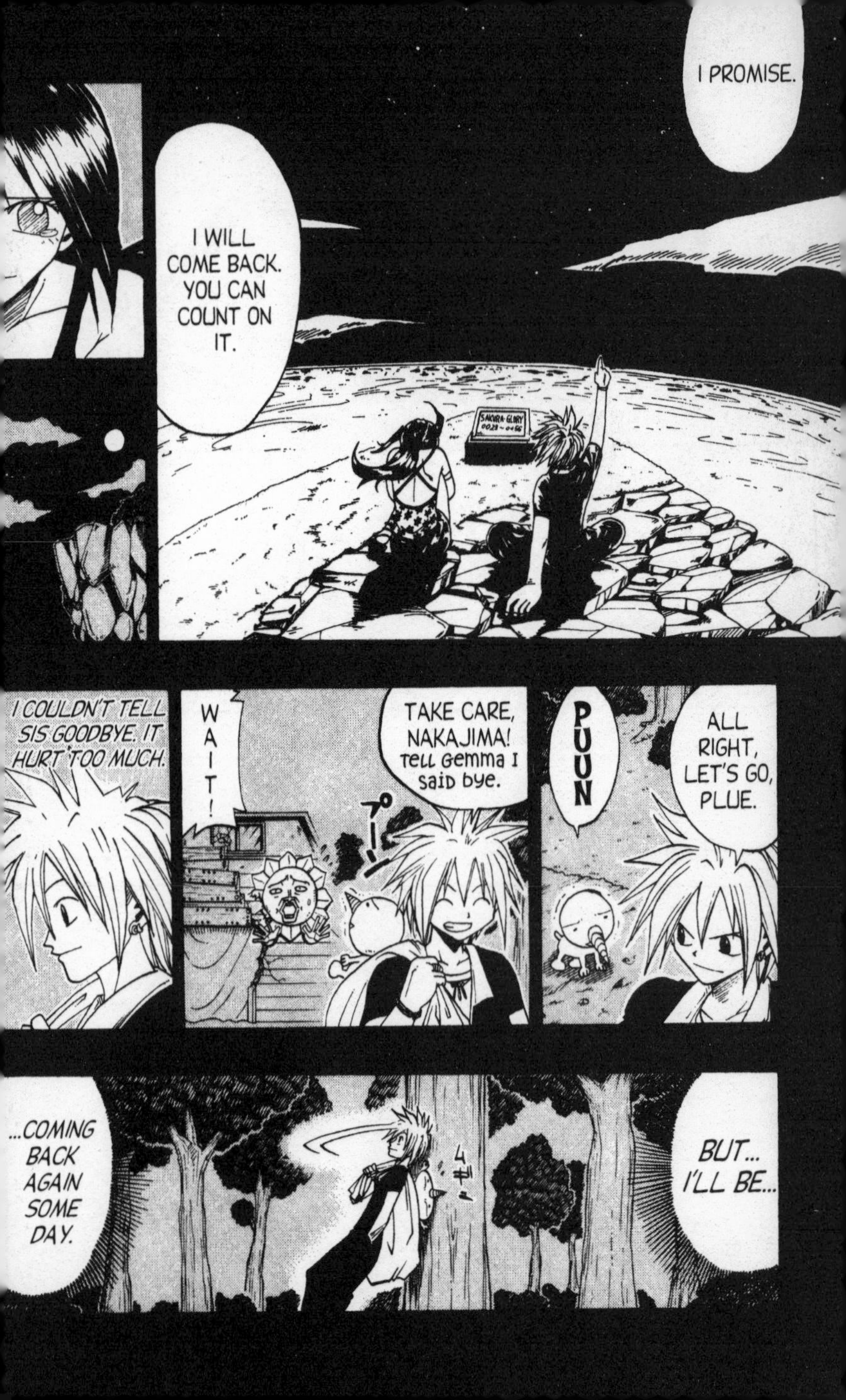
I PROMISE.
I WILL COME BACK. YOU CAN COUNT ON IT.
SAKURA·GLORY
ALL RIGHT, LET'S GO, PLUE.
PUUN
TAKE CARE, NAKAJIMA! Tell Gemma I said bye.
WAIT!
I COULDN'T TELL SIS GOODBYE. IT HURT TOO MUCH.
BUT... I'LL BE...
...COMING BACK AGAIN SOME DAY.

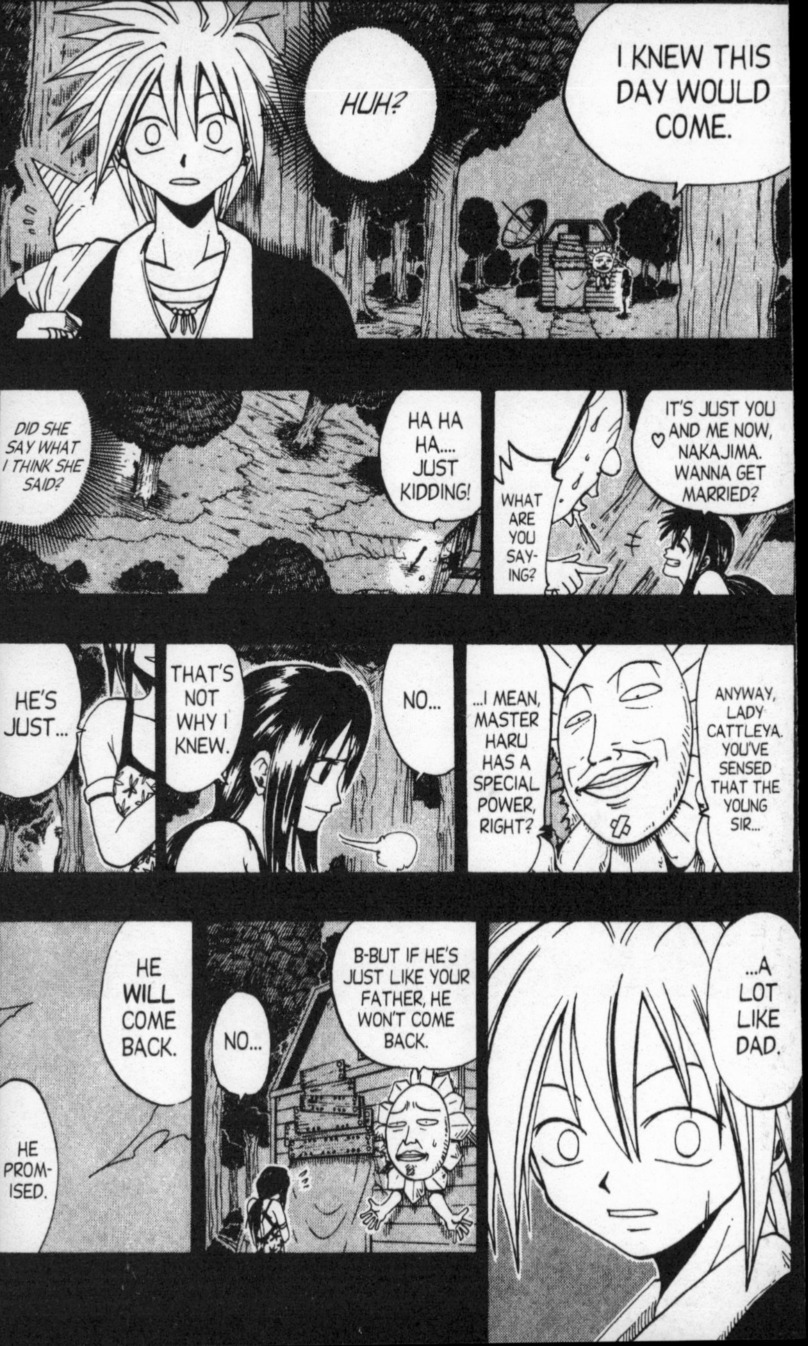
I KNEW THIS DAY WOULD COME.
HUH?
IT'S JUST YOU AND ME NOW, NAKAJIMA. WANNA GET MARRIED?
WHAT ARE YOU SAY-ING?
HA HA HA.... JUST KIDDING!
DID SHE SAY WHAT I THINK SHE SAID?
ANYWAY, LADY CATTLEYA. YOU'VE SENSED THAT THE YOUNG SIR...
...I MEAN, MASTER HARU HAS A SPECIAL POWER, RIGHT?
NO...
THAT'S NOT WHY I KNEW.
HE'S JUST...
...A LOT LIKE DAD.
B-BUT IF HE'S JUST LIKE YOUR FATHER, HE WON'T COME BACK.
NO...
HE WILL COME BACK.
HE PROM-ISED.

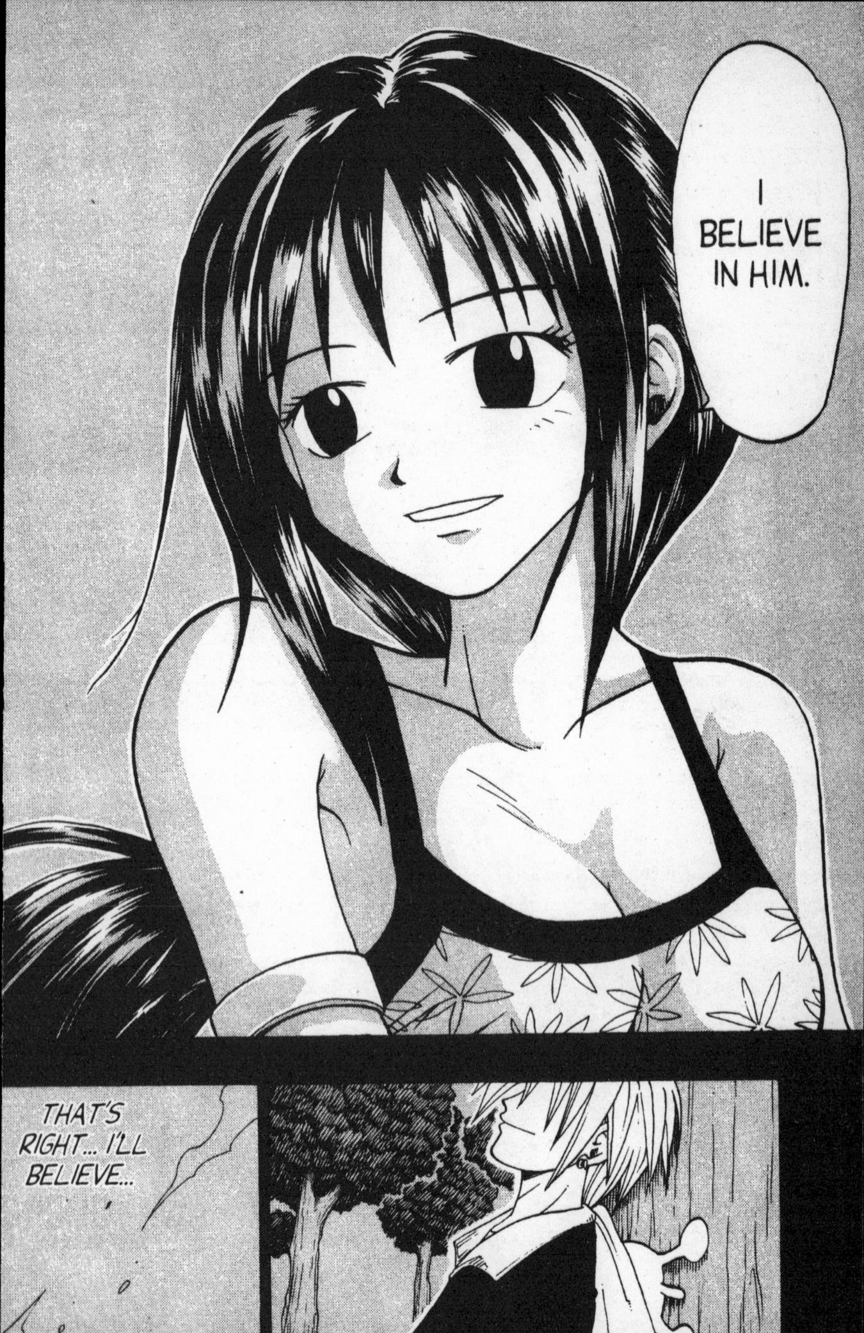
I BELIEVE IN HIM.
THAT'S RIGHT... I'LL BELIEVE...

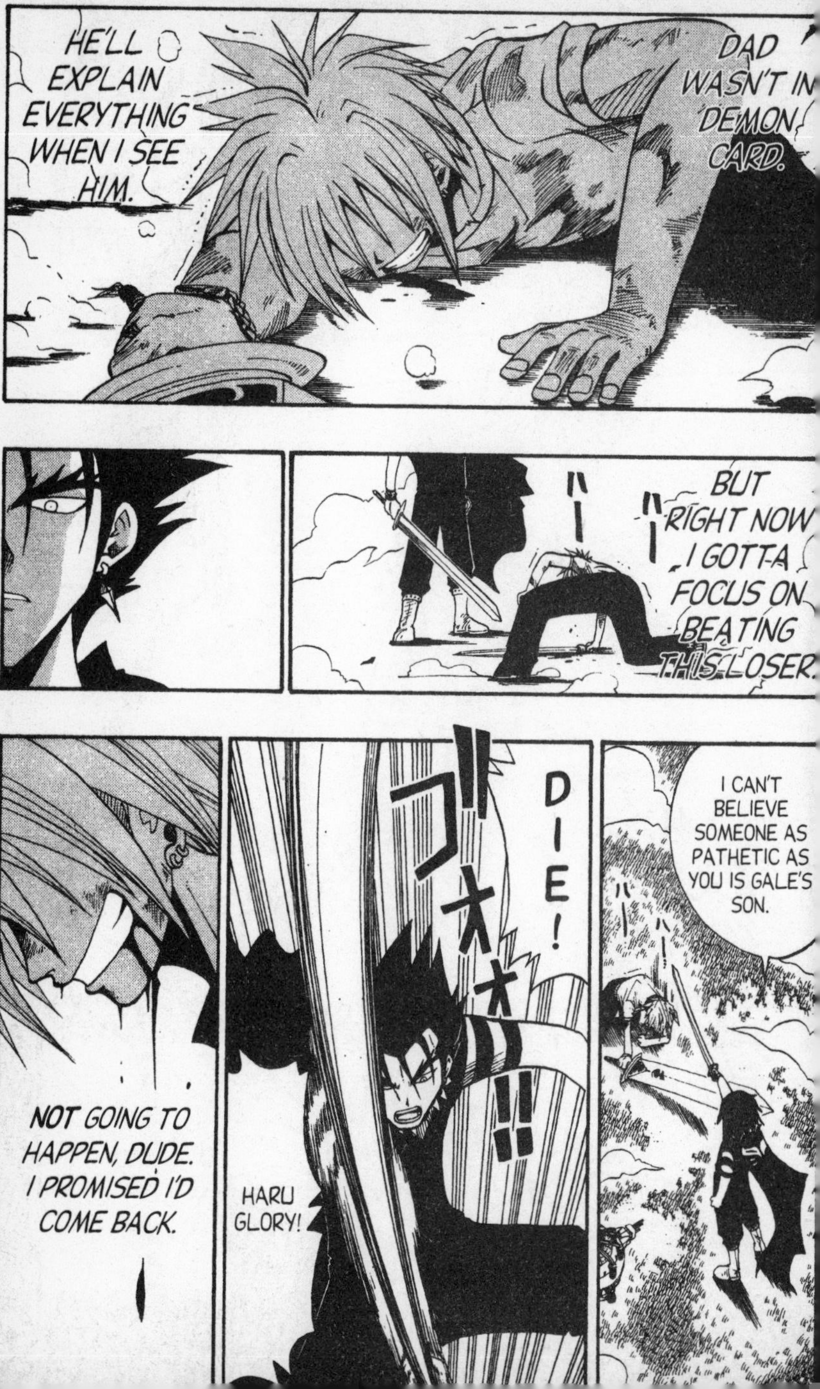
DAD WASN'T IN DEMON CARD.
HE'LL EXPLAIN EVERYTHING WHEN I SEE HIM.
BUT RIGHT NOW I GOTTA FOCUS ON BEATING THIS LOSER.
I CAN'T BELIEVE SOMEONE AS PATHETIC AS YOU IS GALE'S SON.
DIE!
HARU GLORY!
NOT GOING TO HAPPEN, DUDE. I PROMISED I'D COME BACK.

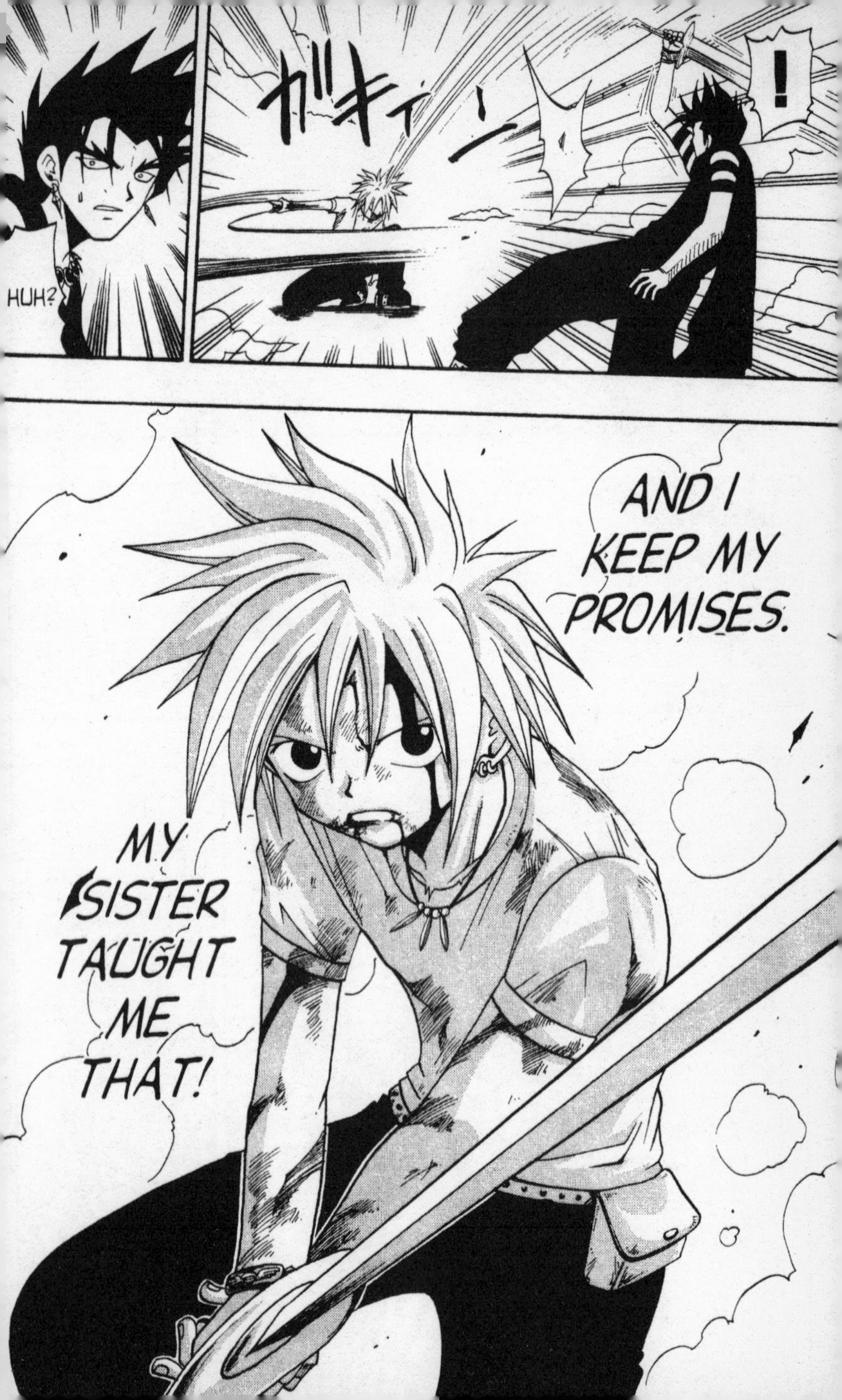
ガキィー
!
HUH?
AND I KEEP MY PROMISES.
MY SISTER TAUGHT ME THAT!

RAVE MASTER™

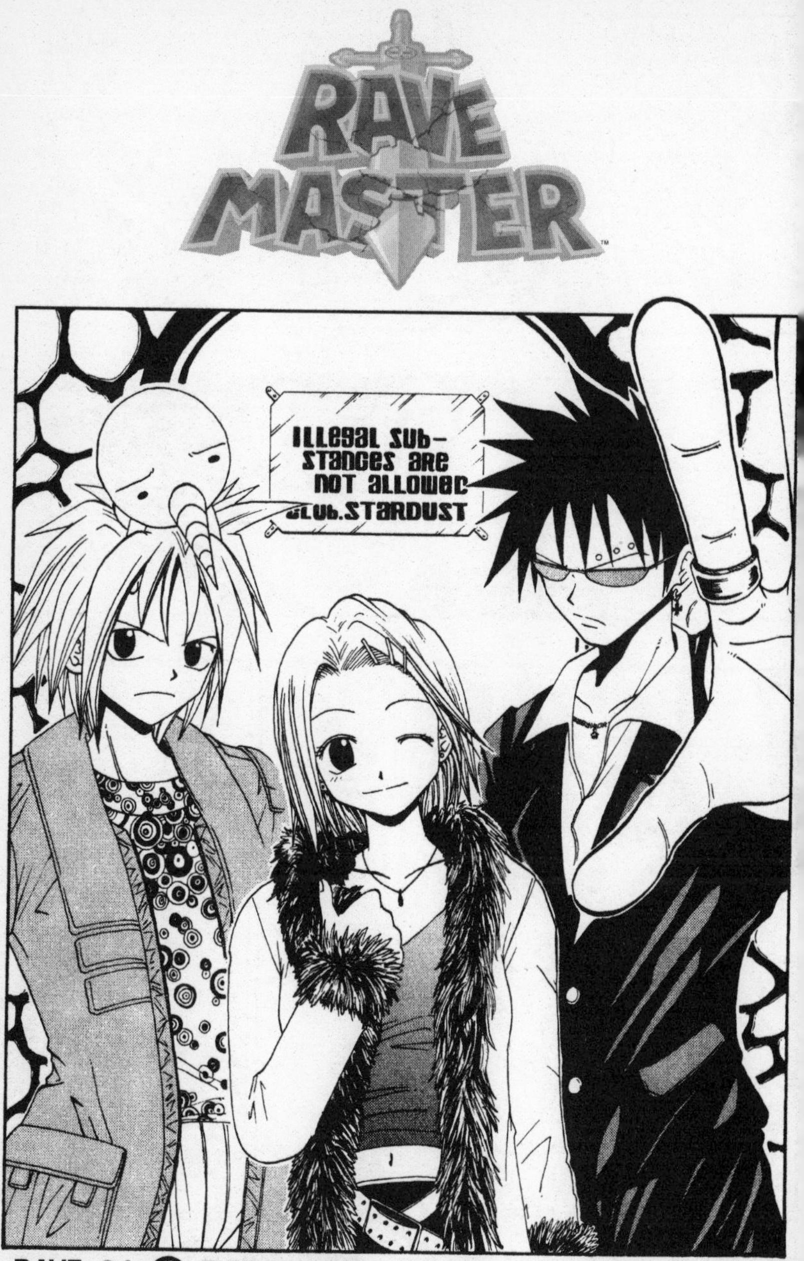
ILLEGAL SUB-
STANCES ARE
NOT ALLOWED
CLUB.STARDUST

RAVE: 34 ✚ FIERCE PRIDE

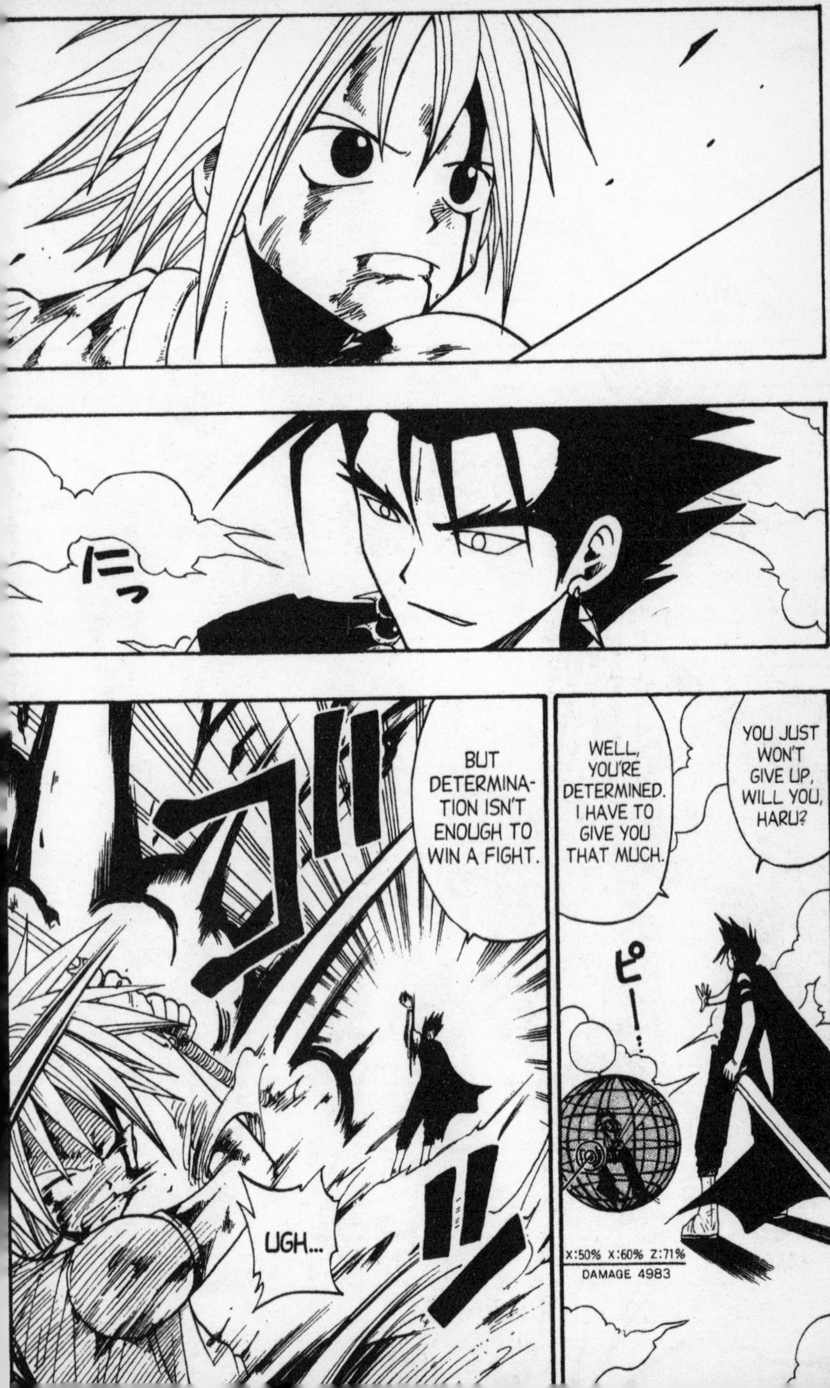
にっ
YOU JUST WON'T GIVE UP, WILL YOU, HARU?
WELL, YOU'RE DETERMINED. I HAVE TO GIVE YOU THAT MUCH.
ピー…
X:50% X:60% Z:71%
DAMAGE 4983
BUT DETERMINATION ISN'T ENOUGH TO WIN A FIGHT.
UGH...

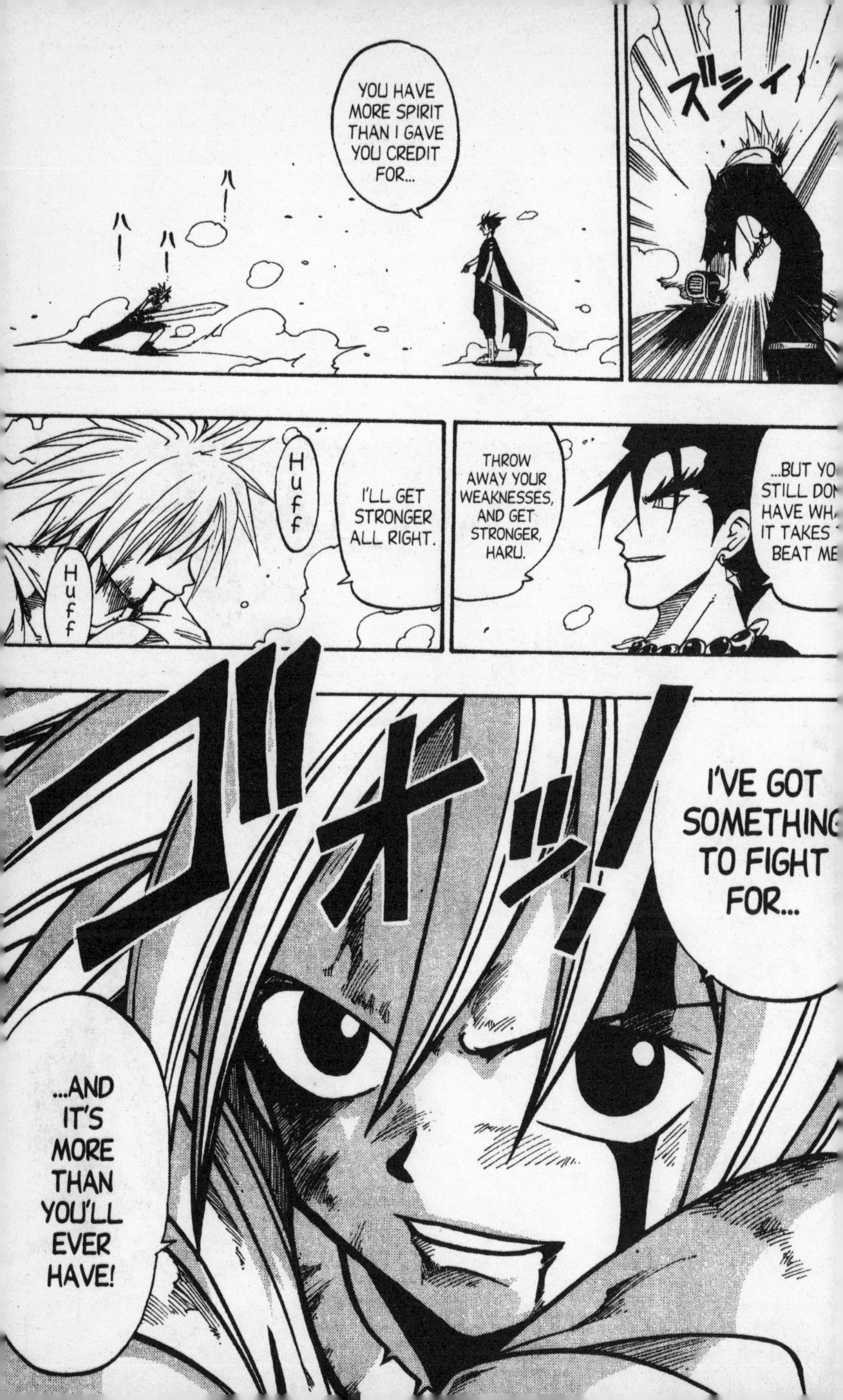
ズシィ
YOU HAVE MORE SPIRIT THAN I GAVE YOU CREDIT FOR...
ハー
ハー
ハー
...BUT YO STILL DON HAVE WHA IT TAKES T BEAT ME
THROW AWAY YOUR WEAKNESSES, AND GET STRONGER, HARU.
I'LL GET STRONGER ALL RIGHT.
Huff
Huff
ゴオッ
I'VE GOT SOMETHING TO FIGHT FOR...
...AND IT'S MORE THAN YOU'LL EVER HAVE!

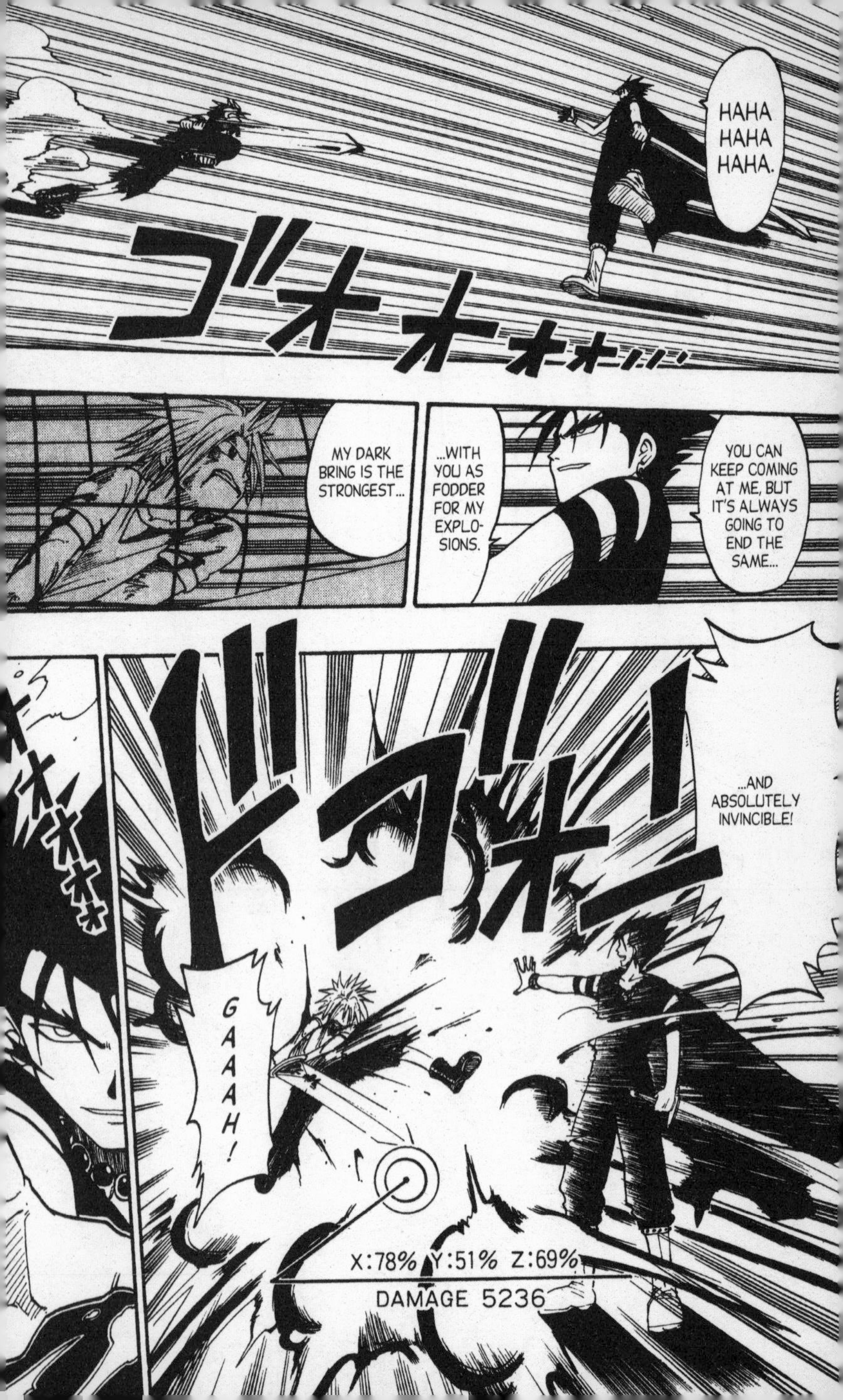
HAHA HAHA HAHA.
ゴオオオオ
YOU CAN KEEP COMING AT ME, BUT IT'S ALWAYS GOING TO END THE SAME...
...WITH YOU AS FODDER FOR MY EXPLOSIONS.
MY DARK BRING IS THE STRONGEST...
...AND ABSOLUTELY INVINCIBLE!
ドゴオーン
GAAAAH!
X:78% Y:51% Z:69%
DAMAGE 5236

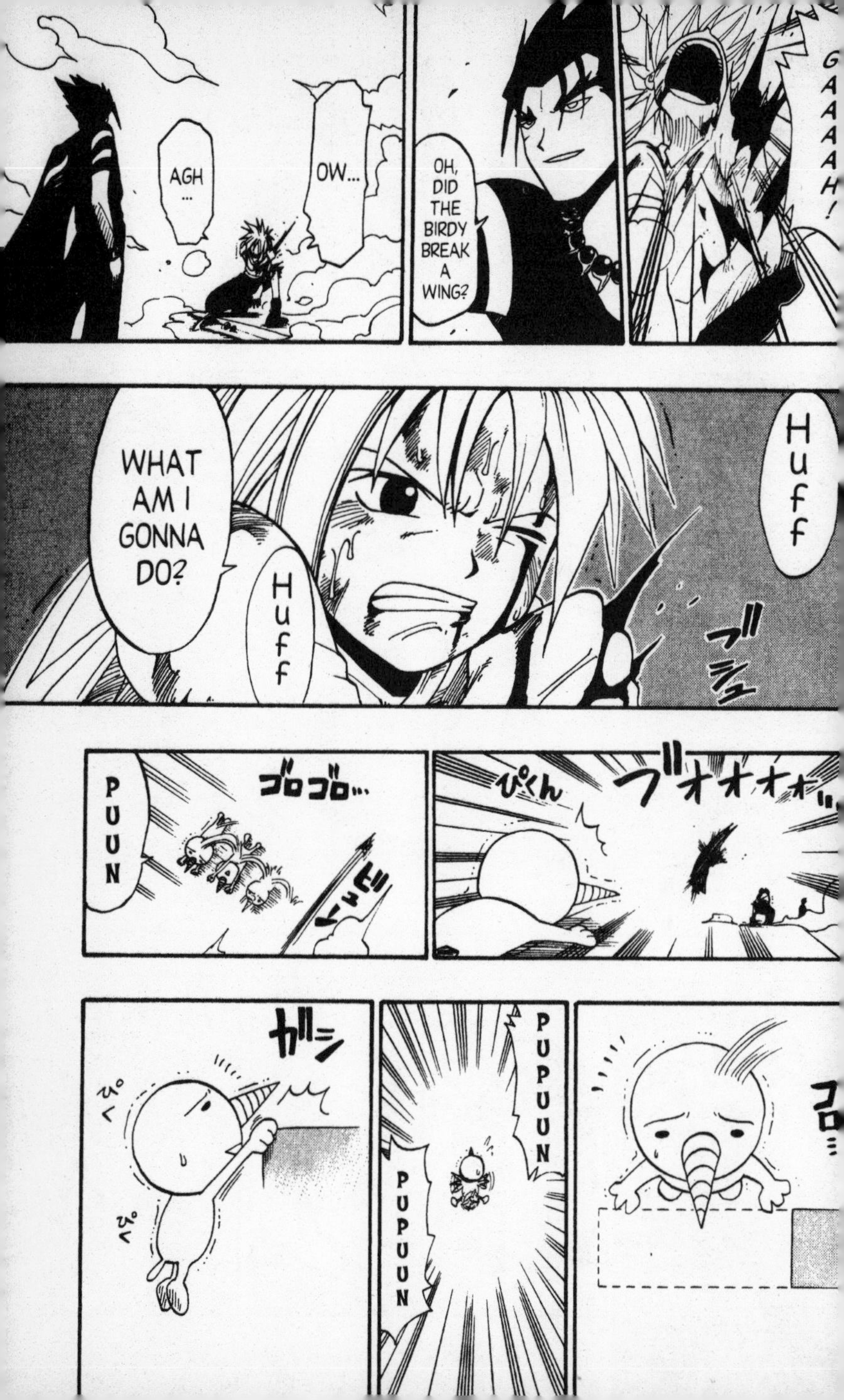

GAAAAAH!
OH, DID THE BIRDY BREAK A WING?
OW...
AGH ...
Huff
WHAT AM I GONNA DO?
Huff
ブシュ
ぴくん
ブオオオオ...
ゴロゴロ...
PUUN
コロ...
PUPUUN
PUPUUN
ガシ
ぴく
ぴく

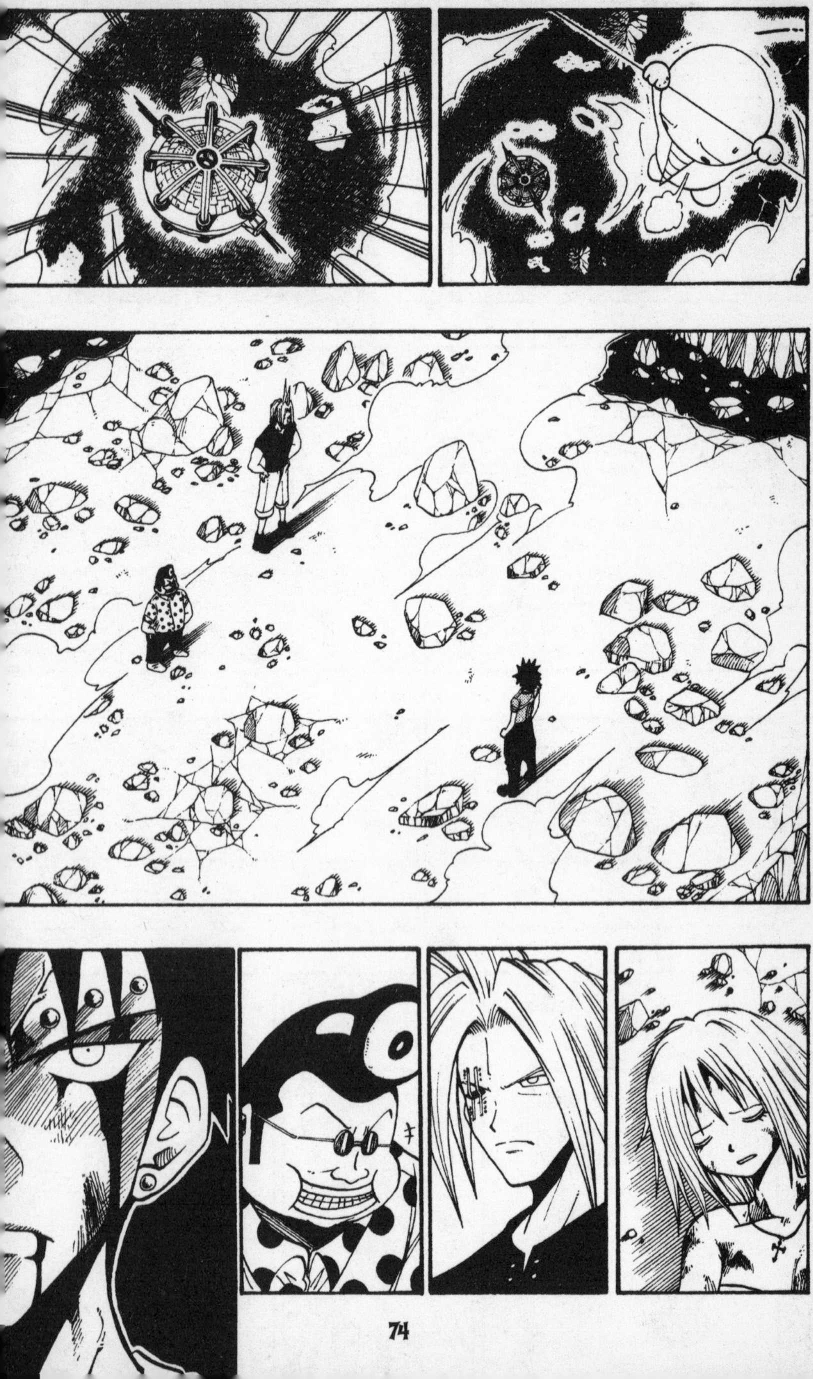

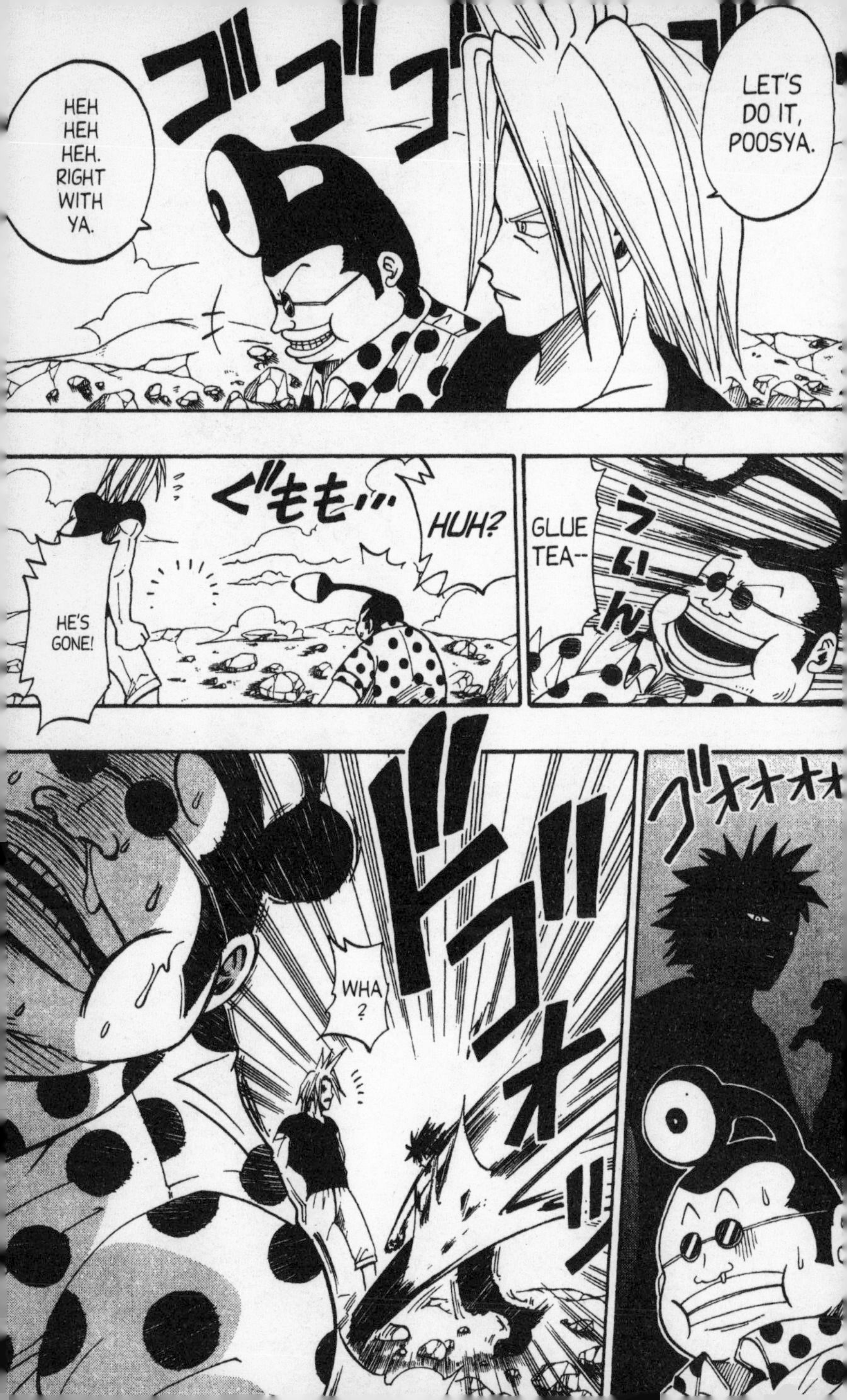
LET'S DO IT, POOSYA.
HEH HEH HEH. RIGHT WITH YA.
GLUE TEA--
HUH?
HE'S GONE!
WHA ?

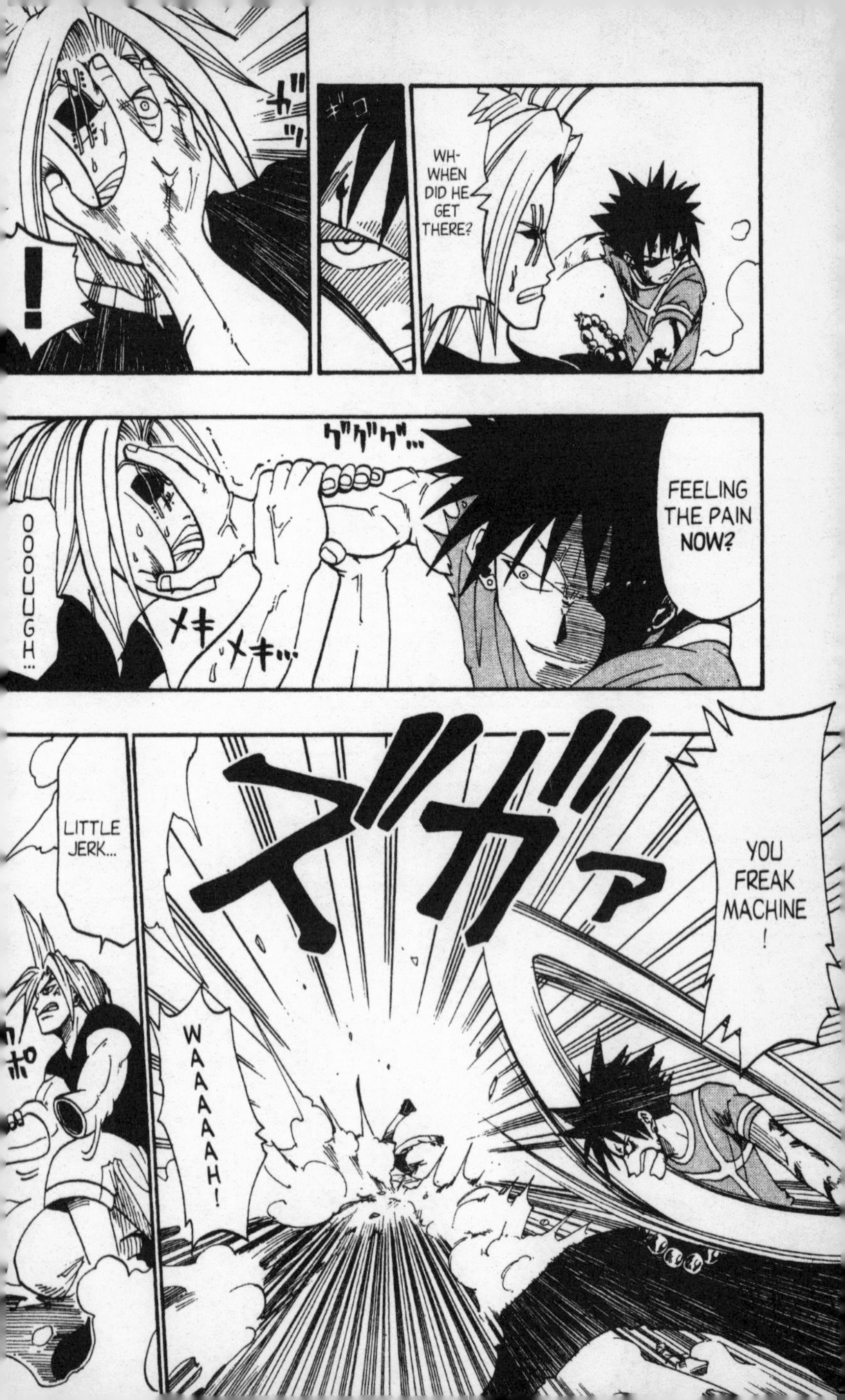

WH- WHEN DID HE GET THERE?
!
FEELING THE PAIN NOW?
OOOOUUGH...
YOU FREAK MACHINE!
WAAAAAH!
LITTLE JERK...

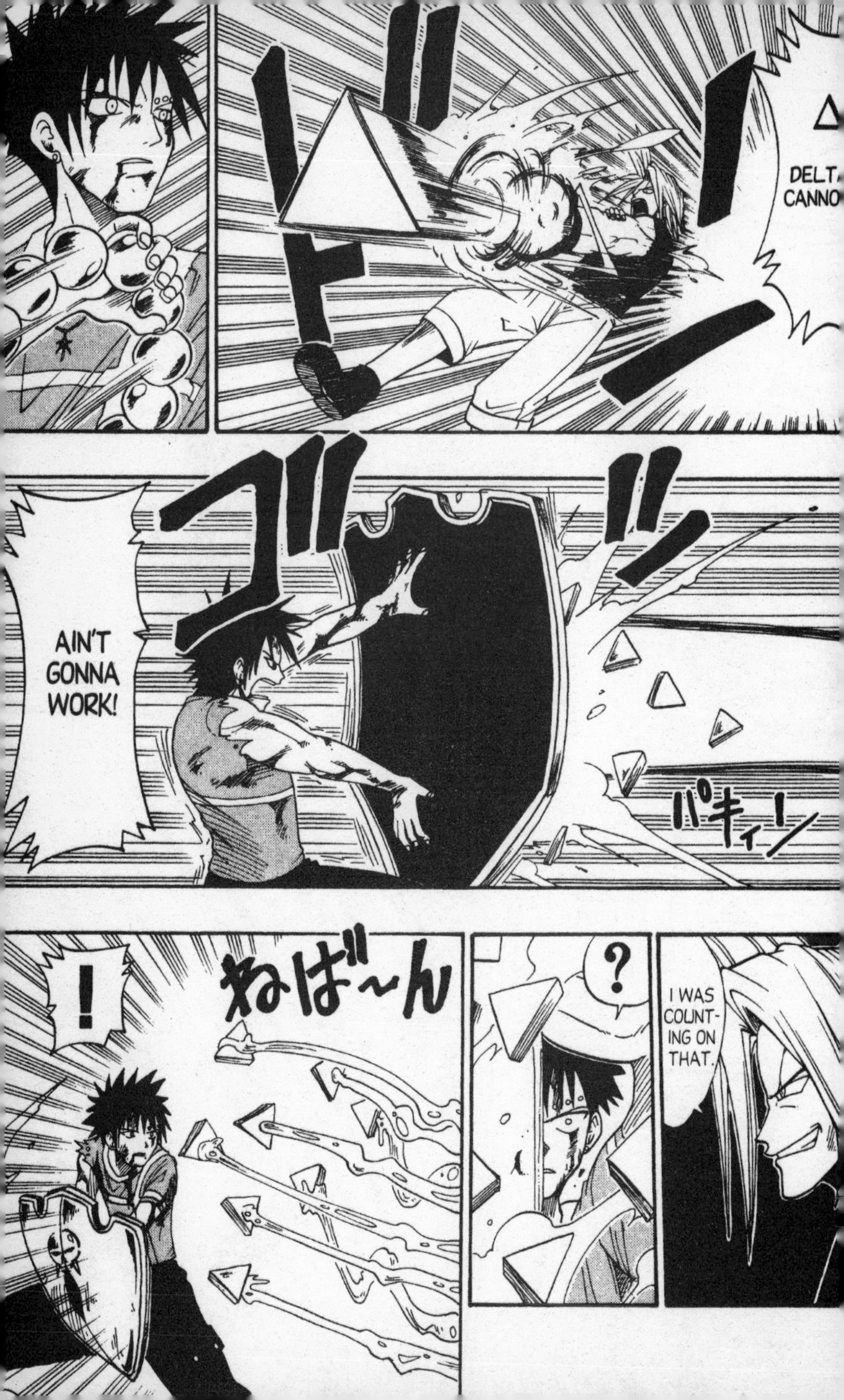
△
DELT CANNO
ゴン
パキィ！
AIN'T GONNA WORK!
I WAS COUNTING ON THAT.
?
!
ねば～ん

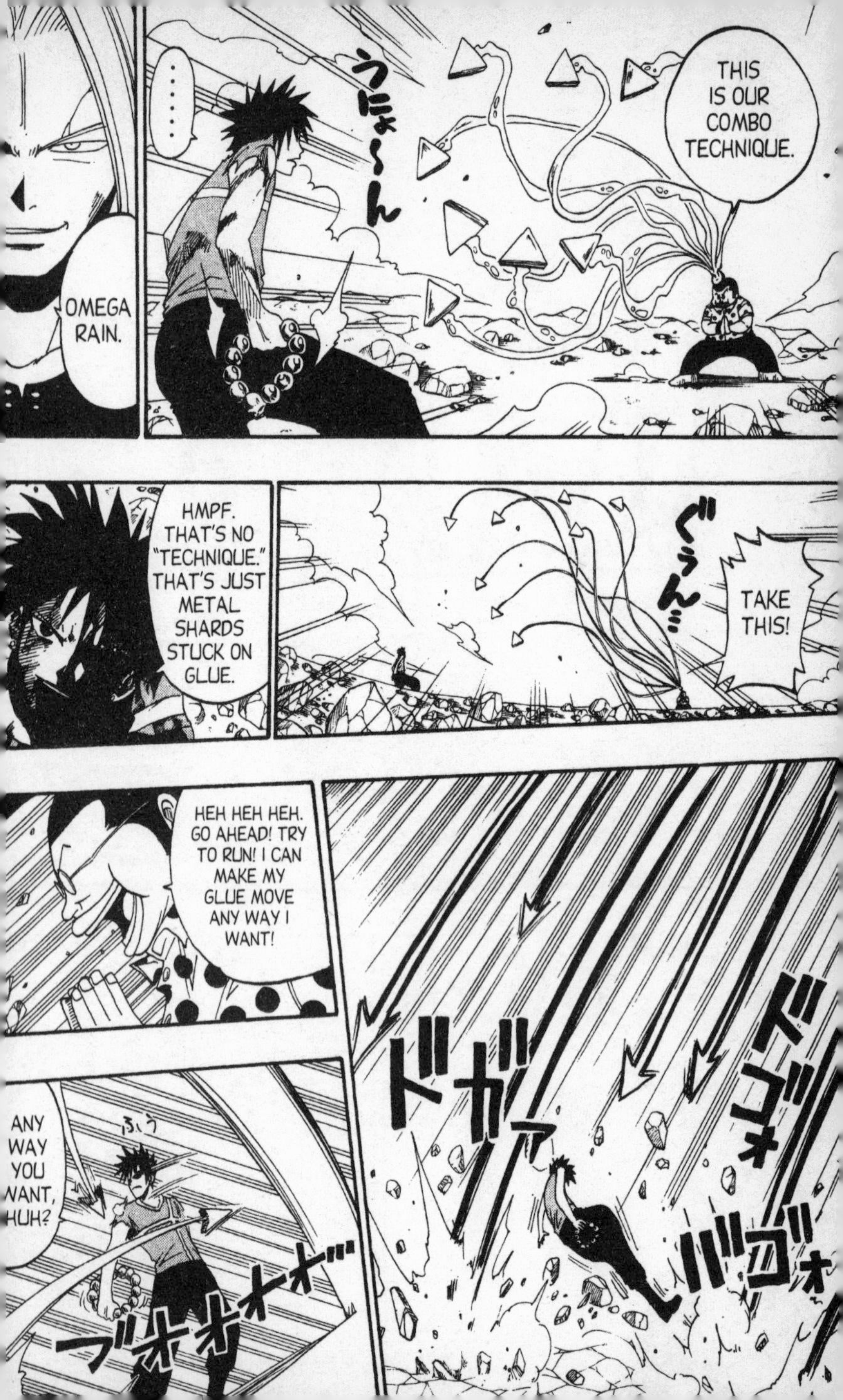

THIS IS OUR COMBO TECHNIQUE.
うにょ~ん
......
OMEGA RAIN.
TAKE THIS!
ぐうん
HMPF. THAT'S NO "TECHNIQUE." THAT'S JUST METAL SHARDS STUCK ON GLUE.
ドゴォ
バゴォ
ドガァ
HEH HEH HEH. GO AHEAD! TRY TO RUN! I CAN MAKE MY GLUE MOVE ANY WAY I WANT!
ANY WAY YOU WANT, HUH?
ふう

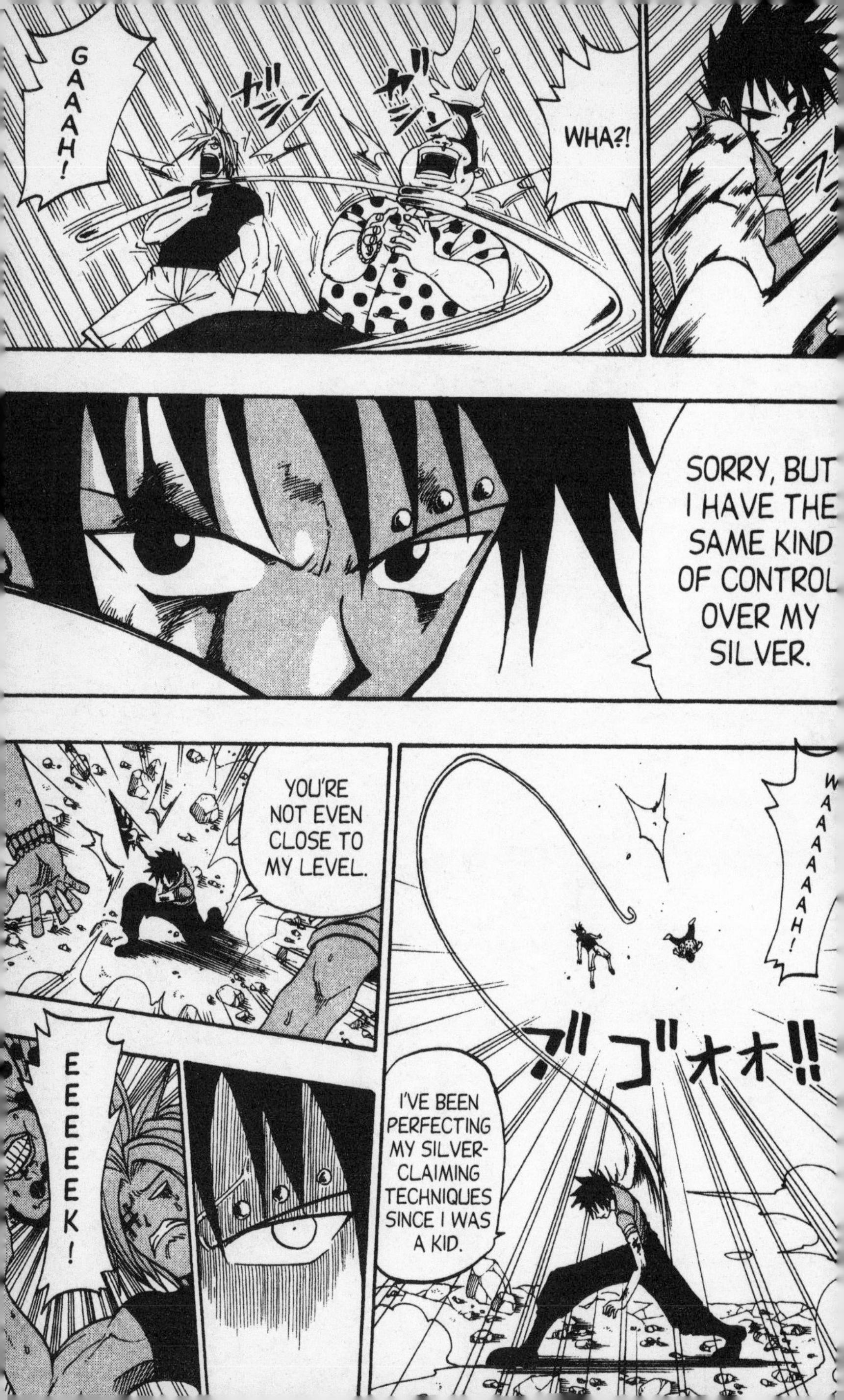
WHA?!
GAAAH!
SORRY, BUT I HAVE THE SAME KIND OF CONTROL OVER MY SILVER.
WAAAAAAAH!
ブゴオオ!!
I'VE BEEN PERFECTING MY SILVER-CLAIMING TECHNIQUES SINCE I WAS A KID.
YOU'RE NOT EVEN CLOSE TO MY LEVEL.
EEEEEEK!

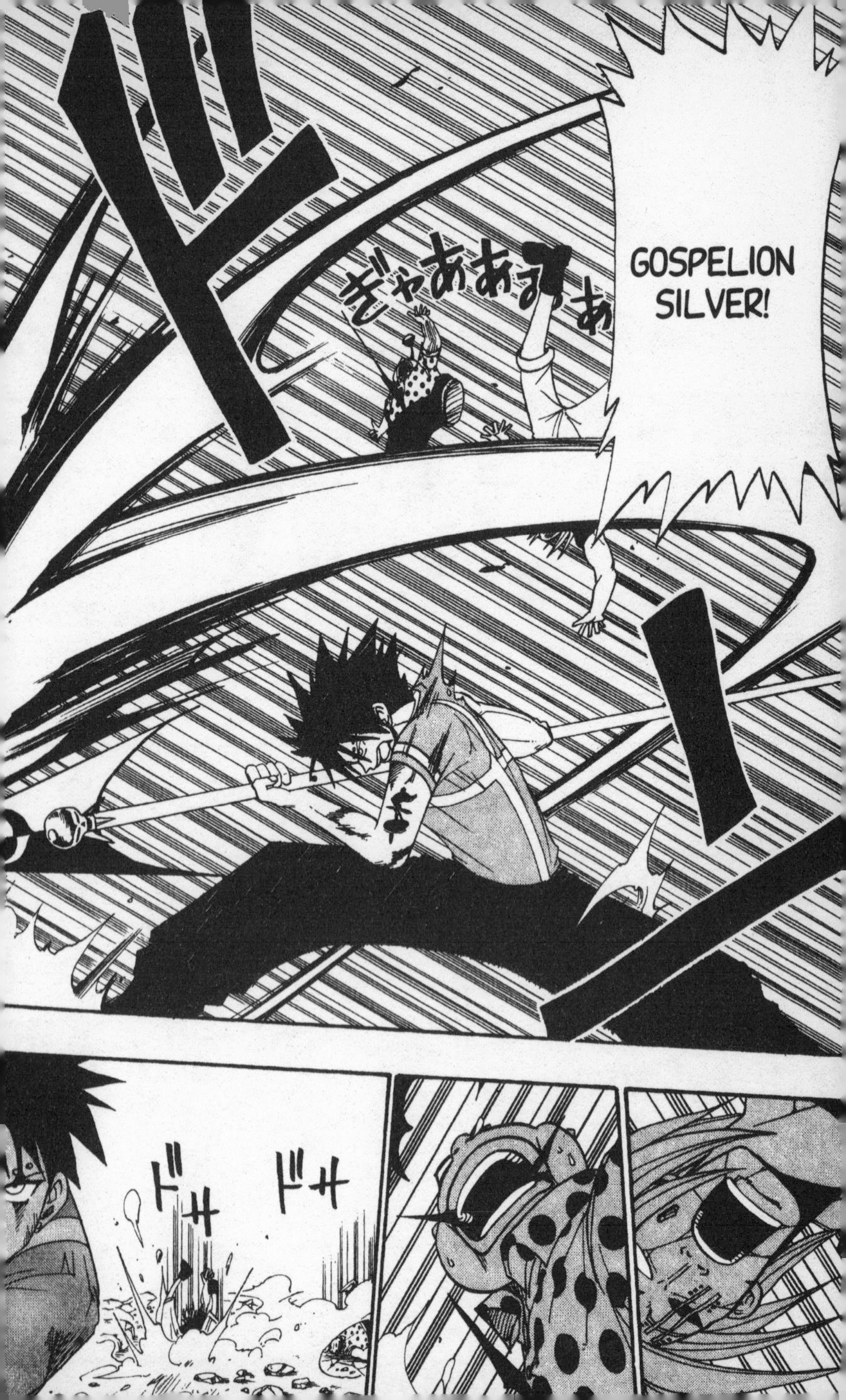
GOSPELION SILVER!
ぎゃあああ あ
ドサ
ドサ

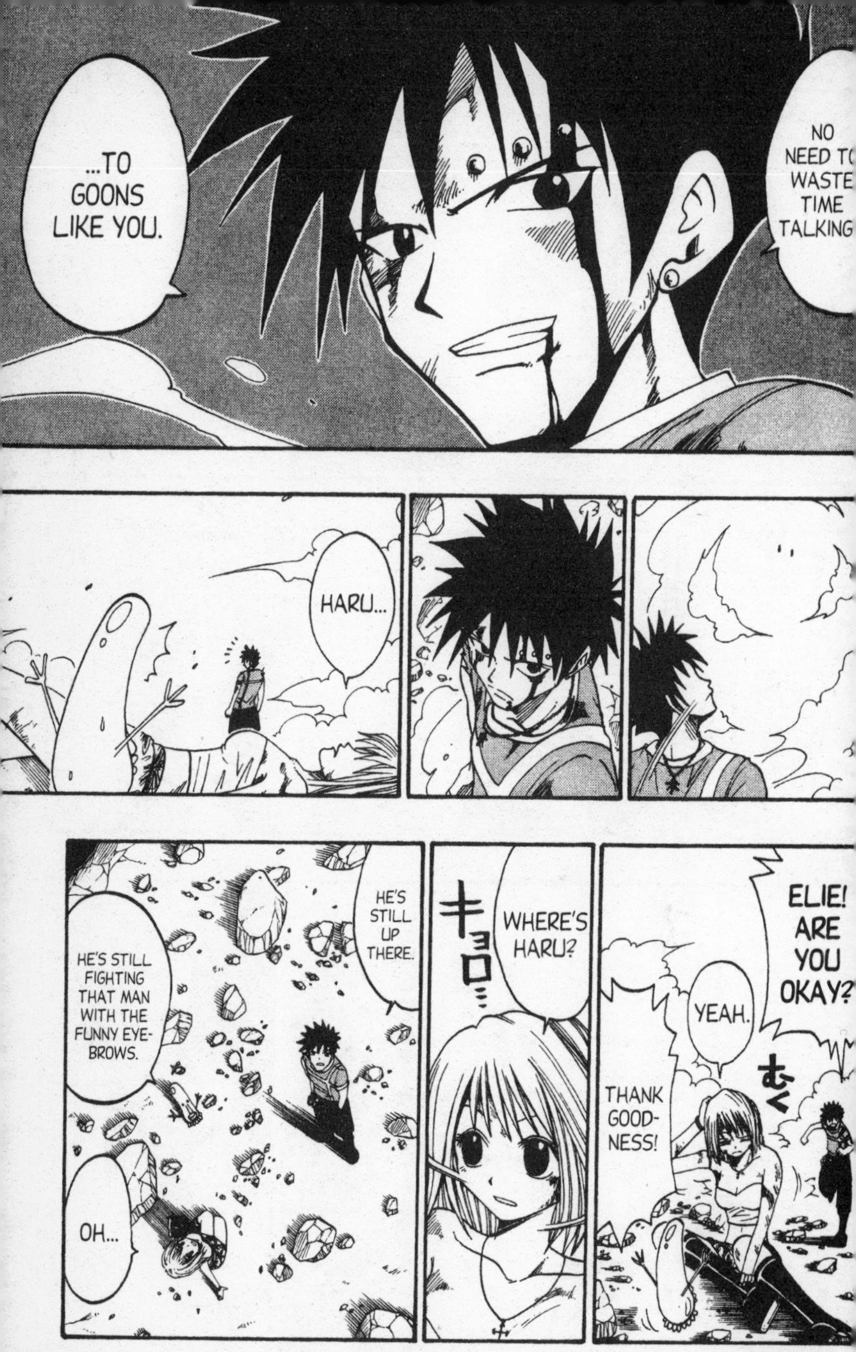
NO NEED TO WASTE TIME TALKING
...TO GOONS LIKE YOU.
HARU...
ELIE! ARE YOU OKAY?
YEAH.
むく
THANK GOODNESS!
キョロ
WHERE'S HARU?
HE'S STILL UP THERE.
HE'S STILL FIGHTING THAT MAN WITH THE FUNNY EYE-BROWS.
OH...

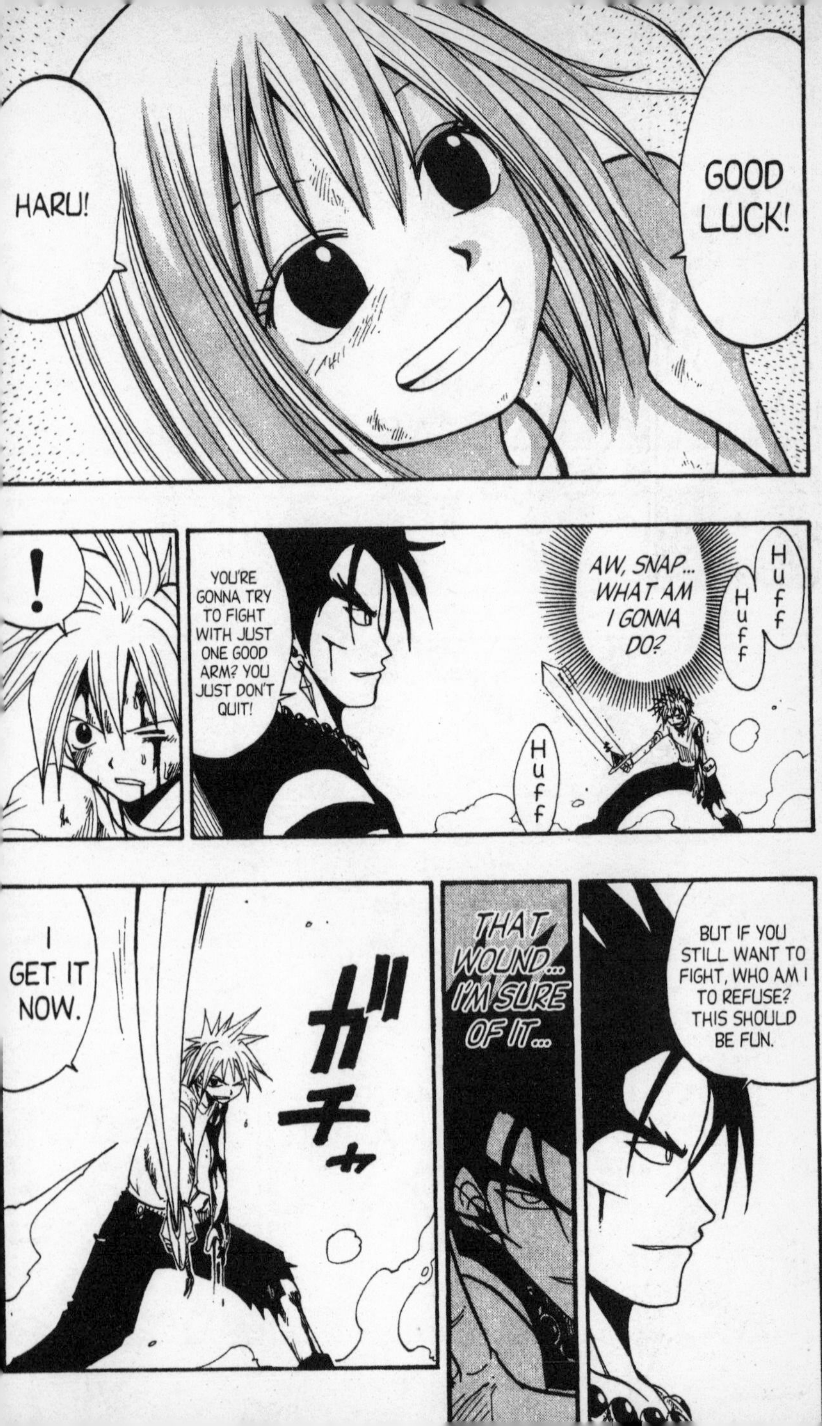

GOOD LUCK!
HARU!
Huff
Huff
AW, SNAP... WHAT AM I GONNA DO?
Huff
YOU'RE GONNA TRY TO FIGHT WITH JUST ONE GOOD ARM? YOU JUST DON'T QUIT!
!
BUT IF YOU STILL WANT TO FIGHT, WHO AM I TO REFUSE? THIS SHOULD BE FUN.
THAT WOUND... I'M SURE OF IT...
ガチャ
I GET IT NOW.

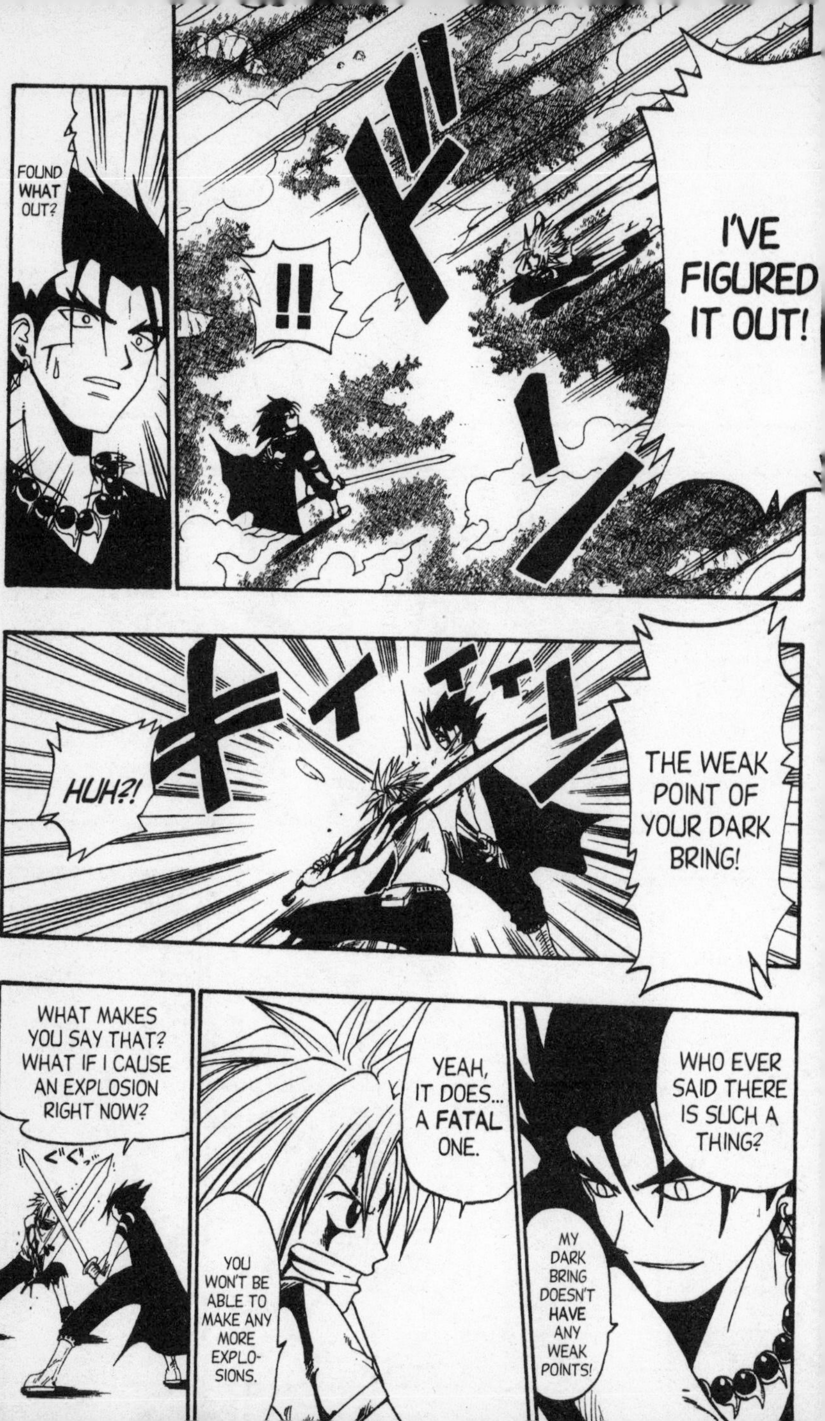
I'VE FIGURED IT OUT!
!!
FOUND WHAT OUT?
THE WEAK POINT OF YOUR DARK BRING!
HUH?!
WHO EVER SAID THERE IS SUCH A THING?
MY DARK BRING DOESN'T HAVE ANY WEAK POINTS!
YEAH, IT DOES... A FATAL ONE.
YOU WON'T BE ABLE TO MAKE ANY MORE EXPLOSIONS.
WHAT MAKES YOU SAY THAT? WHAT IF I CAUSE AN EXPLOSION RIGHT NOW?

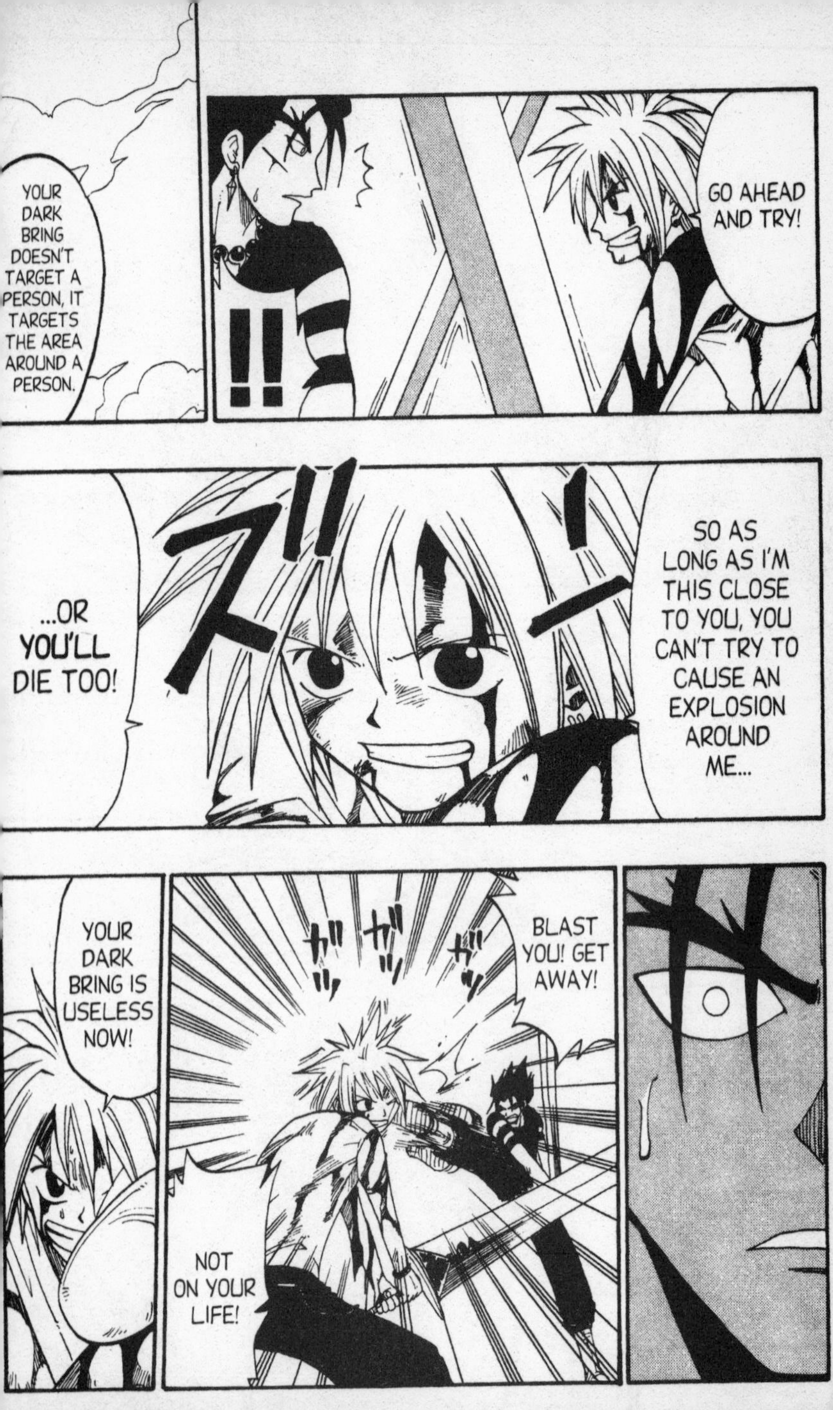

GO AHEAD AND TRY!
!!
YOUR DARK BRING DOESN'T TARGET A PERSON, IT TARGETS THE AREA AROUND A PERSON.
SO AS LONG AS I'M THIS CLOSE TO YOU, YOU CAN'T TRY TO CAUSE AN EXPLOSION AROUND ME...
ズー
...OR YOU'LL DIE TOO!
BLAST YOU! GET AWAY!
ガガガ
NOT ON YOUR LIFE!
YOUR DARK BRING IS USELESS NOW!

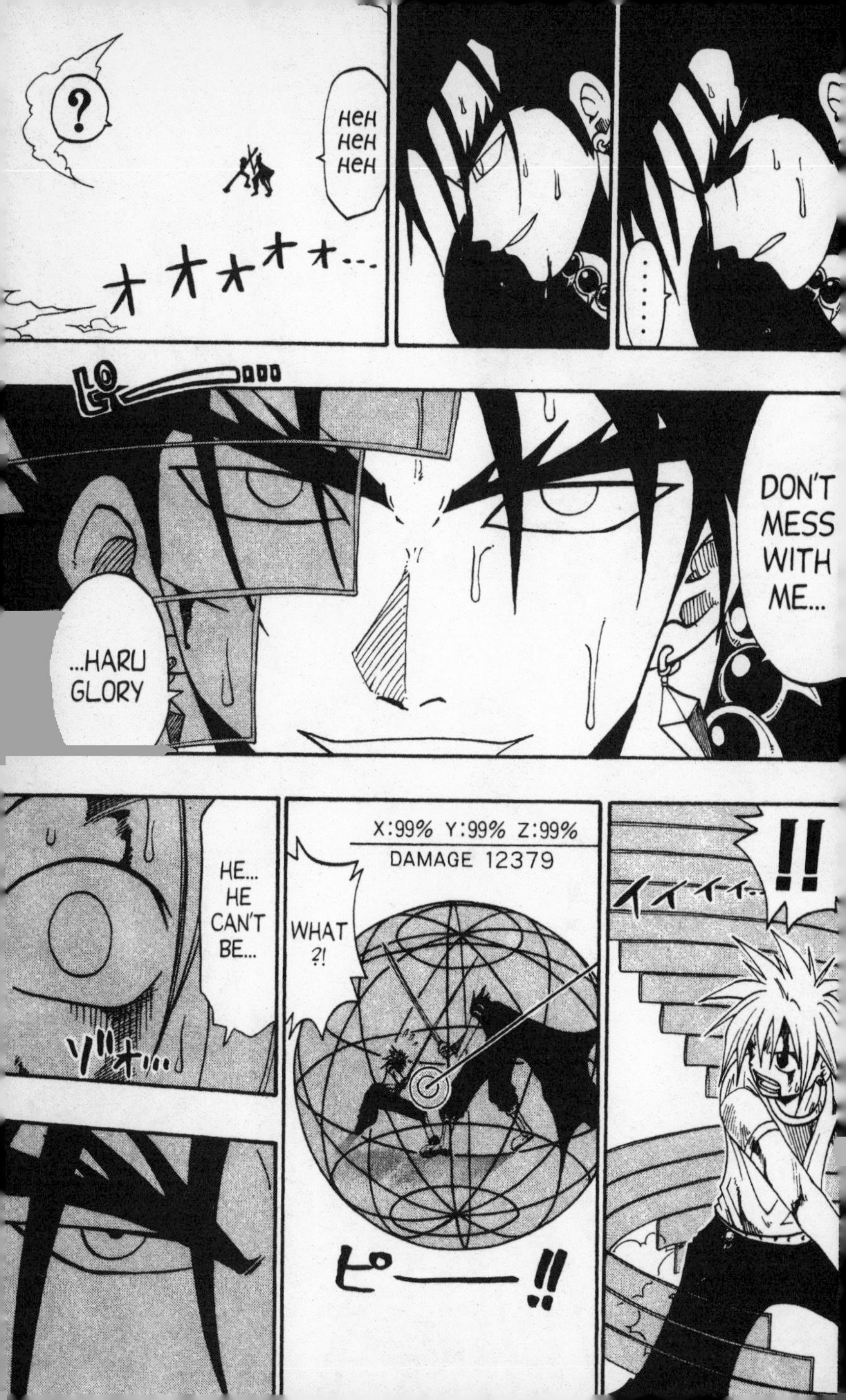
......
HEH HEH HEH
?
オオオオオ…
ピ———
DON'T MESS WITH ME...
...HARU GLORY
!!
イイイイ…
X:99% Y:99% Z:99%
DAMAGE 12379
WHAT ?!
ピー——!!
HE... HE CAN'T BE...
ゾオ…

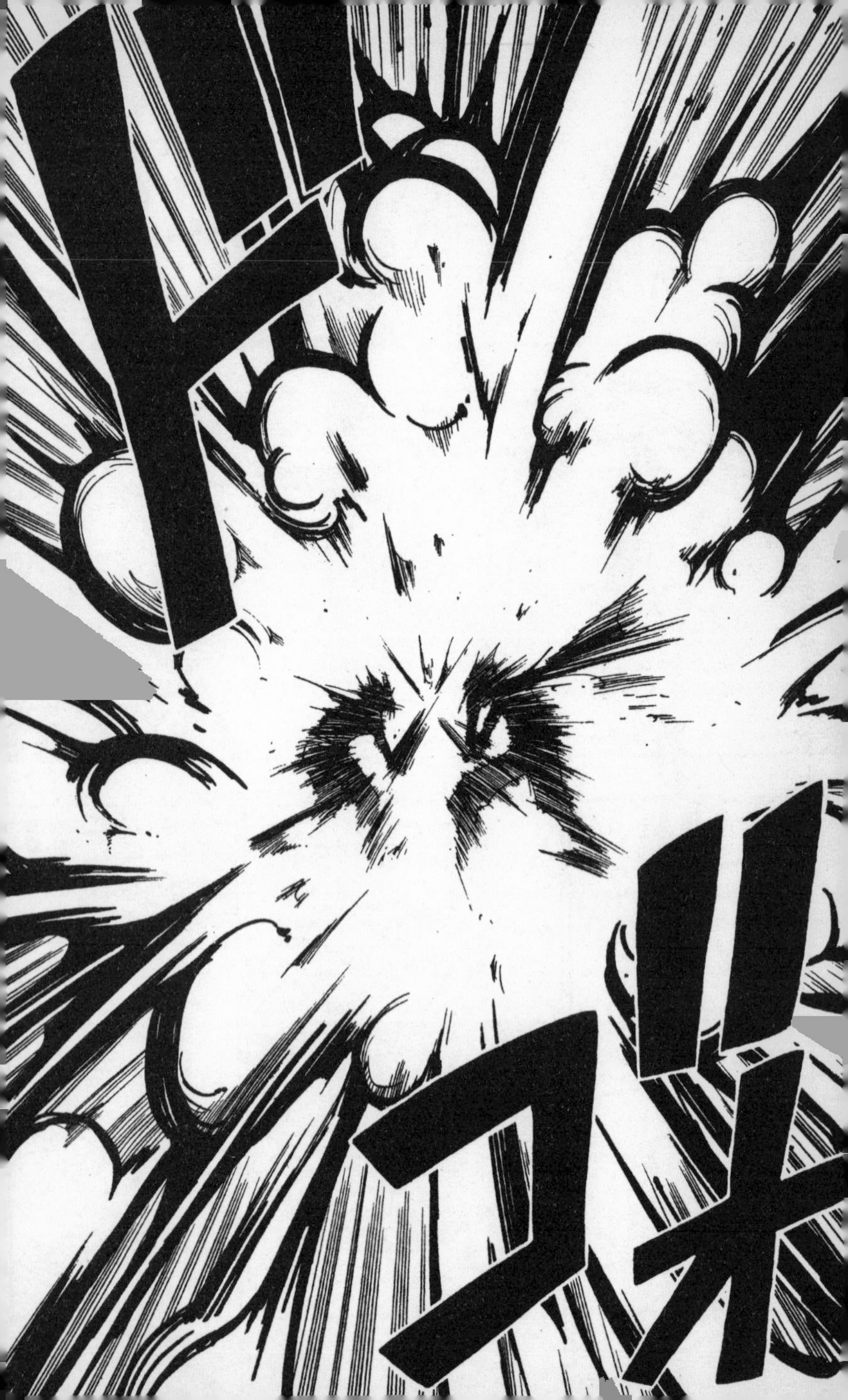
ドゴオ

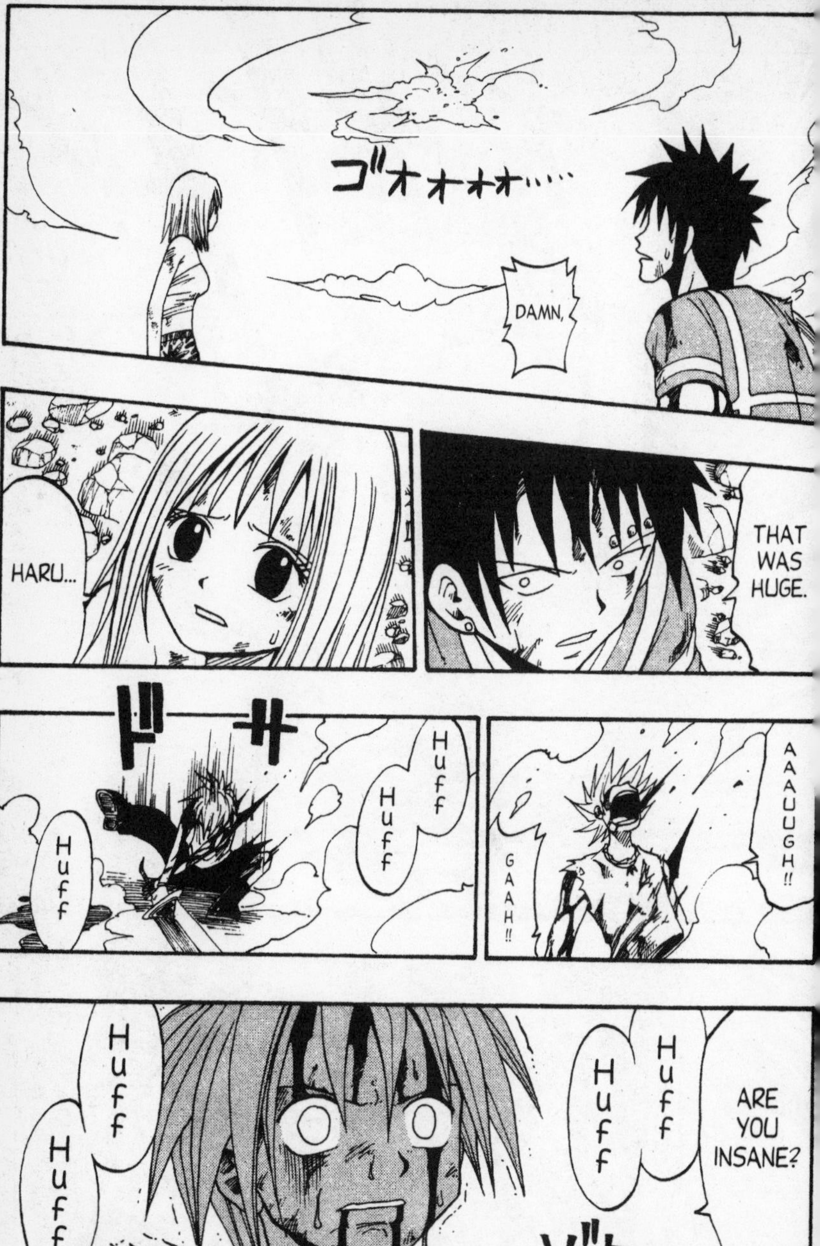
ゴオオオオ……
DAMN,
THAT WAS HUGE.
HARU...
AAAUUGH!!
GAAH!!
ドサ
Huff Huff
Huff Huff
ARE YOU INSANE?
Huff Huff
ゾクッ
Huff Huff

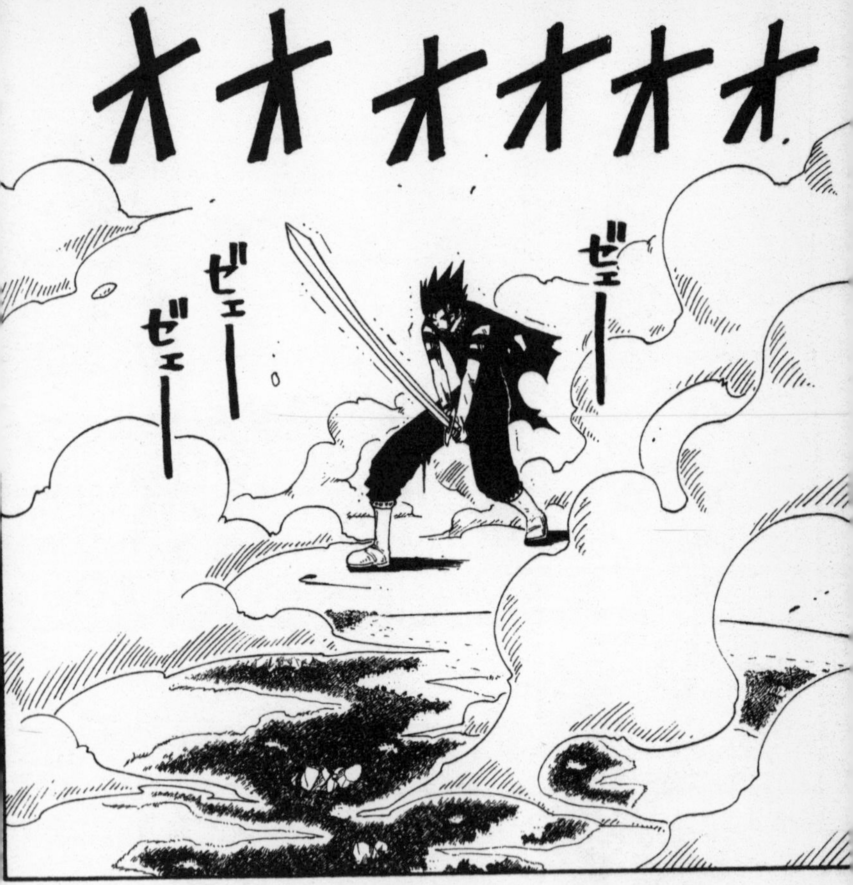
オオオオオオ
ゼェー
ゼェー
ゼェー

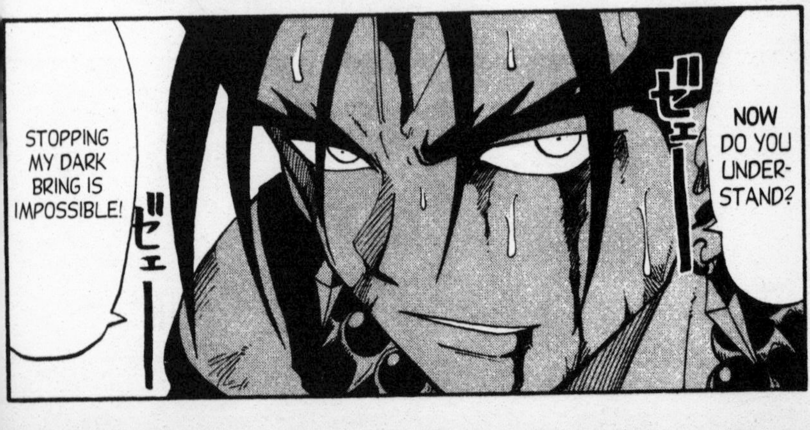
NOW DO YOU UNDER-STAND?
ゼェー
STOPPING MY DARK BRING IS IMPOSSIBLE!
ゼェー

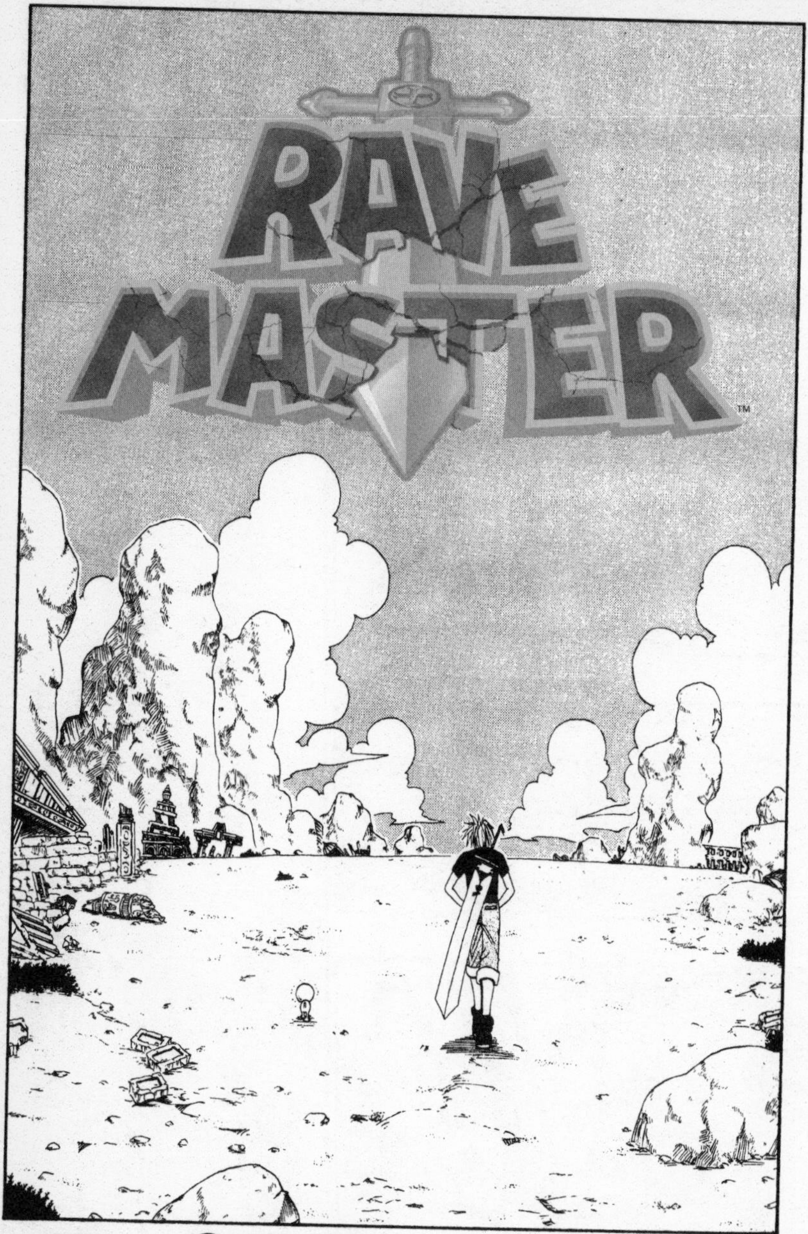
RAVE MASTER™

RAVE: 35 ✚ SAD SKIES

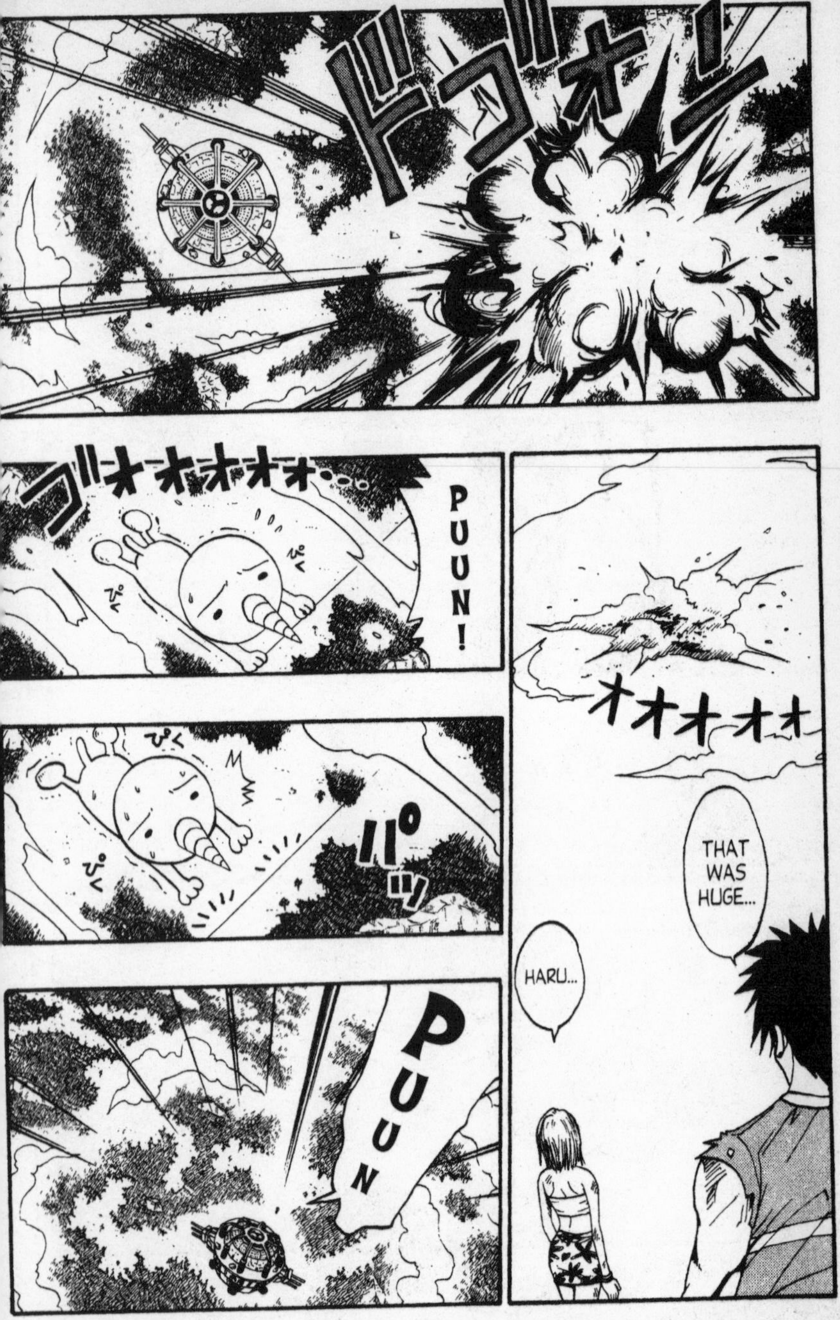
ドゴォン
オオオオオオ
THAT WAS HUGE...
HARU...
ゴオオオオオ…
PUUN!
ぴく
ぴく
ぴく
パッ
ぴく
PUUN

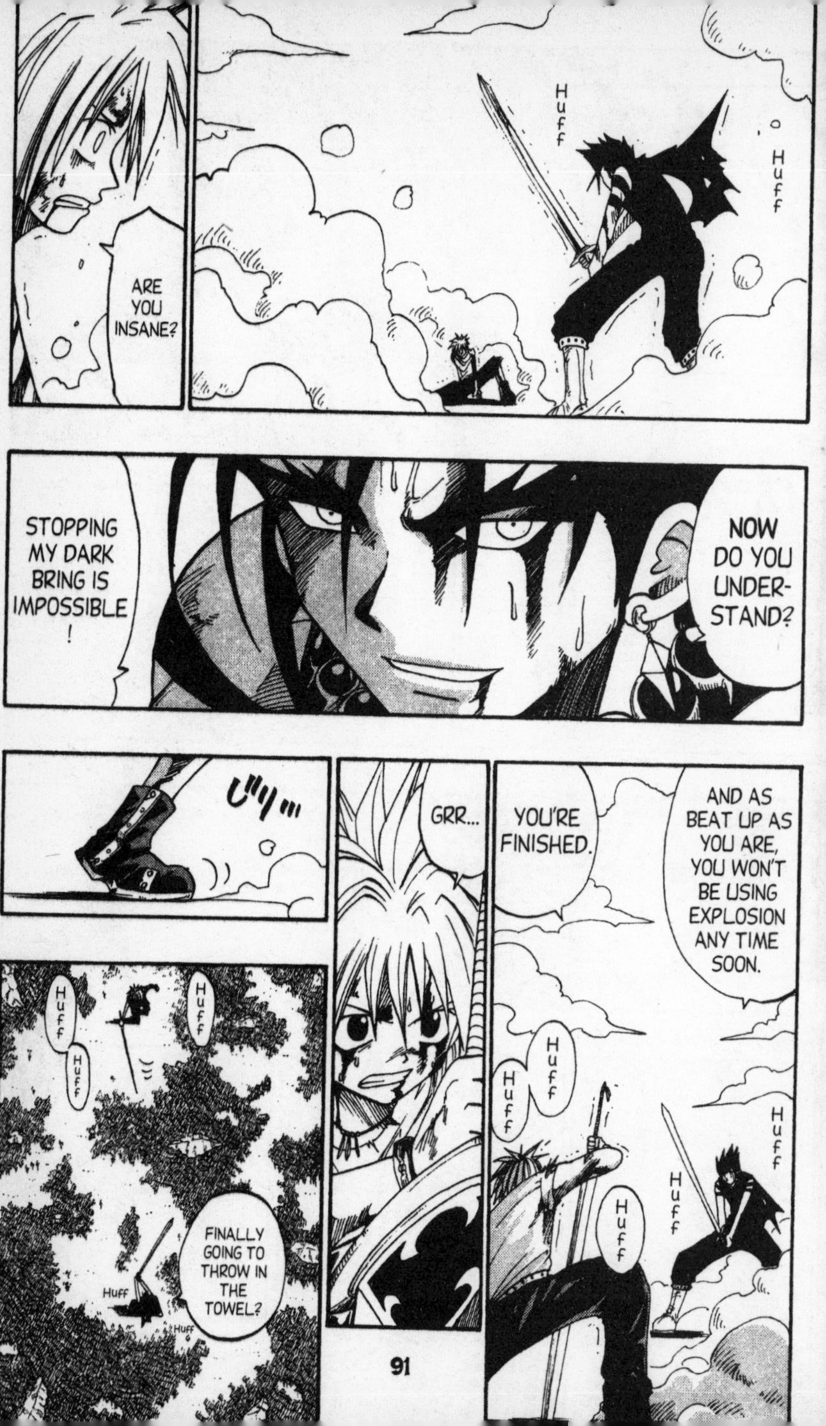
Huff
Huff
ARE YOU INSANE?
NOW DO YOU UNDERSTAND?
STOPPING MY DARK BRING IS IMPOSSIBLE!
AND AS BEAT UP AS YOU ARE, YOU WON'T BE USING EXPLOSION ANY TIME SOON.
YOU'RE FINISHED.
Huff
Huff
Huff
Huff
Huff
GRR...
Huff
Huff
Huff
FINALLY GOING TO THROW IN THE TOWEL?
Huff
Huff

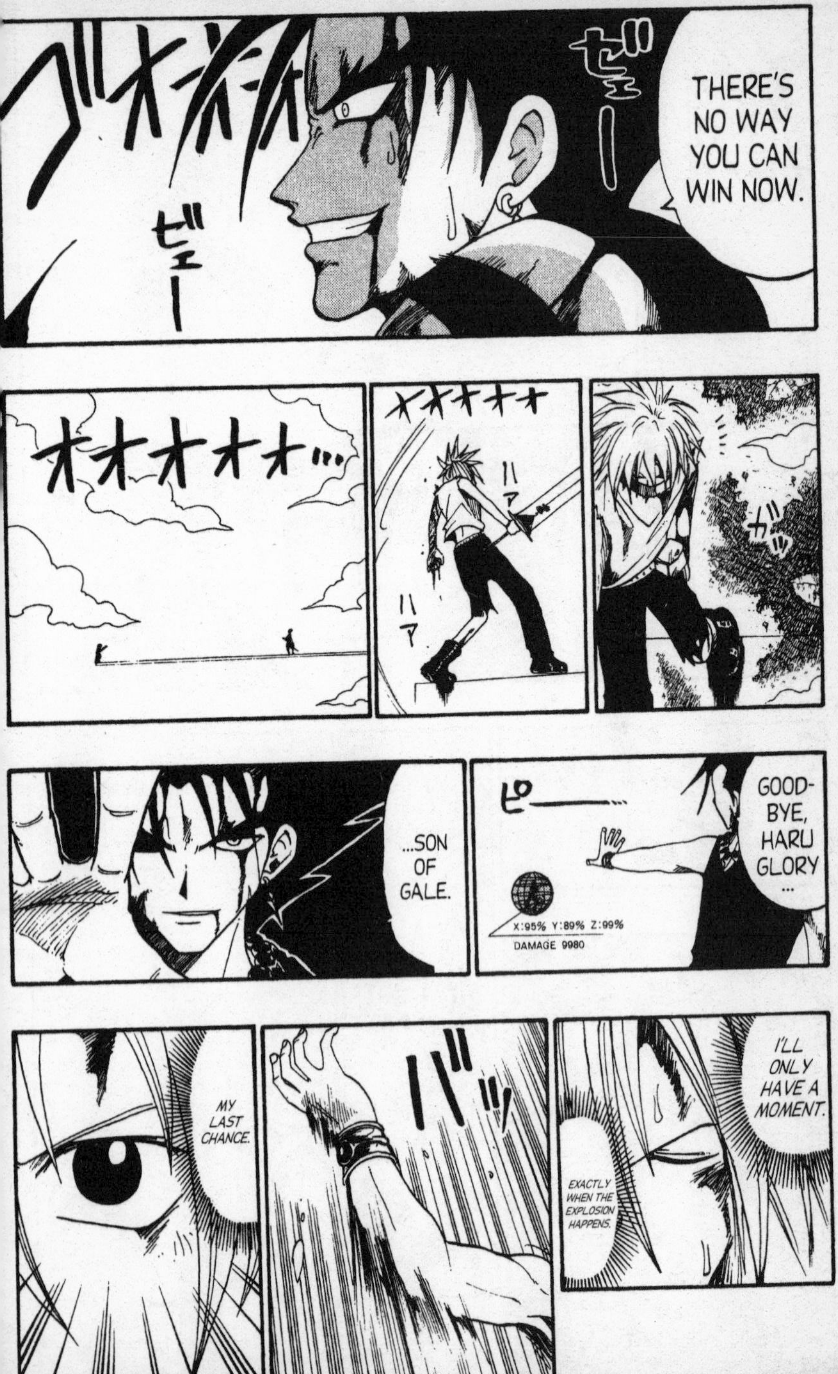
ゼェー
THERE'S NO WAY YOU CAN WIN NOW.
ビュー
ガッ
オオオオオオ
ハア
ハア
オオオオオ…
ピー…
GOOD-BYE, HARU GLORY...
X:95% Y:89% Z:99%
DAMAGE 9980
...SON OF GALE.
I'LL ONLY HAVE A MOMENT.
EXACTLY WHEN THE EXPLOSION HAPPENS.
バッ
MY LAST CHANCE.

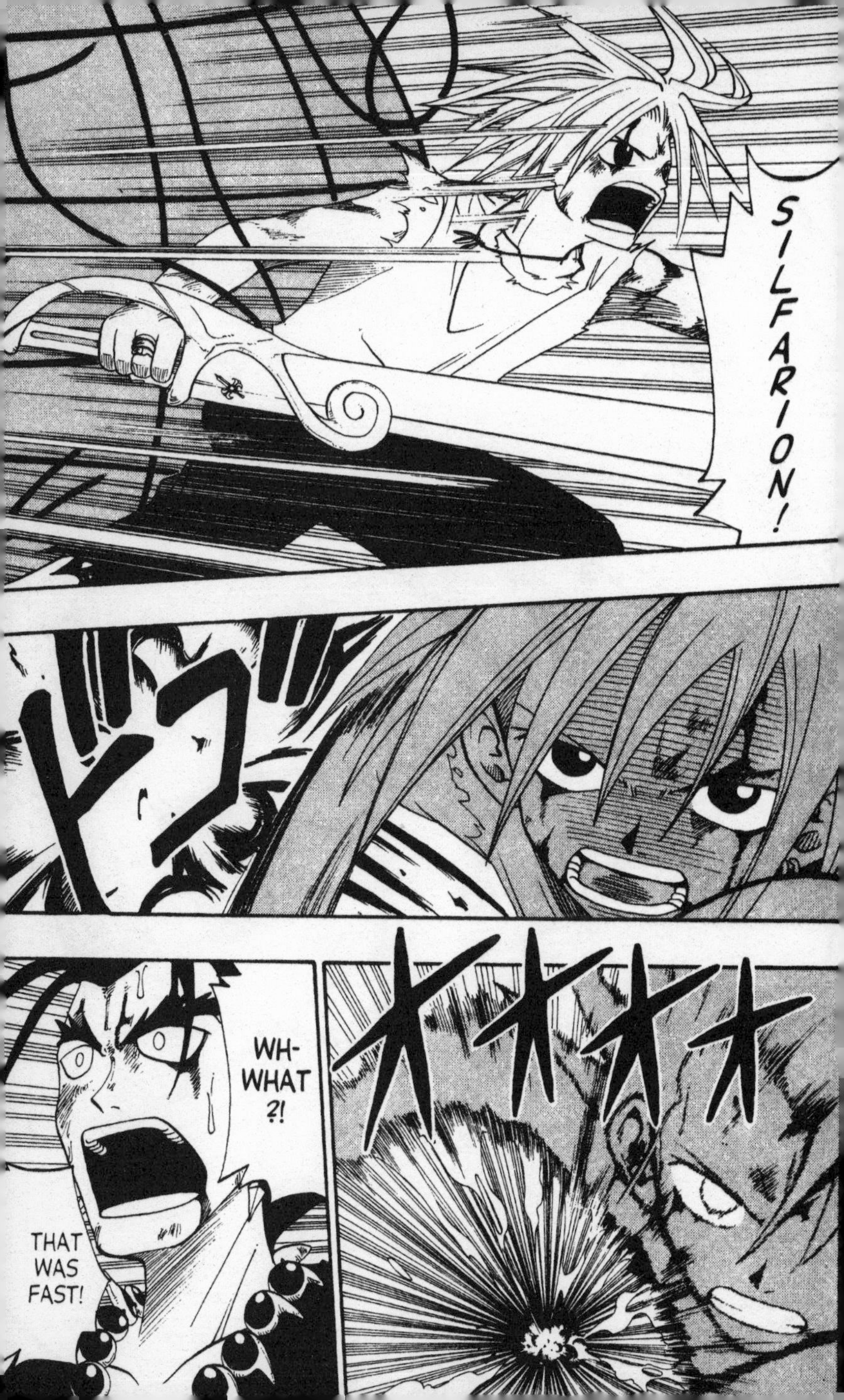
SILFARION!
オオオオ
WH-WHAT?!
THAT WAS FAST!

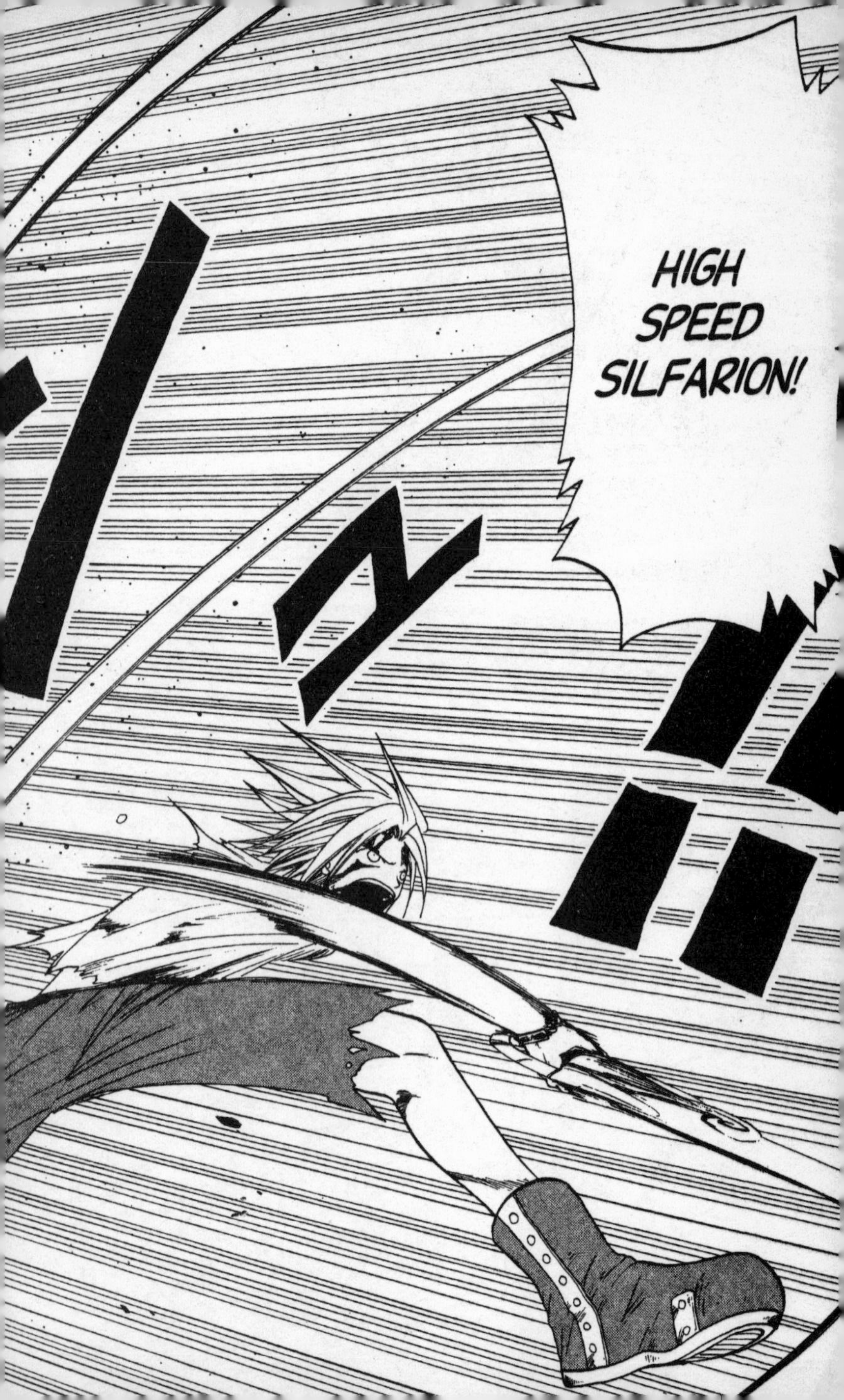
HIGH SPEED SILFARION!

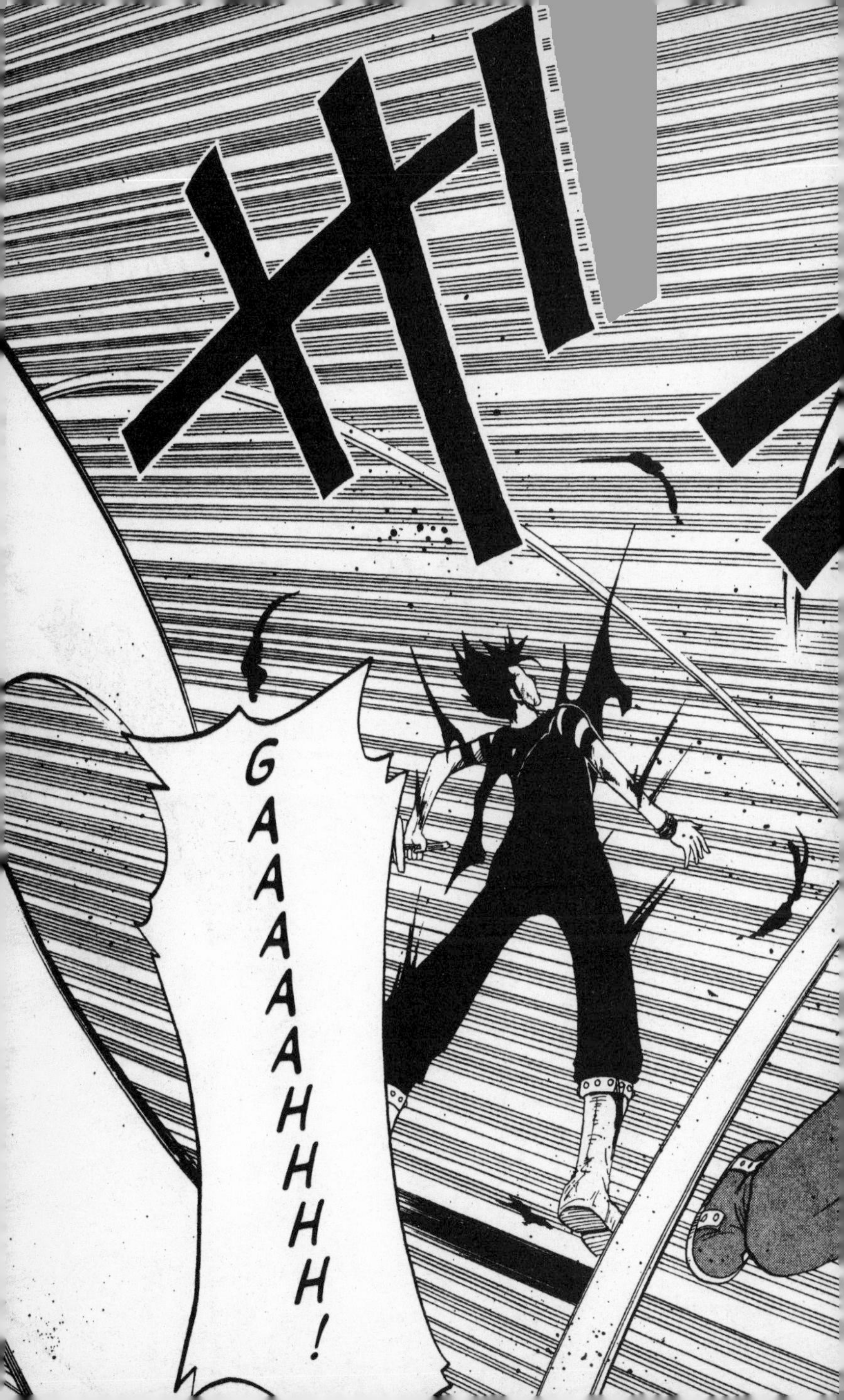
GAAAAAHHHHH!

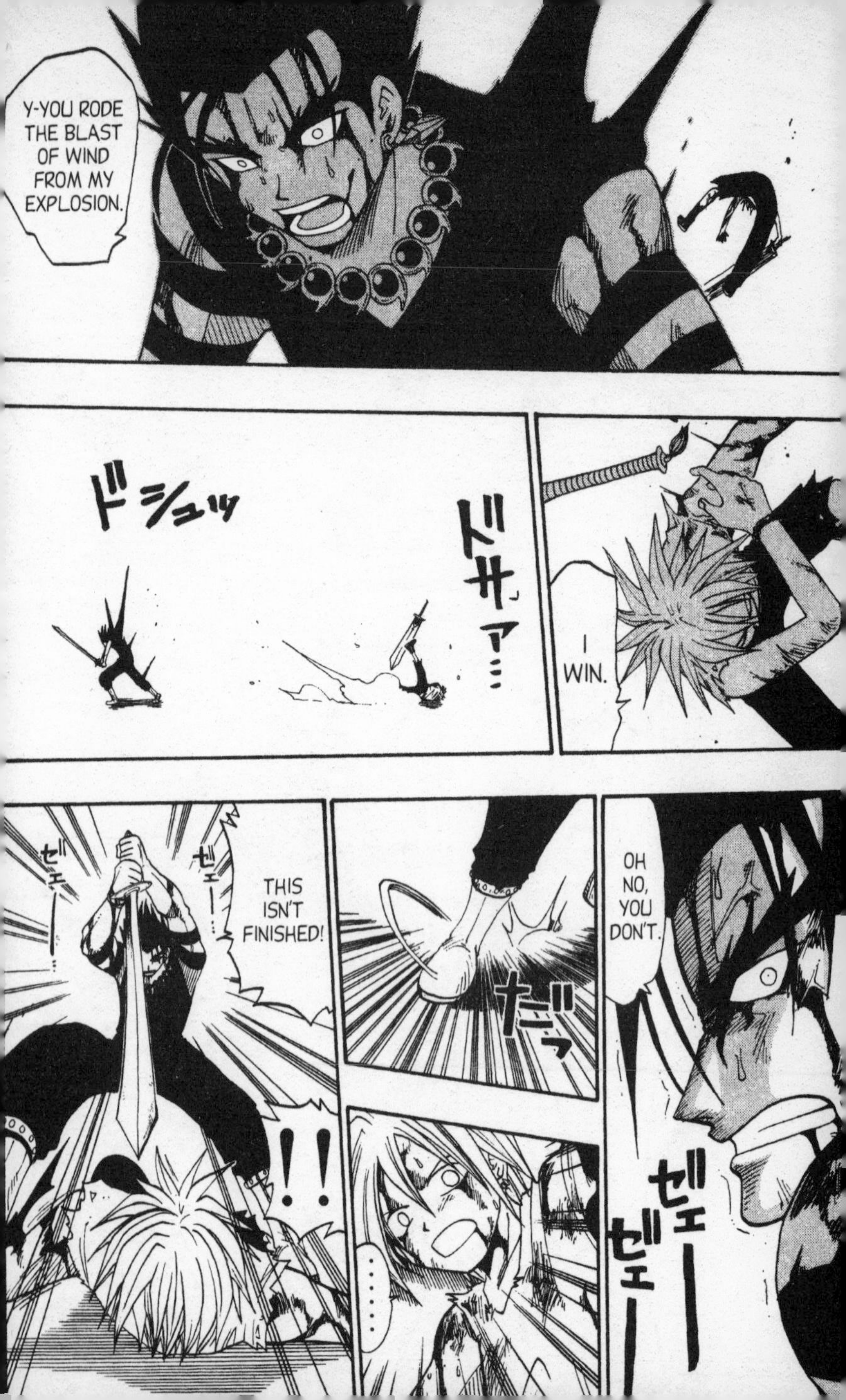
Y-YOU RODE THE BLAST OF WIND FROM MY EXPLOSION.
I WIN.
ドサァ…
ドシュッ
OH NO, YOU DON'T.
ゼェー
ゼェー
!!
……
THIS ISN'T FINISHED!
ゼェー…
ゼェー…

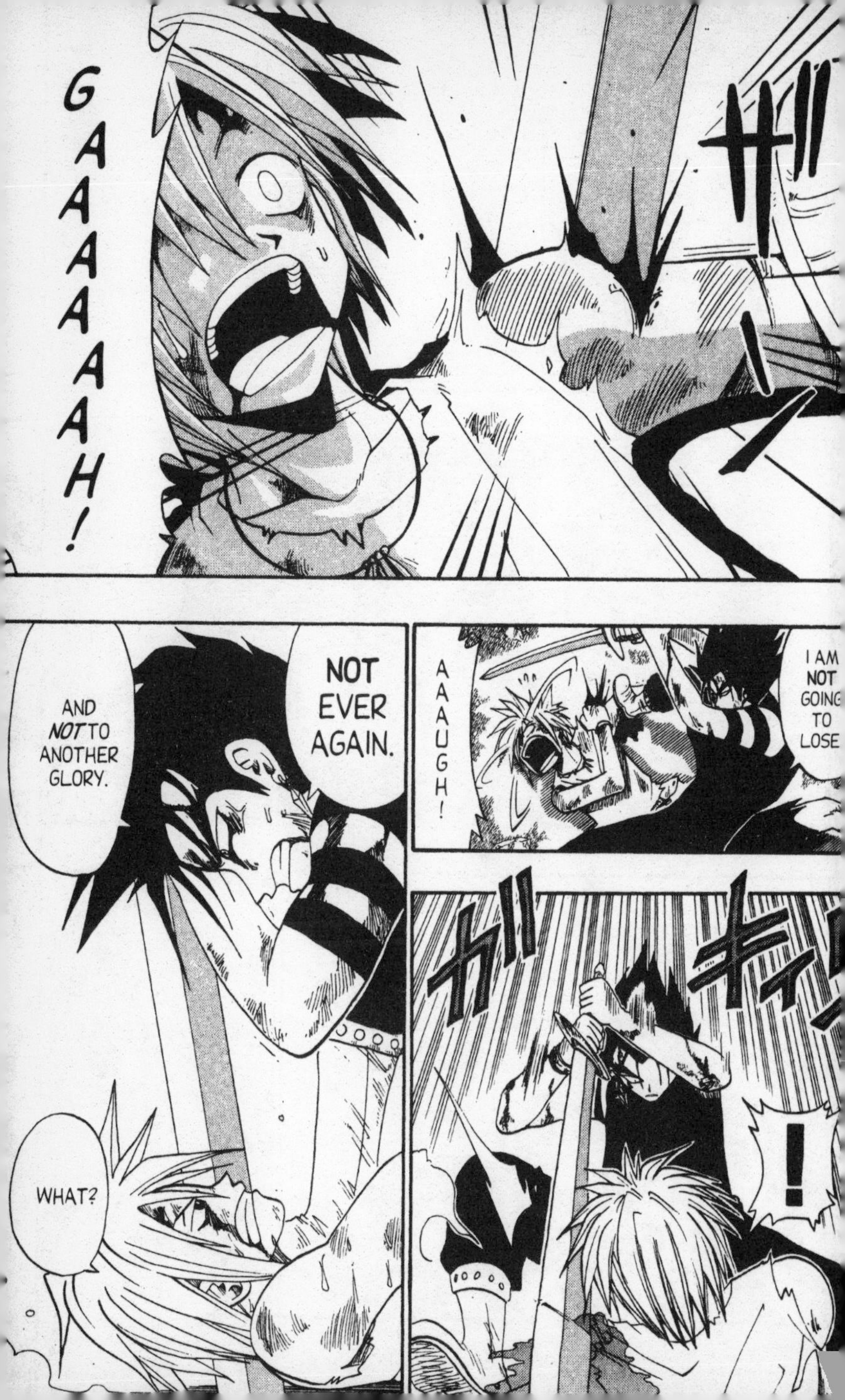
GAAAAAAAH!
I AM NOT GOING TO LOSE
AAAUGH!
!
NOT EVER AGAIN.
AND *NOT* TO ANOTHER GLORY.
WHAT?

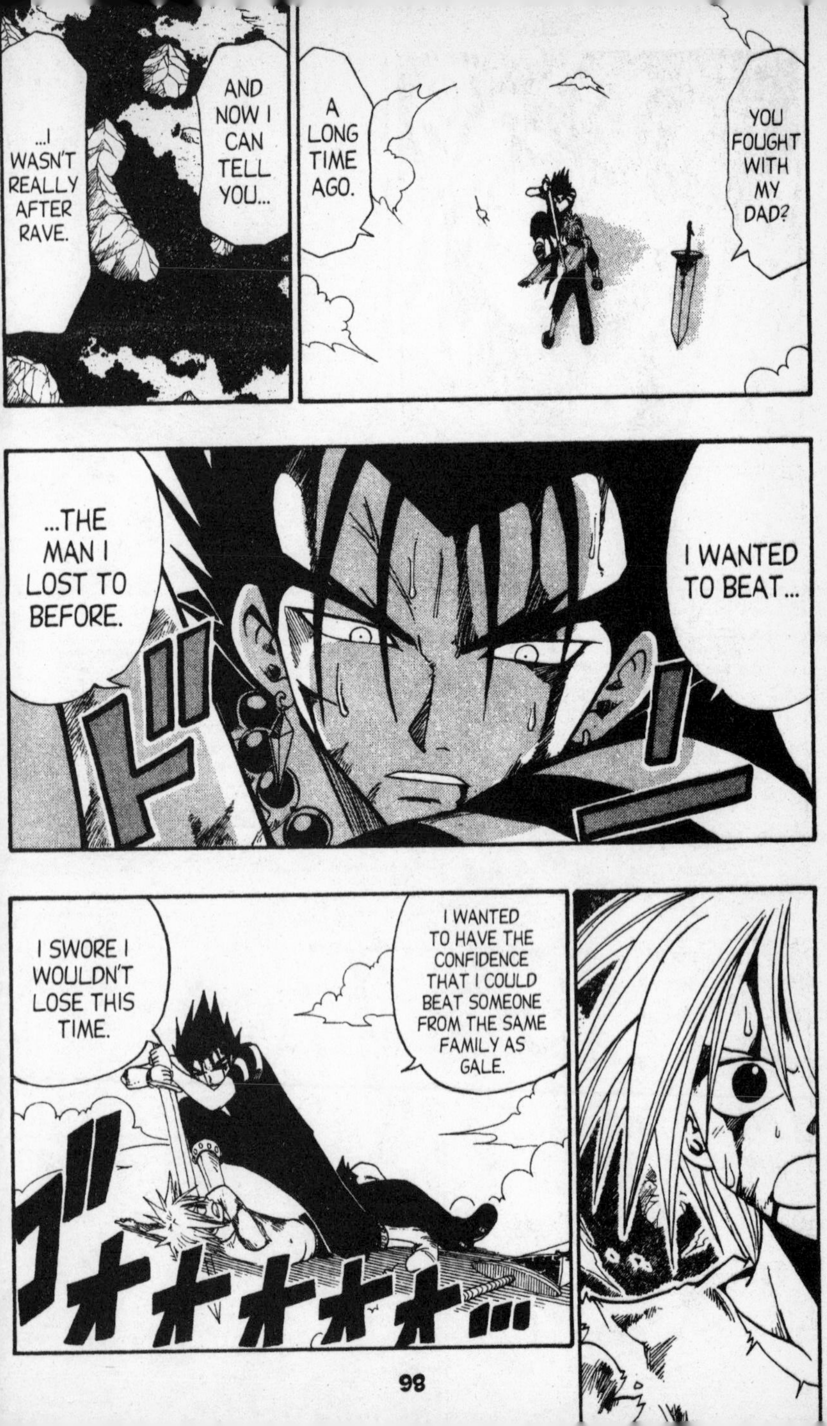
YOU FOUGHT WITH MY DAD?
A LONG TIME AGO.
AND NOW I CAN TELL YOU...
...I WASN'T REALLY AFTER RAVE.
I WANTED TO BEAT...
...THE MAN I LOST TO BEFORE.
ド
I WANTED TO HAVE THE CONFIDENCE THAT I COULD BEAT SOMEONE FROM THE SAME FAMILY AS GALE.
I SWORE I WOULDN'T LOSE THIS TIME.
ゴオオオオ…

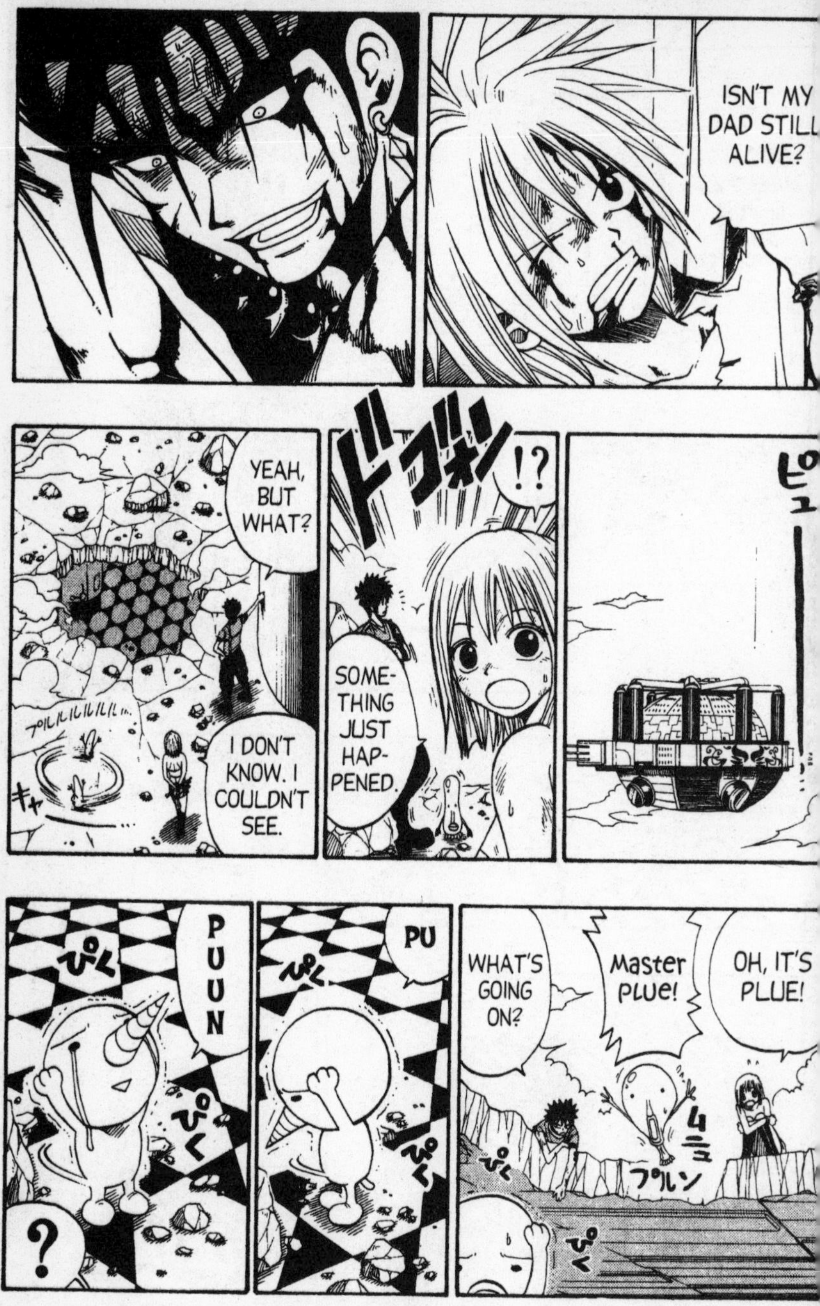
ISN'T MY DAD STILL ALIVE?
ピュー
ドゴォン
!?
SOME-THING JUST HAP-PENED.
YEAH, BUT WHAT?
I DON'T KNOW. I COULDN'T SEE.
プルルルルル…
キャ
OH, IT'S PLUE!
Master PLUE!
WHAT'S GOING ON?
ムニュ
プルン
ぴく
ぴく
PU
ぴく
ぴく
ぴく
PUUN
ぴく
ぴく
?

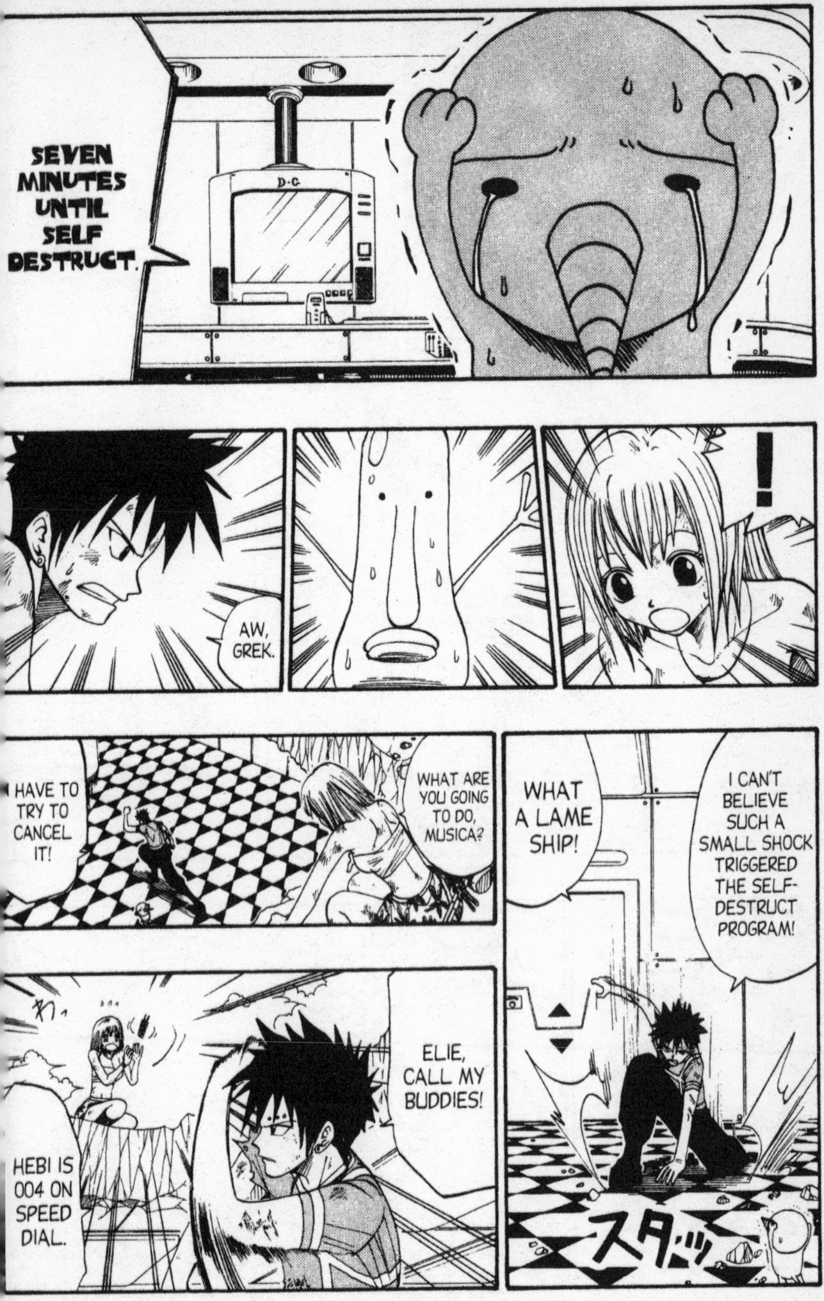
SEVEN MINUTES UNTIL SELF DESTRUCT.
!
AW, GREK.
I CAN'T BELIEVE SUCH A SMALL SHOCK TRIGGERED THE SELF-DESTRUCT PROGRAM!
WHAT A LAME SHIP!
スタッ
WHAT ARE YOU GOING TO DO, MUSICA?
I HAVE TO TRY TO CANCEL IT!
ELIE, CALL MY BUDDIES!
HEBI IS 004 ON SPEED DIAL.

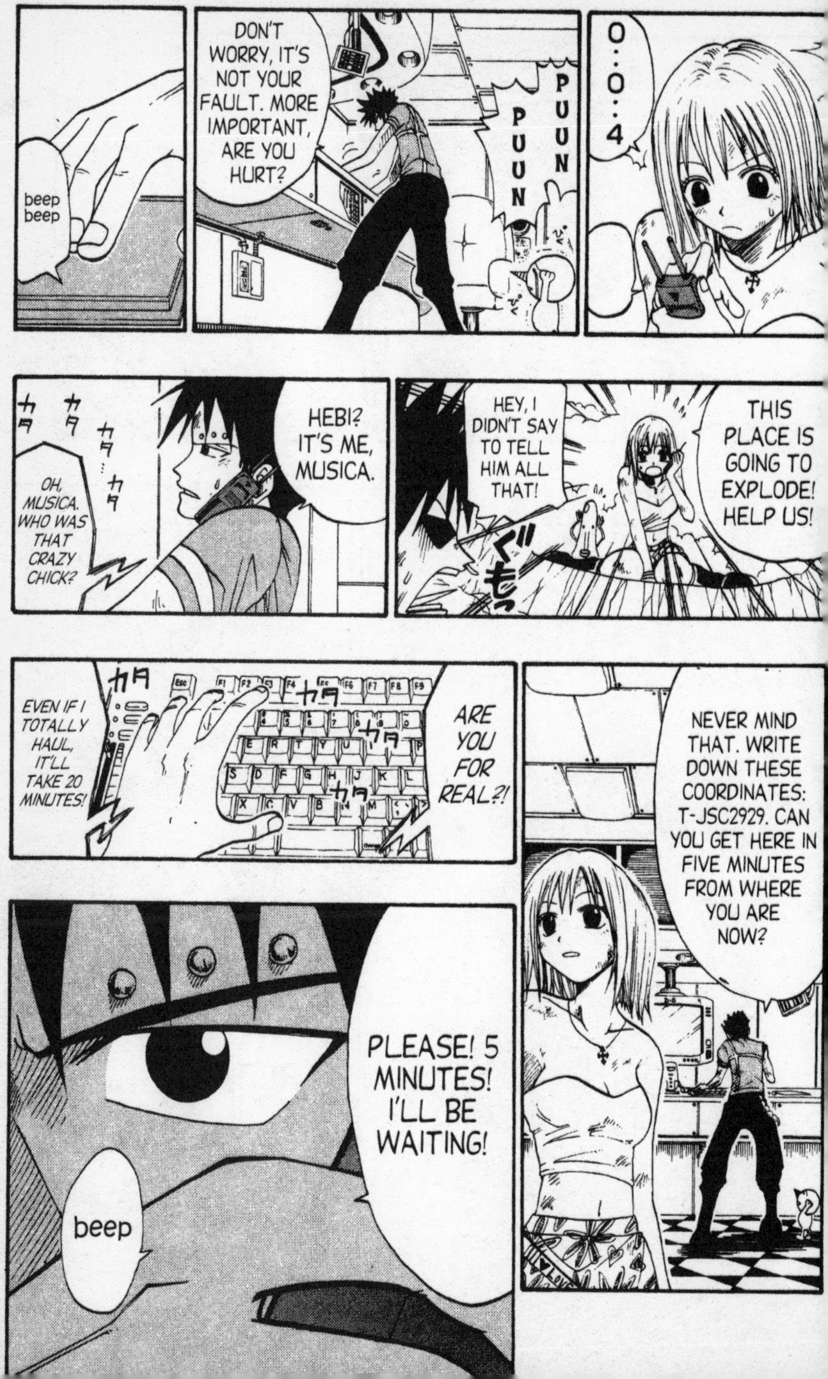
O...O...4
PUUN PUUN
DON'T WORRY, IT'S NOT YOUR FAULT. MORE IMPORTANT, ARE YOU HURT?
beep beep
THIS PLACE IS GOING TO EXPLODE! HELP US!
HEY, I DIDN'T SAY TO TELL HIM ALL THAT!
HEBI? IT'S ME, MUSICA.
OH, MUSICA. WHO WAS THAT CRAZY CHICK?
NEVER MIND THAT. WRITE DOWN THESE COORDINATES: T-JSC2929. CAN YOU GET HERE IN FIVE MINUTES FROM WHERE YOU ARE NOW?
ARE YOU FOR REAL?!
EVEN IF I TOTALLY HAUL, IT'LL TAKE 20 MINUTES!
PLEASE! 5 MINUTES! I'LL BE WAITING!
beep

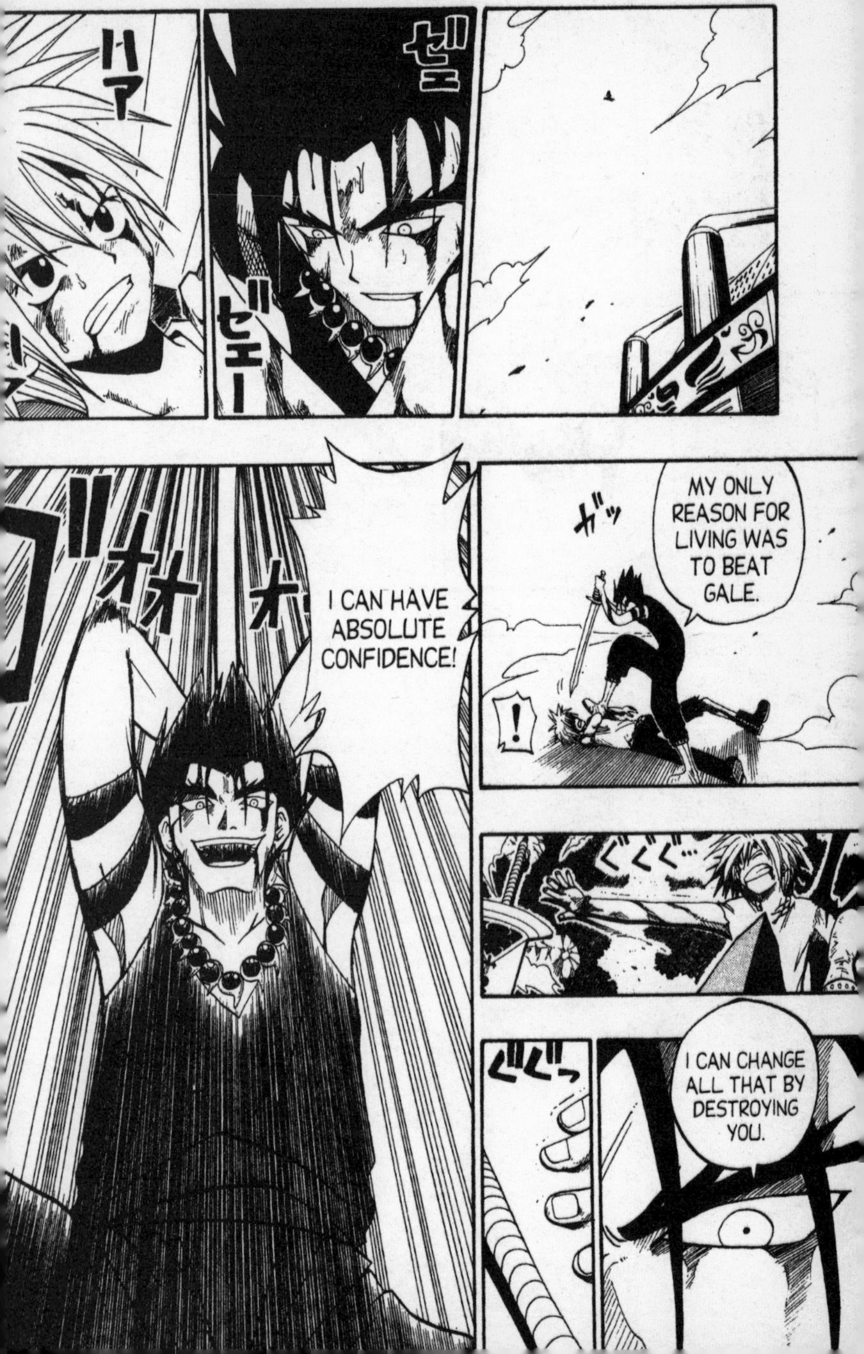
ゼェ
ゼェー
ハア
ガッ
MY ONLY REASON FOR LIVING WAS TO BEAT GALE.
!
ぐぐぐ…
ぐぐっ
I CAN CHANGE ALL THAT BY DESTROYING YOU.
ゴオオ
オ
I CAN HAVE ABSOLUTE CONFIDENCE!

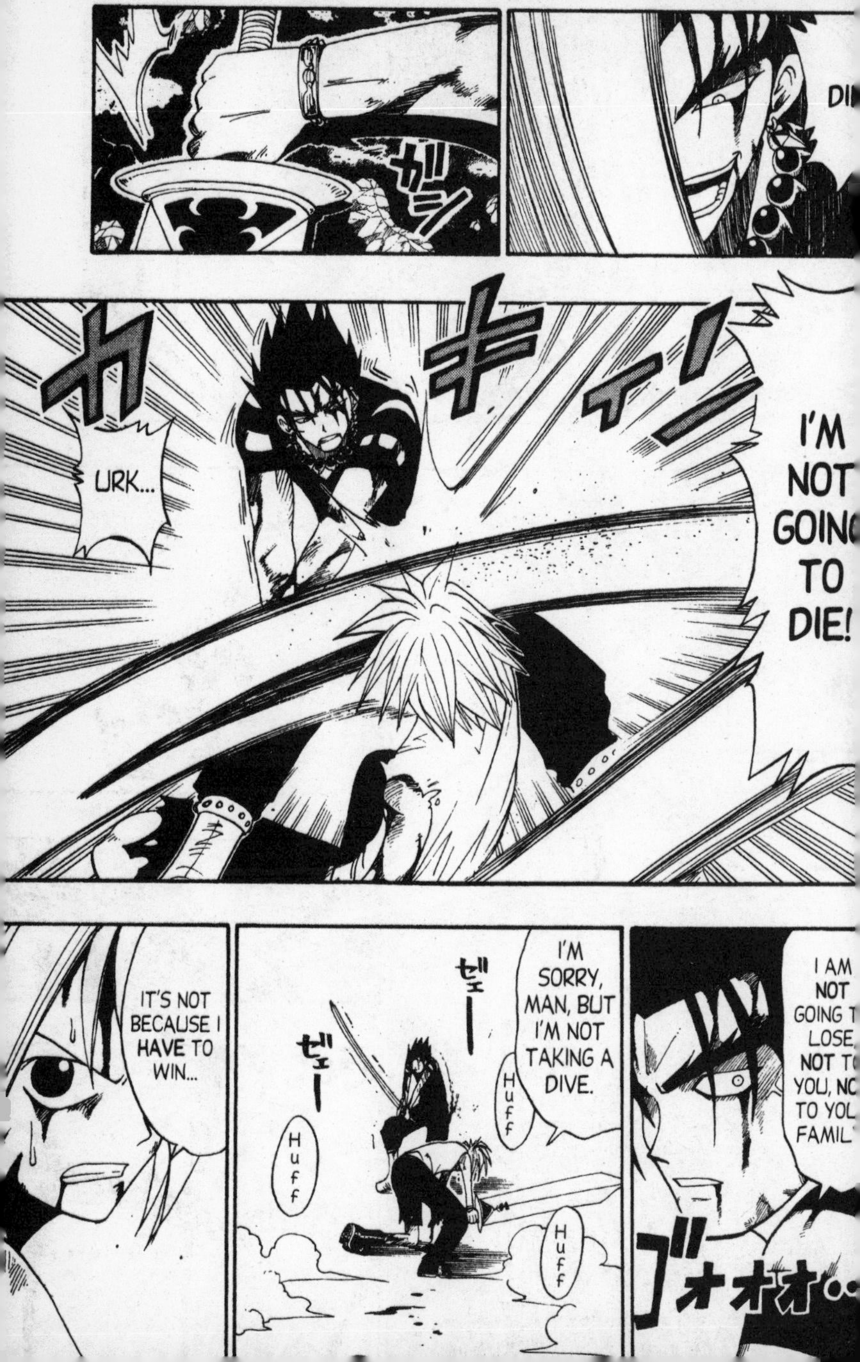
DI
I'M NOT GOIN TO DIE!
URK...
I AM NOT GOING T LOSE. NOT T YOU, NO TO YOU FAMIL
I'M SORRY, MAN, BUT I'M NOT TAKING A DIVE.
Huff
Huff
Huff
IT'S NOT BECAUSE I HAVE TO WIN...

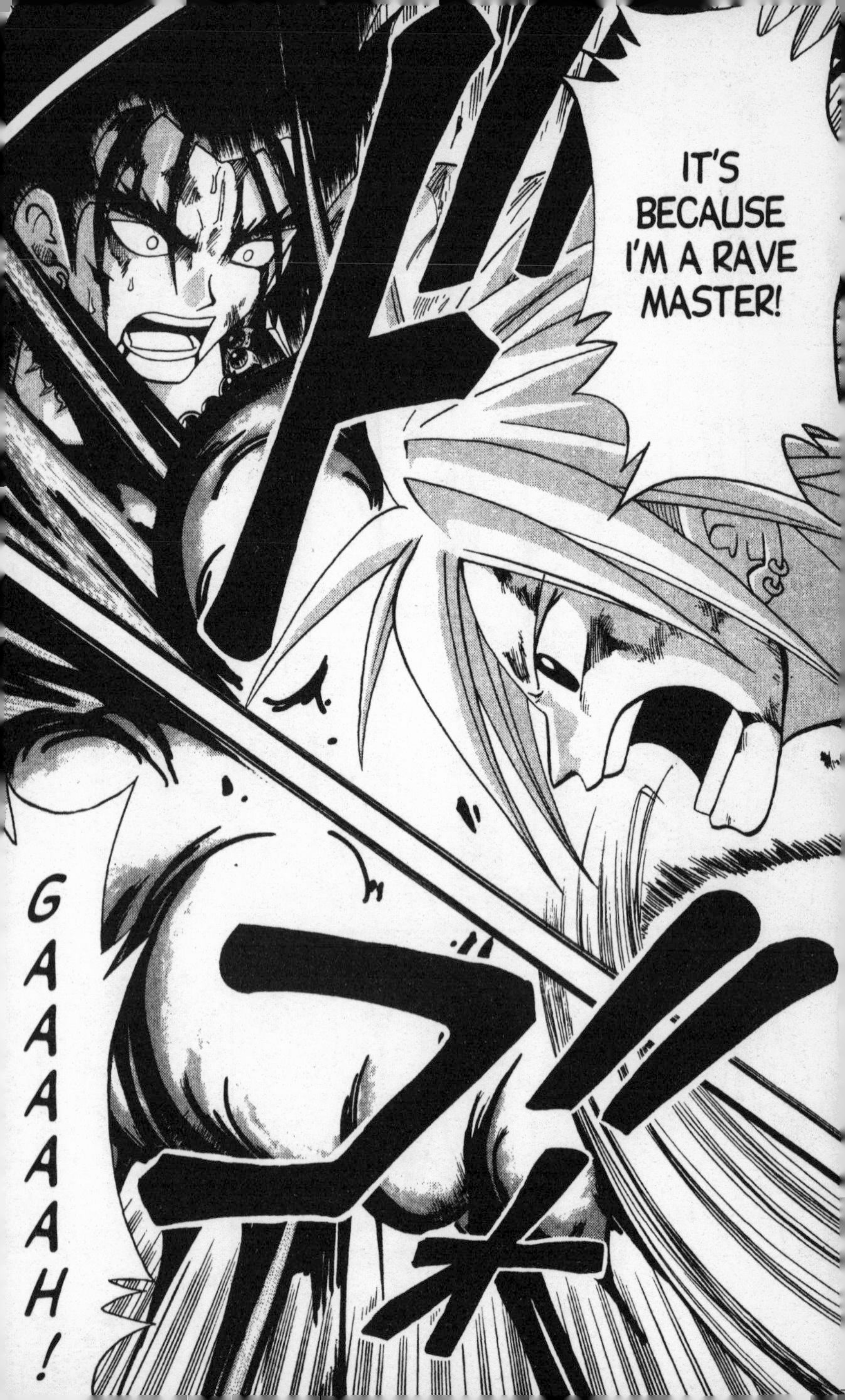
IT'S BECAUSE I'M A RAVE MASTER!
GAAAAAAH!

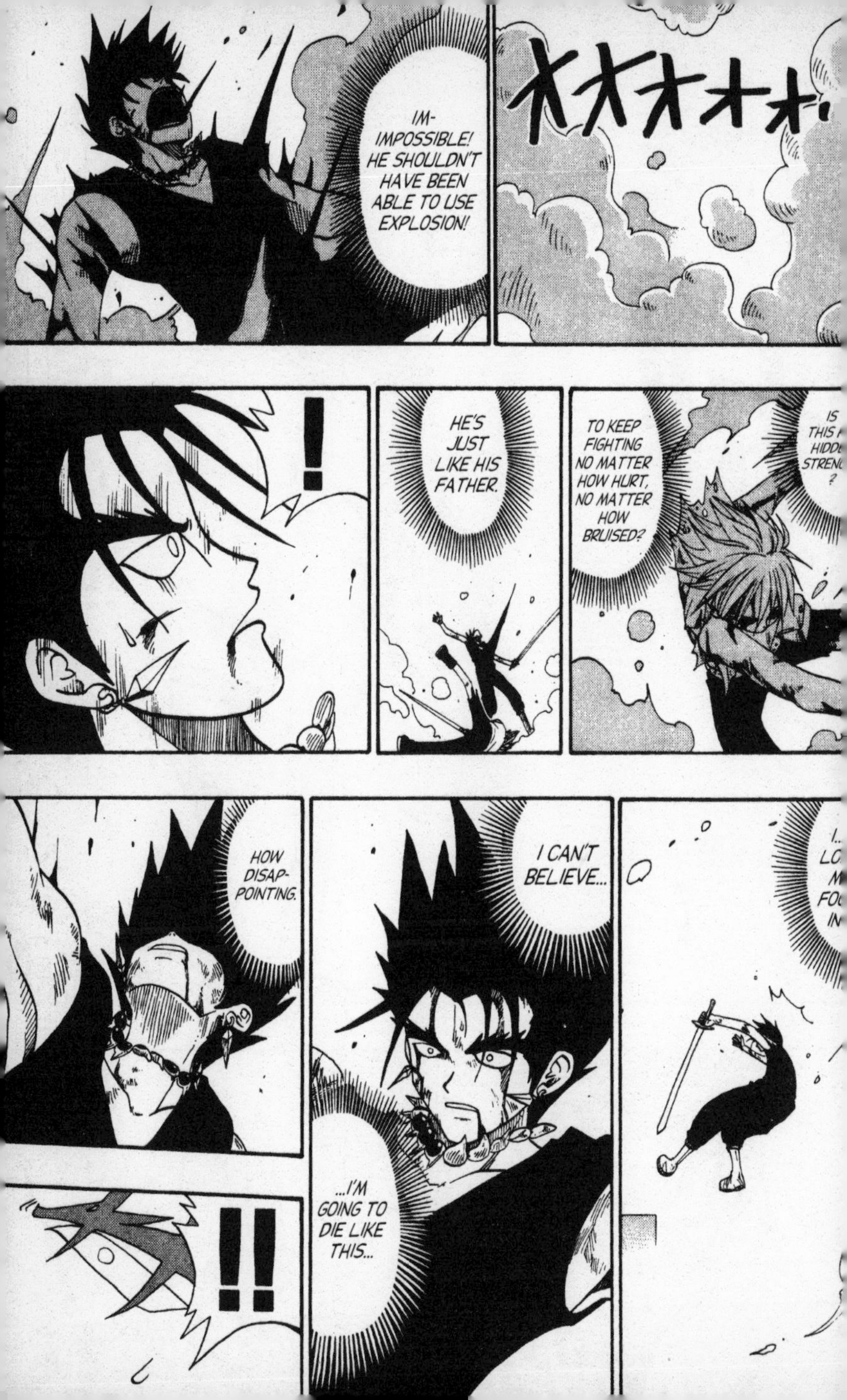

オオオオオ
IM- IMPOSSIBLE! HE SHOULDN'T HAVE BEEN ABLE TO USE EXPLOSION!
IS THIS
TO KEEP FIGHTING NO MATTER HOW HURT, NO MATTER HOW BRUISED?
HE'S JUST LIKE HIS FATHER.
!
I CAN'T BELIEVE...
...I'M GOING TO DIE LIKE THIS...
HOW DISAP- POINTING.
!!

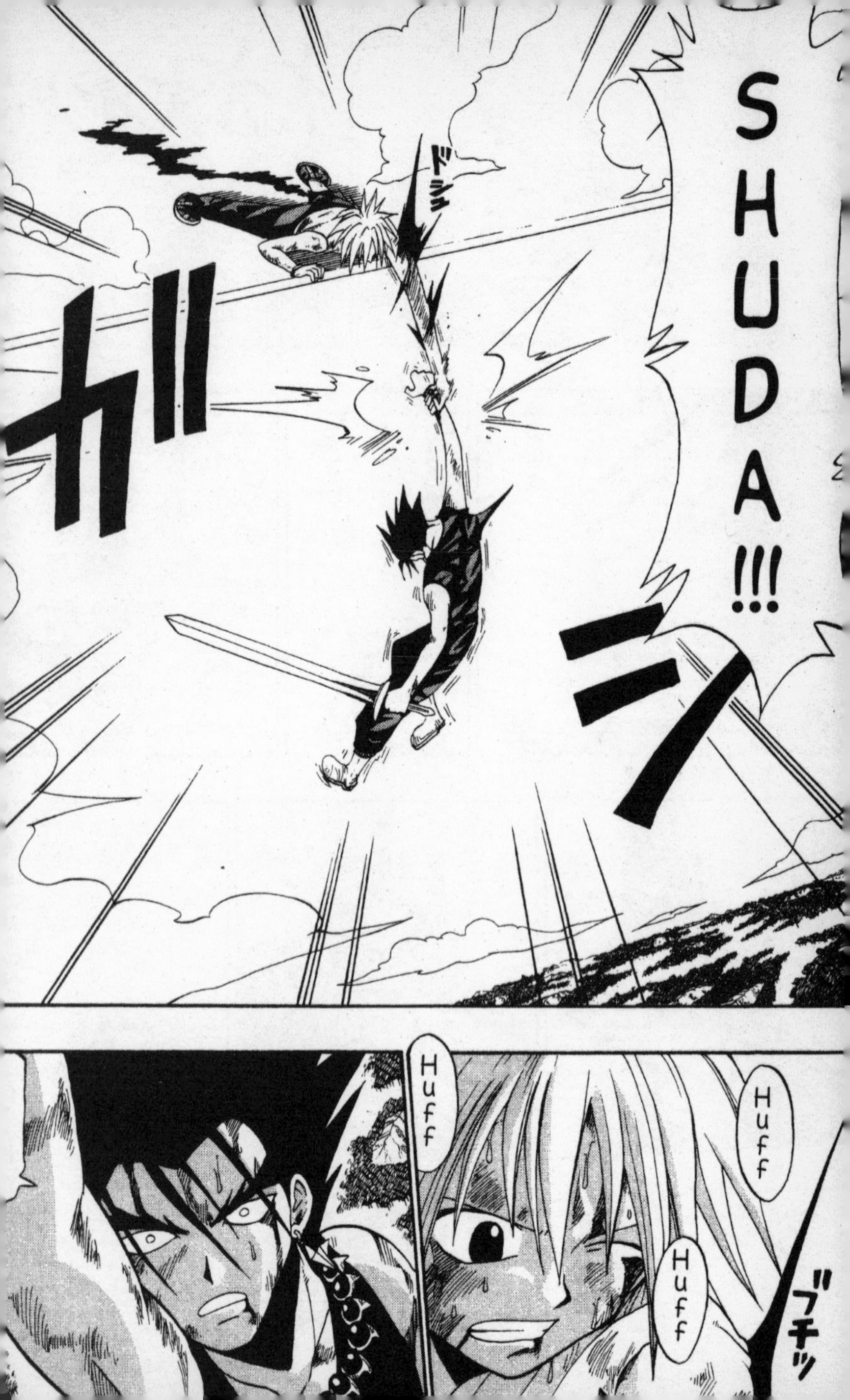
SHUDA!!!
ドシュ
ガン
Huff
Huff
ブチッ
Huff

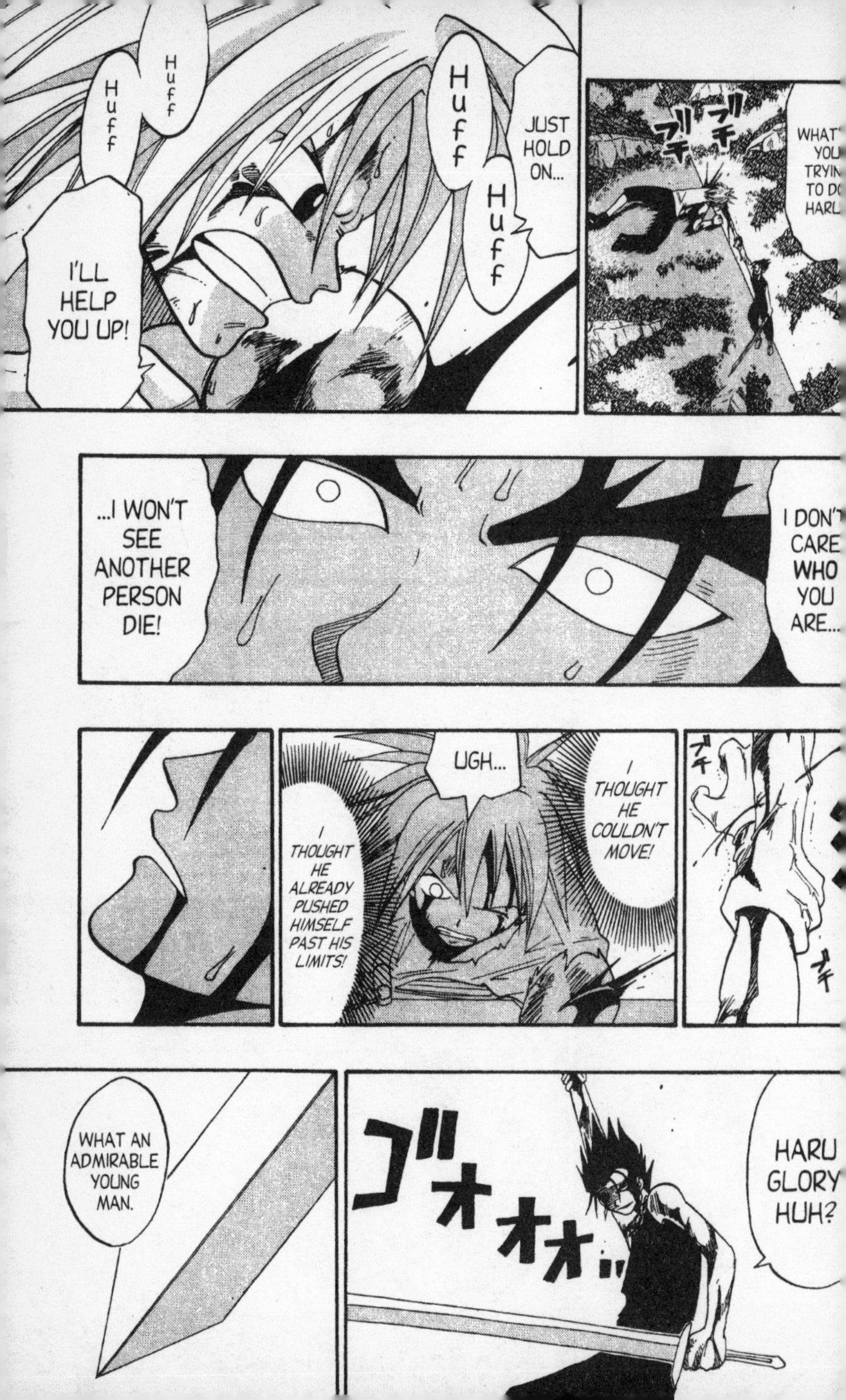
ブチ ブチ
WHAT' YOU TRYIN TO DO HARU
JUST HOLD ON...
Huff Huff
Huff Huff
Huff
Huff
I'LL HELP YOU UP!
I DON'T CARE WHO YOU ARE...
...I WON'T SEE ANOTHER PERSON DIE!
ブチ
ブチ
UGH...
I THOUGHT HE COULDN'T MOVE!
I THOUGHT HE ALREADY PUSHED HIMSELF PAST HIS LIMITS!
HARU GLORY HUH?
ゴオオオ..
WHAT AN ADMIRABLE YOUNG MAN.

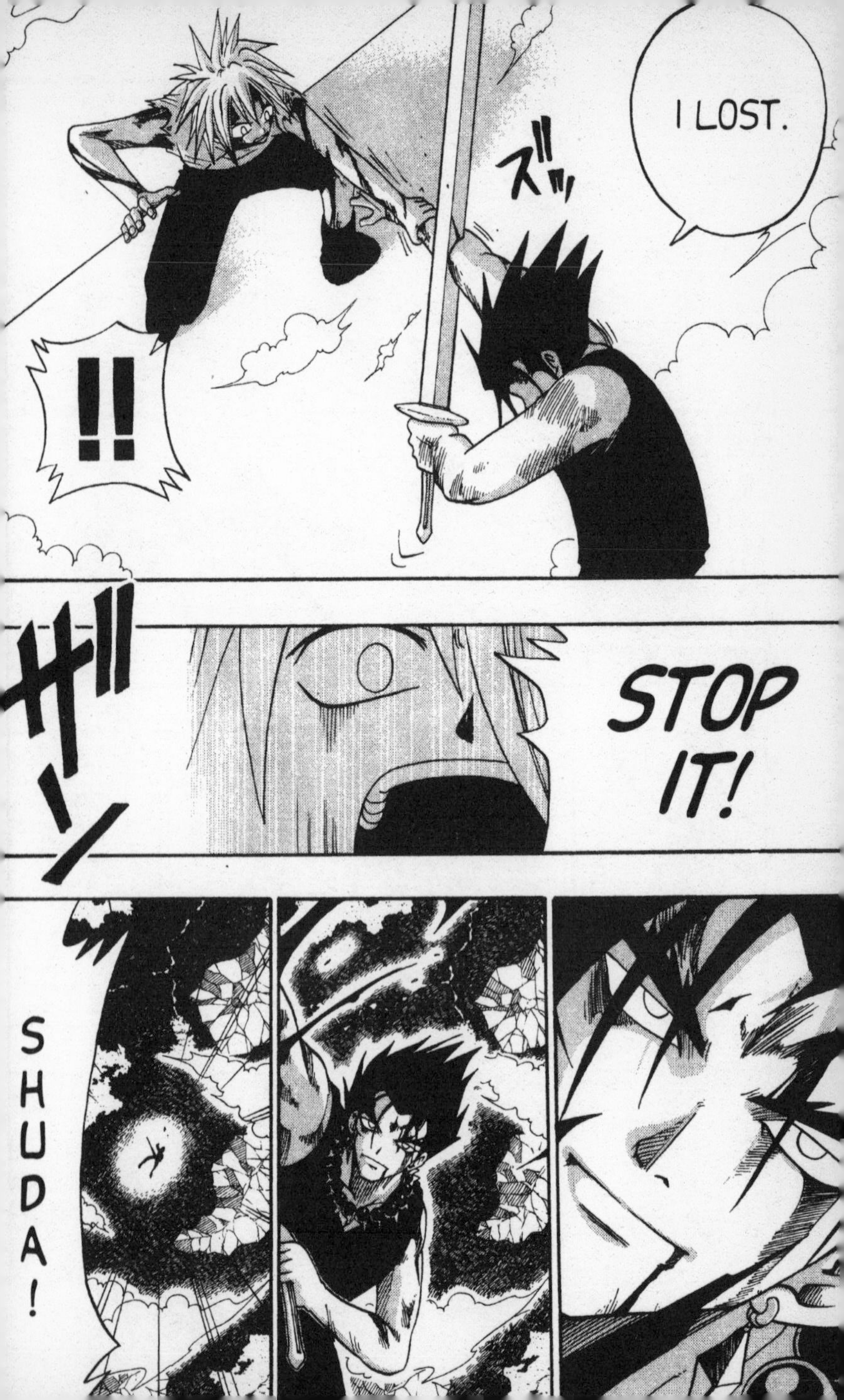
I LOST.
!!
STOP IT!
SHUDA!

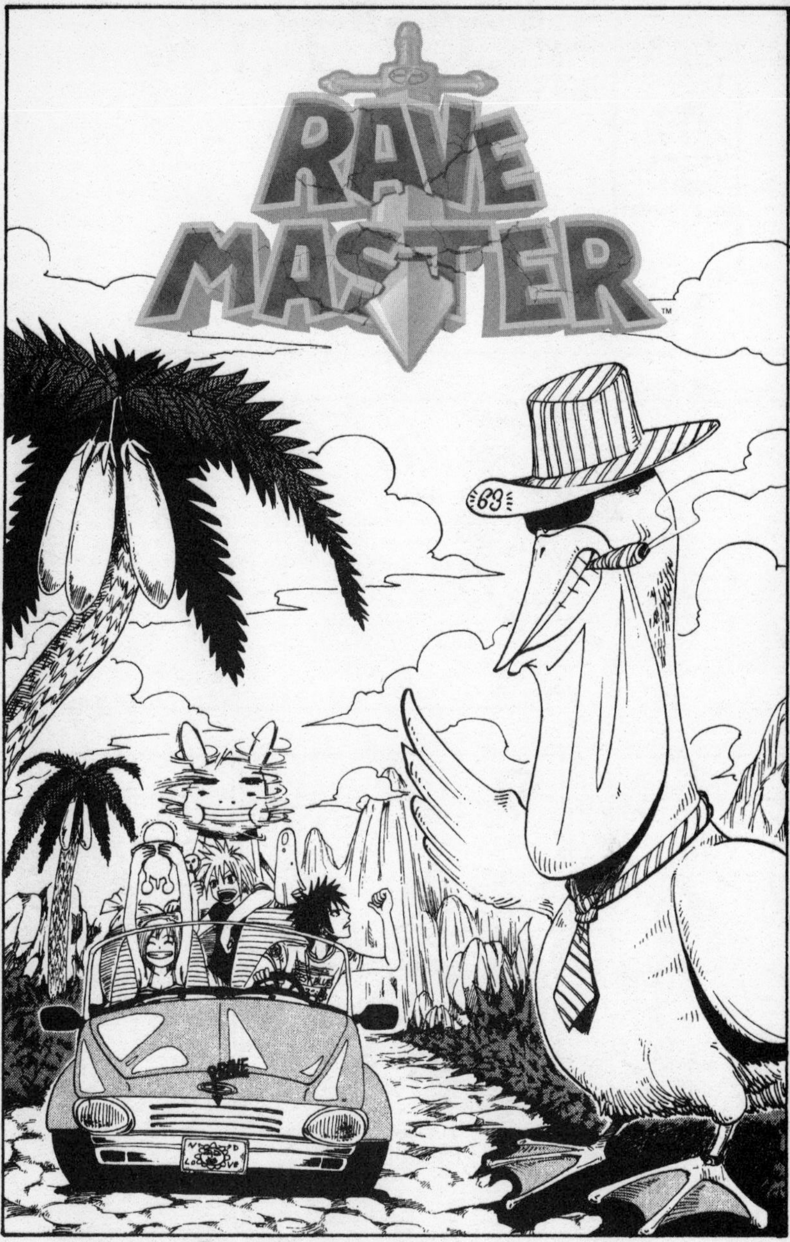
RAVE MASTER™

RAVE: 36 ✠ AN IRON HEART

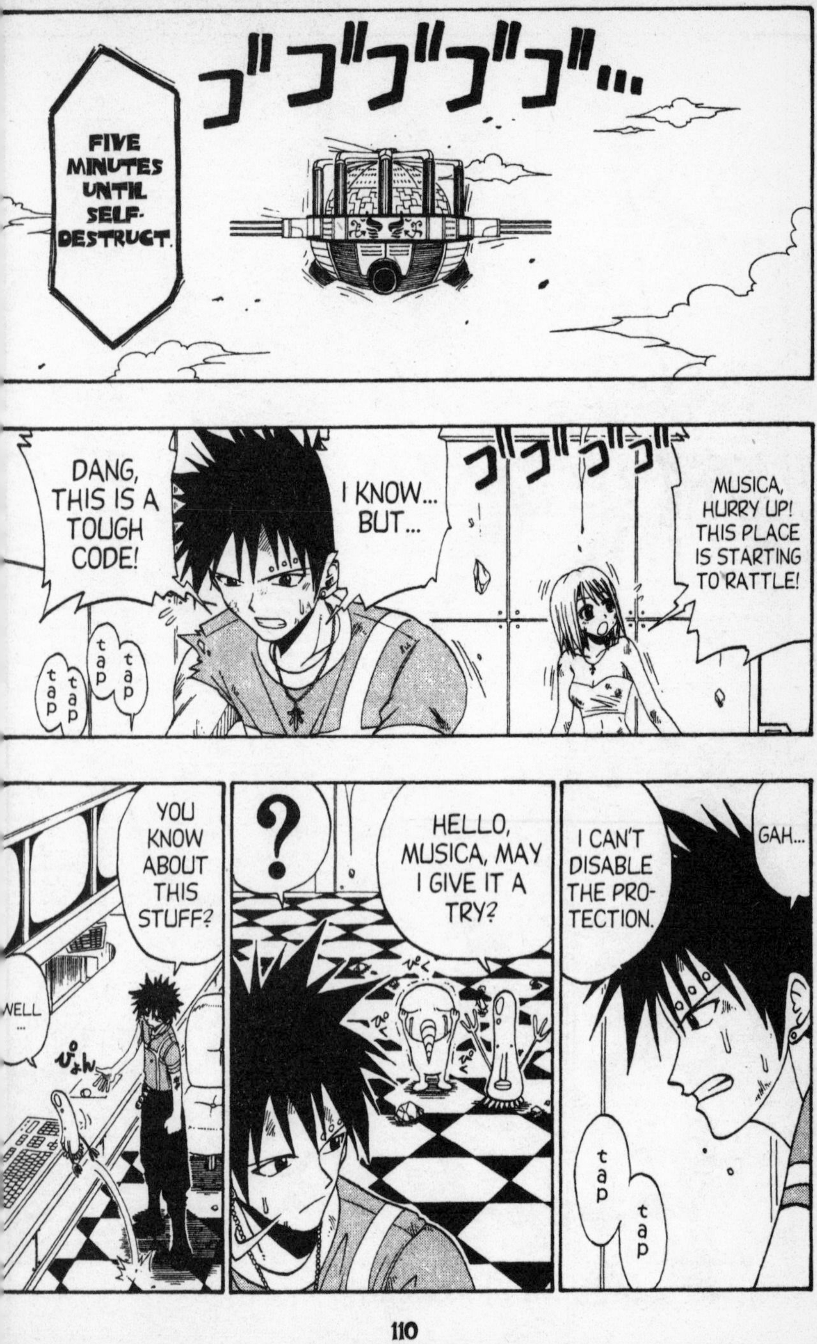
ゴゴゴゴゴ...
FIVE MINUTES UNTIL SELF-DESTRUCT.
MUSICA, HURRY UP! THIS PLACE IS STARTING TO RATTLE!
ゴゴゴゴ
I KNOW... BUT...
DANG, THIS IS A TOUGH CODE!
tap tap
tap tap
GAH...
I CAN'T DISABLE THE PROTECTION.
tap tap
HELLO, MUSICA, MAY I GIVE IT A TRY?
?
YOU KNOW ABOUT THIS STUFF?
WELL ...
ぴょん

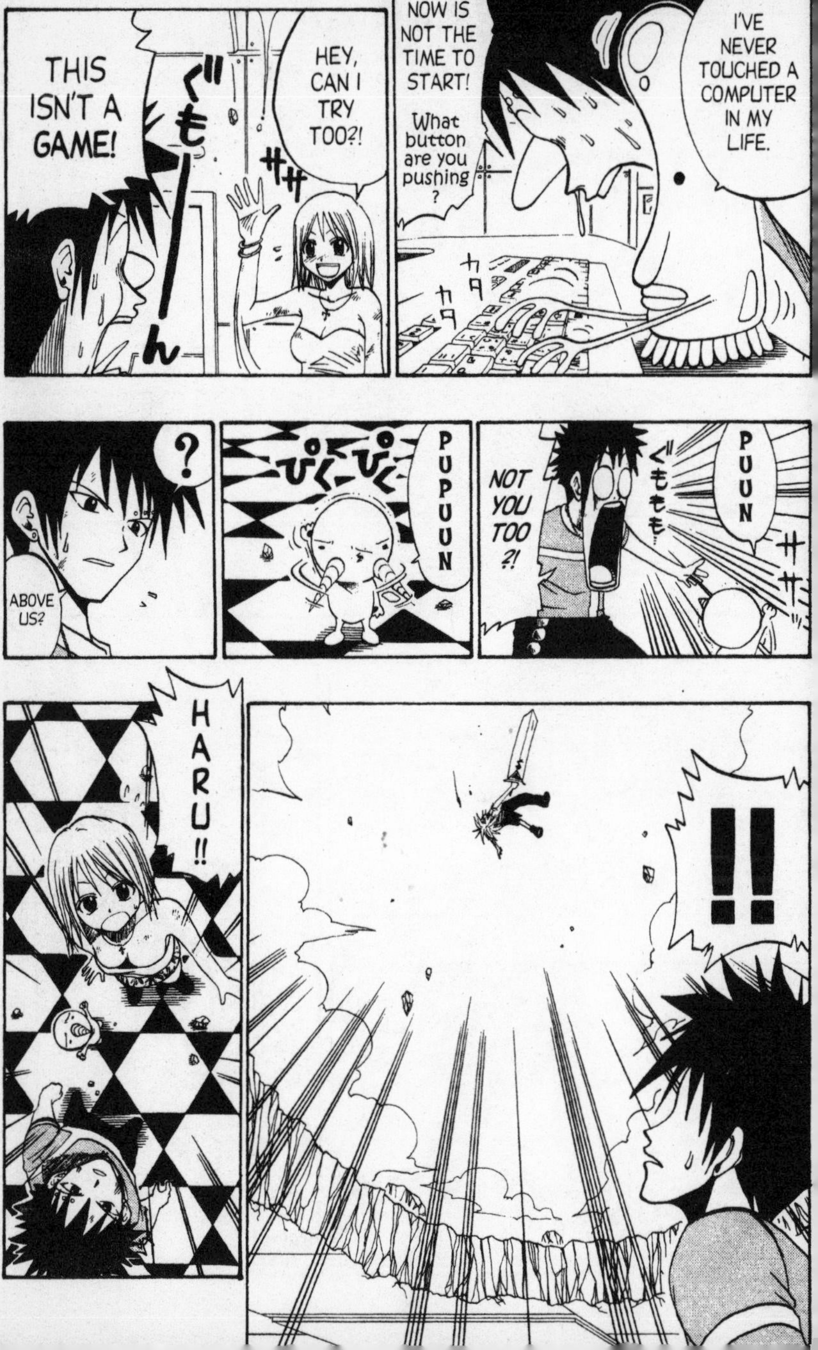
I'VE NEVER TOUCHED A COMPUTER IN MY LIFE.
NOW IS NOT THE TIME TO START!
What button are you pushing?
カタ
カタ
HEY, CAN I TRY TOO?!
ササ
THIS ISN'T A GAME!
ぐもーん
PUUN
ぐももも…
NOT YOU TOO?!
PUPUUUN
ぴくーぴく
?
ABOVE US?
!!
HARU!!

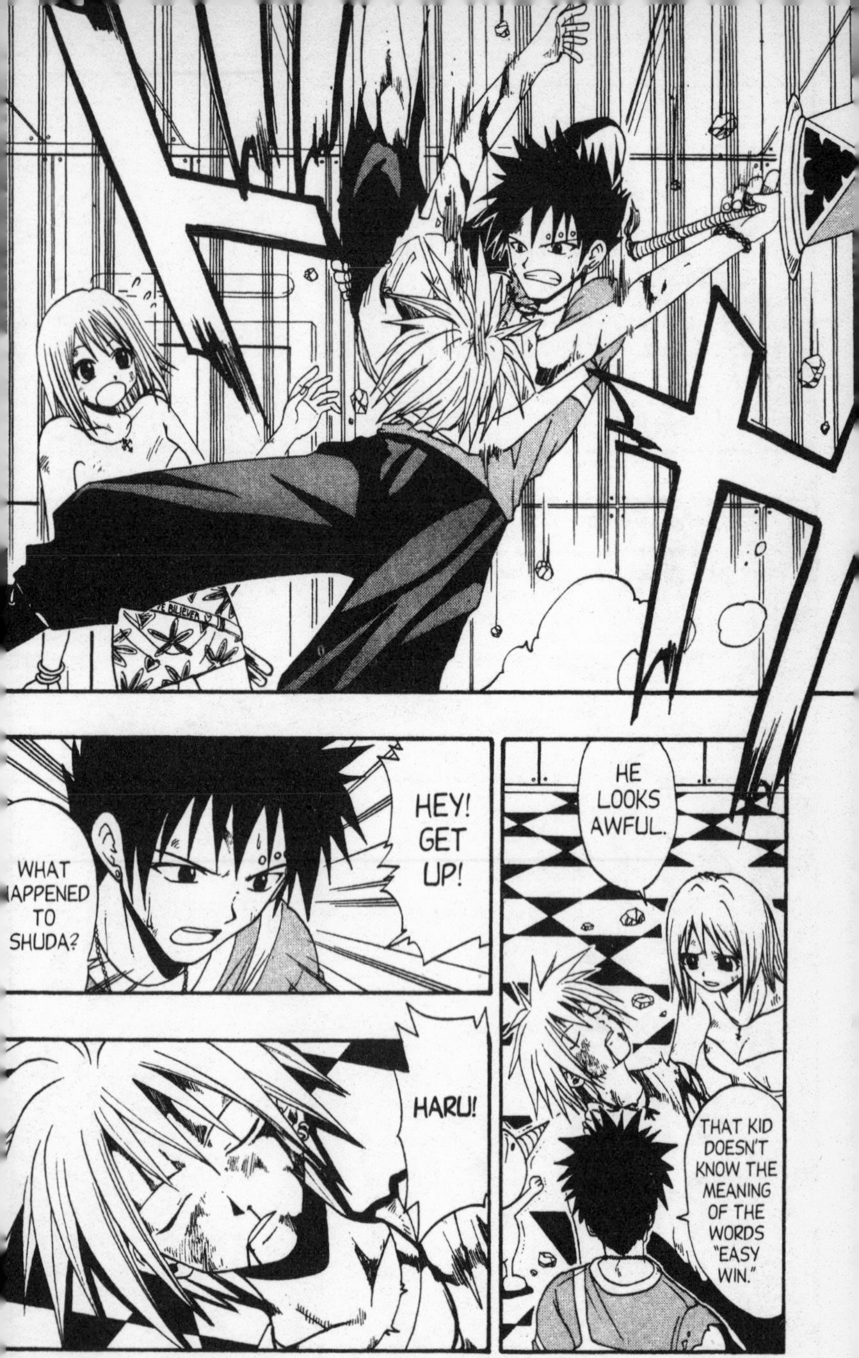
HE LOOKS AWFUL.
THAT KID DOESN'T KNOW THE MEANING OF THE WORDS "EASY WIN."
HEY! GET UP!
WHAT HAPPENED TO SHUDA?
HARU!

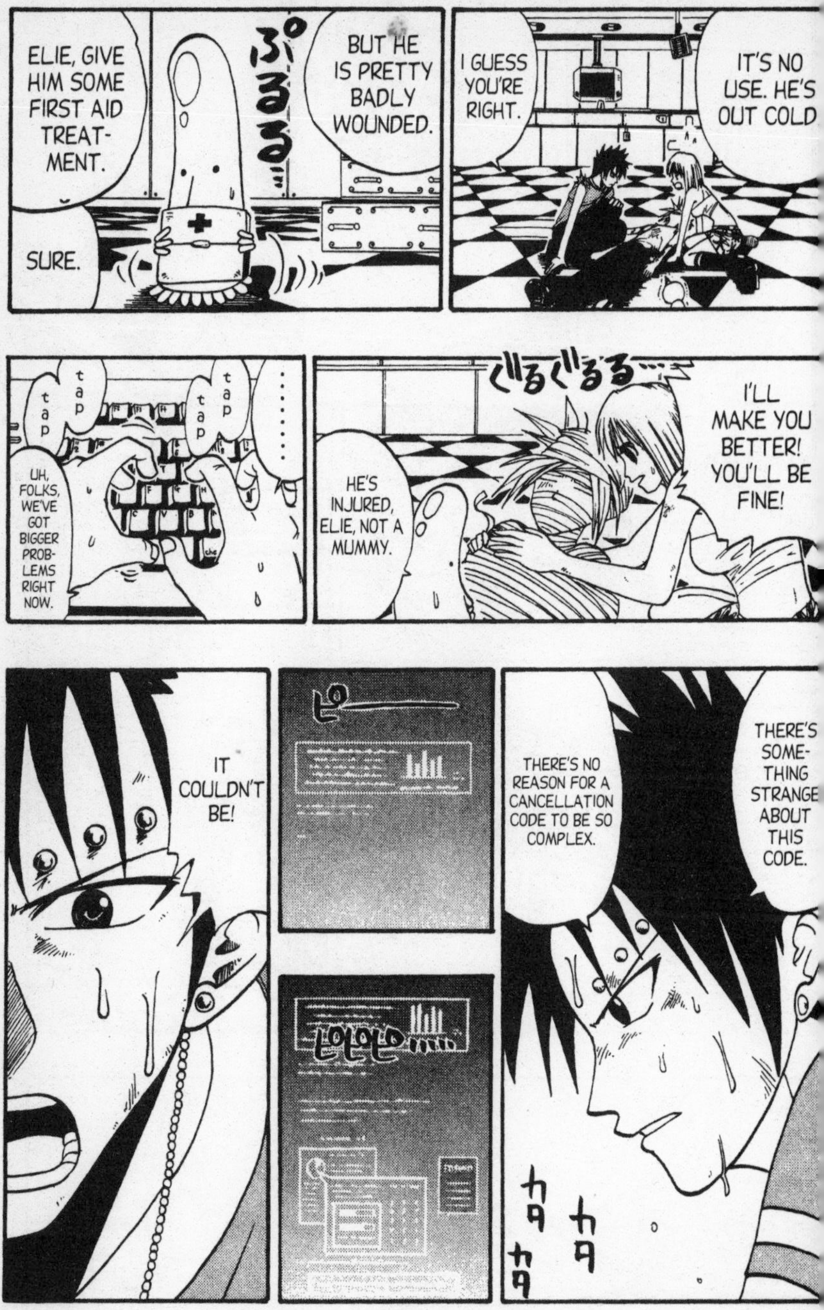

IT'S NO USE. HE'S OUT COLD
I GUESS YOU'RE RIGHT.
BUT HE IS PRETTY BADLY WOUNDED.
ぷるる
ELIE, GIVE HIM SOME FIRST AID TREATMENT.
SURE.
ぐるぐるる…
I'LL MAKE YOU BETTER! YOU'LL BE FINE!
HE'S INJURED, ELIE, NOT A MUMMY.
......
tap tap
tap tap
UH, FOLKS, WE'VE GOT BIGGER PROBLEMS RIGHT NOW.
THERE'S SOMETHING STRANGE ABOUT THIS CODE.
THERE'S NO REASON FOR A CANCELLATION CODE TO BE SO COMPLEX.
カタ カタ カタ
ピ—
ピロピロ…
IT COULDN'T BE!

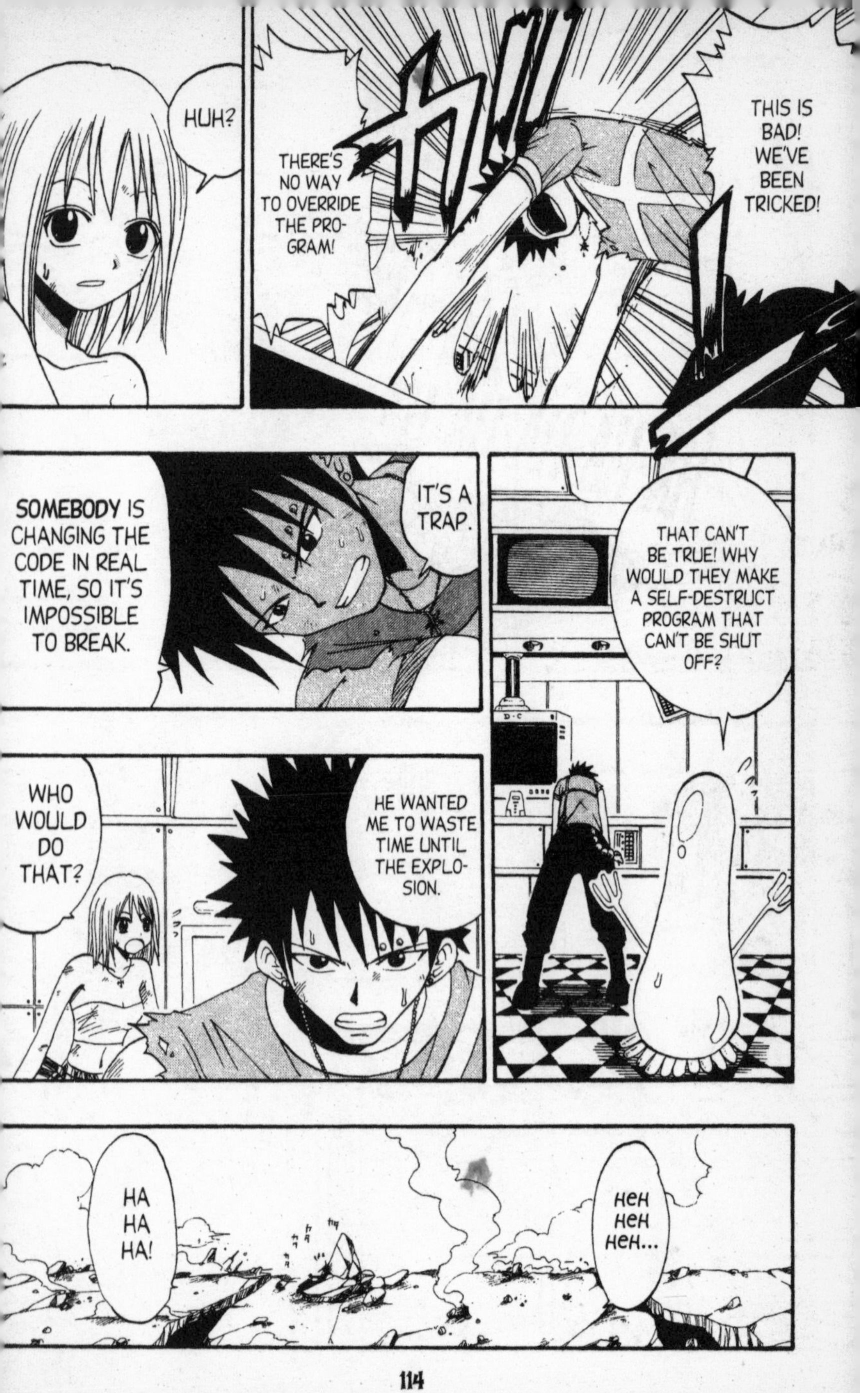
THIS IS BAD! WE'VE BEEN TRICKED!
THERE'S NO WAY TO OVERRIDE THE PRO- GRAM!
HUH?
THAT CAN'T BE TRUE! WHY WOULD THEY MAKE A SELF-DESTRUCT PROGRAM THAT CAN'T BE SHUT OFF?
IT'S A TRAP.
SOMEBODY IS CHANGING THE CODE IN REAL TIME, SO IT'S IMPOSSIBLE TO BREAK.
HE WANTED ME TO WASTE TIME UNTIL THE EXPLO- SION.
WHO WOULD DO THAT?
HEH HEH HEH...
HA HA HA!

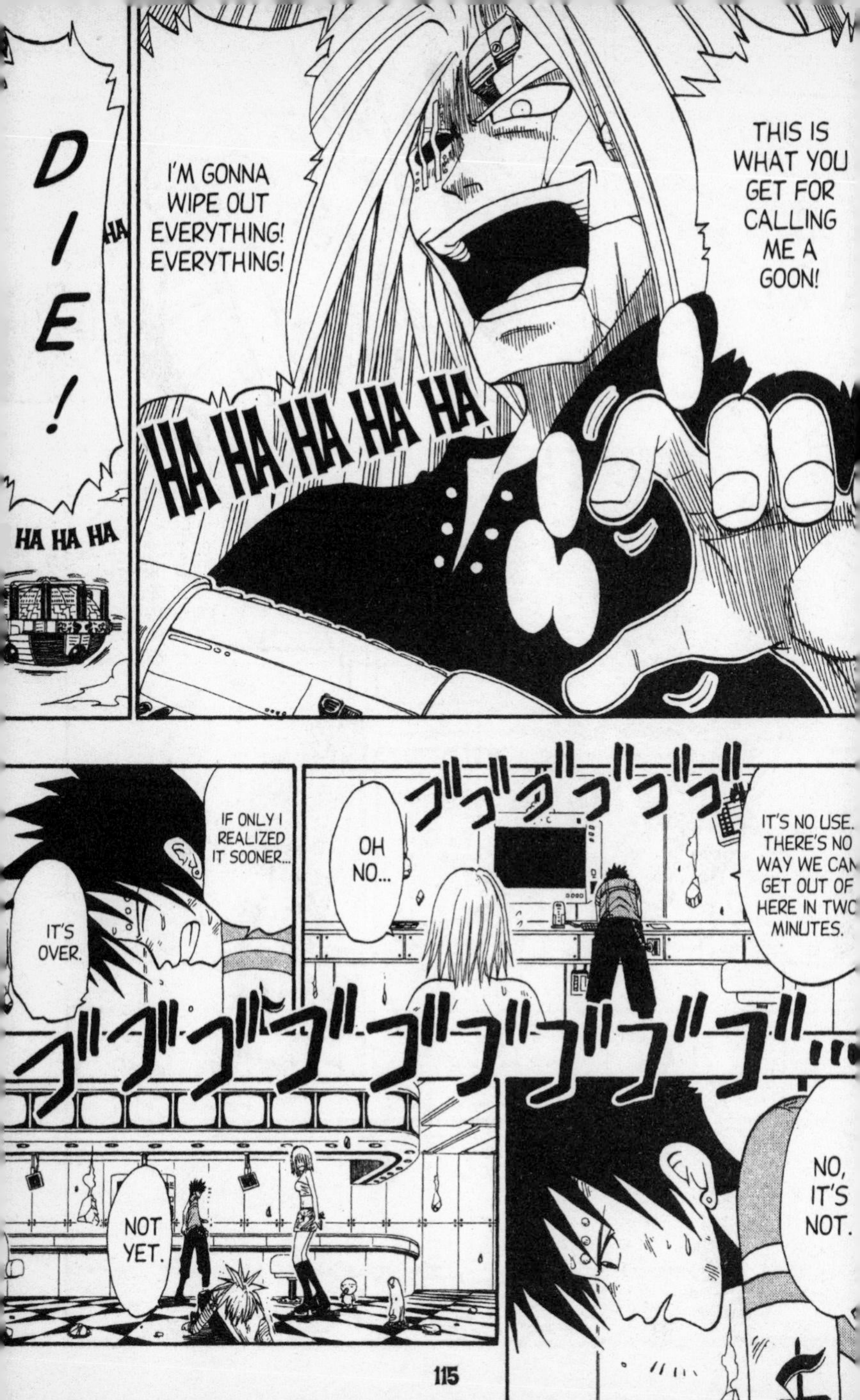
THIS IS WHAT YOU GET FOR CALLING ME A GOON!
I'M GONNA WIPE OUT EVERYTHING! EVERYTHING!
HA HA HA HA HA
HA
DIE!
HA HA HA
ゴゴゴゴゴ
IT'S NO USE. THERE'S NO WAY WE CAN GET OUT OF HERE IN TWO MINUTES.
OH NO...
IF ONLY I REALIZED IT SOONER...
IT'S OVER.
ゴゴゴゴゴゴゴゴゴ...
NO, IT'S NOT.
NOT YET.

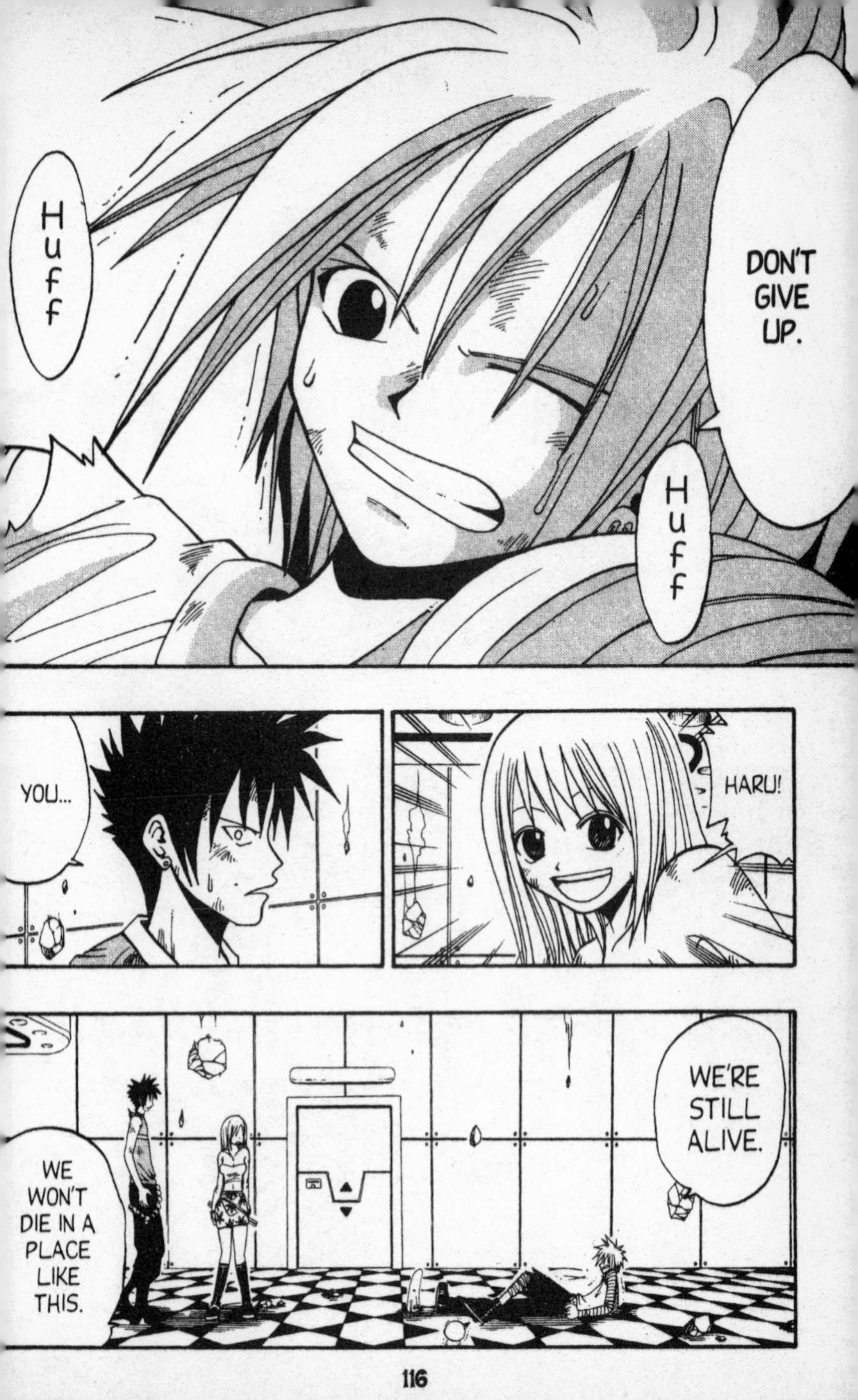
DON'T GIVE UP.
Huff
Huff
HARU!
YOU...
WE'RE STILL ALIVE.
WE WON'T DIE IN A PLACE LIKE THIS.

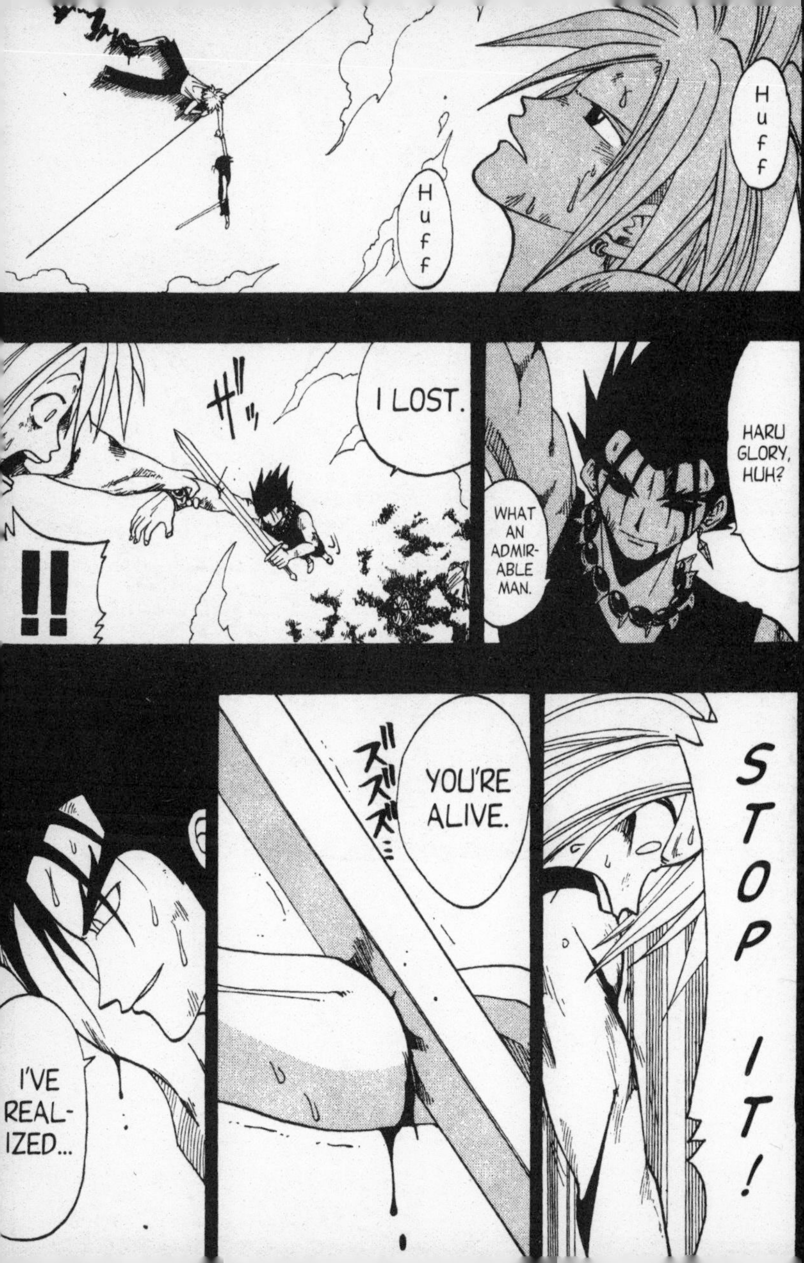
Huff
Huff
HARU GLORY, HUH?
WHAT AN ADMIRABLE MAN.
I LOST.
ザッ
!!
STOP IT!
YOU'RE ALIVE.
ズズズ
I'VE REALIZED...

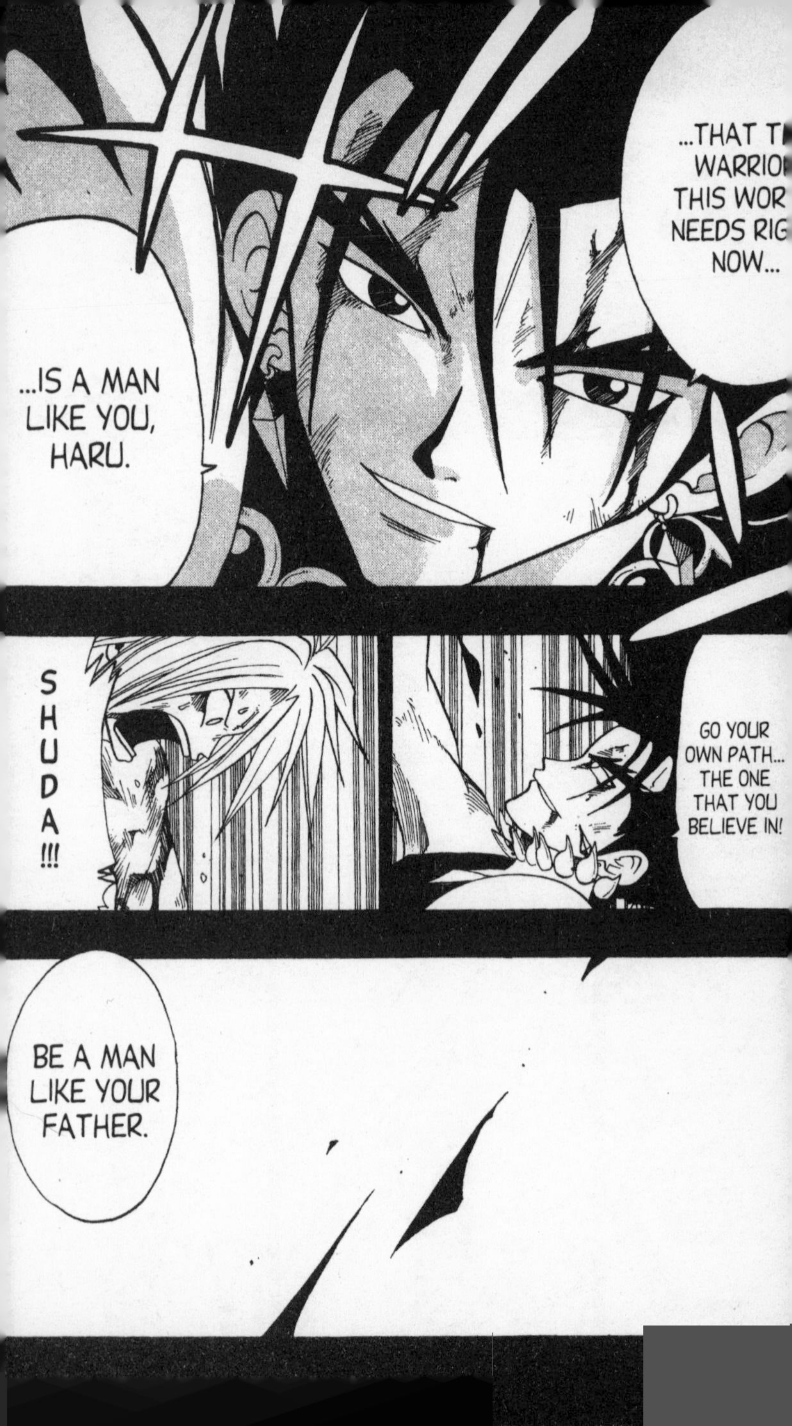
...THAT T WARRIO THIS WOR NEEDS RIG NOW...
...IS A MAN LIKE YOU, HARU.
GO YOUR OWN PATH... THE ONE THAT YOU BELIEVE IN!
SHUDA!!!
BE A MAN LIKE YOUR FATHER.

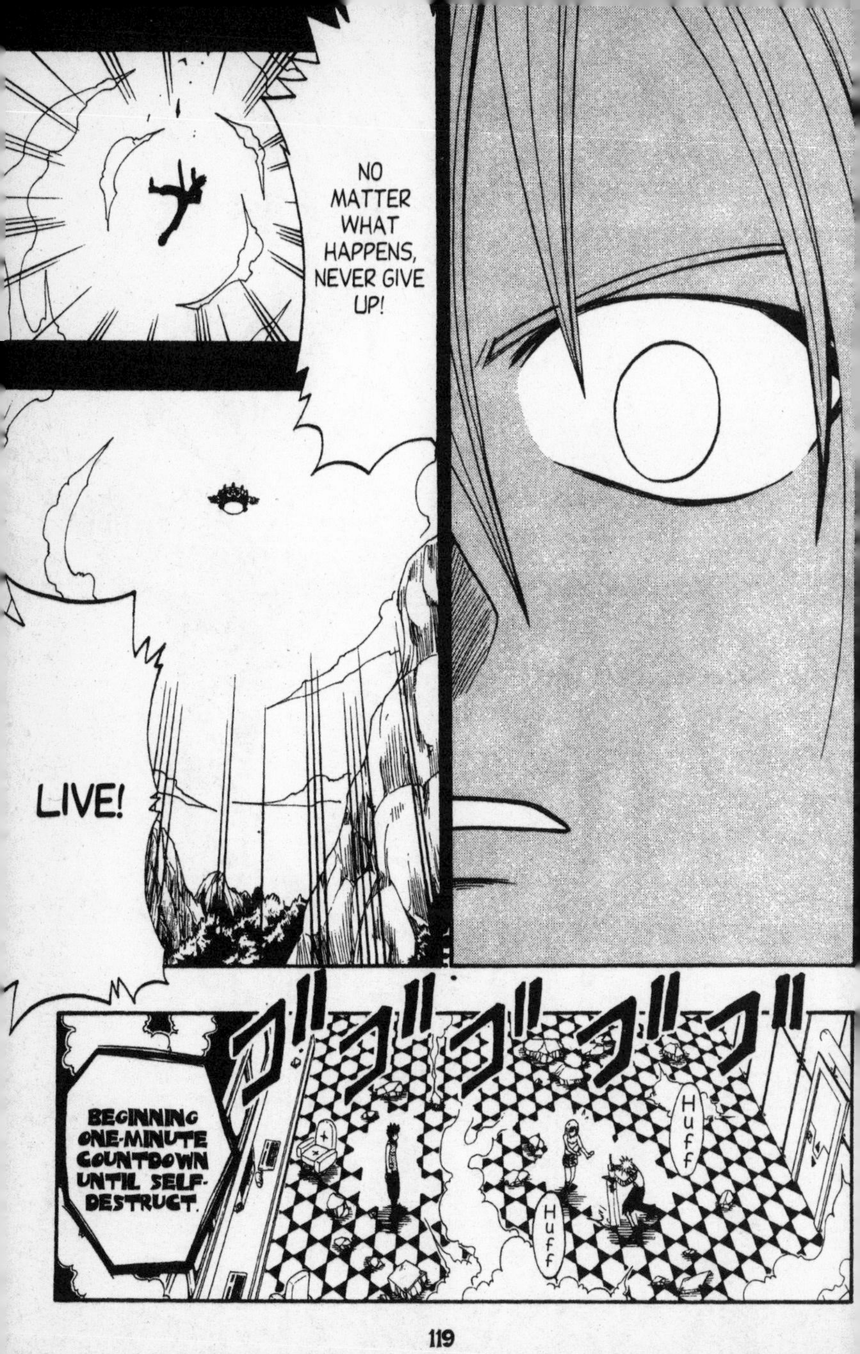
NO MATTER WHAT HAPPENS, NEVER GIVE UP!
LIVE!
ゴゴゴゴゴ
Huff
Huff
BEGINNING ONE-MINUTE COUNTDOWN UNTIL SELF-DESTRUCT.

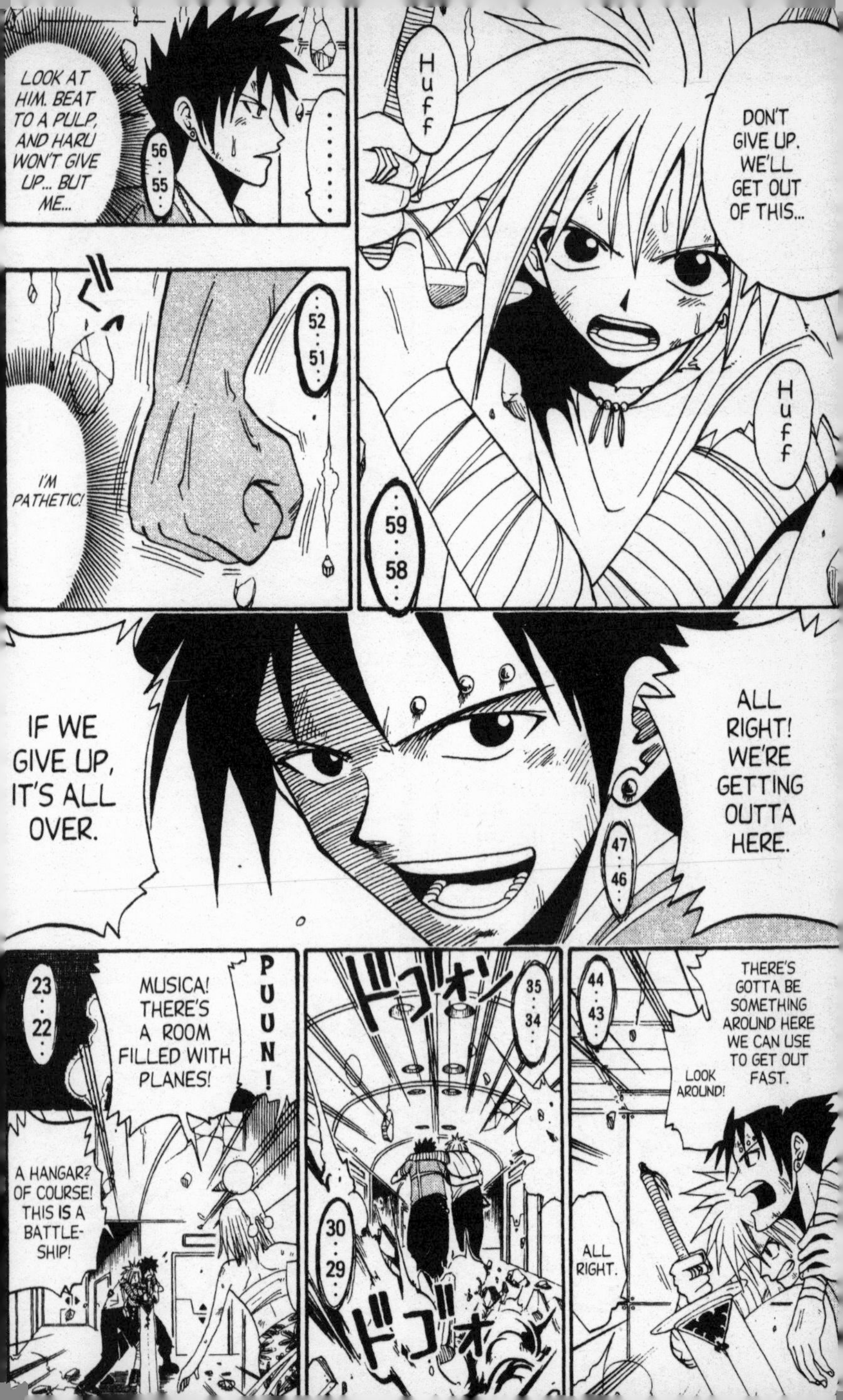
Huff
......
DON'T GIVE UP. WE'LL GET OUT OF THIS...
Huff
...59...58...
LOOK AT HIM. BEAT TO A PULP, AND HARU WON'T GIVE UP... BUT ME...
56...55...
...52...51...
I'M PATHETIC!
ALL RIGHT! WE'RE GETTING OUTTA HERE.
IF WE GIVE UP, IT'S ALL OVER.
47...46...
44...43...
THERE'S GOTTA BE SOMETHING AROUND HERE WE CAN USE TO GET OUT FAST.
LOOK AROUND!
ALL RIGHT.
ドゴォン
35...34...
30...29...
ドゴォ
PUUN!
MUSICA! THERE'S A ROOM FILLED WITH PLANES!
23...22...
A HANGAR? OF COURSE! THIS IS A BATTLE-SHIP!

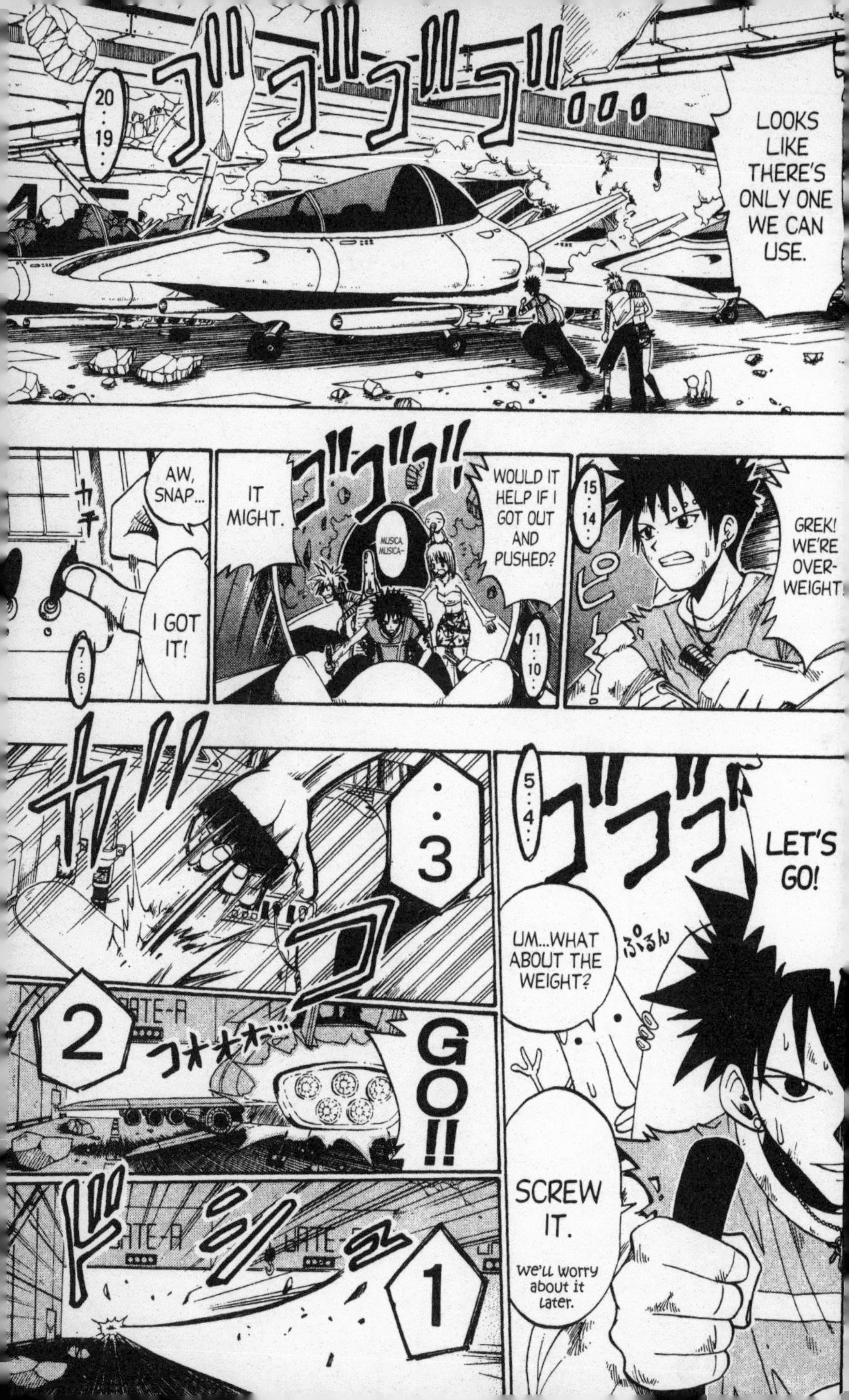
LOOKS LIKE THERE'S ONLY ONE WE CAN USE.
20... 19...
ゴゴゴ...
GREK! WE'RE OVER-WEIGHT.
15... 14...
WOULD IT HELP IF I GOT OUT AND PUSHED?
IT MIGHT.
MUSICA, MUSICA~
11... 10...
AW, SNAP...
I GOT IT!
カチ
7... 6...
5... 4...
LET'S GO!
UM...WHAT ABOUT THE WEIGHT?
ぷるん
SCREW IT.
We'll worry about it later.
3
2
GATE-A
GO!!
1

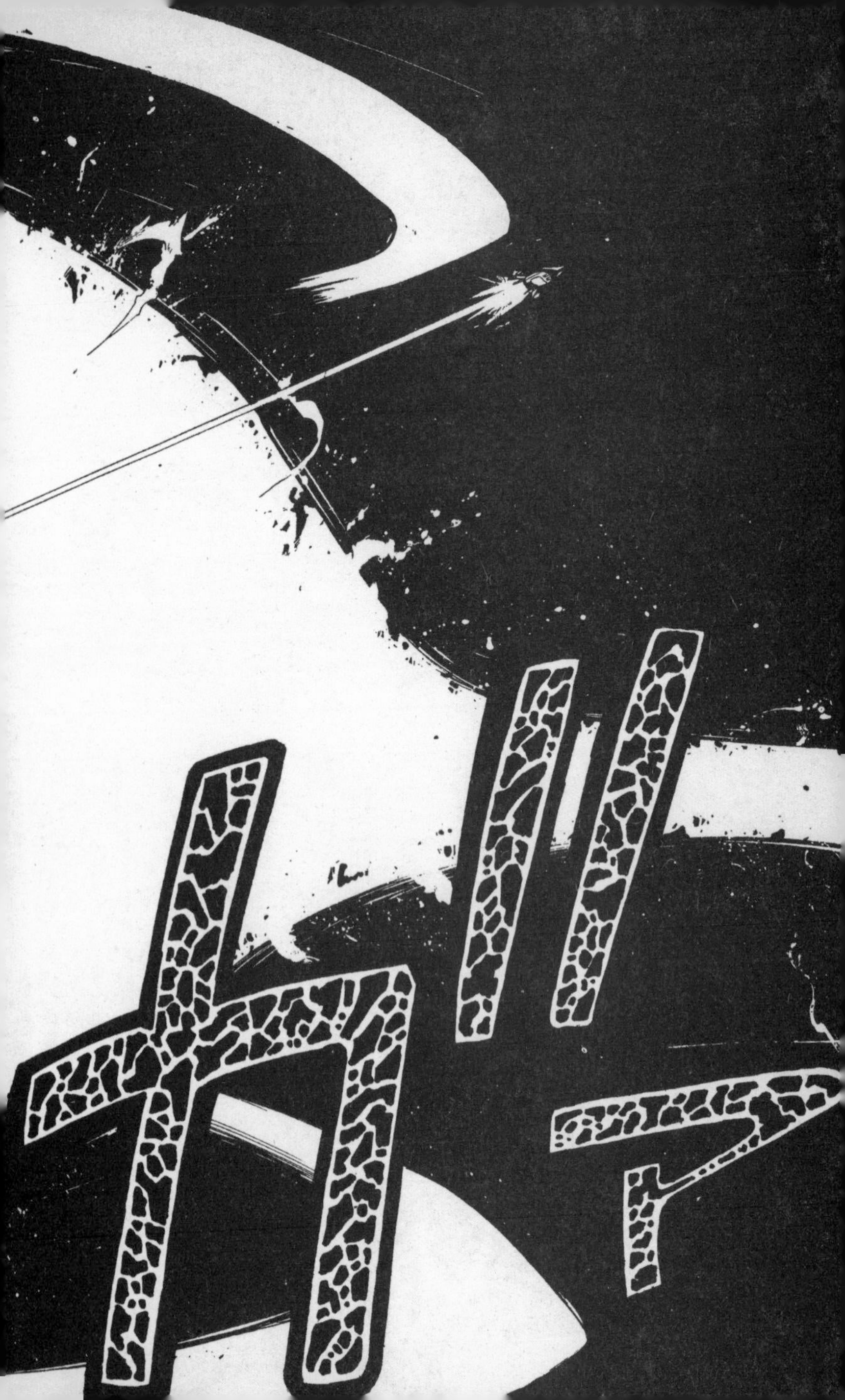
ガァ

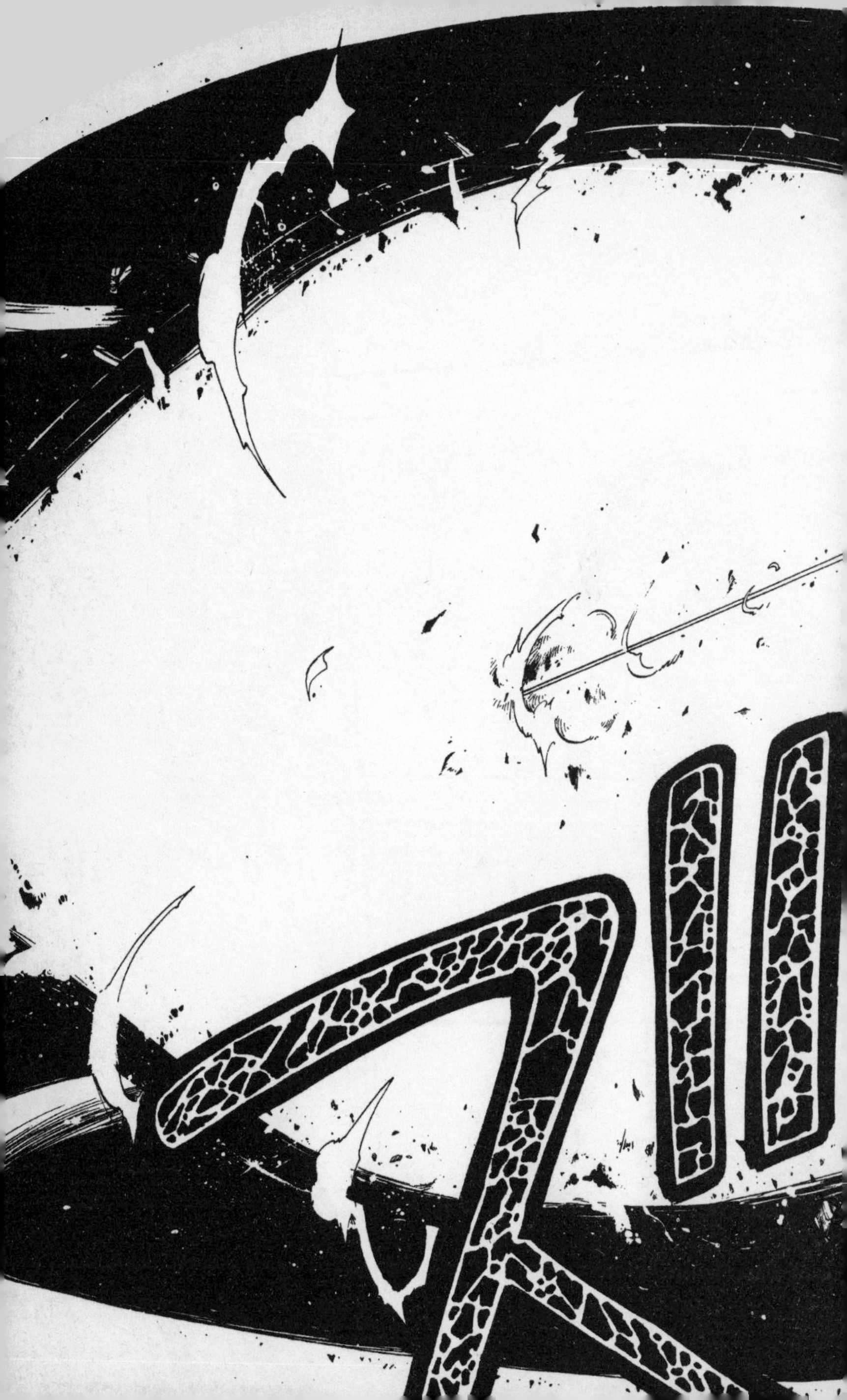

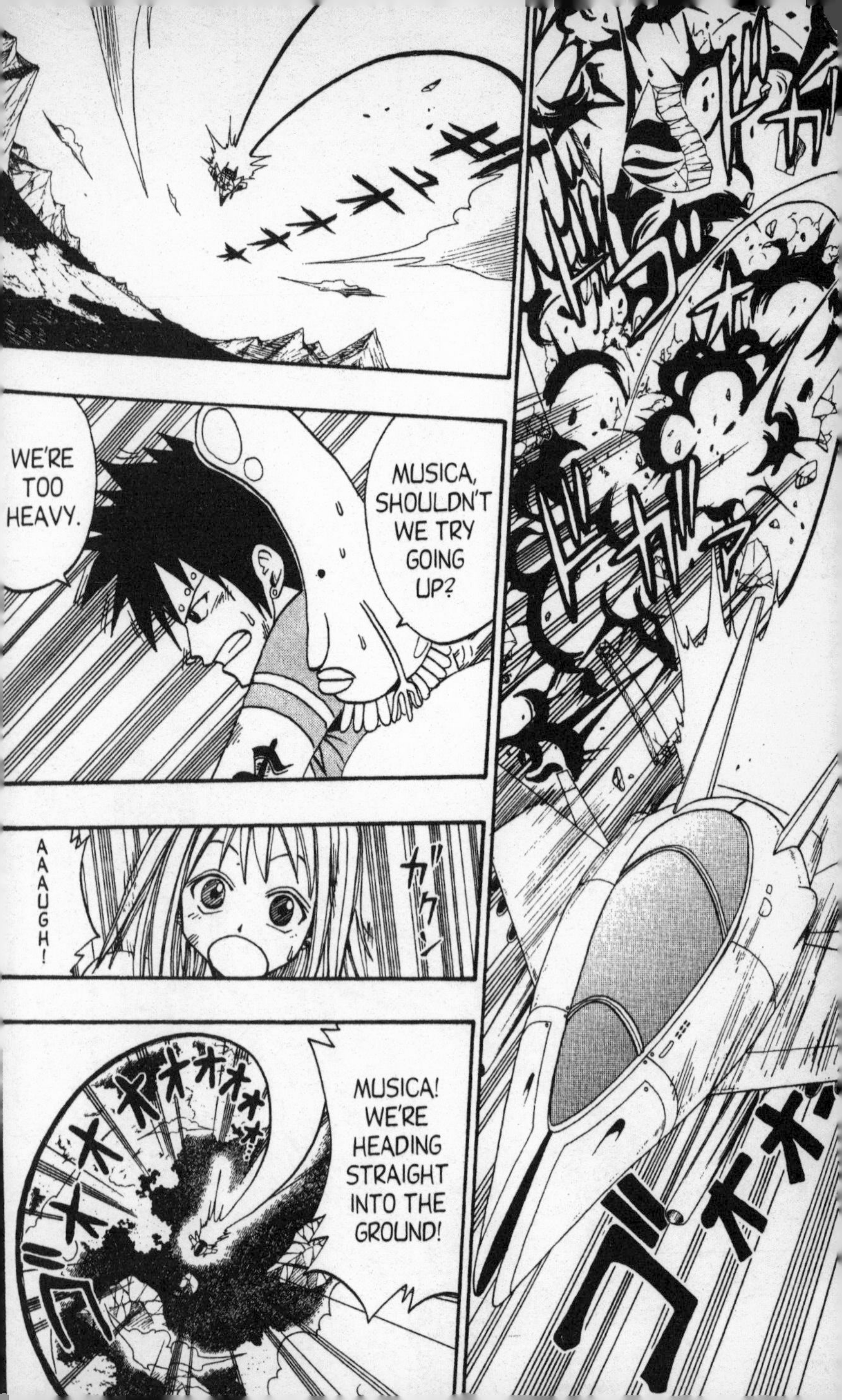
MUSICA, SHOULDN'T WE TRY GOING UP?
WE'RE TOO HEAVY.
AAAUGH!
MUSICA! WE'RE HEADING STRAIGHT INTO THE GROUND!

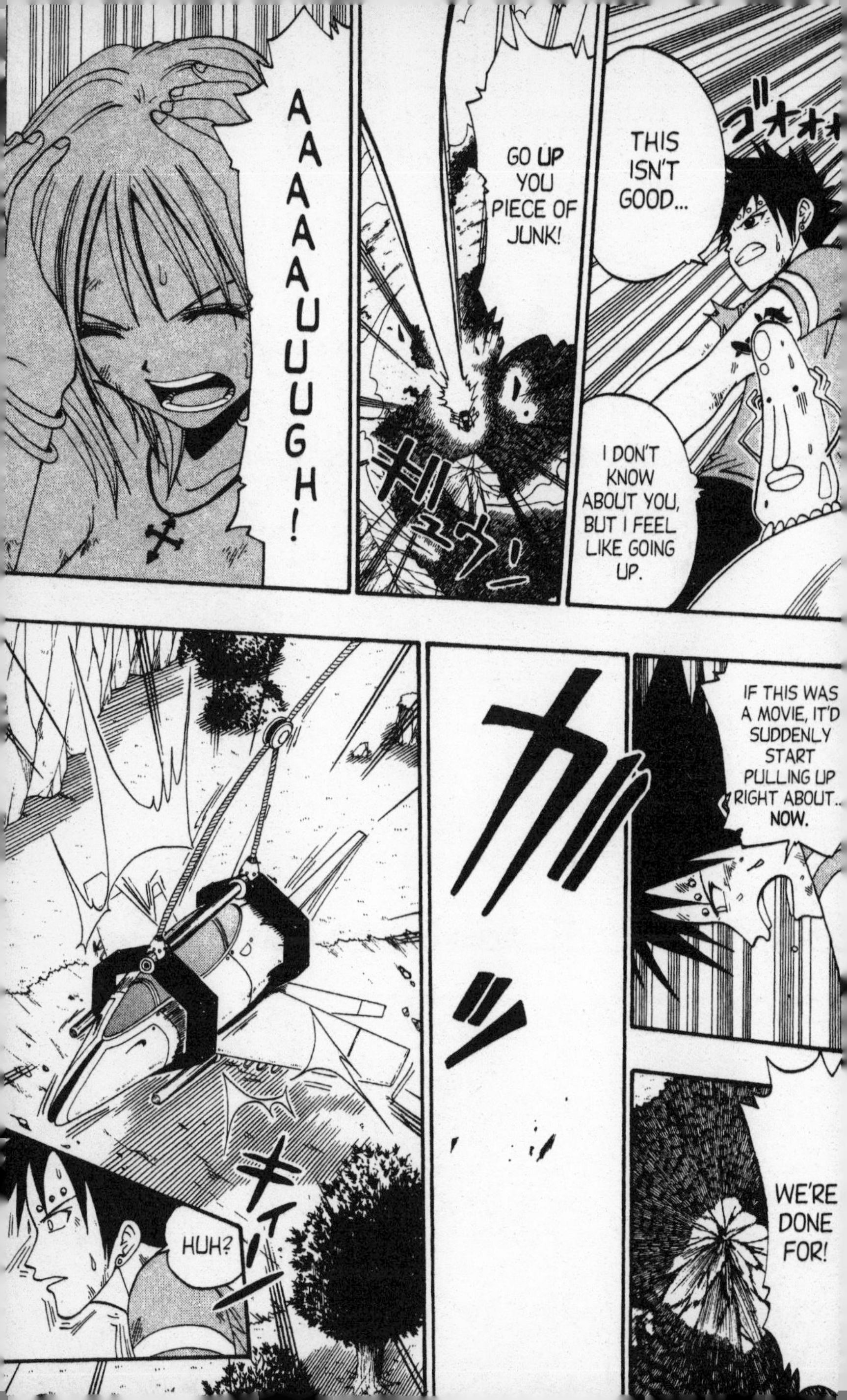
THIS ISN'T GOOD...
I DON'T KNOW ABOUT YOU, BUT I FEEL LIKE GOING UP.
GO UP YOU PIECE OF JUNK!
AAAAAUUUUGH!
IF THIS WAS A MOVIE, IT'D SUDDENLY START PULLING UP RIGHT ABOUT.. NOW.
WE'RE DONE FOR!
カッ
HUH?

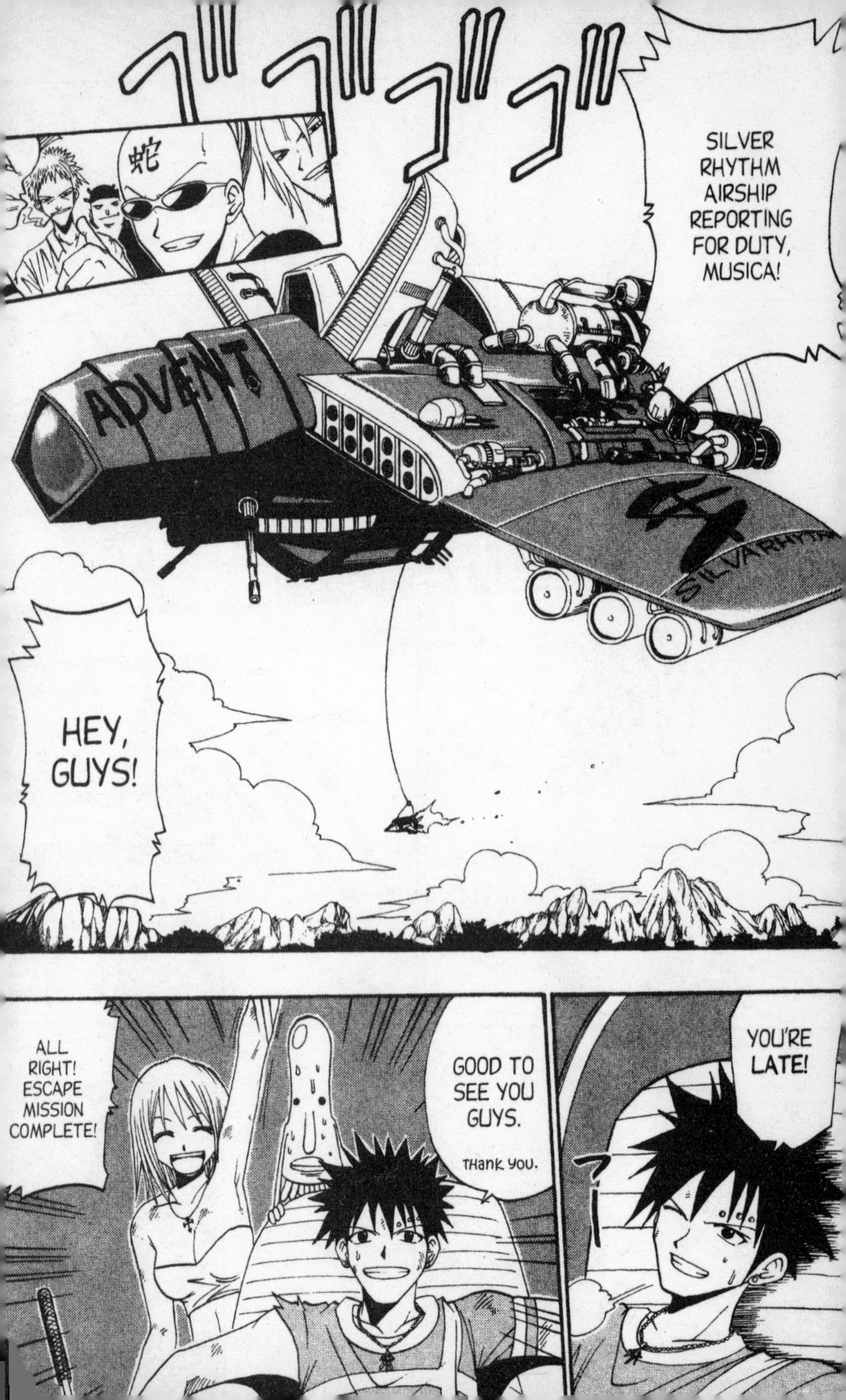
ゴゴゴゴ
SILVER RHYTHM AIRSHIP REPORTING FOR DUTY, MUSICA!
蛇
ADVENT
HEY, GUYS!
YOU'RE LATE!
GOOD TO SEE YOU GUYS.
THANK YOU.
ALL RIGHT! ESCAPE MISSION COMPLETE!

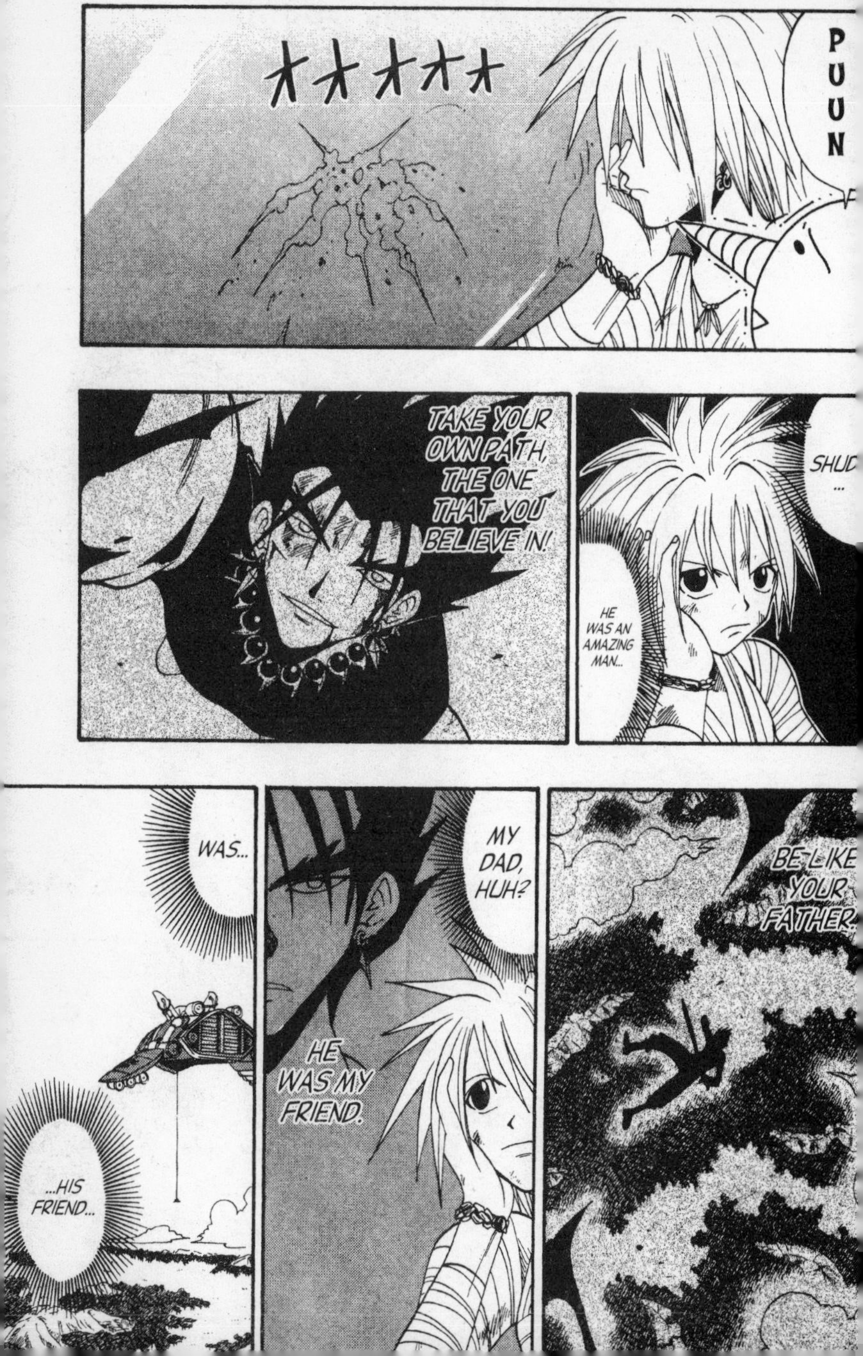
PUUN
SHUD ...
HE WAS AN AMAZING MAN...
TAKE YOUR OWN PATH, THE ONE THAT YOU BELIEVE IN!
BE LIKE YOUR FATHER...
MY DAD, HUH?
HE WAS MY FRIEND.
WAS...
...HIS FRIEND...

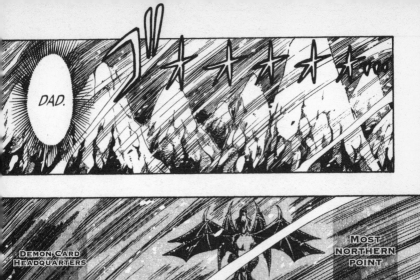

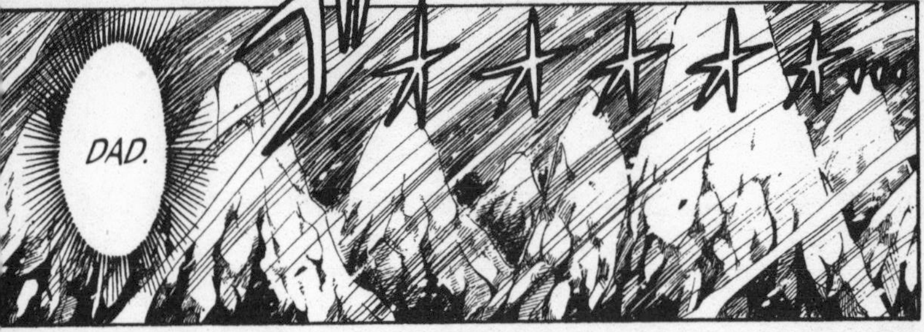
ゴォォォォォ…
DAD.

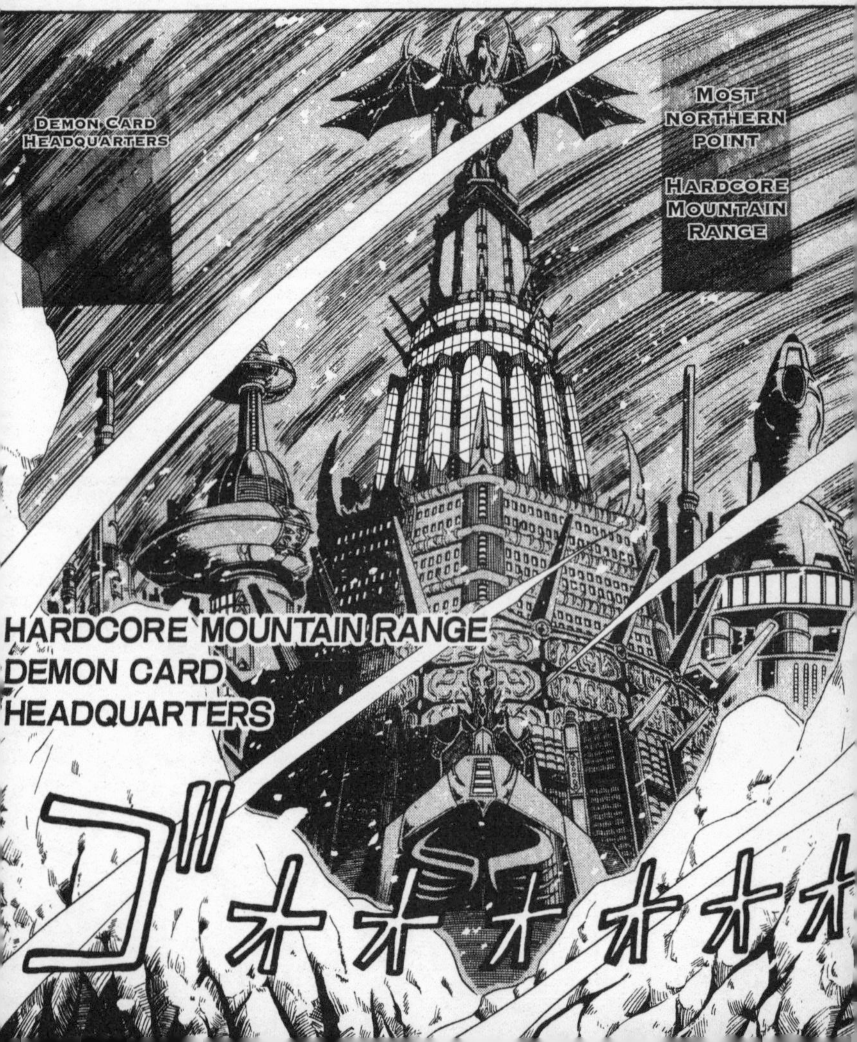
MOST NORTHERN POINT
HARDCORE MOUNTAIN RANGE
DEMON CARD HEADQUARTERS
HARDCORE MOUNTAIN RANGE DEMON CARD HEADQUARTERS
ゴォォォォォォ

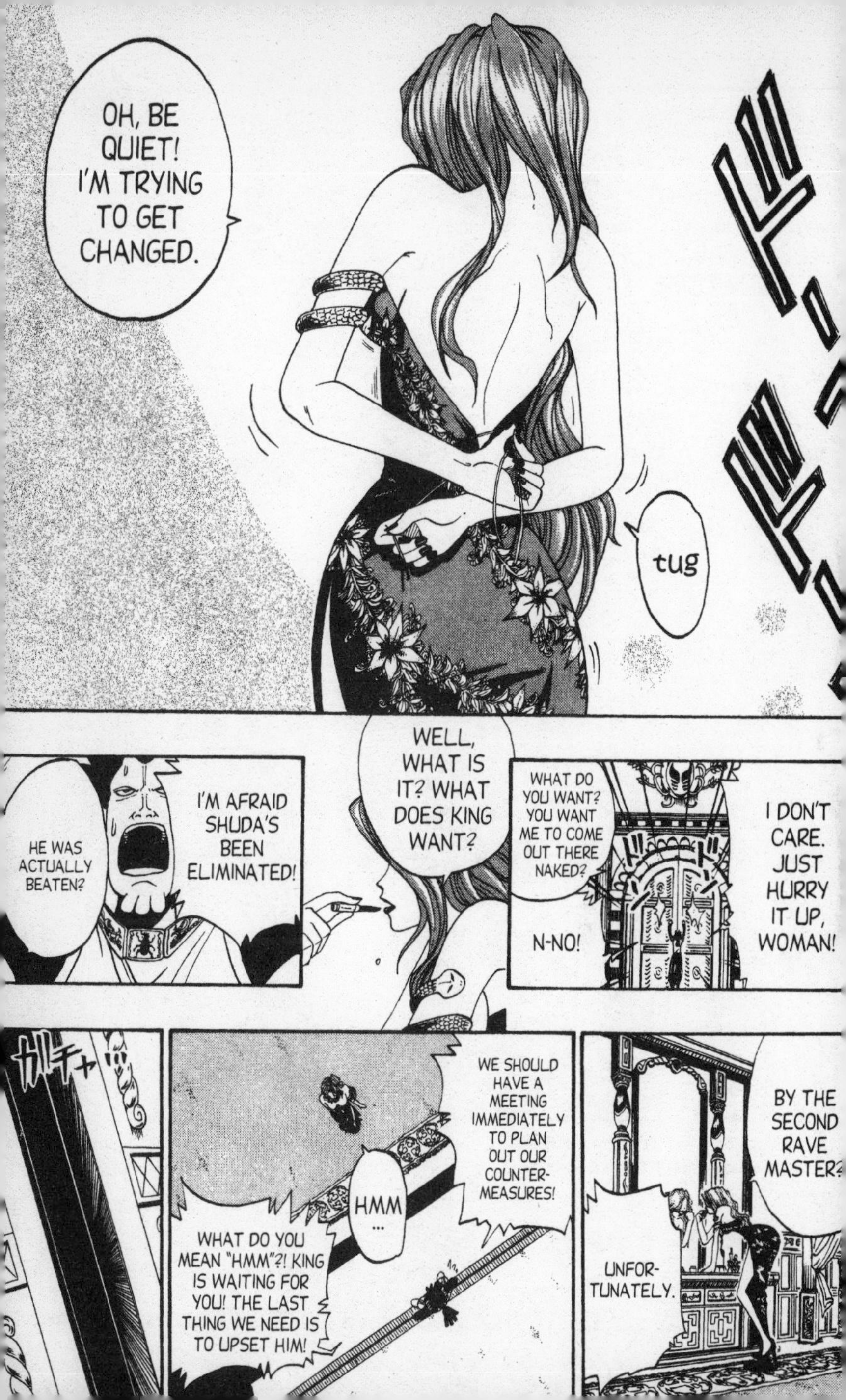
OH, BE QUIET! I'M TRYING TO GET CHANGED.
tug
I DON'T CARE. JUST HURRY IT UP, WOMAN!
WHAT DO YOU WANT? YOU WANT ME TO COME OUT THERE NAKED?
N-NO!
WELL, WHAT IS IT? WHAT DOES KING WANT?
I'M AFRAID SHUDA'S BEEN ELIMINATED!
HE WAS ACTUALLY BEATEN?
BY THE SECOND RAVE MASTER?
UNFORTUNATELY.
WE SHOULD HAVE A MEETING IMMEDIATELY TO PLAN OUT OUR COUNTER-MEASURES!
HMM...
WHAT DO YOU MEAN "HMM"?! KING IS WAITING FOR YOU! THE LAST THING WE NEED IS TO UPSET HIM!
ガチャ

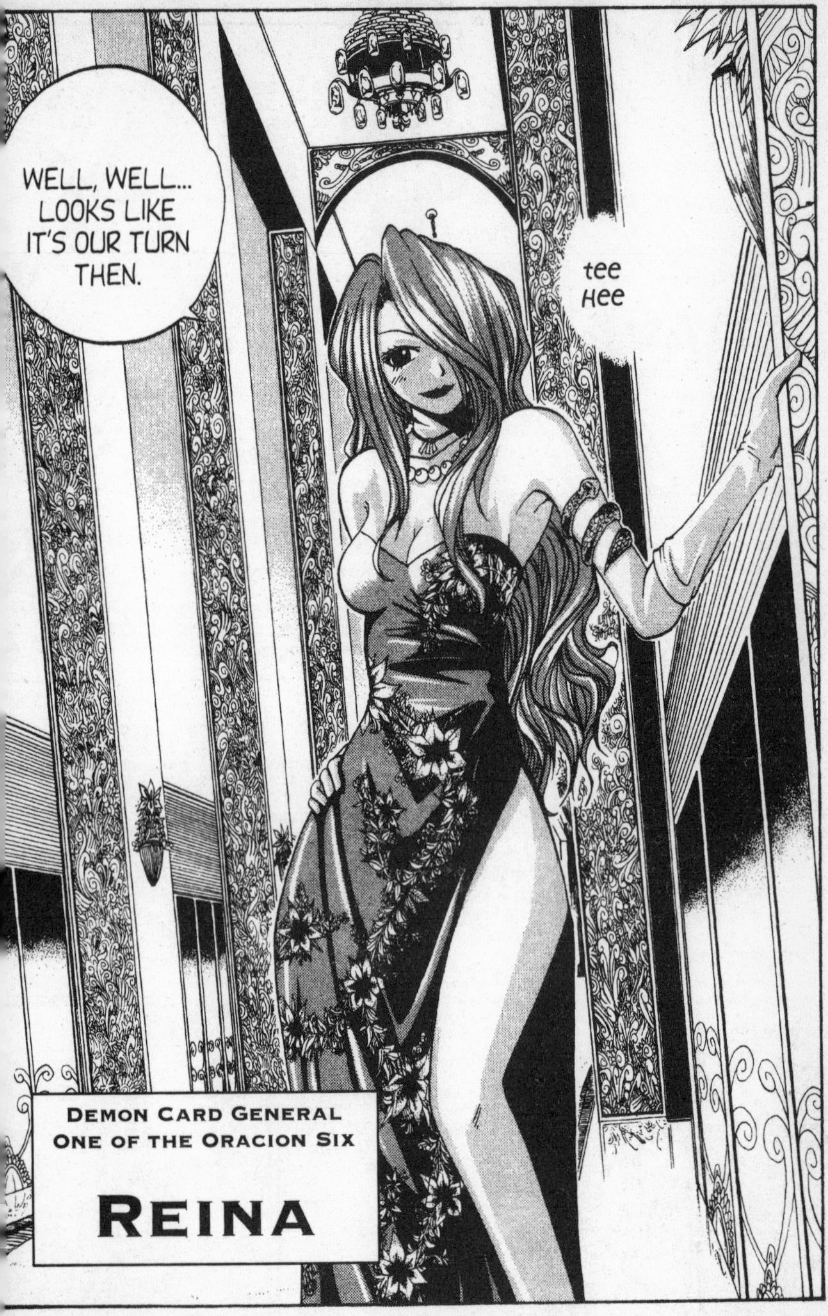
tee Hee
WELL, WELL... LOOKS LIKE IT'S OUR TURN THEN.
DEMON CARD GENERAL
ONE OF THE ORACION SIX
REINA

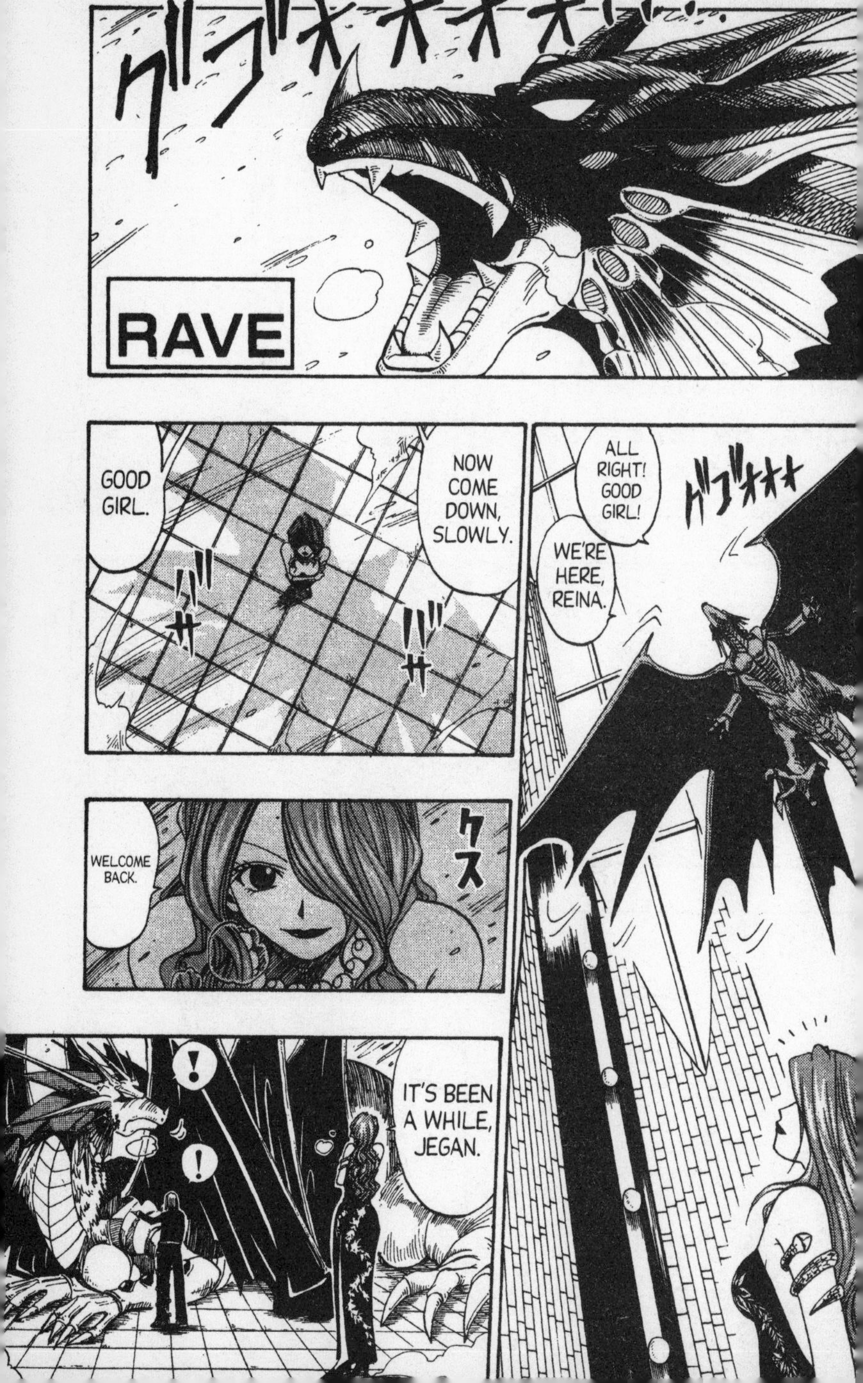
グゴオオオオ
RAVE
ALL RIGHT! GOOD GIRL!
WE'RE HERE, REINA.
グゴオオオ
NOW COME DOWN, SLOWLY.
GOOD GIRL.
バサ
バサ
WELCOME BACK.
クス
IT'S BEEN A WHILE, JEGAN.
!
!

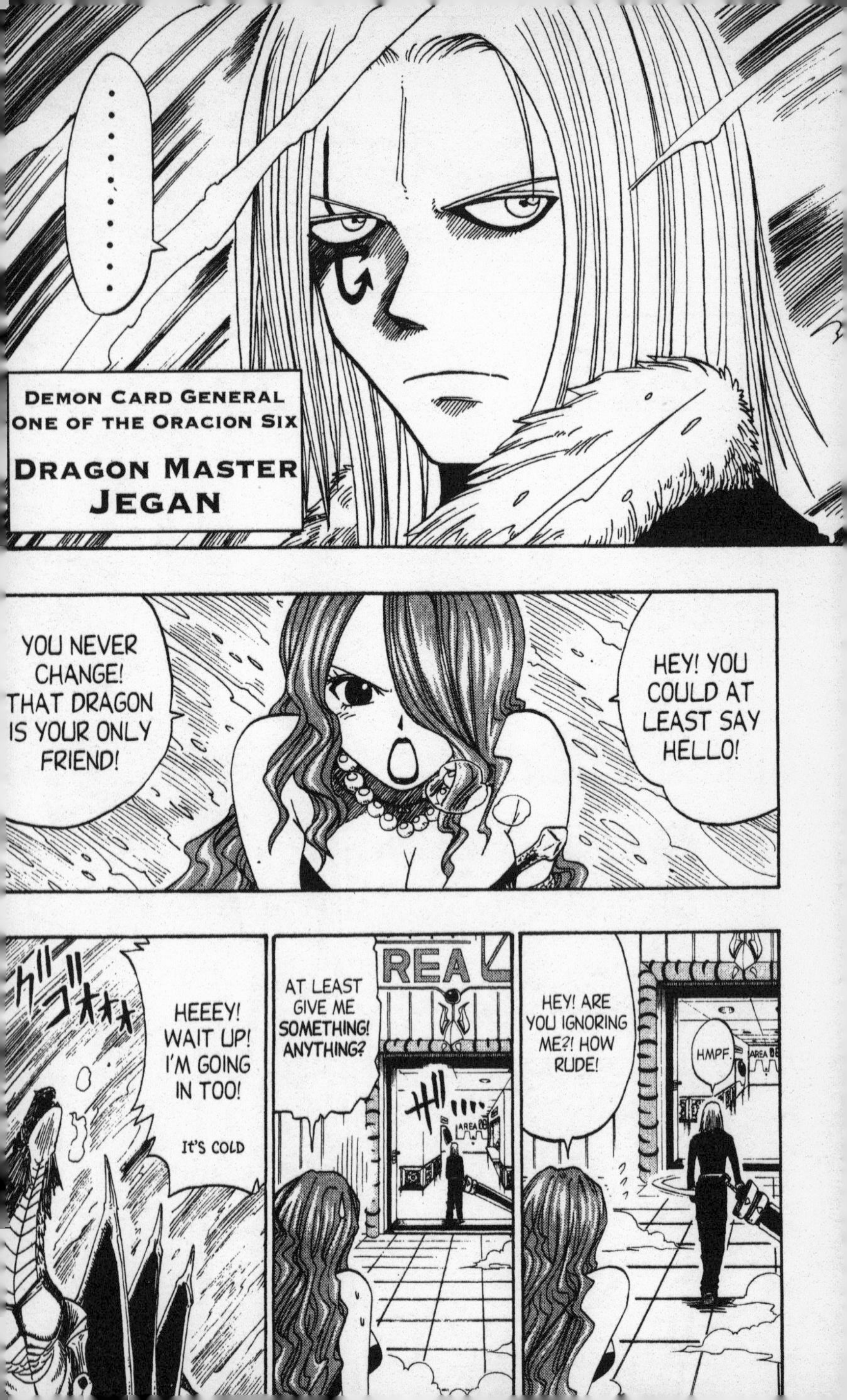
......
DEMON CARD GENERAL
ONE OF THE ORACION SIX
DRAGON MASTER JEGAN
HEY! YOU COULD AT LEAST SAY HELLO!
YOU NEVER CHANGE! THAT DRAGON IS YOUR ONLY FRIEND!
HMPF.
HEY! ARE YOU IGNORING ME?! HOW RUDE!
REA
AT LEAST GIVE ME SOMETHING! ANYTHING?
HEEEY! WAIT UP! I'M GOING IN TOO!
IT'S COLD

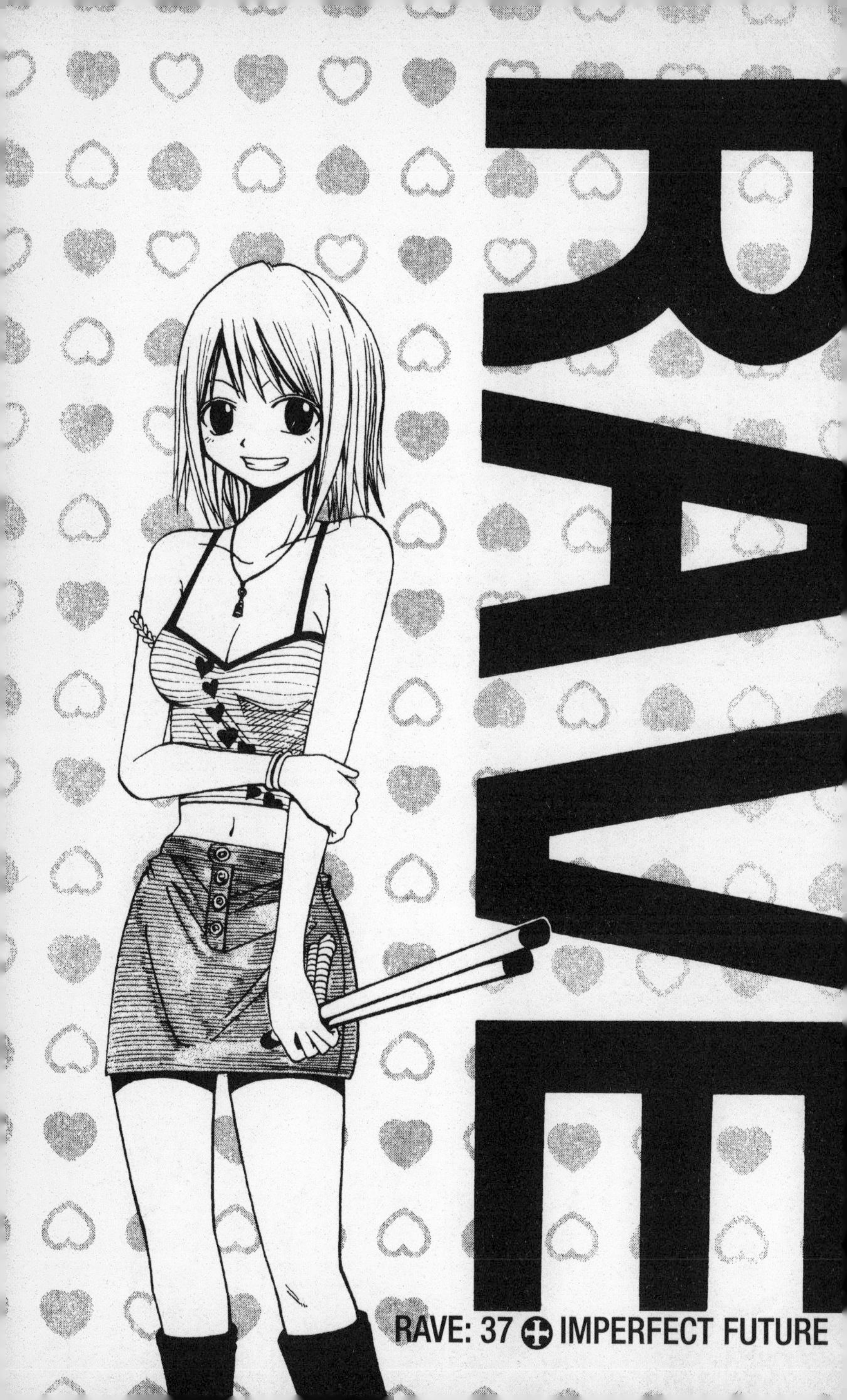
RAVE

RAVE: 37 ✚ IMPERFECT FUTURE

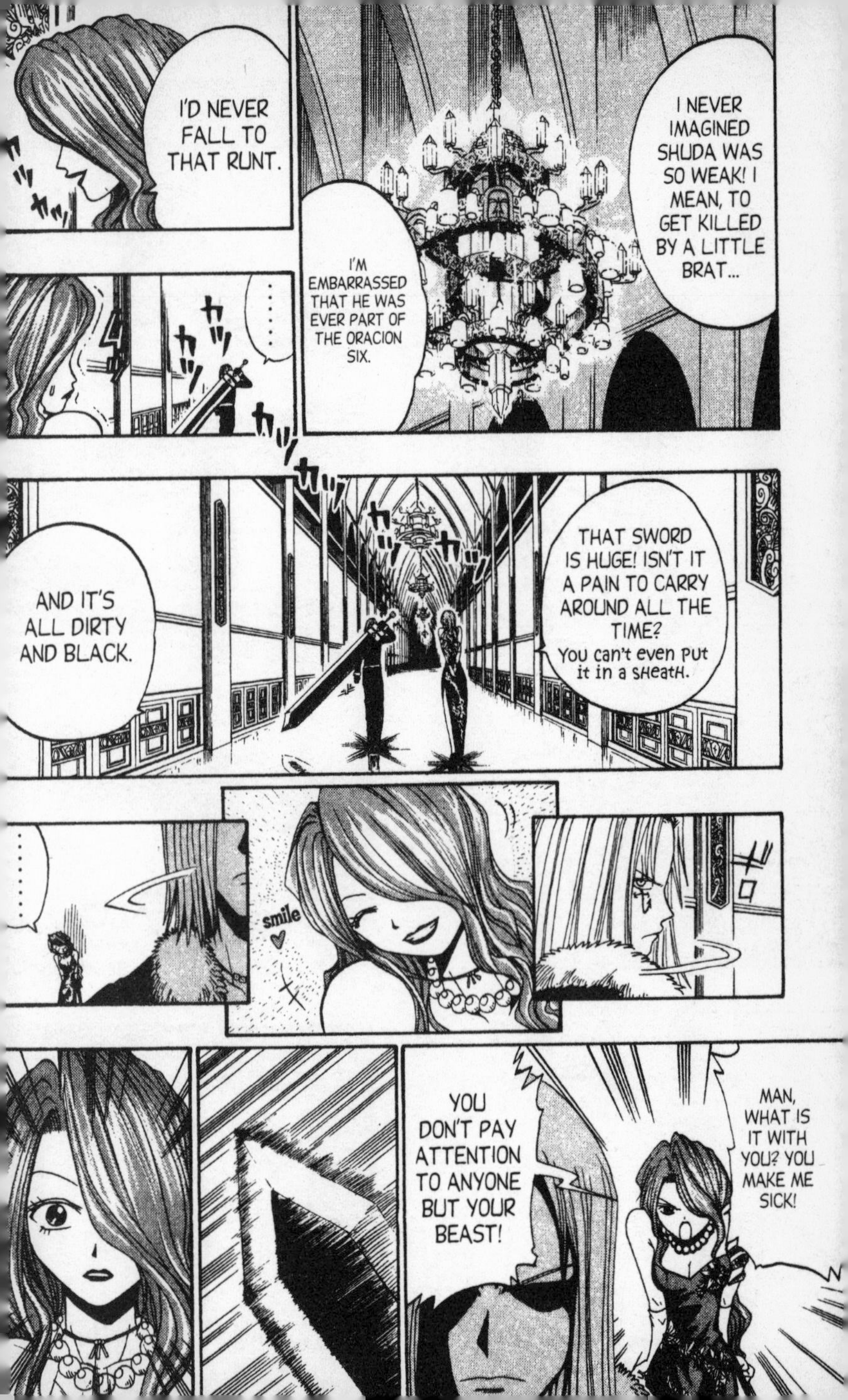
I NEVER IMAGINED SHUDA WAS SO WEAK! I MEAN, TO GET KILLED BY A LITTLE BRAT...
I'M EMBARRASSED THAT HE WAS EVER PART OF THE ORACION SIX.
I'D NEVER FALL TO THAT RUNT.
......
THAT SWORD IS HUGE! ISN'T IT A PAIN TO CARRY AROUND ALL THE TIME? You can't even put it in a sheath.
AND IT'S ALL DIRTY AND BLACK.
smile
......
MAN, WHAT IS IT WITH YOU? YOU MAKE ME SICK!
YOU DON'T PAY ATTENTION TO ANYONE BUT YOUR BEAST!

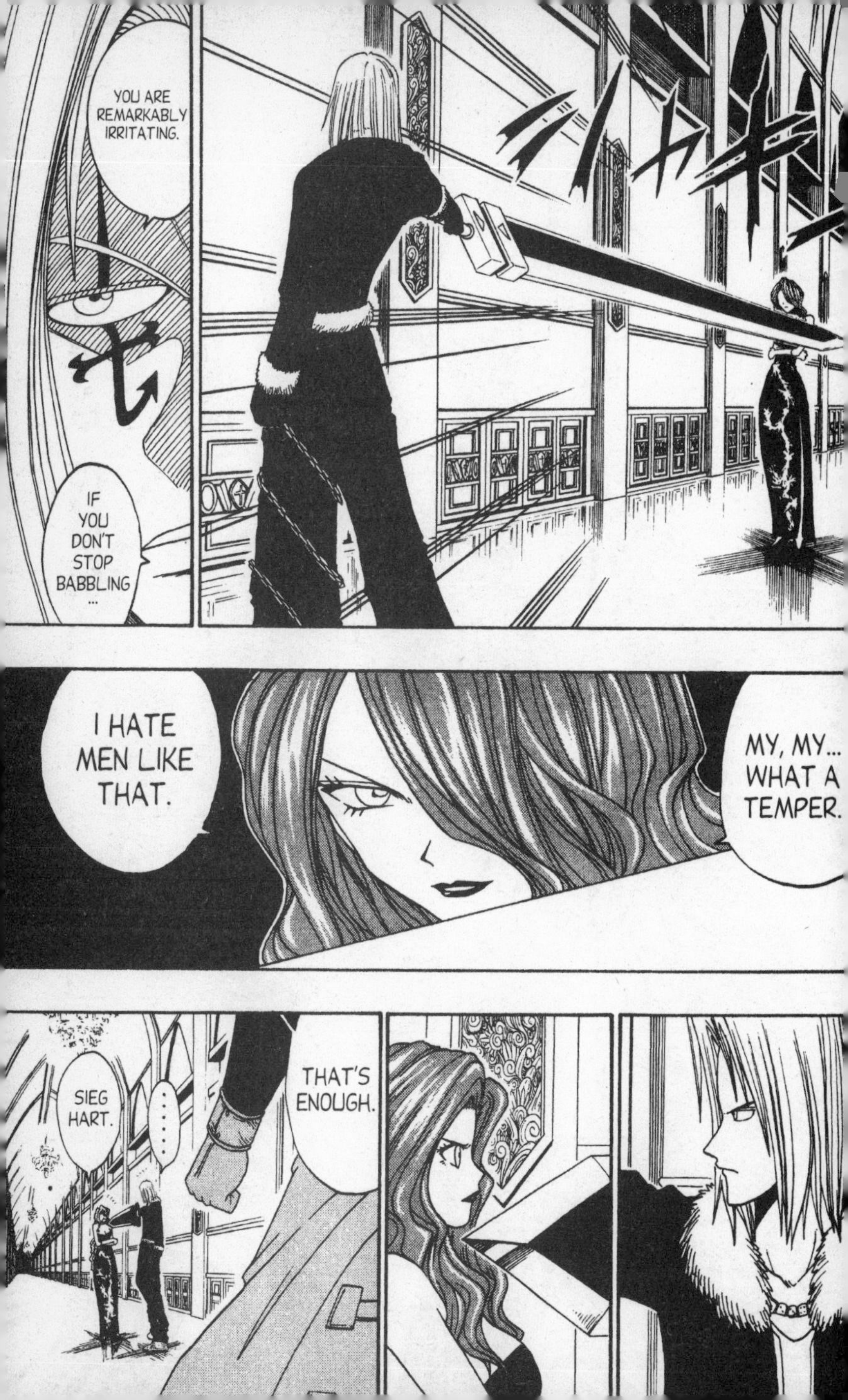

YOU ARE REMARKABLY IRRITATING.
IF YOU DON'T STOP BABBLING ...
MY, MY... WHAT A TEMPER.
I HATE MEN LIKE THAT.
THAT'S ENOUGH.
......
SIEG HART.

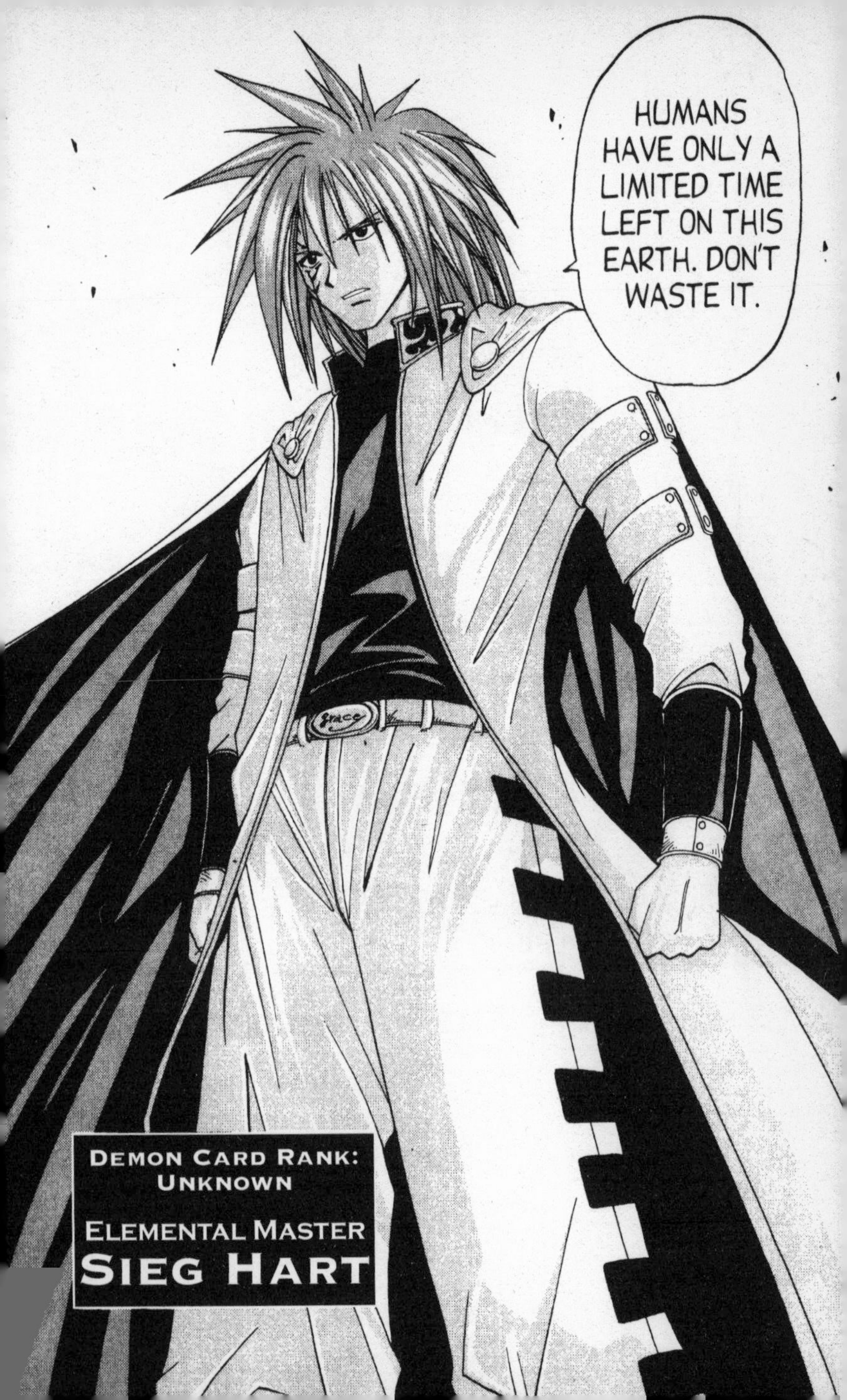
HUMANS HAVE ONLY A LIMITED TIME LEFT ON THIS EARTH. DON'T WASTE IT.
DEMON CARD RANK: UNKNOWN
ELEMENTAL MASTER
SIEG HART

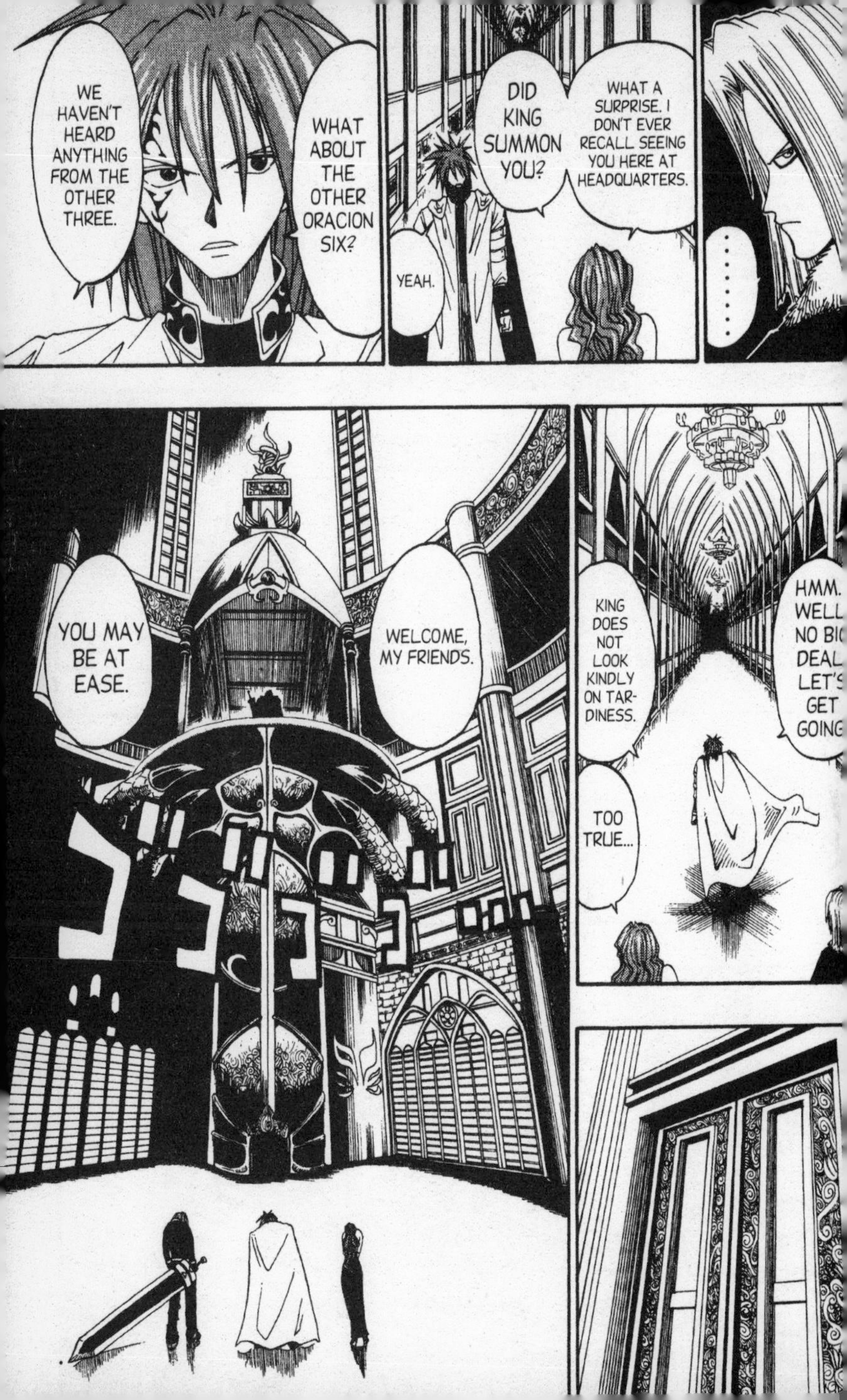
......
WHAT A SURPRISE. I DON'T EVER RECALL SEEING YOU HERE AT HEADQUARTERS.
DID KING SUMMON YOU?
YEAH.
WHAT ABOUT THE OTHER ORACION SIX?
WE HAVEN'T HEARD ANYTHING FROM THE OTHER THREE.
HMM. WELL NO BI DEAL LET'S GET GOING
KING DOES NOT LOOK KINDLY ON TARDINESS.
TOO TRUE...
WELCOME, MY FRIENDS.
YOU MAY BE AT EASE.

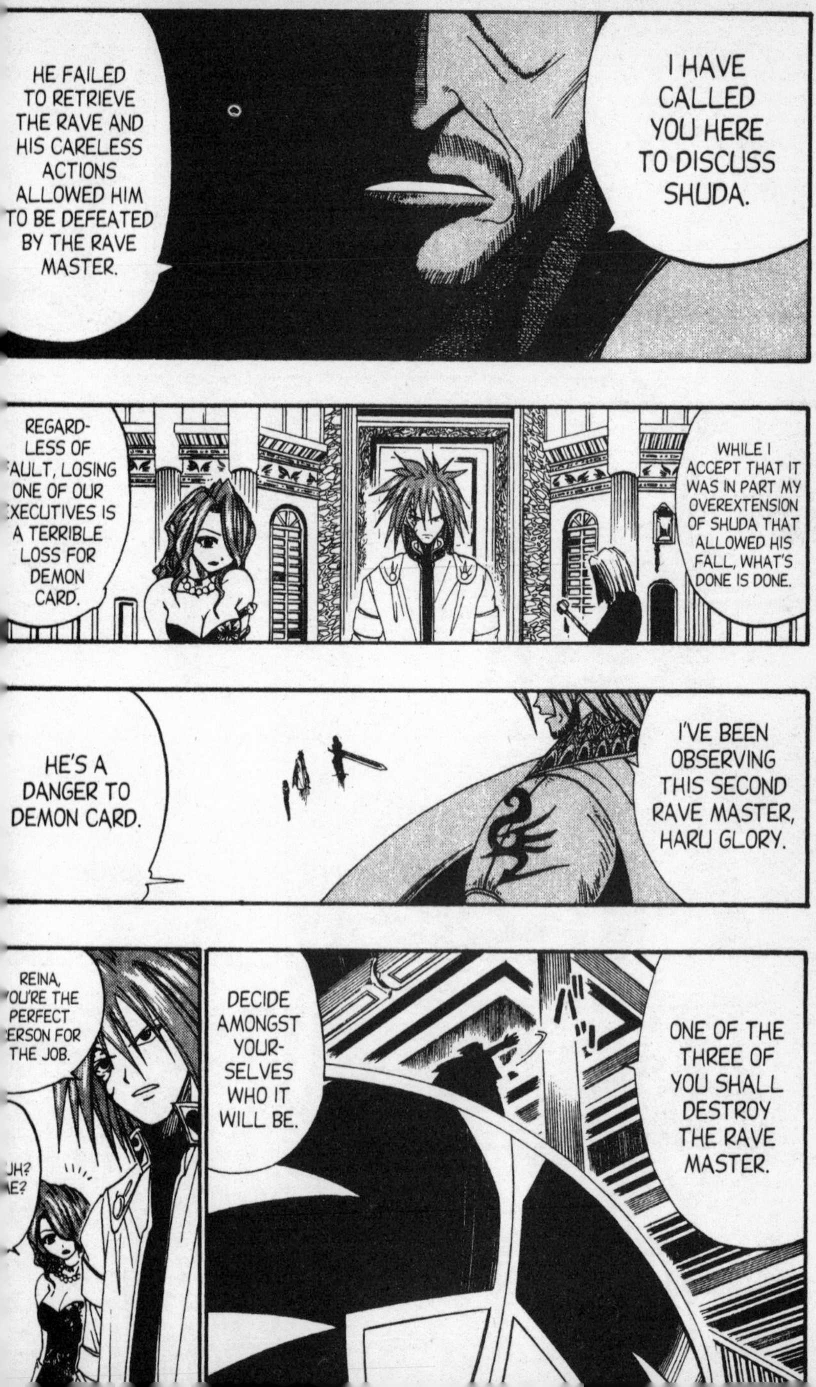
I HAVE CALLED YOU HERE TO DISCUSS SHUDA.
HE FAILED TO RETRIEVE THE RAVE AND HIS CARELESS ACTIONS ALLOWED HIM TO BE DEFEATED BY THE RAVE MASTER.
WHILE I ACCEPT THAT IT WAS IN PART MY OVEREXTENSION OF SHUDA THAT ALLOWED HIS FALL, WHAT'S DONE IS DONE.
REGARD-LESS OF AULT, LOSING ONE OF OUR XECUTIVES IS A TERRIBLE LOSS FOR DEMON CARD.
I'VE BEEN OBSERVING THIS SECOND RAVE MASTER, HARU GLORY.
HE'S A DANGER TO DEMON CARD.
ONE OF THE THREE OF YOU SHALL DESTROY THE RAVE MASTER.
DECIDE AMONGST YOUR-SELVES WHO IT WILL BE.
REINA, OU'RE THE PERFECT ERSON FOR THE JOB.
UH? E?

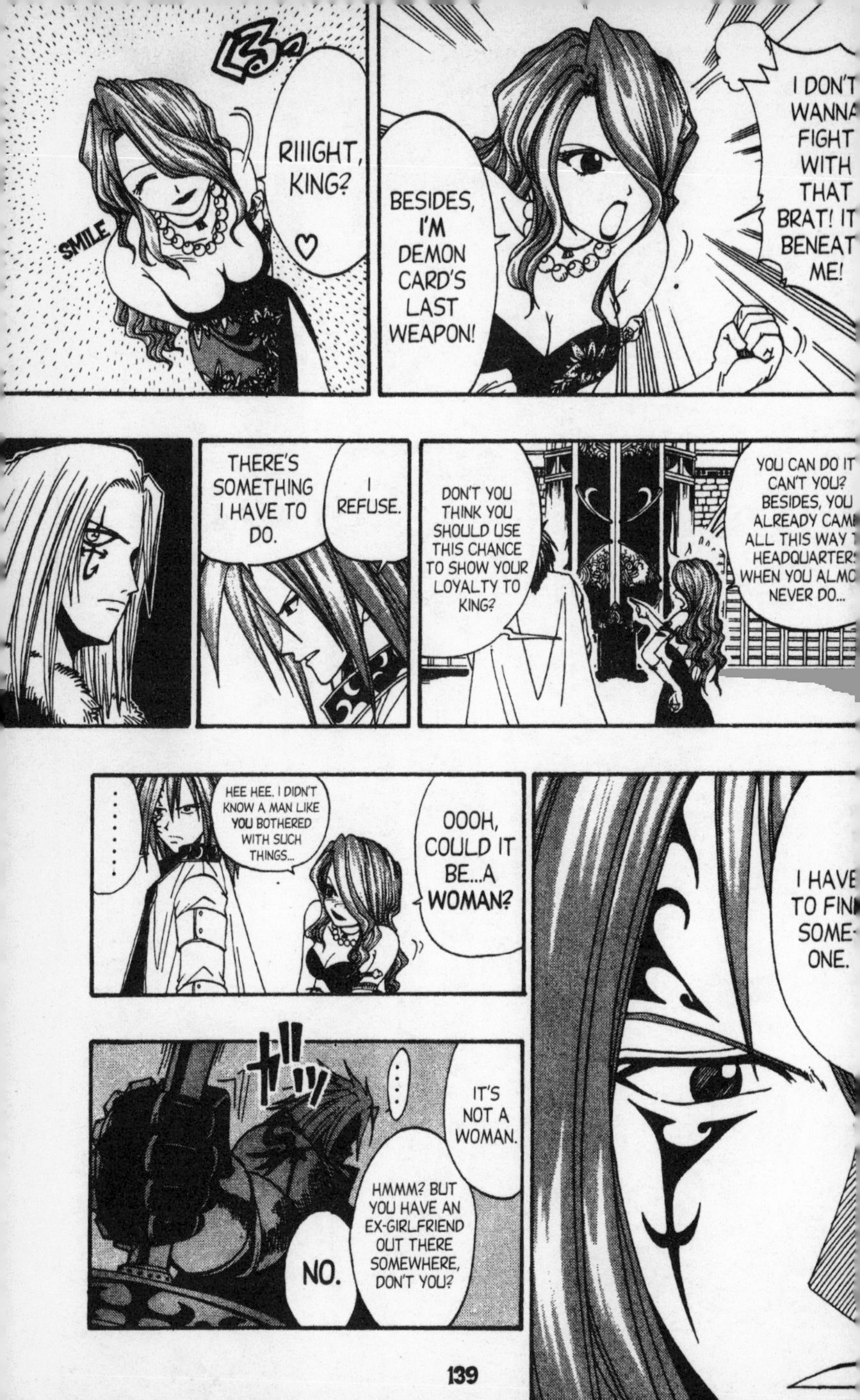
I DON'T WANNA FIGHT WITH THAT BRAT! IT BENEAT ME!
BESIDES, I'M DEMON CARD'S LAST WEAPON!
RIIIGHT, KING? ♡
SMILE
YOU CAN DO IT CAN'T YOU? BESIDES, YOU ALREADY CAM ALL THIS WAY T HEADQUARTER WHEN YOU ALMO NEVER DO...
DON'T YOU THINK YOU SHOULD USE THIS CHANCE TO SHOW YOUR LOYALTY TO KING?
I REFUSE.
THERE'S SOMETHING I HAVE TO DO.
I HAVE TO FIN SOME-ONE.
OOOH, COULD IT BE...A WOMAN?
HEE HEE. I DIDN'T KNOW A MAN LIKE YOU BOTHERED WITH SUCH THINGS...
......
IT'S NOT A WOMAN.
...
HMMM? BUT YOU HAVE AN EX-GIRLFRIEND OUT THERE SOMEWHERE, DON'T YOU?
NO.

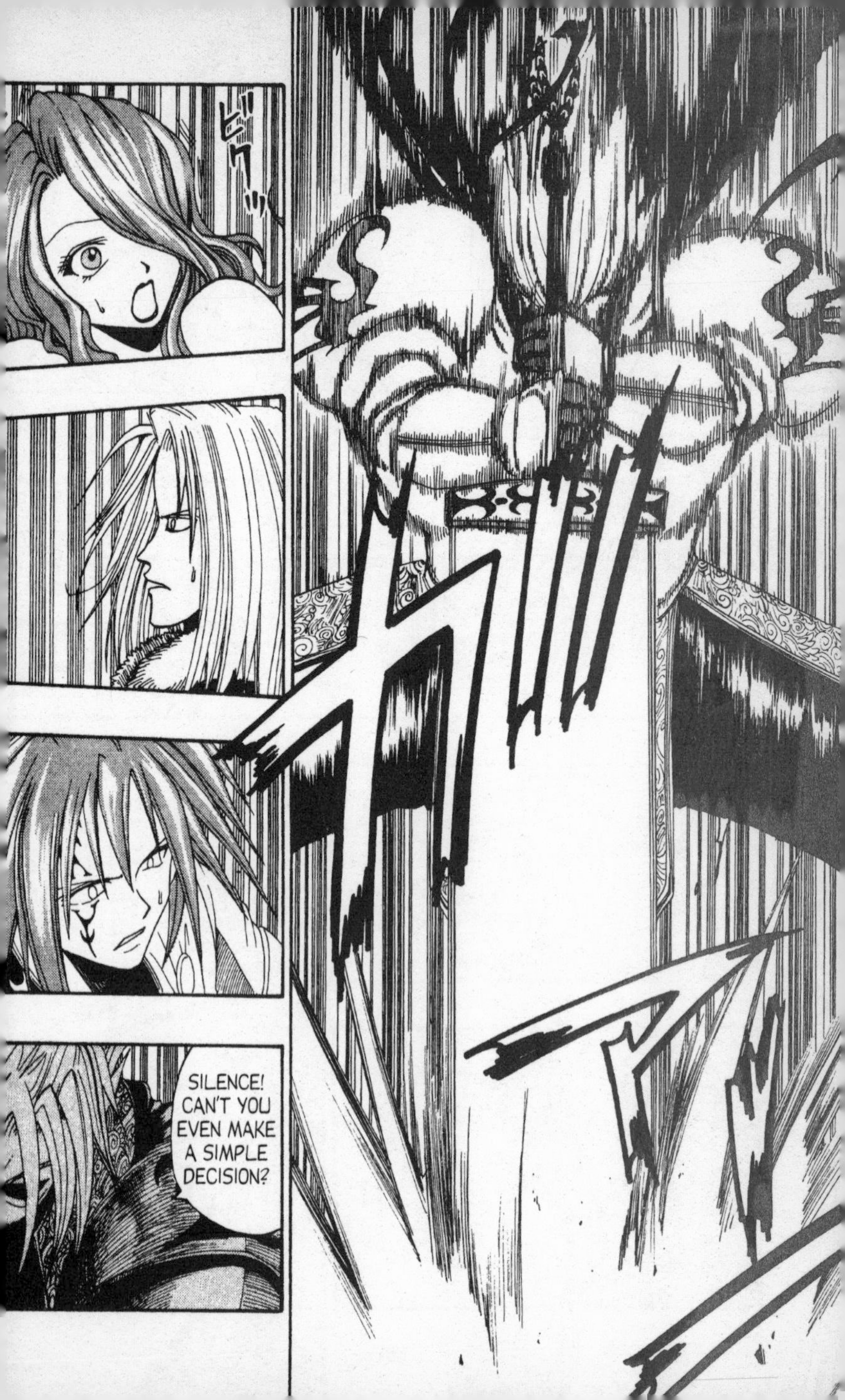
ビクッ
SILENCE! CAN'T YOU EVEN MAKE A SIMPLE DECISION?

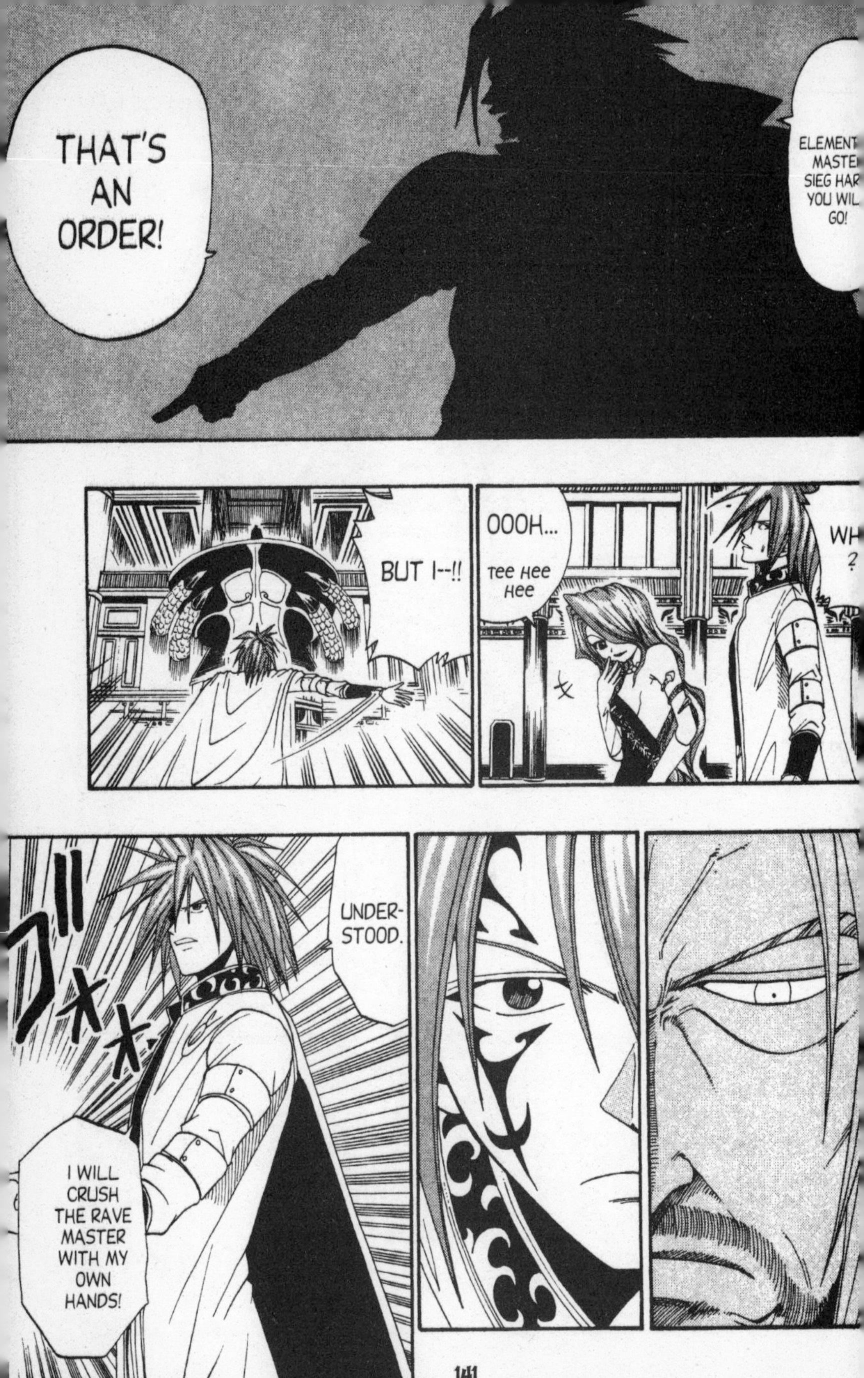
ELEMENT MASTE SIEG HAR YOU WIL GO!
THAT'S AN ORDER!
WH ?
OOOH...
TEE HEE HEE
BUT I--!!
UNDER-STOOD.
I WILL CRUSH THE RAVE MASTER WITH MY OWN HANDS!

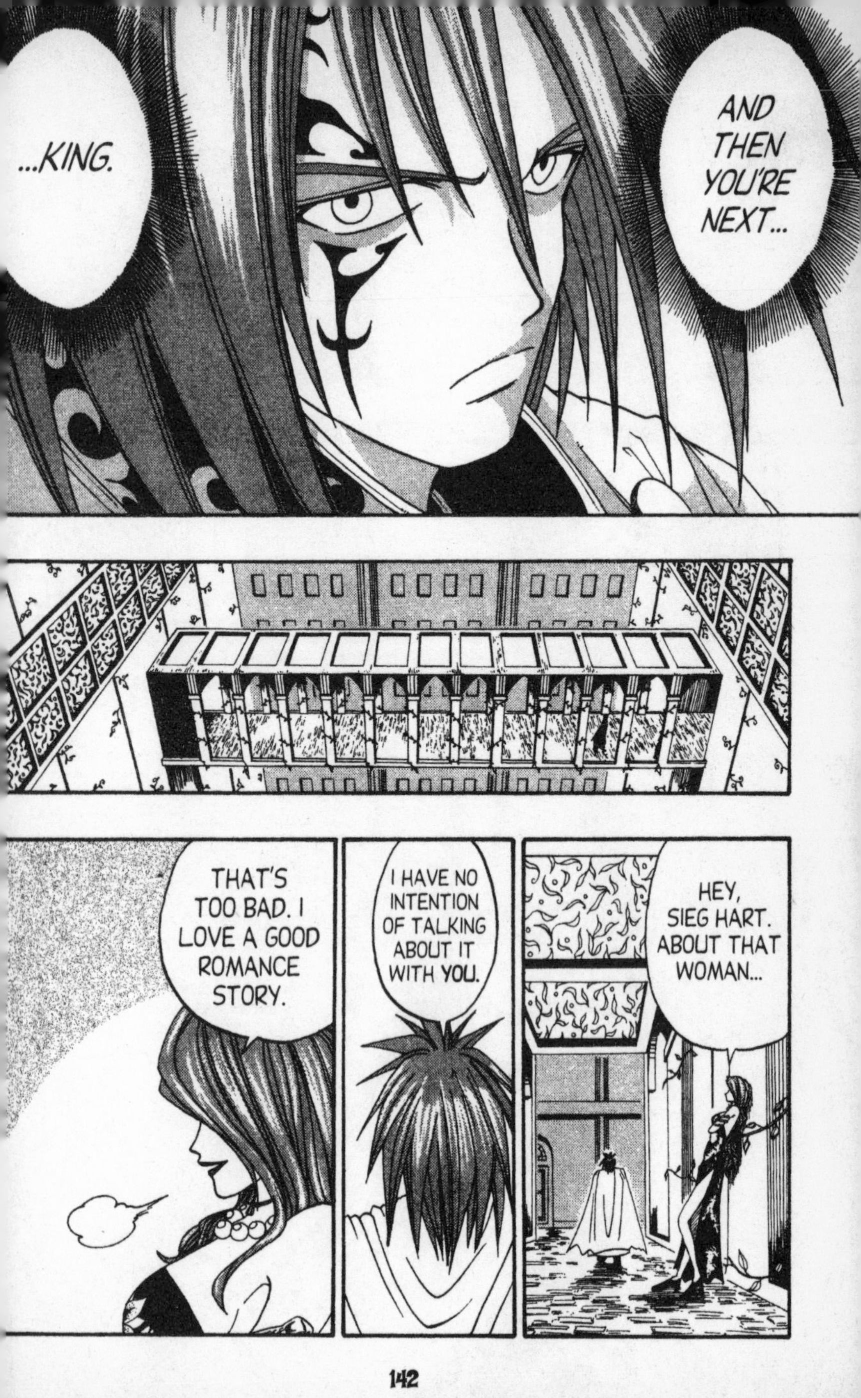
AND THEN YOU'RE NEXT...
...KING.
HEY, SIEG HART. ABOUT THAT WOMAN...
I HAVE NO INTENTION OF TALKING ABOUT IT WITH YOU.
THAT'S TOO BAD. I LOVE A GOOD ROMANCE STORY.

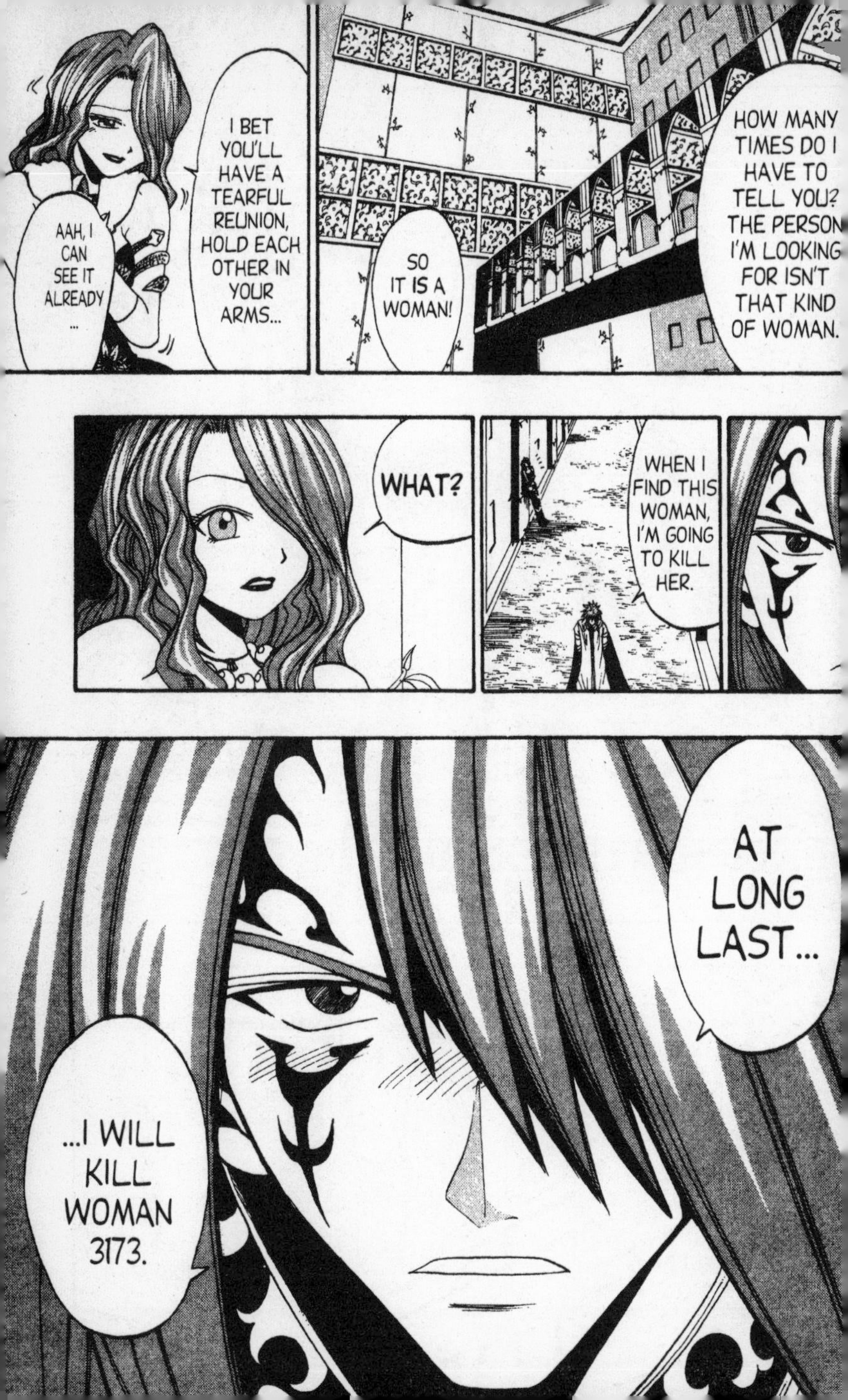
HOW MANY TIMES DO I HAVE TO TELL YOU? THE PERSON I'M LOOKING FOR ISN'T THAT KIND OF WOMAN.
SO IT IS A WOMAN!
I BET YOU'LL HAVE A TEARFUL REUNION, HOLD EACH OTHER IN YOUR ARMS...
AAH, I CAN SEE IT ALREADY ...
WHEN I FIND THIS WOMAN, I'M GOING TO KILL HER.
WHAT?
AT LONG LAST...
...I WILL KILL WOMAN 3173.

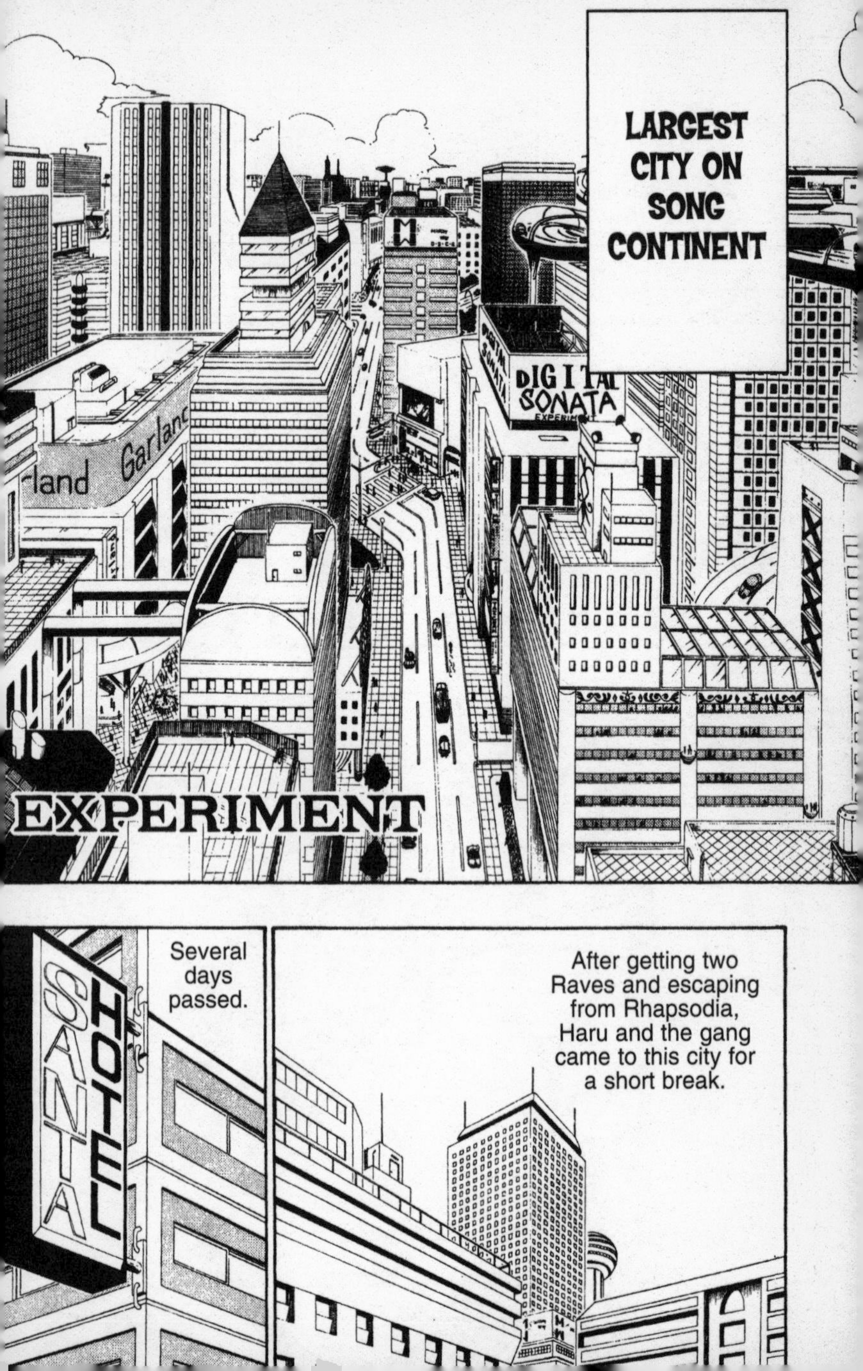
LARGEST CITY ON SONG CONTINENT
EXPERIMENT
DIGITAL SONATA
Garland
After getting two Raves and escaping from Rhapsodia, Haru and the gang came to this city for a short break.
Several days passed.
HOTEL
SANTA

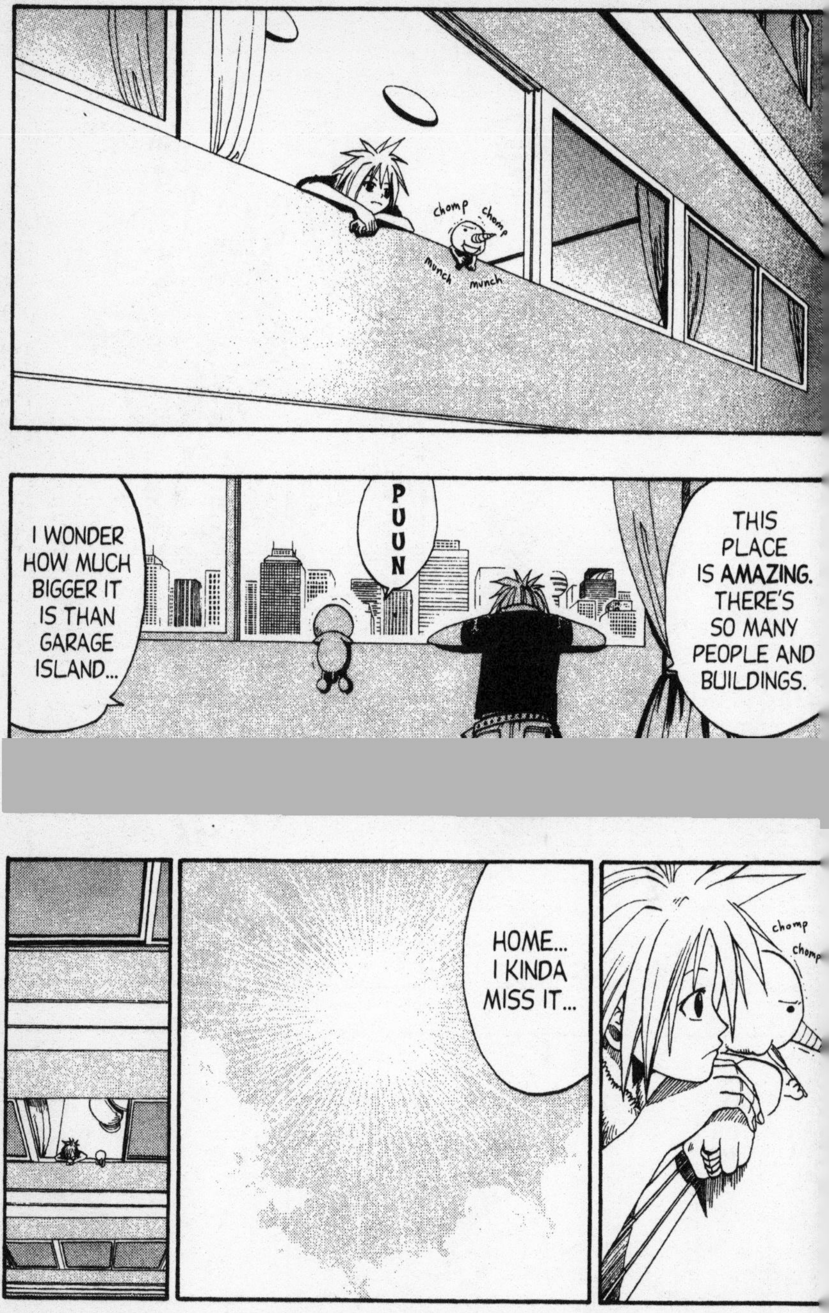
chomp chomp
munch munch
THIS PLACE IS AMAZING. THERE'S SO MANY PEOPLE AND BUILDINGS.
PUUN
I WONDER HOW MUCH BIGGER IT IS THAN GARAGE ISLAND...
chomp chomp
HOME... I KINDA MISS IT...

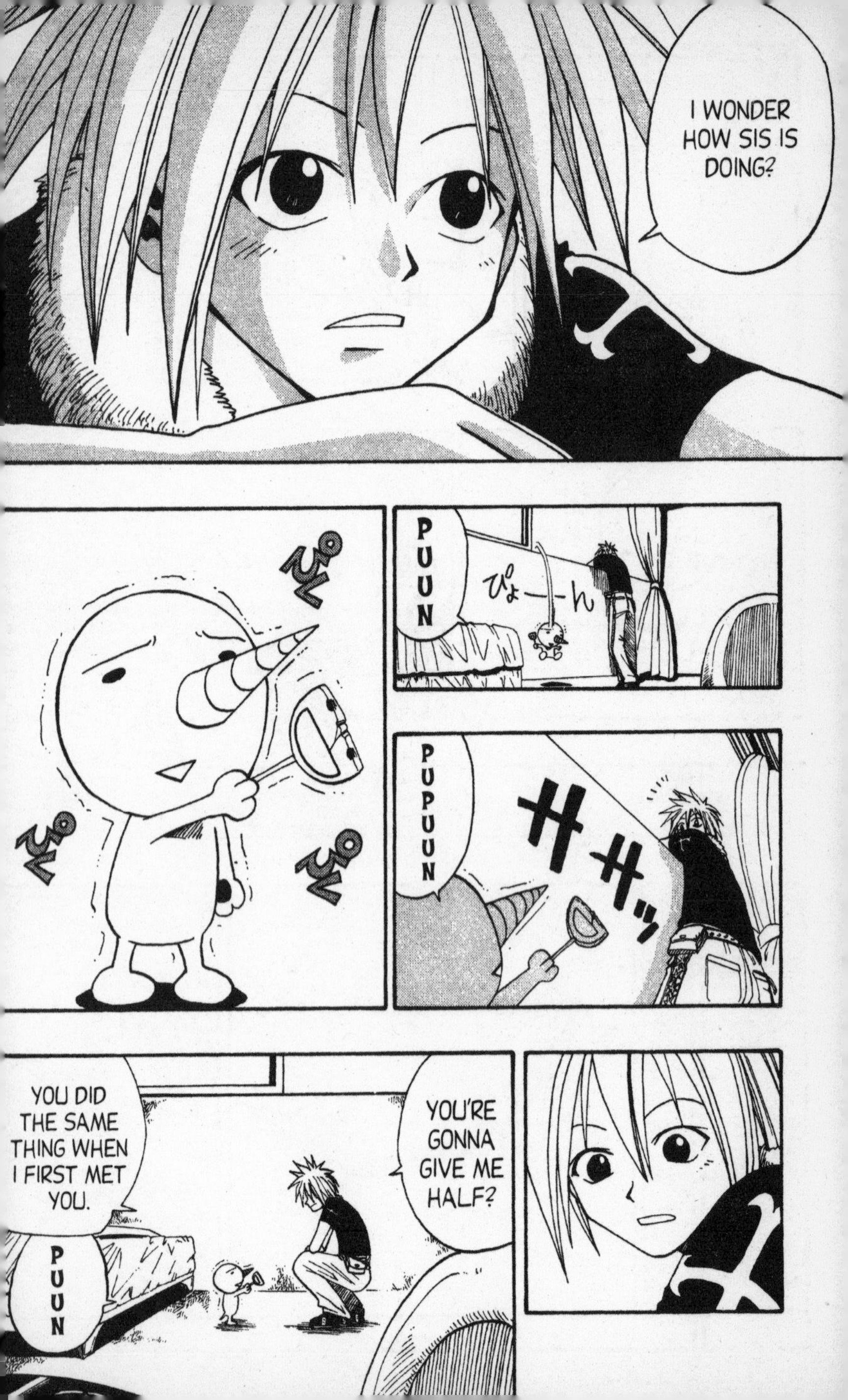
I WONDER HOW SIS IS DOING?
PUUN
ぴょーーん
PUPUUN
ササッ
YOU'RE GONNA GIVE ME HALF?
YOU DID THE SAME THING WHEN I FIRST MET YOU.
PUUN

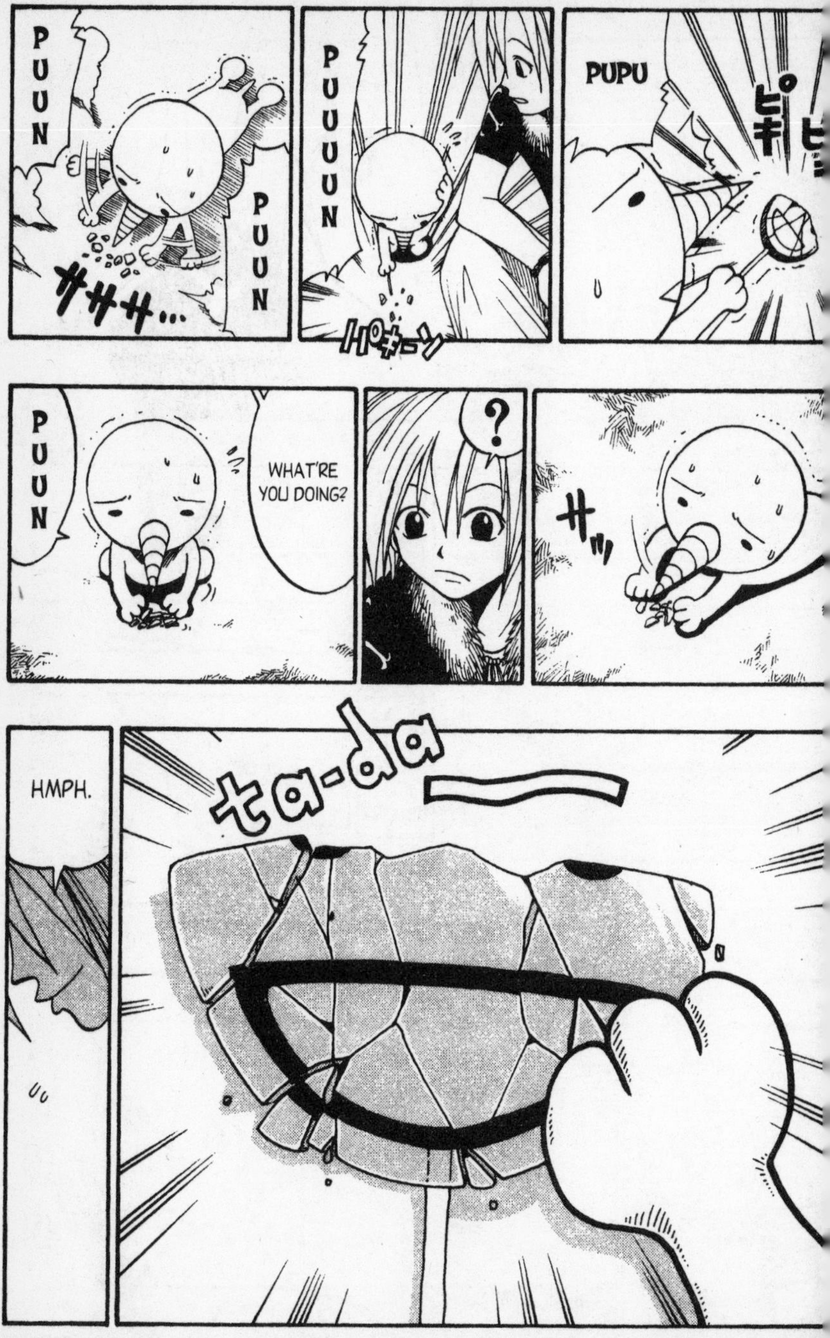
PUPU
PUUUUUN
パキーン
PUUN
PUUN
サササ…
サッ
?
WHAT'RE YOU DOING?
PUUN
ta-da
HMPH.

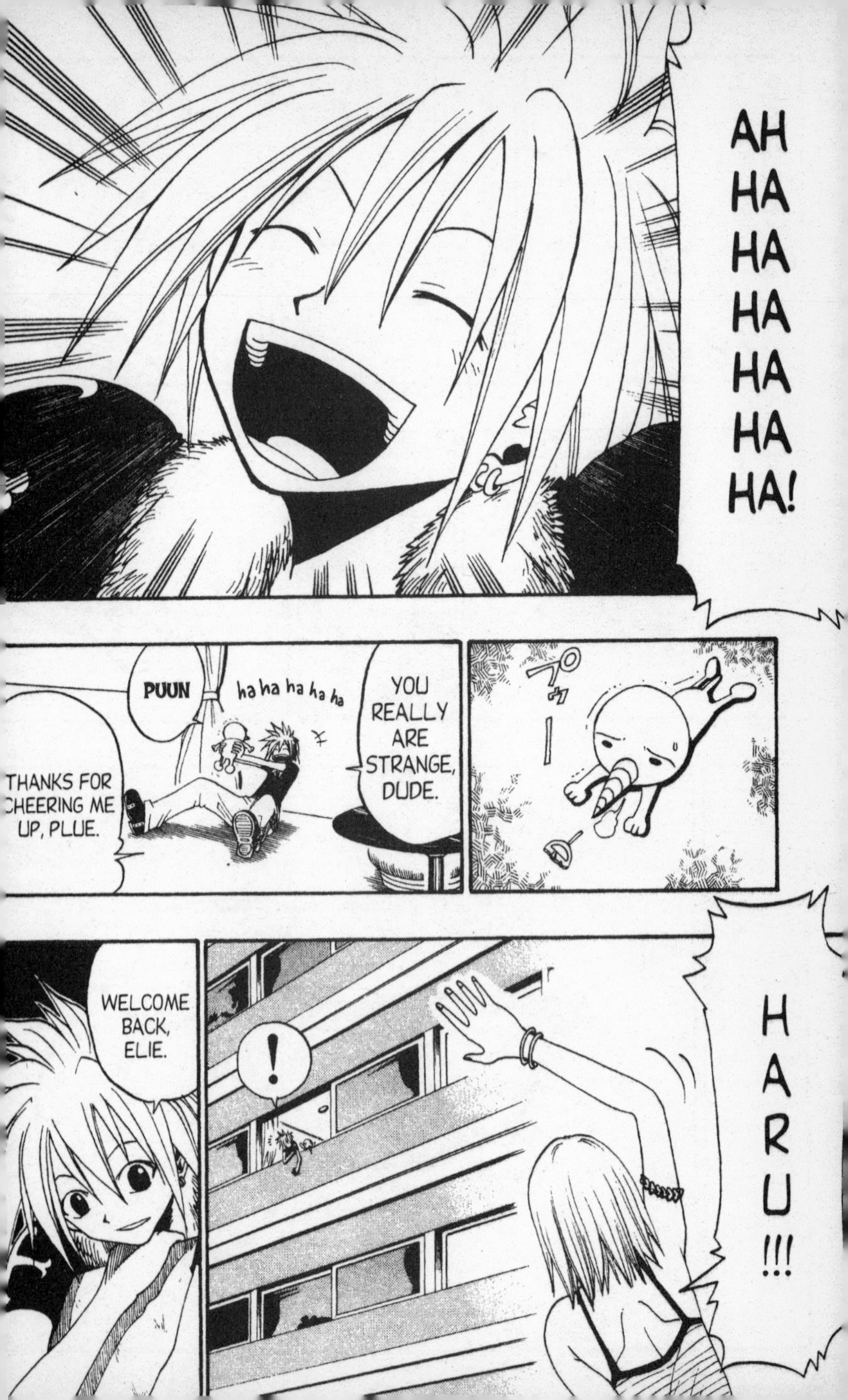
AH HA HA HA HA HA HA!
YOU REALLY ARE STRANGE, DUDE.
ha ha ha ha ha
PUUN
THANKS FOR CHEERING ME UP, PLUE.
HARU!!!
!
WELCOME BACK, ELIE.

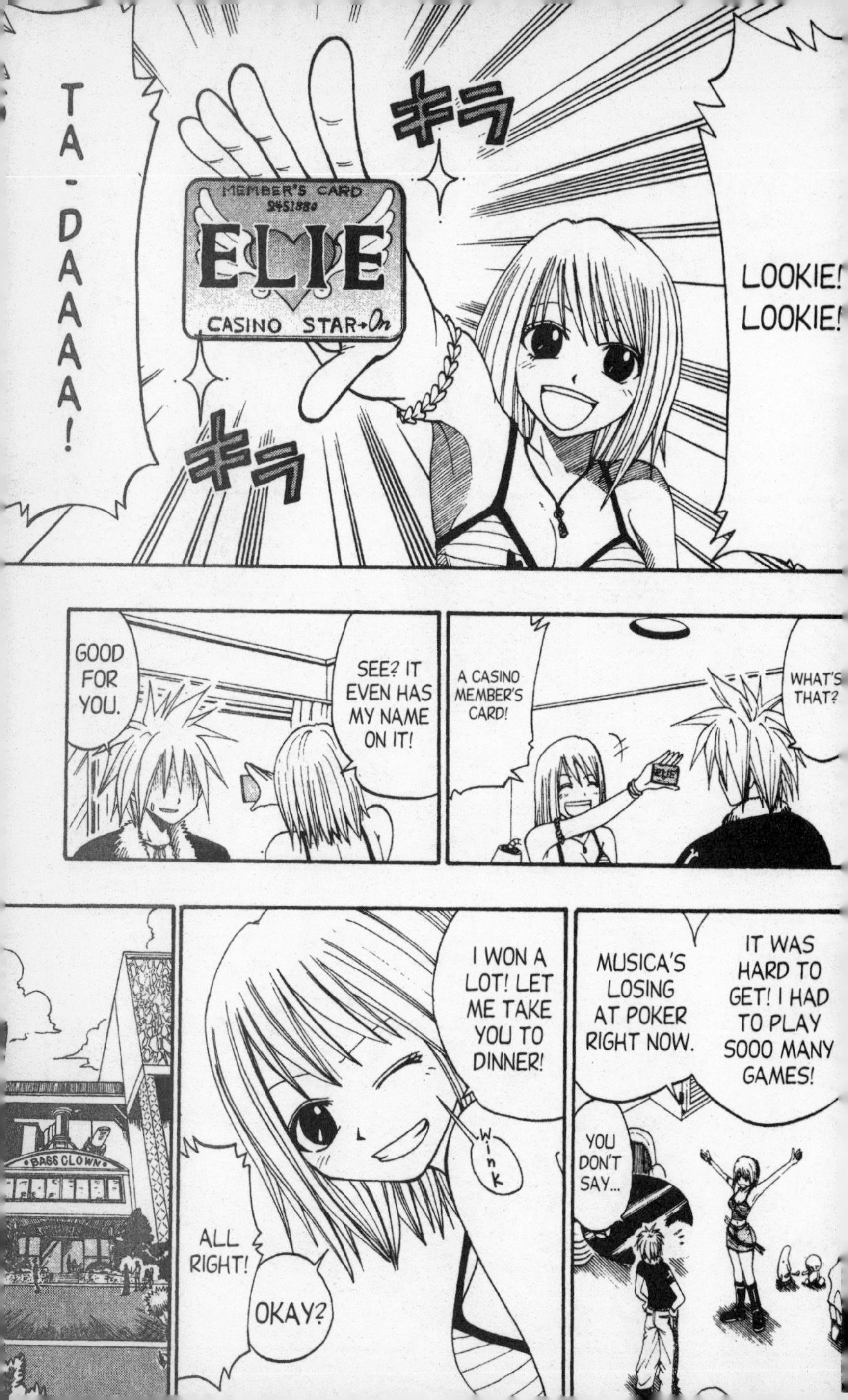
LOOKIE! LOOKIE!
TA-DAAAAA!
キラ
MEMBER'S CARD
ELIE
CASINO STAR→On
キラ
WHAT'S THAT?
A CASINO MEMBER'S CARD!
SEE? IT EVEN HAS MY NAME ON IT!
GOOD FOR YOU.
IT WAS HARD TO GET! I HAD TO PLAY SOOO MANY GAMES!
MUSICA'S LOSING AT POKER RIGHT NOW.
YOU DON'T SAY...
I WON A LOT! LET ME TAKE YOU TO DINNER!
Wink
OKAY?
ALL RIGHT!
BASS CLOWN

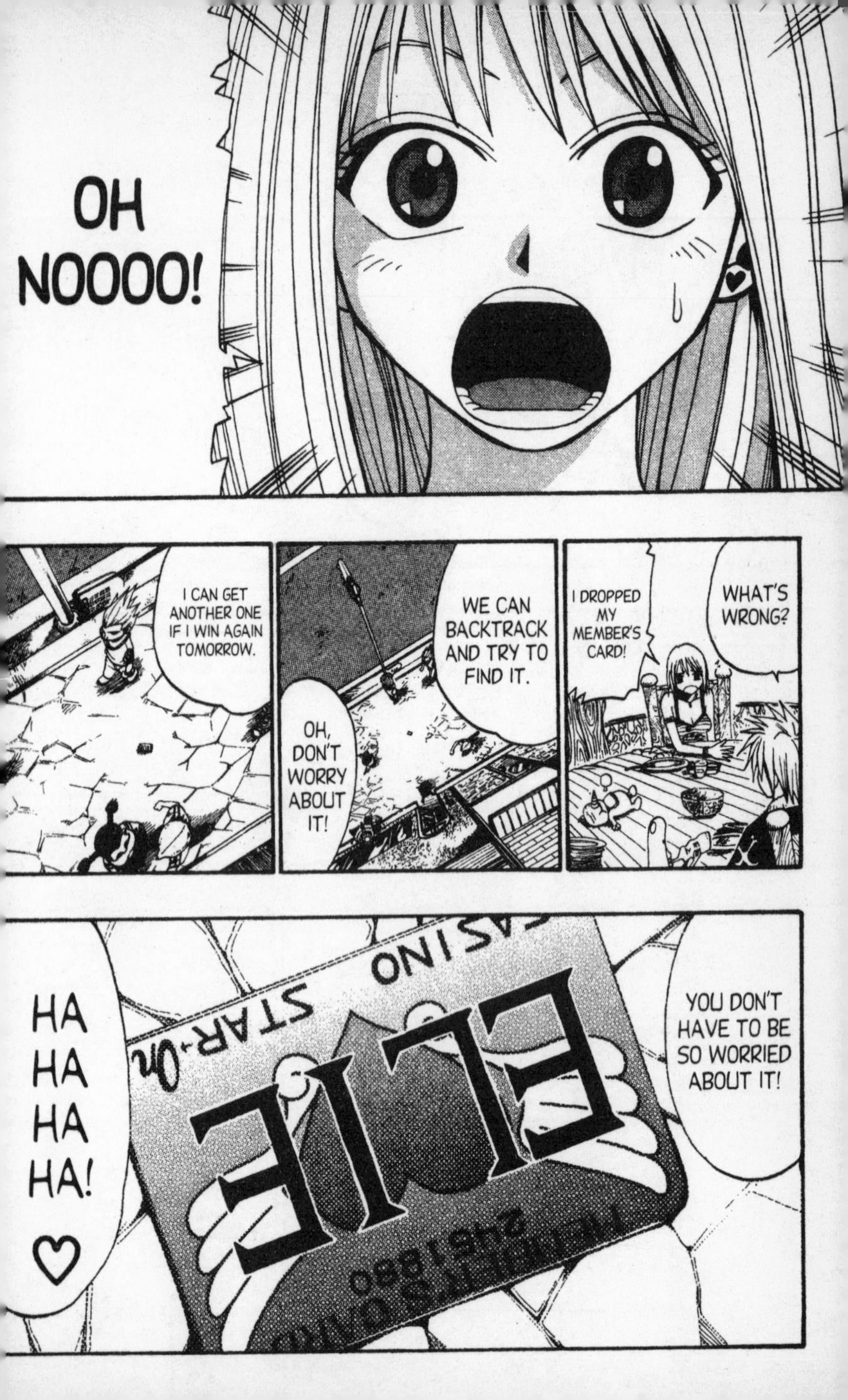
OH NOOOO!
WHAT'S WRONG?
I DROPPED MY MEMBER'S CARD!
WE CAN BACKTRACK AND TRY TO FIND IT.
OH, DON'T WORRY ABOUT IT!
I CAN GET ANOTHER ONE IF I WIN AGAIN TOMORROW.
YOU DON'T HAVE TO BE SO WORRIED ABOUT IT!
HA HA HA HA! ♡

ONE OF THE ORACION SIX: BAKUEN NO SHUDA

WEAPONS: MAINLY HIS DARK BRING, FULL METAL-VALSYAR FLAME - BALLETTÄNZER ZEFFREA

BIRTHDAY / AGE: AUGUST 19, 0037 / 29
HEIGHT / WEIGHT / BLOOD TYPE: 180 CM / 70 KG / A
BIRTHPLACE: UNKNOWN
HOBBIES: FIGHTING
SPECIAL SKILLS: PLAYING WITH FIRE
LIKES: THE SKY
HATES: GALE GLORY

DESCRIPTION
BAKUEN NO SHUDA... I JUST MADE UP THE WORD "BAKUEN." (LAUGH) IT'S A COMBINATION OF THE JAPANESE WORDS FOR "EXPLOSION" AND "FLAME."

WALZER MEANS "WALTZ" IN GERMAN. AND BALLETTÄNZER MEANS "BALLERINA."

SO, YOU'RE PROBABLY WONDERING WHEN I'M GOING TO REVEAL SHUDA'S CONNECTION TO GALE (HARU'S FATHER). THERE'S ALSO SOMETHING IMPORTANT IN HIS PAST THAT DOESN'T HAVE TO DO WITH SHUDA. I REALLY WANT TO SAY IT, BUT THE EDITOR TOLD ME NOT TO FOR NOW, SO I HAVE TO KEEP IT A SECRET.

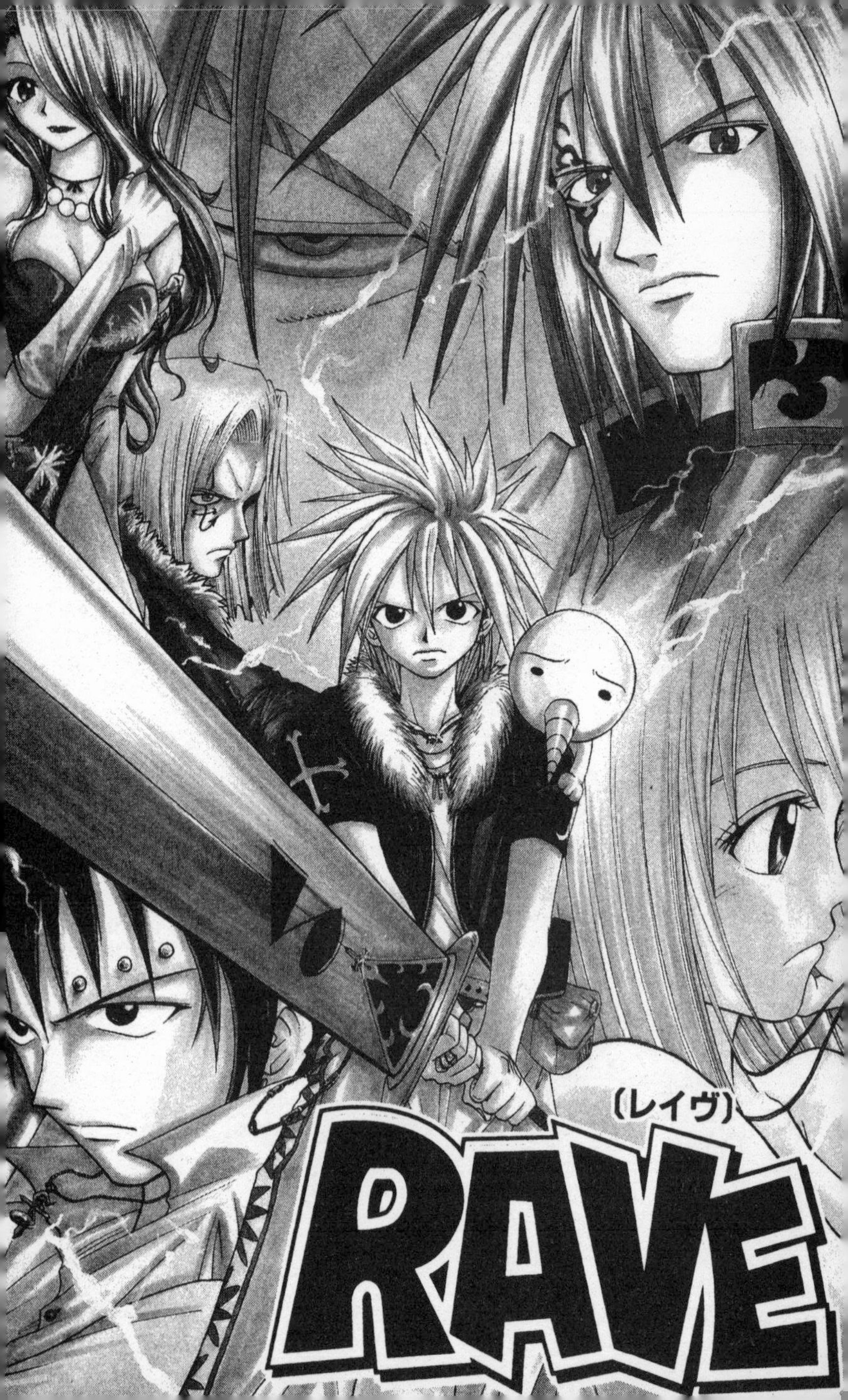
(レイヴ)
RAVE

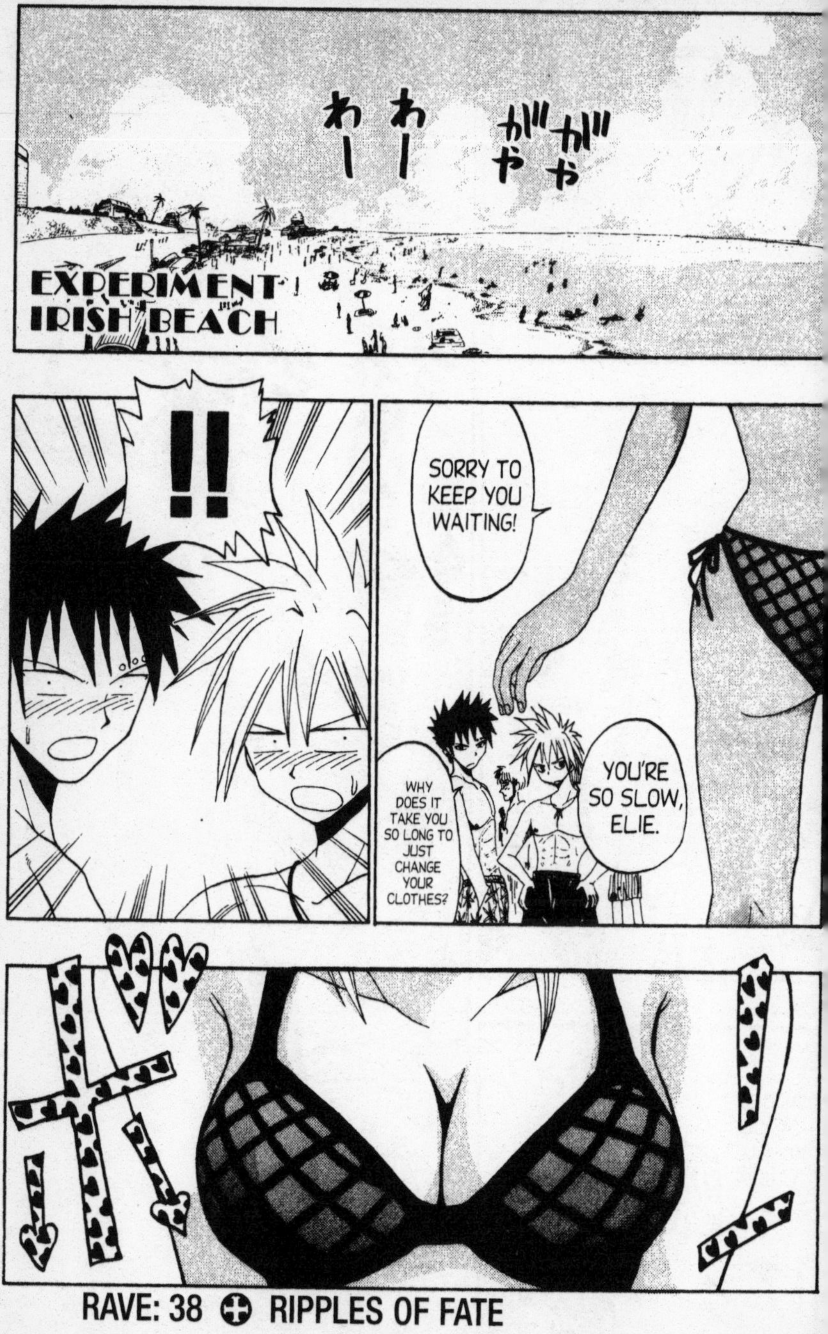
がやがや
わーわー
EXPERIMENT IRISH BEACH
SORRY TO KEEP YOU WAITING!
YOU'RE SO SLOW, ELIE.
WHY DOES IT TAKE YOU SO LONG TO JUST CHANGE YOUR CLOTHES?
!!

RAVE: 38 ✚ RIPPLES OF FATE

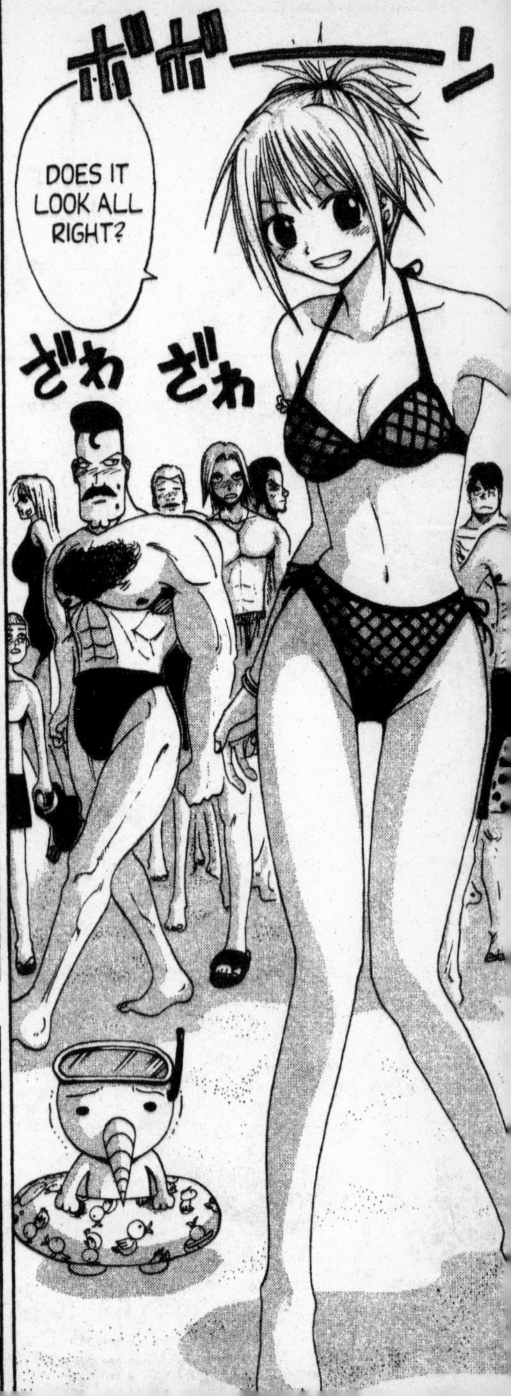
ボボーン
DOES IT LOOK ALL RIGHT?
ざわ ざわ

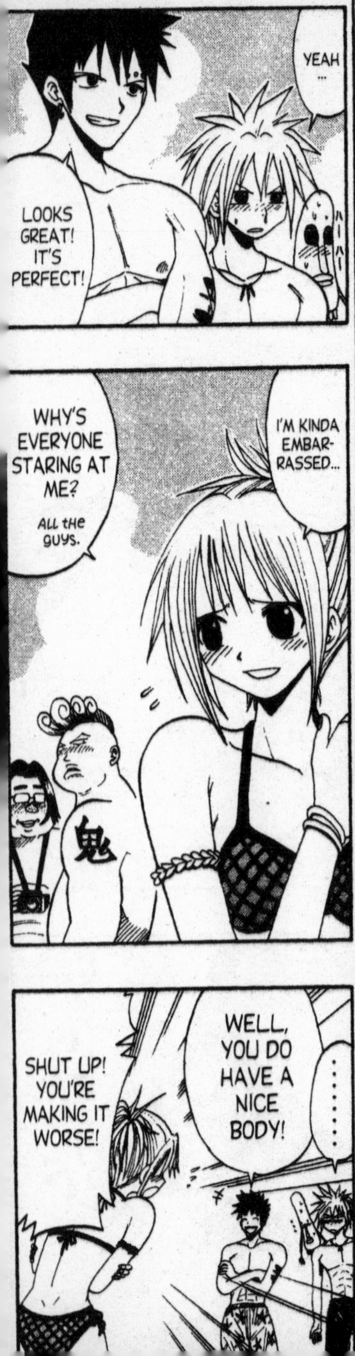
YEAH ...
LOOKS GREAT! IT'S PERFECT!
I'M KINDA EMBARRASSED...
WHY'S EVERYONE STARING AT ME?
All the guys.
......
WELL, YOU DO HAVE A NICE BODY!
SHUT UP! YOU'RE MAKING IT WORSE!

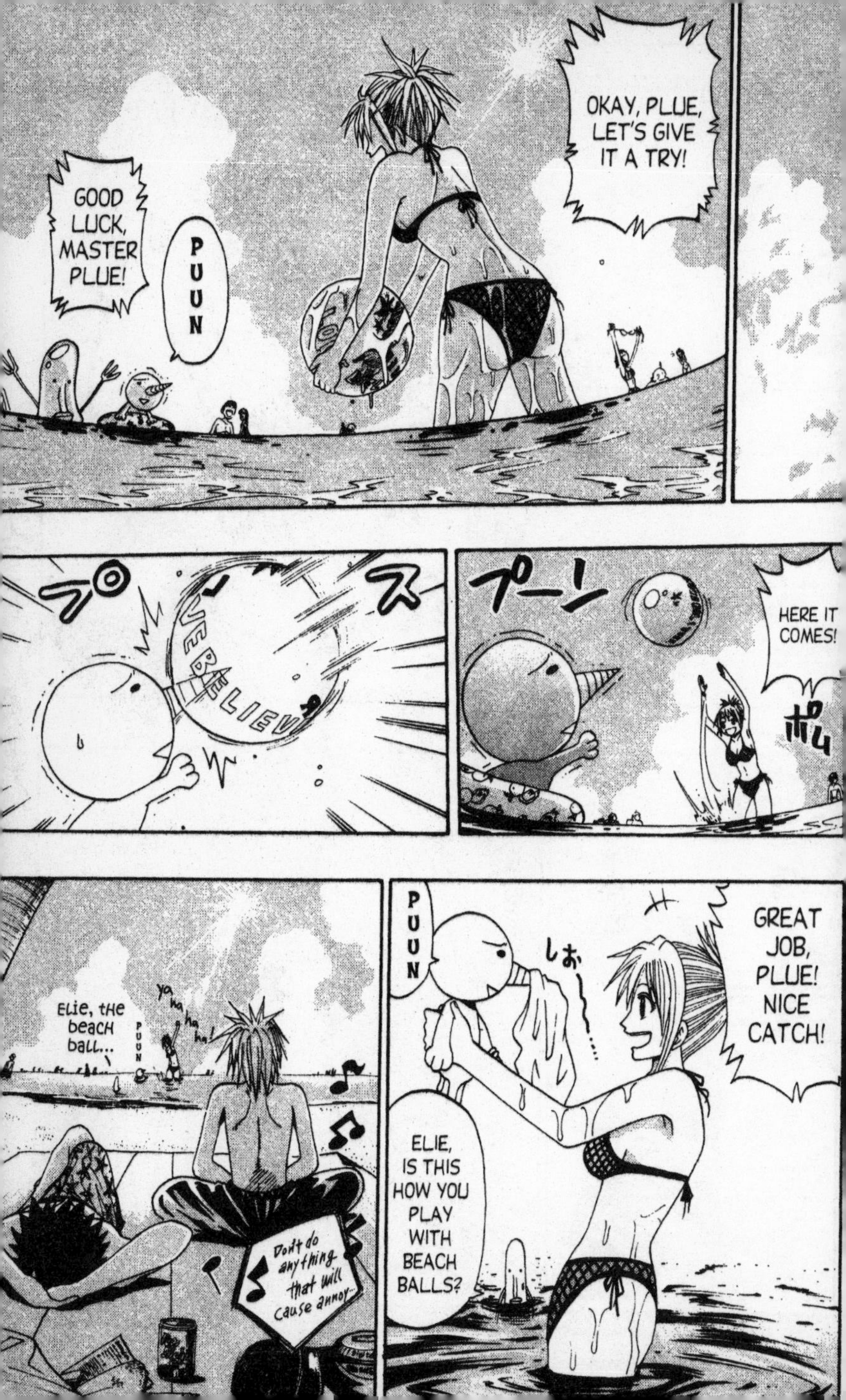
OKAY, PLUE, LET'S GIVE IT A TRY!
PUUN
GOOD LUCK, MASTER PLUE!
プーン
HERE IT COMES!
ポム
プス
VE BELIEV
GREAT JOB, PLUE! NICE CATCH!
しお~…
PUUN
ELIE, IS THIS HOW YOU PLAY WITH BEACH BALLS?
ya ha ha ha!
PUUN
Elie, the beach ball...
Don't do anything that will cause annoy...

HA HA HA HA HA! MAN, THEY'RE GOOFY!
YEAH, TELL ME ABOUT IT.
I KNOW WE'RE IN THE MIDDLE OF A FIGHT WITH DEMON CARD...
...BUT IT'S SO NICE AND PEACEFUL HERE.
ガヤ ガヤ
ガヤ ガヤ
Yaaaah!
PUUN
I HEARD THERE'S A MUSEUM HERE THAT WAS BUILT TO COMMEMORATE PEACE.
MAYBE WE SHOULD CHECK IT OUT.
Are you in earnest or simply joking? the fall of nation!!
YOU MEAN SYMPHONIA MUSEUM?
YEAH, THEY'VE GOT ALL KINDS OF RECORDS AND ARTIFACTS FROM THE IMPERIAL WAR. *

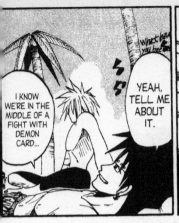

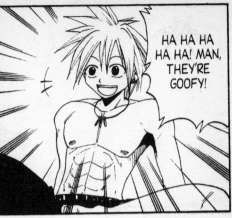

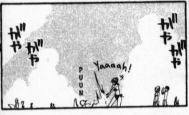

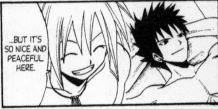

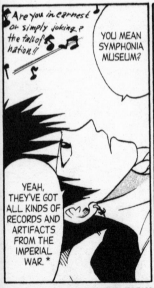

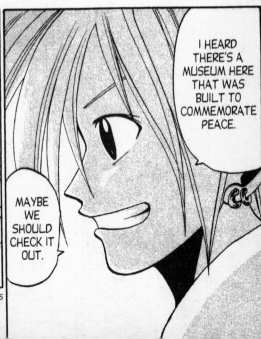

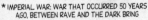

* IMPERIAL WAR: WAR THAT OCCURRED 50 YEARS AGO, BETWEEN RAVE AND THE DARK BRING

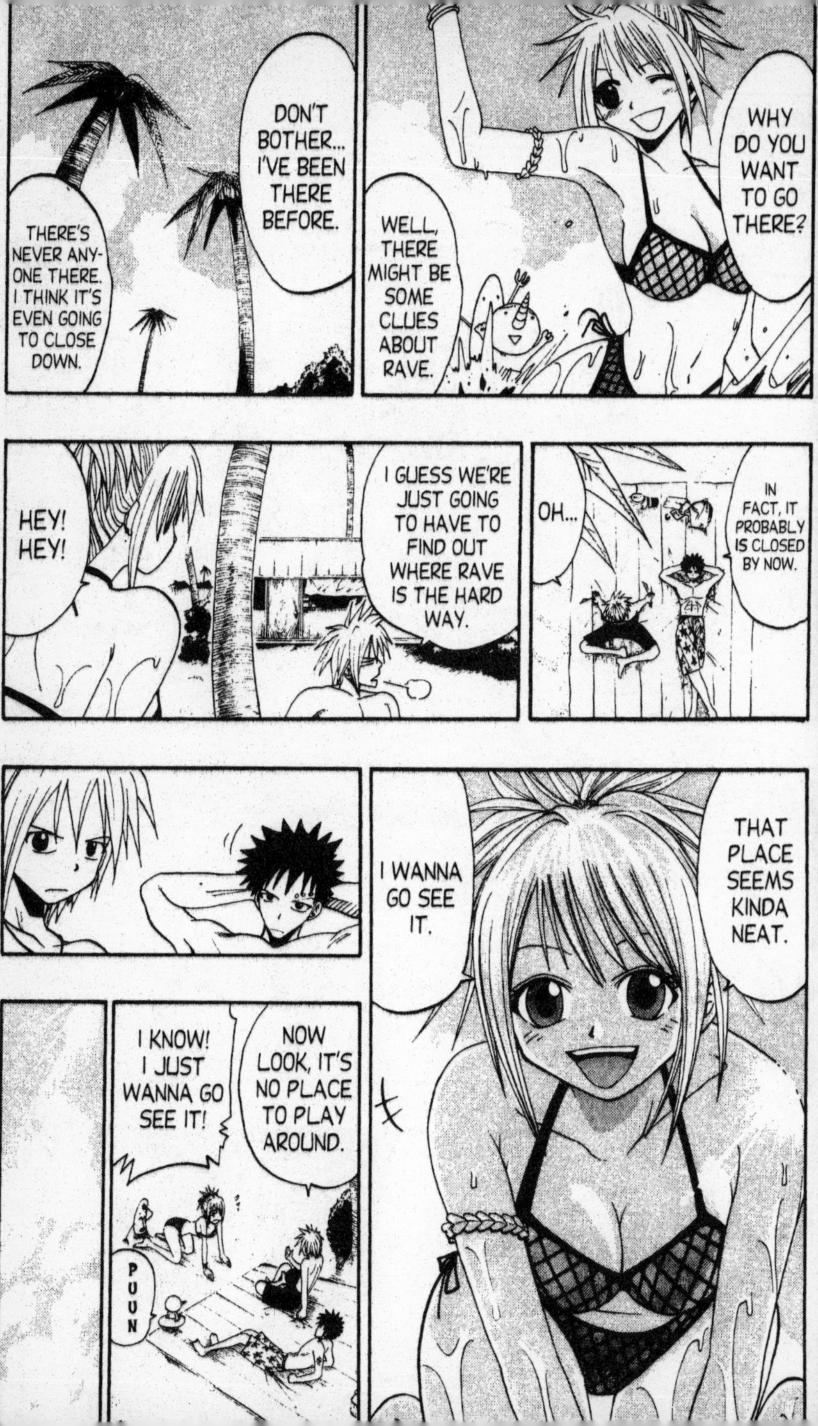
WHY DO YOU WANT TO GO THERE?
WELL, THERE MIGHT BE SOME CLUES ABOUT RAVE.
DON'T BOTHER... I'VE BEEN THERE BEFORE.
THERE'S NEVER ANY-ONE THERE. I THINK IT'S EVEN GOING TO CLOSE DOWN.
IN FACT, IT PROBABLY IS CLOSED BY NOW.
OH...
I GUESS WE'RE JUST GOING TO HAVE TO FIND OUT WHERE RAVE IS THE HARD WAY.
HEY! HEY!
THAT PLACE SEEMS KINDA NEAT.
I WANNA GO SEE IT.
NOW LOOK, IT'S NO PLACE TO PLAY AROUND.
I KNOW! I JUST WANNA GO SEE IT!
PUUN

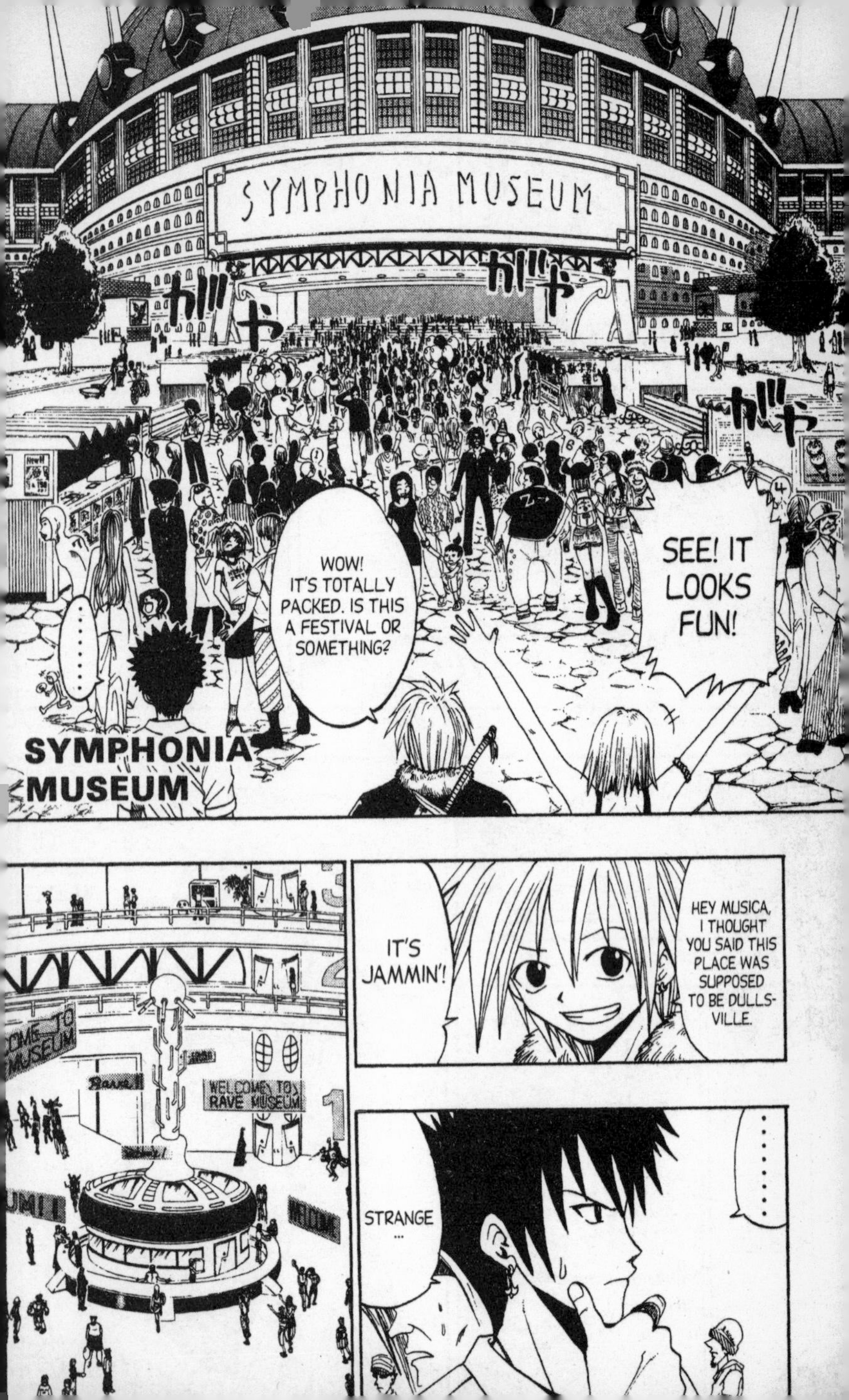
SYMPHONIA MUSEUM
ガヤ
ガヤ
ガヤ
SEE! IT LOOKS FUN!
WOW! IT'S TOTALLY PACKED. IS THIS A FESTIVAL OR SOMETHING?
......
SYMPHONIA MUSEUM
HEY MUSICA, I THOUGHT YOU SAID THIS PLACE WAS SUPPOSED TO BE DULLS-VILLE.
IT'S JAMMIN'!
......
STRANGE ...
COME TO MUSEUM
WELCOME TO RAVE MUSEUM

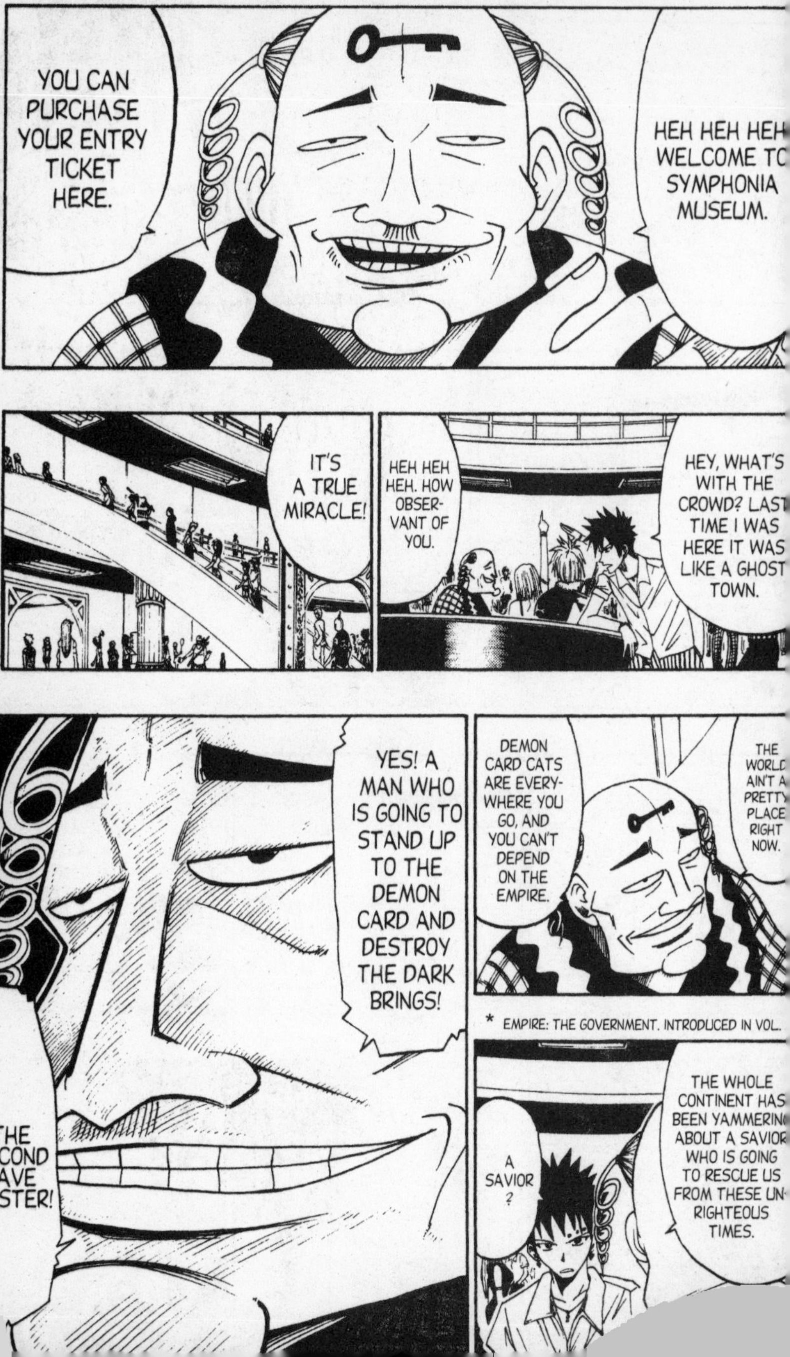
HEH HEH HEH WELCOME TO SYMPHONIA MUSEUM.
YOU CAN PURCHASE YOUR ENTRY TICKET HERE.
HEY, WHAT'S WITH THE CROWD? LAST TIME I WAS HERE IT WAS LIKE A GHOST TOWN.
HEH HEH HEH. HOW OBSER-VANT OF YOU.
IT'S A TRUE MIRACLE!
THE WORLD AIN'T A PRETTY PLACE RIGHT NOW.
DEMON CARD CATS ARE EVERY-WHERE YOU GO, AND YOU CAN'T DEPEND ON THE EMPIRE.
* EMPIRE: THE GOVERNMENT. INTRODUCED IN VOL.
THE WHOLE CONTINENT HAS BEEN YAMMERING ABOUT A SAVIOR WHO IS GOING TO RESCUE US FROM THESE UN-RIGHTEOUS TIMES.
A SAVIOR?
YES! A MAN WHO IS GOING TO STAND UP TO THE DEMON CARD AND DESTROY THE DARK BRINGS!
THE SECOND RAVE MASTER!

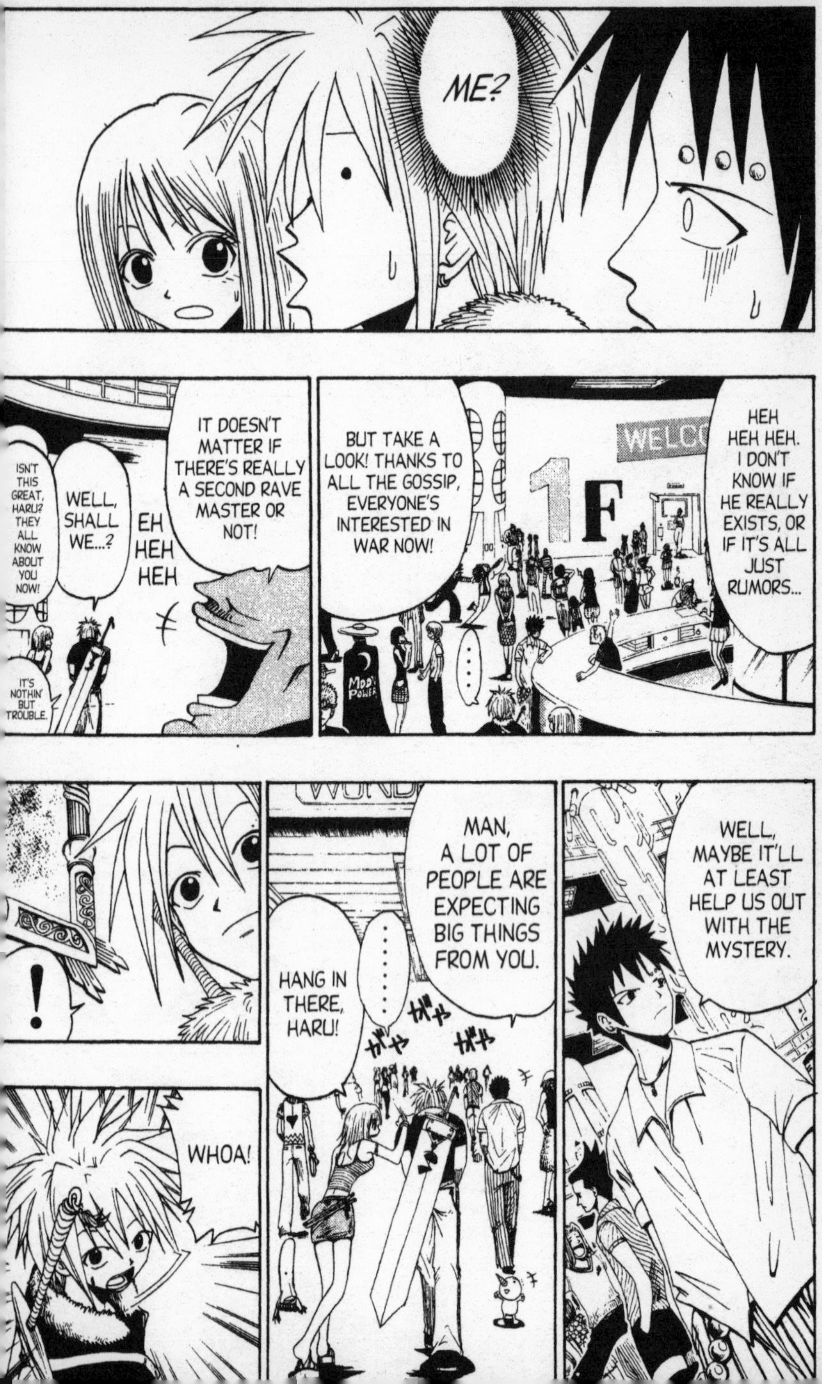
ME?
HEH HEH HEH. I DON'T KNOW IF HE REALLY EXISTS, OR IF IT'S ALL JUST RUMORS...
BUT TAKE A LOOK! THANKS TO ALL THE GOSSIP, EVERYONE'S INTERESTED IN WAR NOW!
......
WELC
1F
MOON POWER
IT DOESN'T MATTER IF THERE'S REALLY A SECOND RAVE MASTER OR NOT!
EH HEH HEH
WELL, SHALL WE...?
ISN'T THIS GREAT, HARU? THEY ALL KNOW ABOUT YOU NOW!
IT'S NOTHIN' BUT TROUBLE.
WELL, MAYBE IT'LL AT LEAST HELP US OUT WITH THE MYSTERY.
MAN, A LOT OF PEOPLE ARE EXPECTING BIG THINGS FROM YOU.
......
HANG IN THERE, HARU!
がや
がや
がや
!
WHOA!

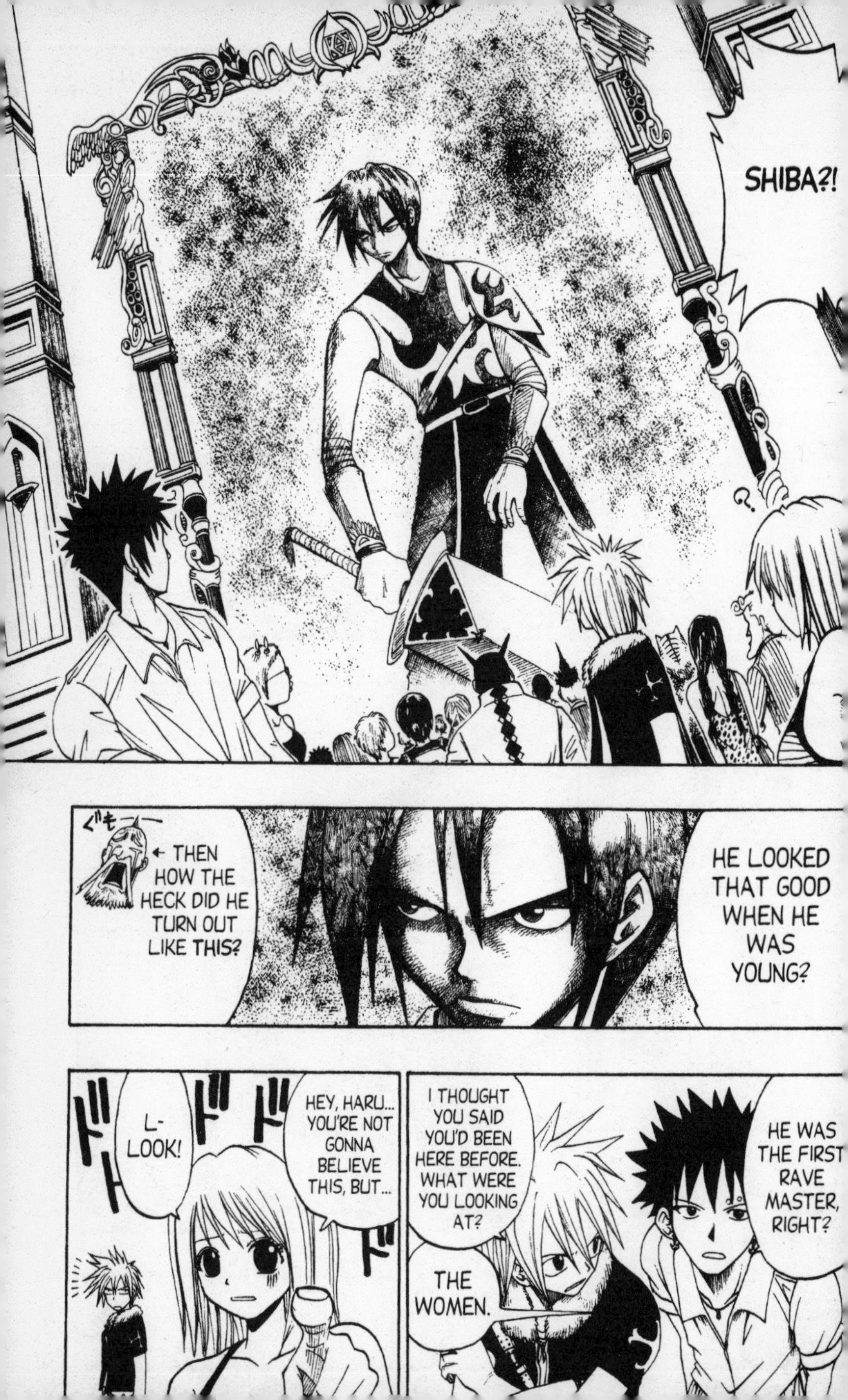
SHIBA?!
HE LOOKED THAT GOOD WHEN HE WAS YOUNG?
ぐもー
← THEN HOW THE HECK DID HE TURN OUT LIKE THIS?
HE WAS THE FIRST RAVE MASTER, RIGHT?
I THOUGHT YOU SAID YOU'D BEEN HERE BEFORE. WHAT WERE YOU LOOKING AT?
THE WOMEN.
HEY, HARU... YOU'RE NOT GONNA BELIEVE THIS, BUT...
L-LOOK!
ドドドドド

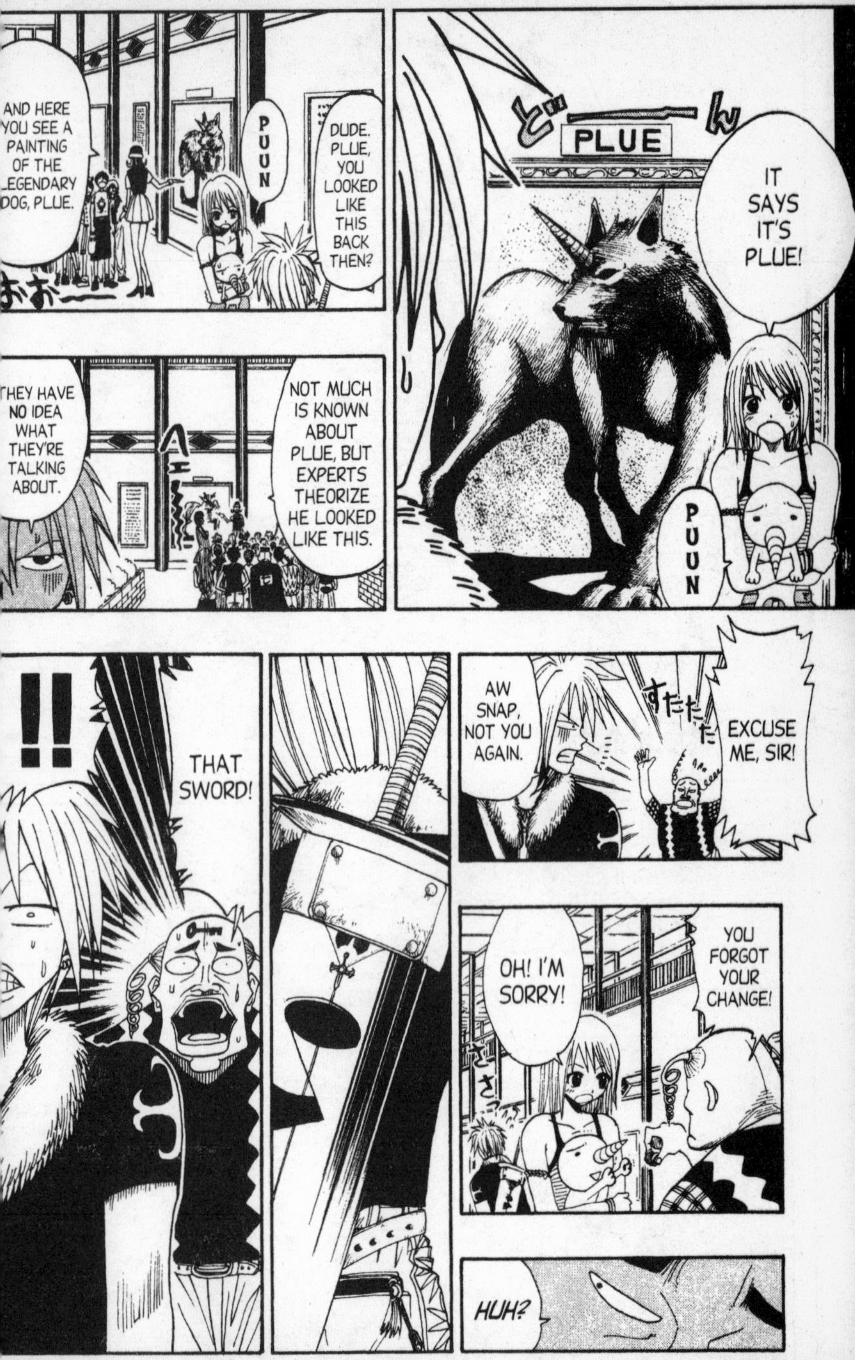
どーーーん
PLUE
IT SAYS IT'S PLUE!
PUUN
DUDE. PLUE, YOU LOOKED LIKE THIS BACK THEN?
PUUN
AND HERE YOU SEE A PAINTING OF THE LEGENDARY DOG, PLUE.
おおーー
NOT MUCH IS KNOWN ABOUT PLUE, BUT EXPERTS THEORIZE HE LOOKED LIKE THIS.
THEY HAVE NO IDEA WHAT THEY'RE TALKING ABOUT.
EXCUSE ME, SIR!
すたたた
AW SNAP, NOT YOU AGAIN.
YOU FORGOT YOUR CHANGE!
OH! I'M SORRY!
ささっ
HUH?
THAT SWORD!
!!

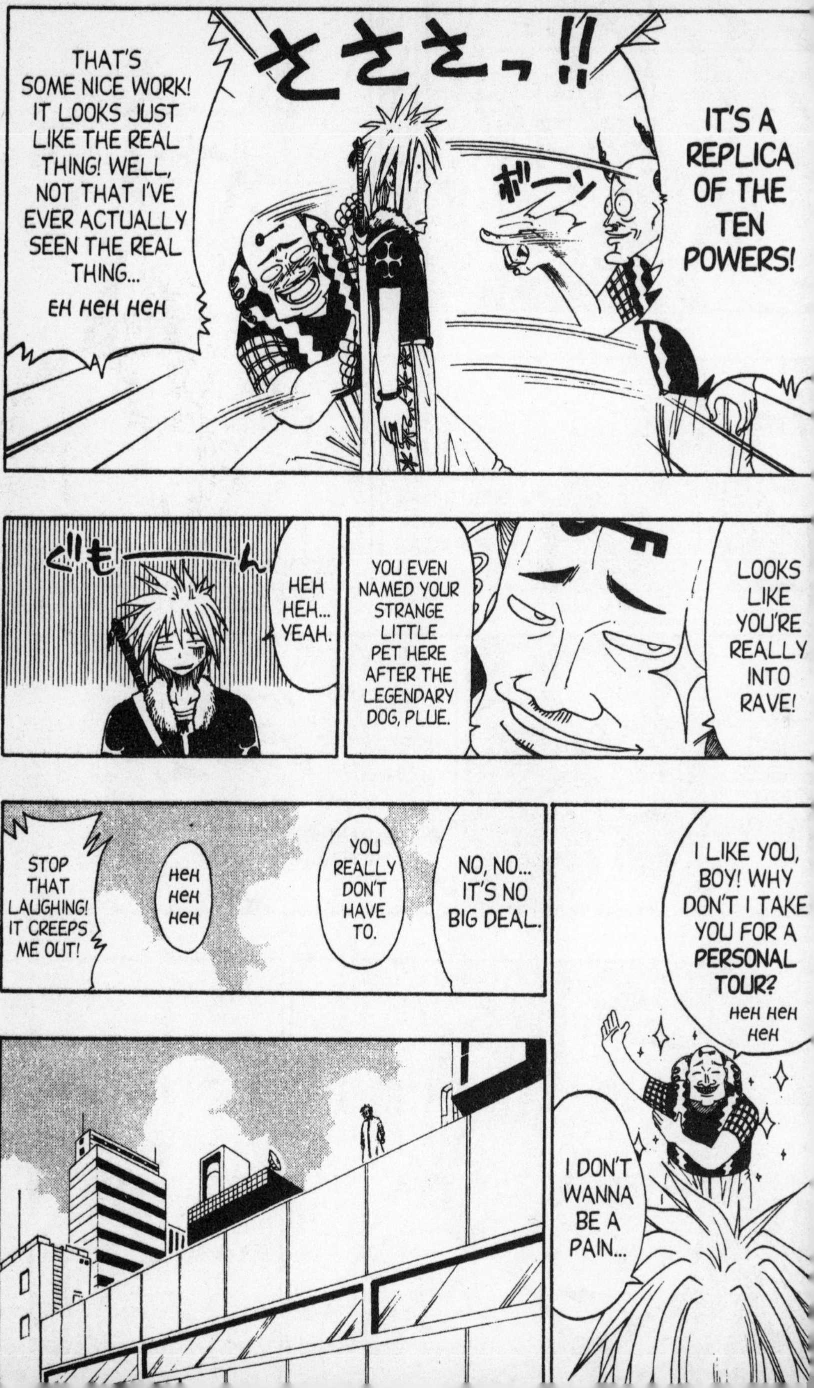

さささっ!!
IT'S A REPLICA OF THE TEN POWERS!
ボーン
THAT'S SOME NICE WORK! IT LOOKS JUST LIKE THE REAL THING! WELL, NOT THAT I'VE EVER ACTUALLY SEEN THE REAL THING... EH HEH HEH
LOOKS LIKE YOU'RE REALLY INTO RAVE!
YOU EVEN NAMED YOUR STRANGE LITTLE PET HERE AFTER THE LEGENDARY DOG, PLUE.
ぐも―――ん
HEH HEH... YEAH.
I LIKE YOU, BOY! WHY DON'T I TAKE YOU FOR A PERSONAL TOUR?
HEH HEH HEH
I DON'T WANNA BE A PAIN...
NO, NO... IT'S NO BIG DEAL.
YOU REALLY DON'T HAVE TO.
HEH HEH HEH
STOP THAT LAUGHING! IT CREEPS ME OUT!

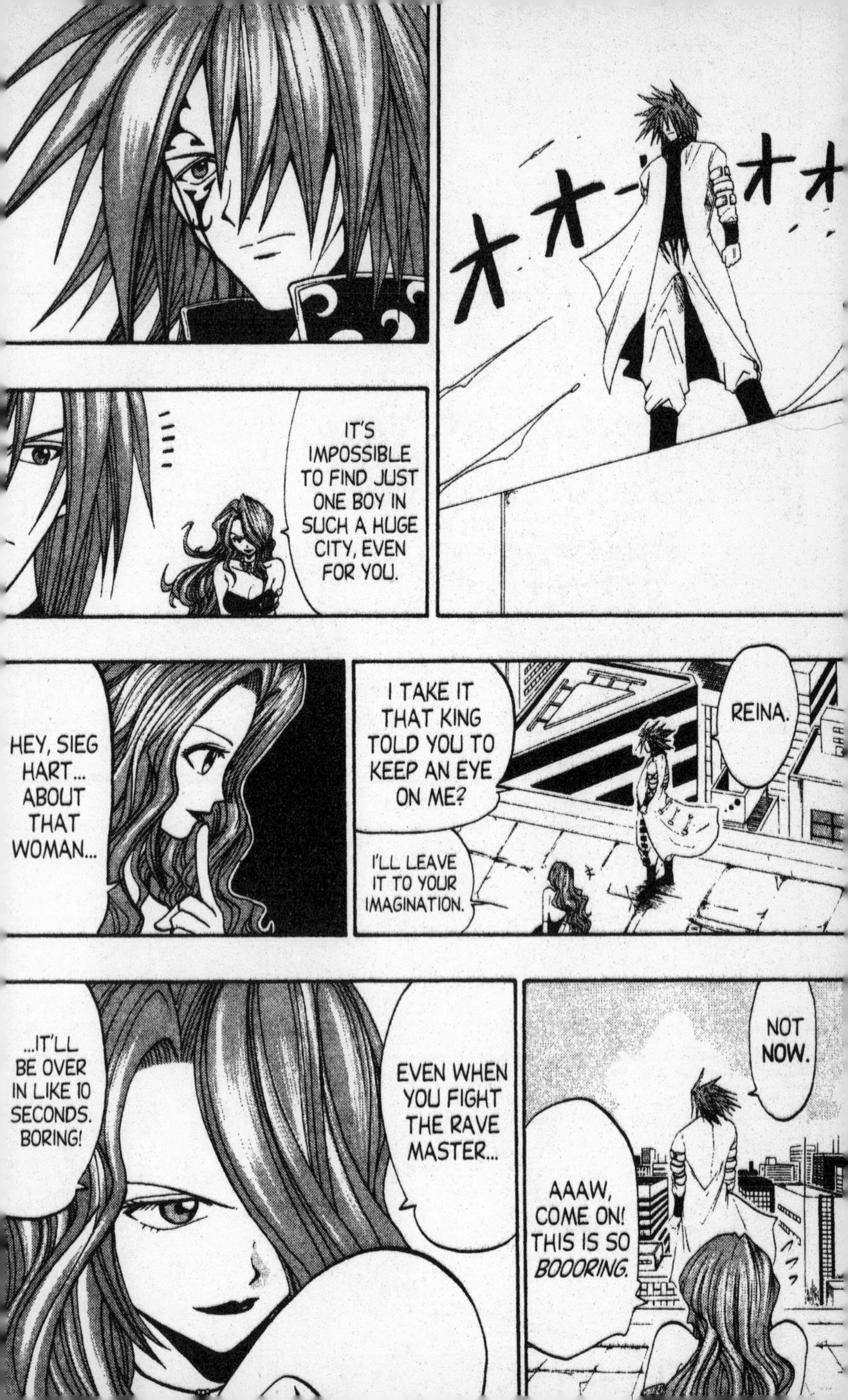
IT'S IMPOSSIBLE TO FIND JUST ONE BOY IN SUCH A HUGE CITY, EVEN FOR YOU.
REINA.
I TAKE IT THAT KING TOLD YOU TO KEEP AN EYE ON ME?
I'LL LEAVE IT TO YOUR IMAGINATION.
HEY, SIEG HART... ABOUT THAT WOMAN...
NOT NOW.
AAAW, COME ON! THIS IS SO *BOOORING.*
EVEN WHEN YOU FIGHT THE RAVE MASTER...
...IT'LL BE OVER IN LIKE 10 SECONDS. BORING!

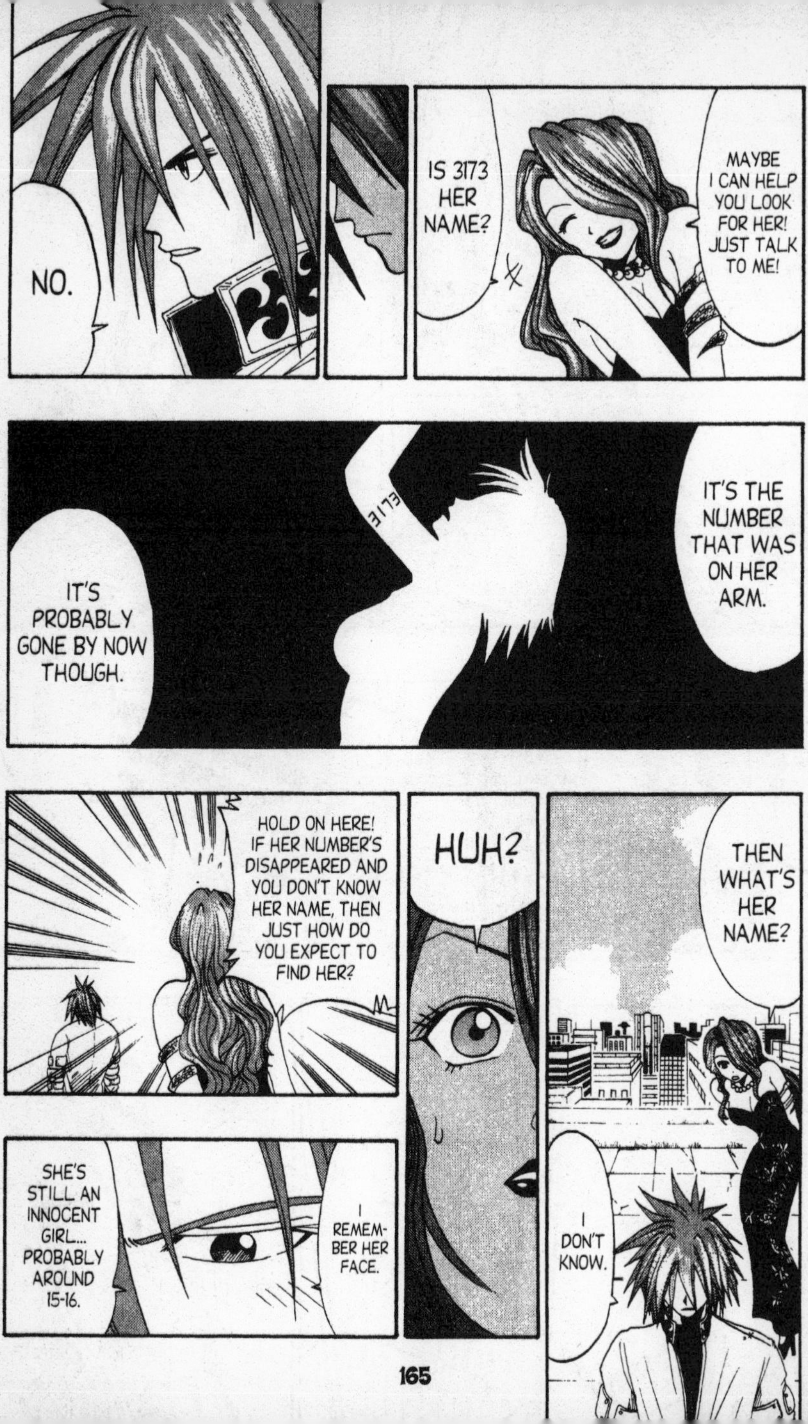
MAYBE I CAN HELP YOU LOOK FOR HER! JUST TALK TO ME!
IS 3173 HER NAME?
NO.
IT'S THE NUMBER THAT WAS ON HER ARM.
ELIE
IT'S PROBABLY GONE BY NOW THOUGH.
THEN WHAT'S HER NAME?
I DON'T KNOW.
HUH?
HOLD ON HERE! IF HER NUMBER'S DISAPPEARED AND YOU DON'T KNOW HER NAME, THEN JUST HOW DO YOU EXPECT TO FIND HER?
I REMEMBER HER FACE.
SHE'S STILL AN INNOCENT GIRL... PROBABLY AROUND 15-16.

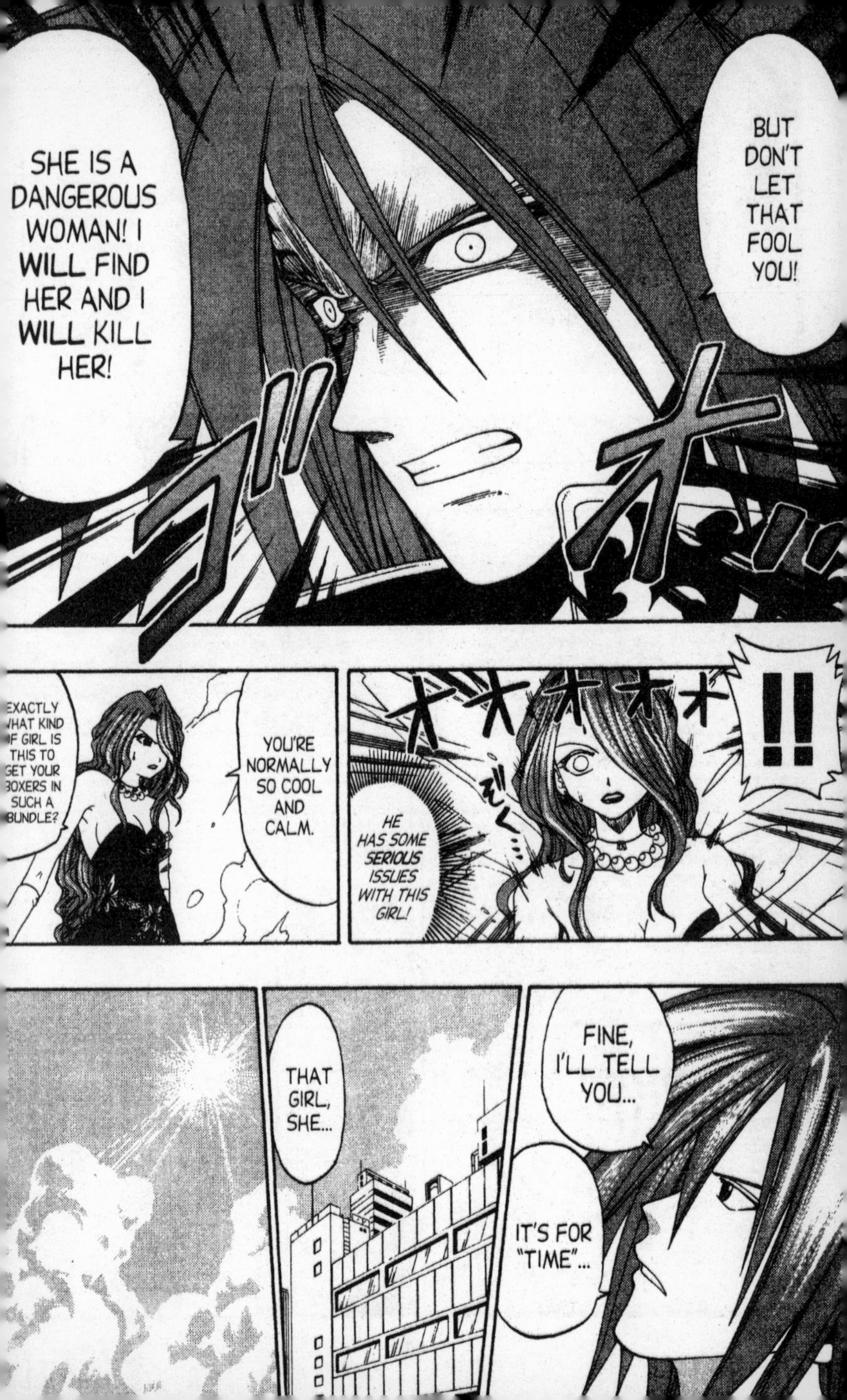
BUT DON'T LET THAT FOOL YOU!
SHE IS A DANGEROUS WOMAN! I WILL FIND HER AND I WILL KILL HER!
!!
HE HAS SOME SERIOUS ISSUES WITH THIS GIRL!
YOU'RE NORMALLY SO COOL AND CALM.
EXACTLY WHAT KIND OF GIRL IS THIS TO GET YOUR BOXERS IN SUCH A BUNDLE?
FINE, I'LL TELL YOU...
IT'S FOR "TIME"...
THAT GIRL, SHE...

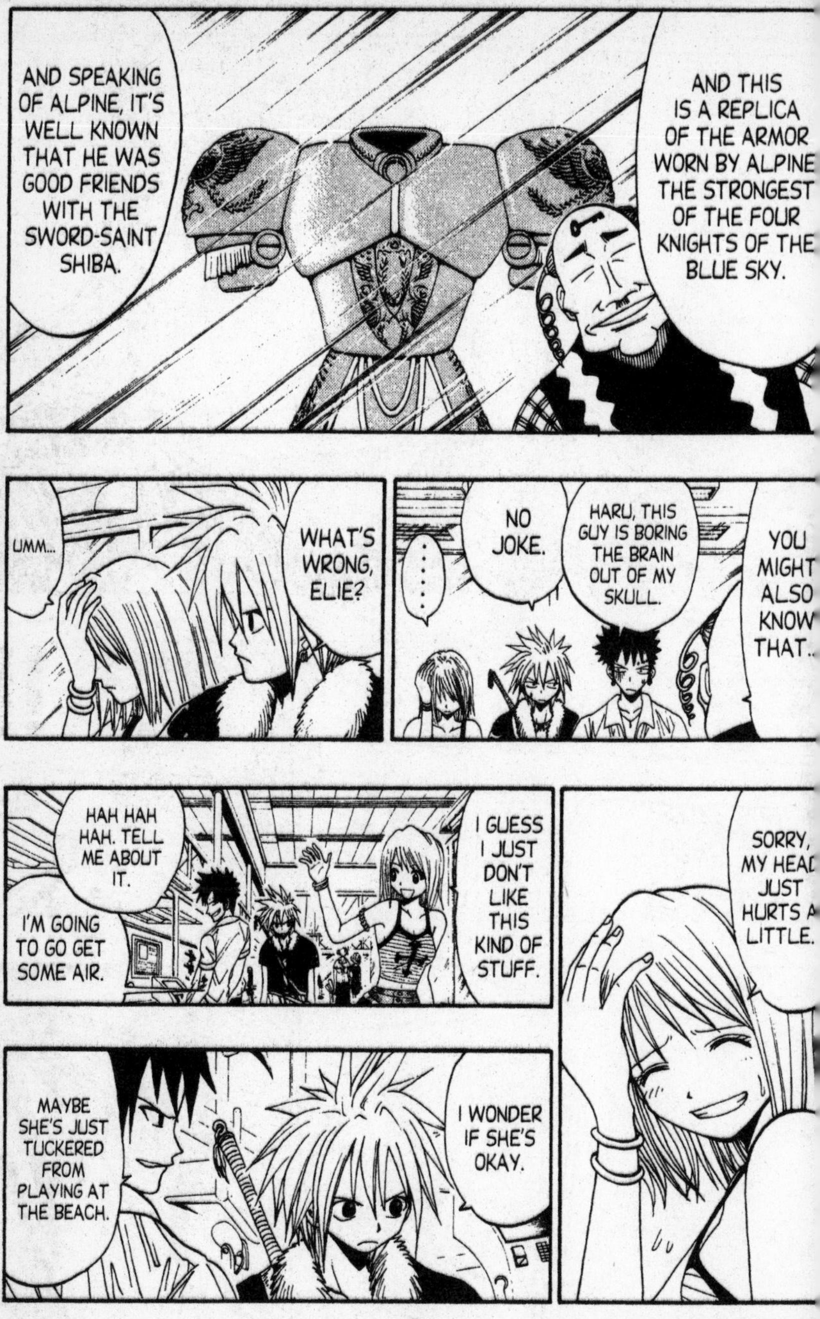
AND THIS IS A REPLICA OF THE ARMOR WORN BY ALPINE THE STRONGEST OF THE FOUR KNIGHTS OF THE BLUE SKY.
AND SPEAKING OF ALPINE, IT'S WELL KNOWN THAT HE WAS GOOD FRIENDS WITH THE SWORD-SAINT SHIBA.
YOU MIGHT ALSO KNOW THAT...
HARU, THIS GUY IS BORING THE BRAIN OUT OF MY SKULL.
NO JOKE.
......
WHAT'S WRONG, ELIE?
UMM...
SORRY, MY HEAD JUST HURTS A LITTLE.
I GUESS I JUST DON'T LIKE THIS KIND OF STUFF.
HAH HAH HAH. TELL ME ABOUT IT.
I'M GOING TO GO GET SOME AIR.
I WONDER IF SHE'S OKAY.
MAYBE SHE'S JUST TUCKERED FROM PLAYING AT THE BEACH.

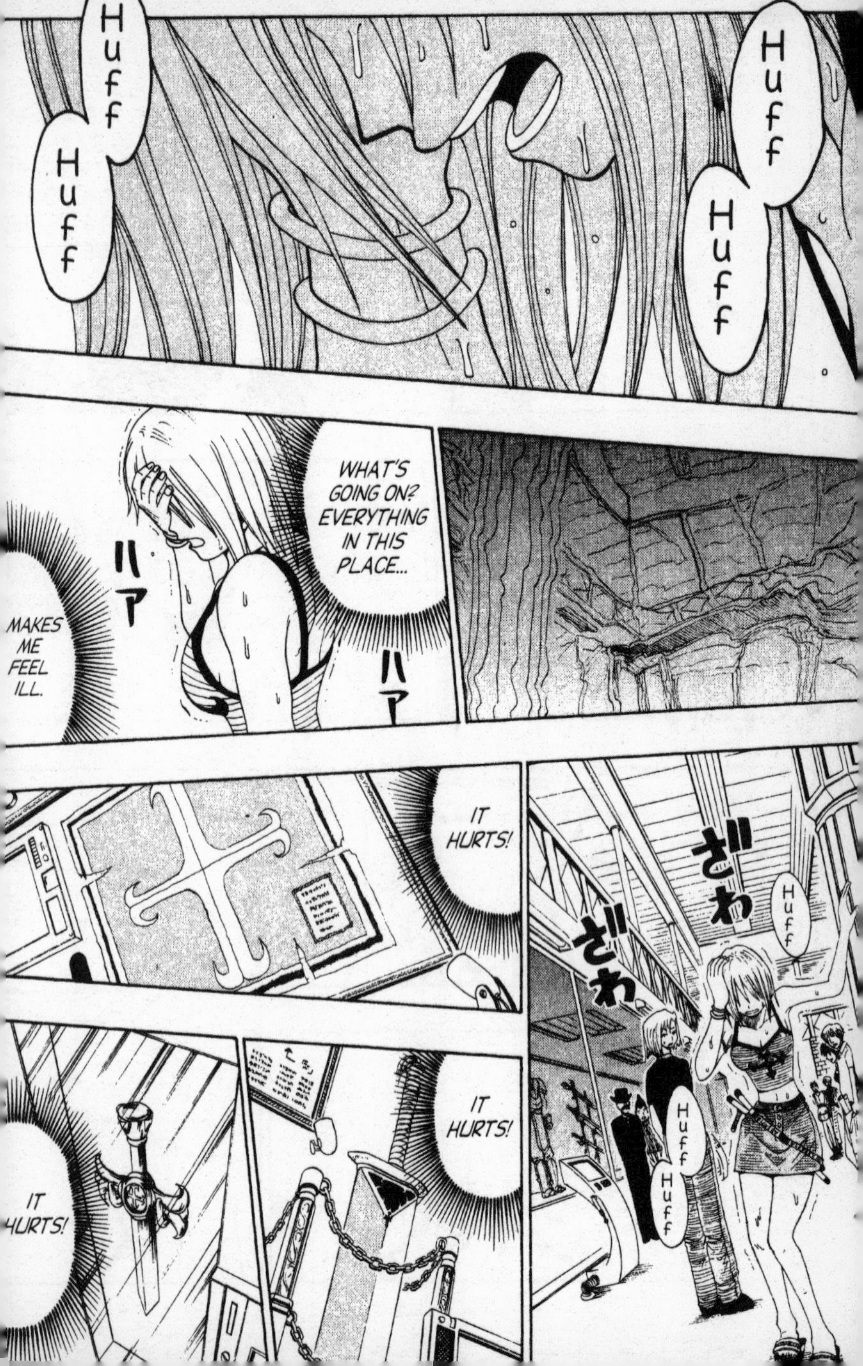

Huff
Huff
Huff
Huff
WHAT'S GOING ON? EVERYTHING IN THIS PLACE...
ハア
ハア
MAKES ME FEEL ILL.
ざわ
ざわ
Huff
Huff
Huff
IT HURTS!
IT HURTS!
IT HURTS!

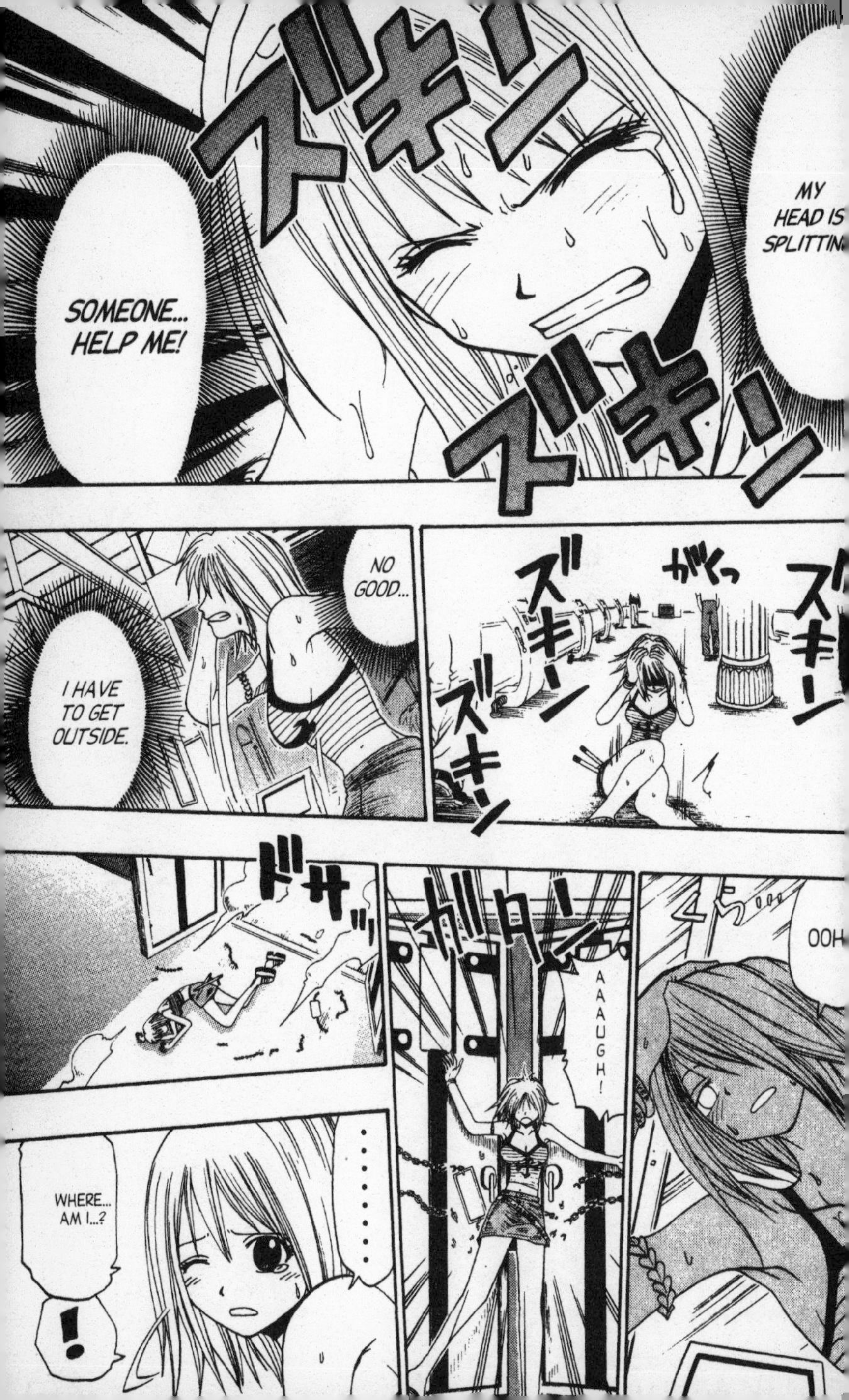
MY HEAD IS SPLITTIN
ズキン
ズキン
SOMEONE... HELP ME!
ズキン
がくっ
ズキン
ズキン
NO GOOD...
I HAVE TO GET OUTSIDE.
くら...
OOH
ガタン
AAAUGH!
ドサッ
......
WHERE... AM I...?
!

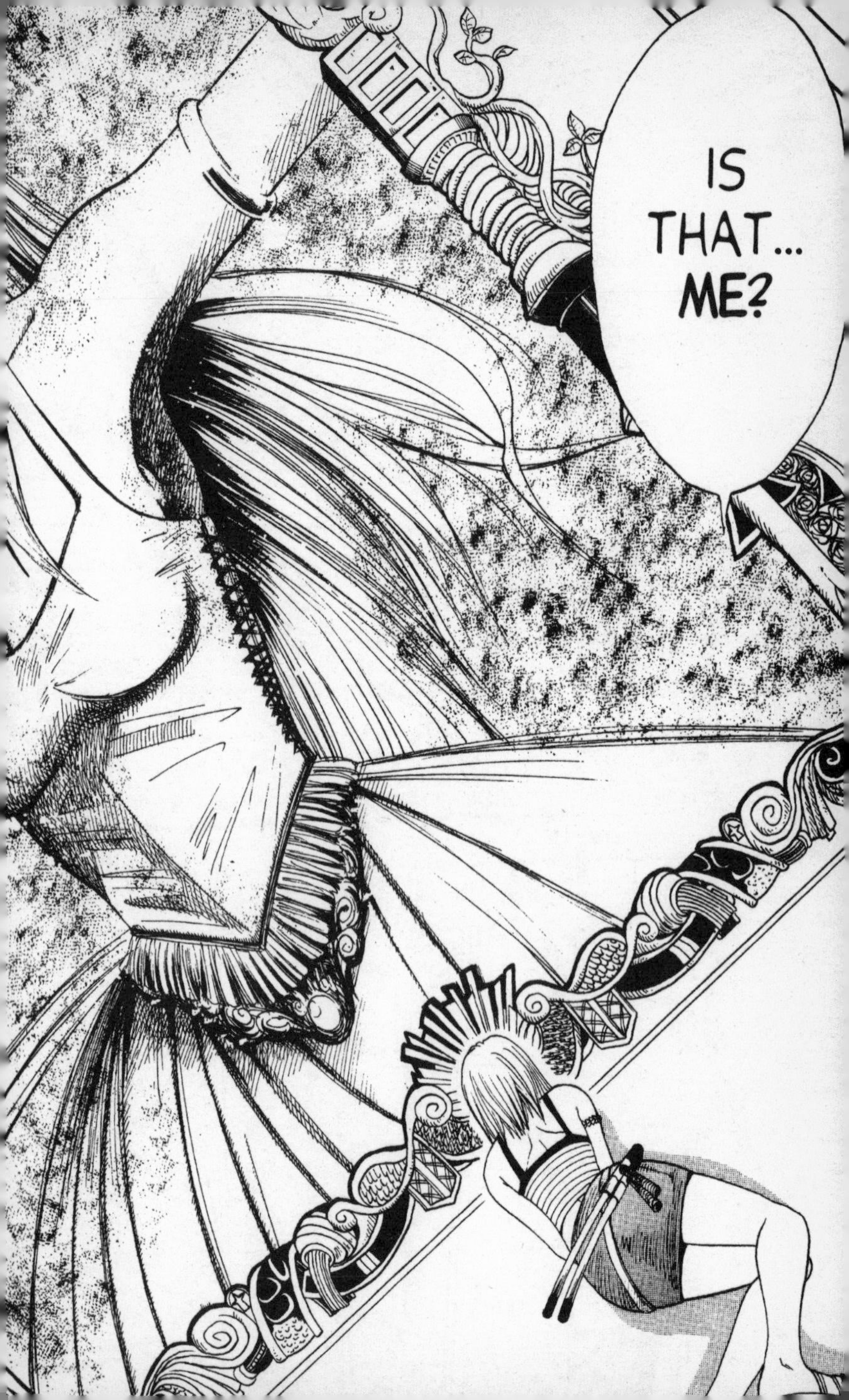
IS THAT... ME?

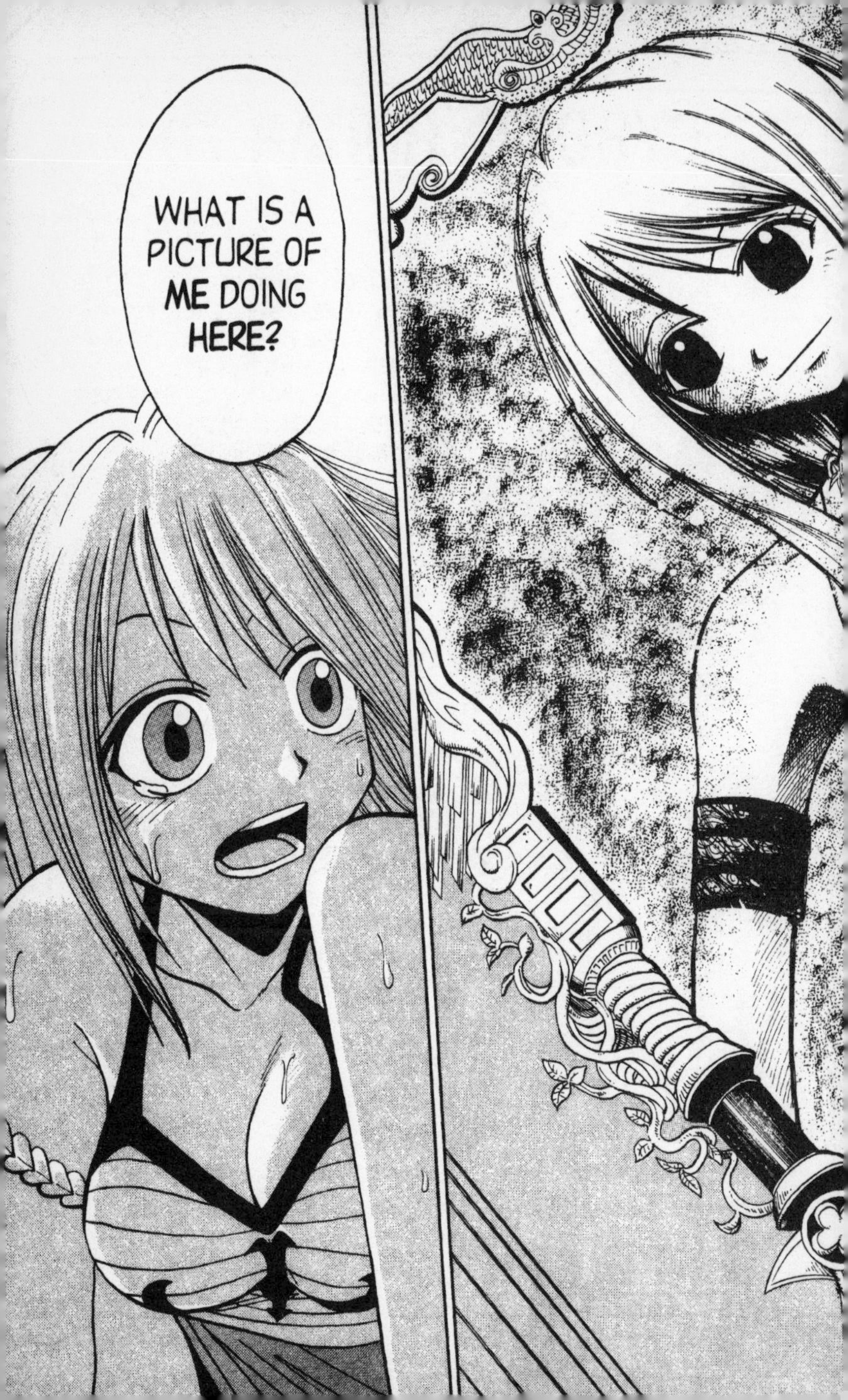
WHAT IS A PICTURE OF ME DOING HERE?

CYBORG: RUGAR 70

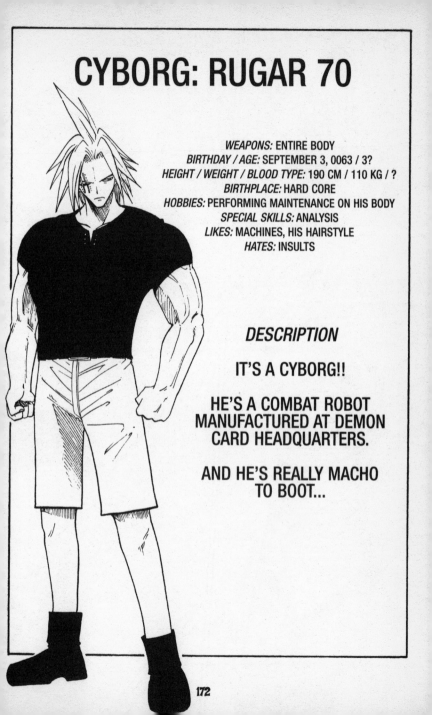

WEAPONS: ENTIRE BODY
BIRTHDAY / AGE: SEPTEMBER 3, 0063 / 3?
HEIGHT / WEIGHT / BLOOD TYPE: 190 CM / 110 KG / ?
BIRTHPLACE: HARD CORE
HOBBIES: PERFORMING MAINTENANCE ON HIS BODY
SPECIAL SKILLS: ANALYSIS
LIKES: MACHINES, HIS HAIRSTYLE
HATES: INSULTS

DESCRIPTION

IT'S A CYBORG!!

HE'S A COMBAT ROBOT
MANUFACTURED AT DEMON
CARD HEADQUARTERS.

AND HE'S REALLY MACHO
TO BOOT...

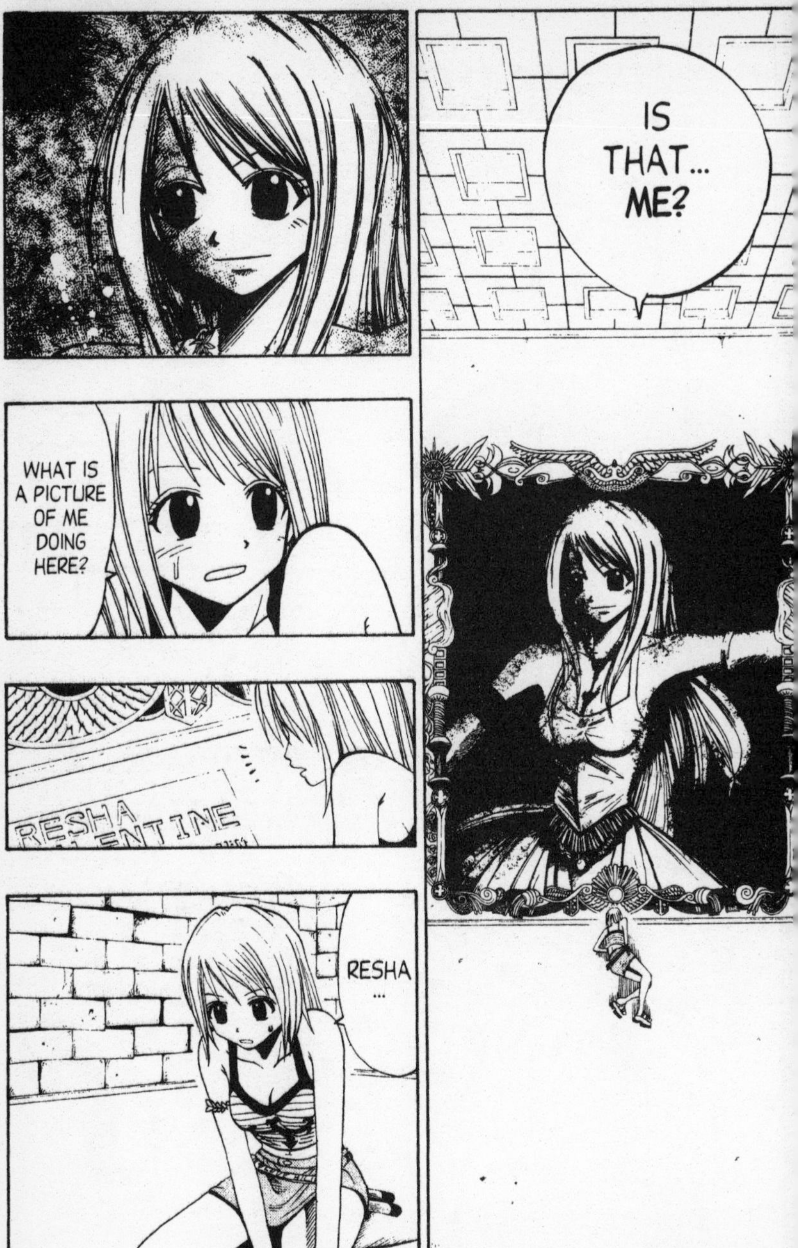
IS THAT... ME?
WHAT IS A PICTURE OF ME DOING HERE?
RESHA
RESHA ...

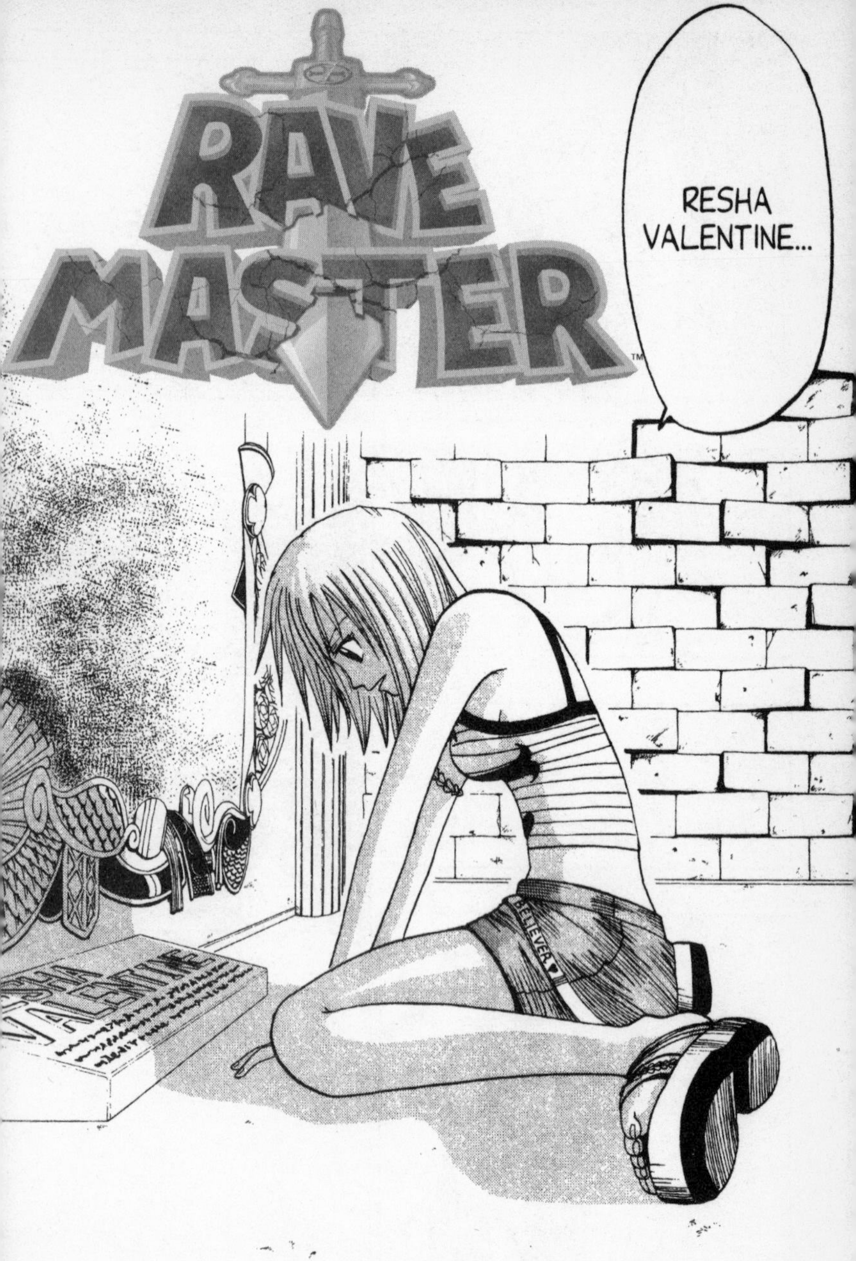
RAVE MASTER
RESHA VALENTINE...
BELIEVER

RAVE: 39 ✠ ELIE AND RESHA

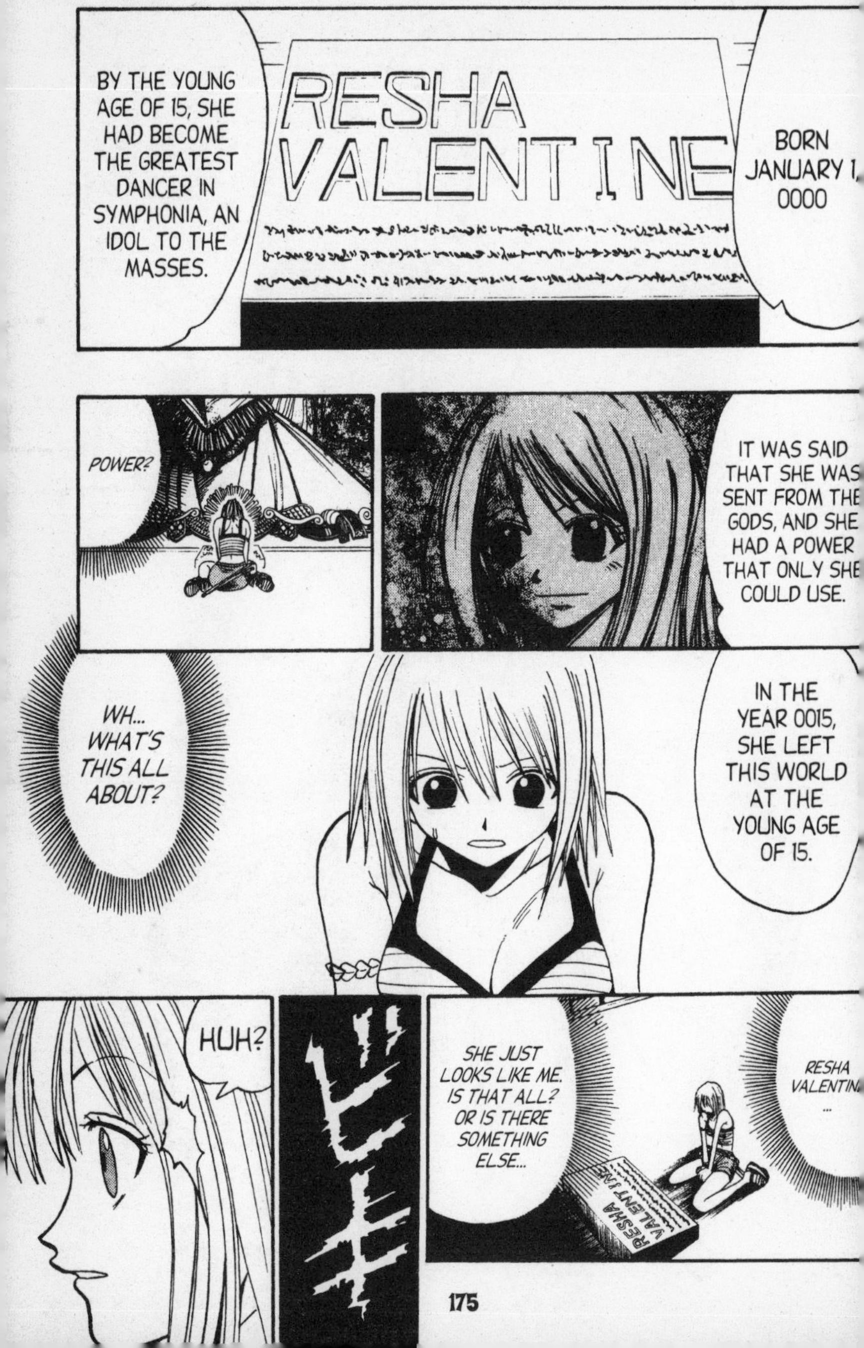
BORN JANUARY 1, 0000
RESHA VALENTINE
BY THE YOUNG AGE OF 15, SHE HAD BECOME THE GREATEST DANCER IN SYMPHONIA, AN IDOL TO THE MASSES.
IT WAS SAID THAT SHE WAS SENT FROM THE GODS, AND SHE HAD A POWER THAT ONLY SHE COULD USE.
POWER?
IN THE YEAR 0015, SHE LEFT THIS WORLD AT THE YOUNG AGE OF 15.
WH... WHAT'S THIS ALL ABOUT?
RESHA VALENTIN...
SHE JUST LOOKS LIKE ME. IS THAT ALL? OR IS THERE SOMETHING ELSE...
RESHA VALENTINE
HUH?

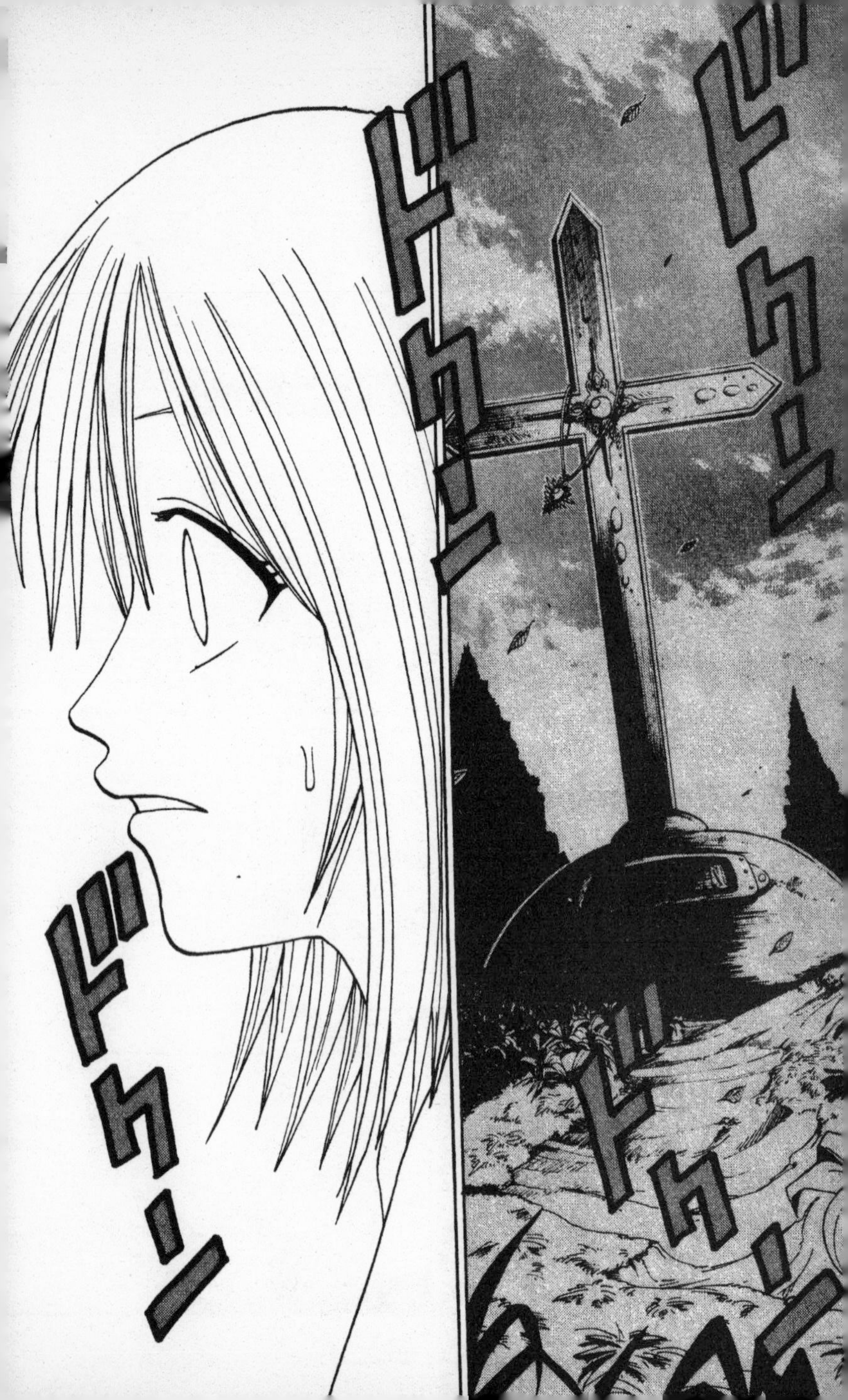
ドクーン
ドクーン
ドクーン
ドクーン

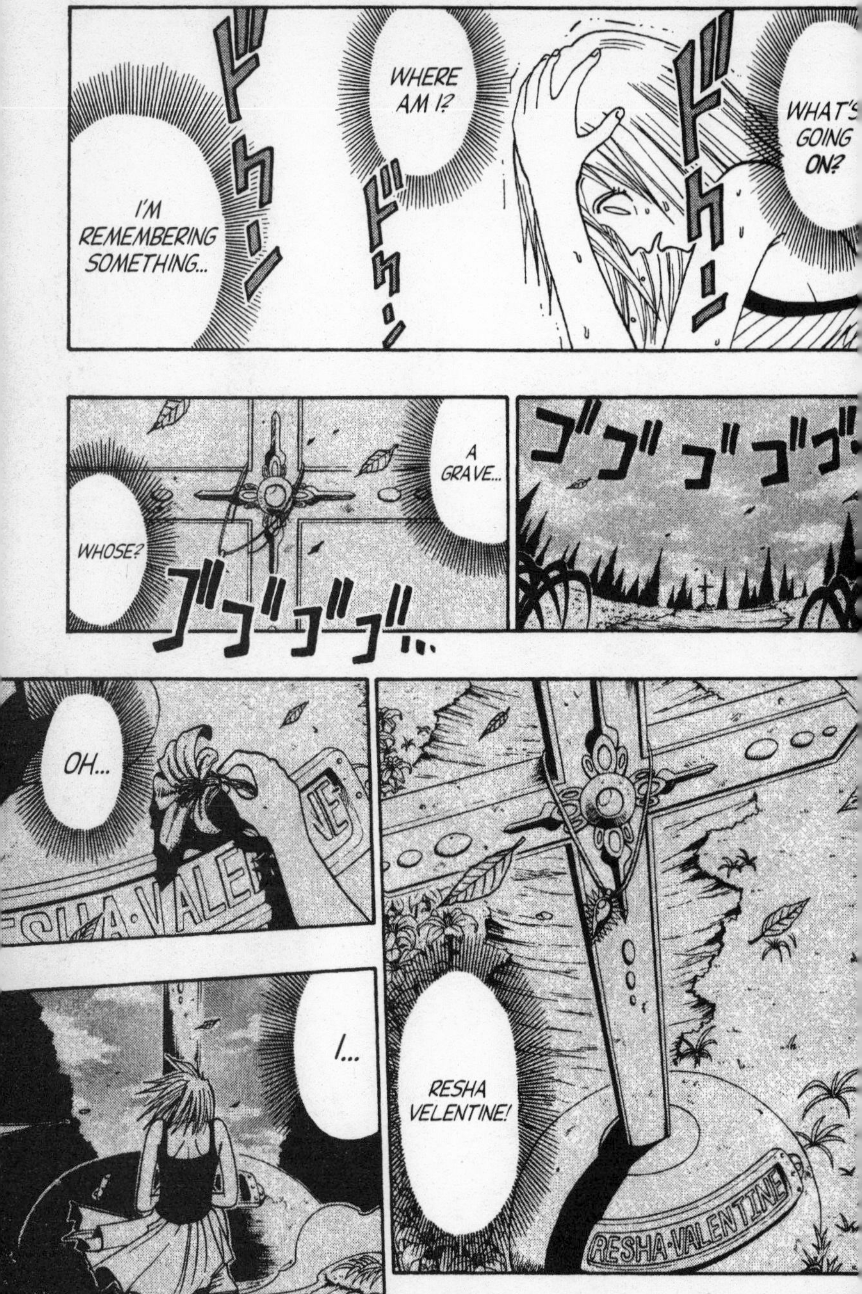

WHAT'S GOING ON?
ドクン
WHERE AM I?
ドクン
I'M REMEMBERING SOMETHING...
ドクン
ゴゴゴゴ
A GRAVE...
WHOSE?
ゴゴゴゴ
RESHA VELENTINE!
RESHA·VALENTINE
OH...
I...

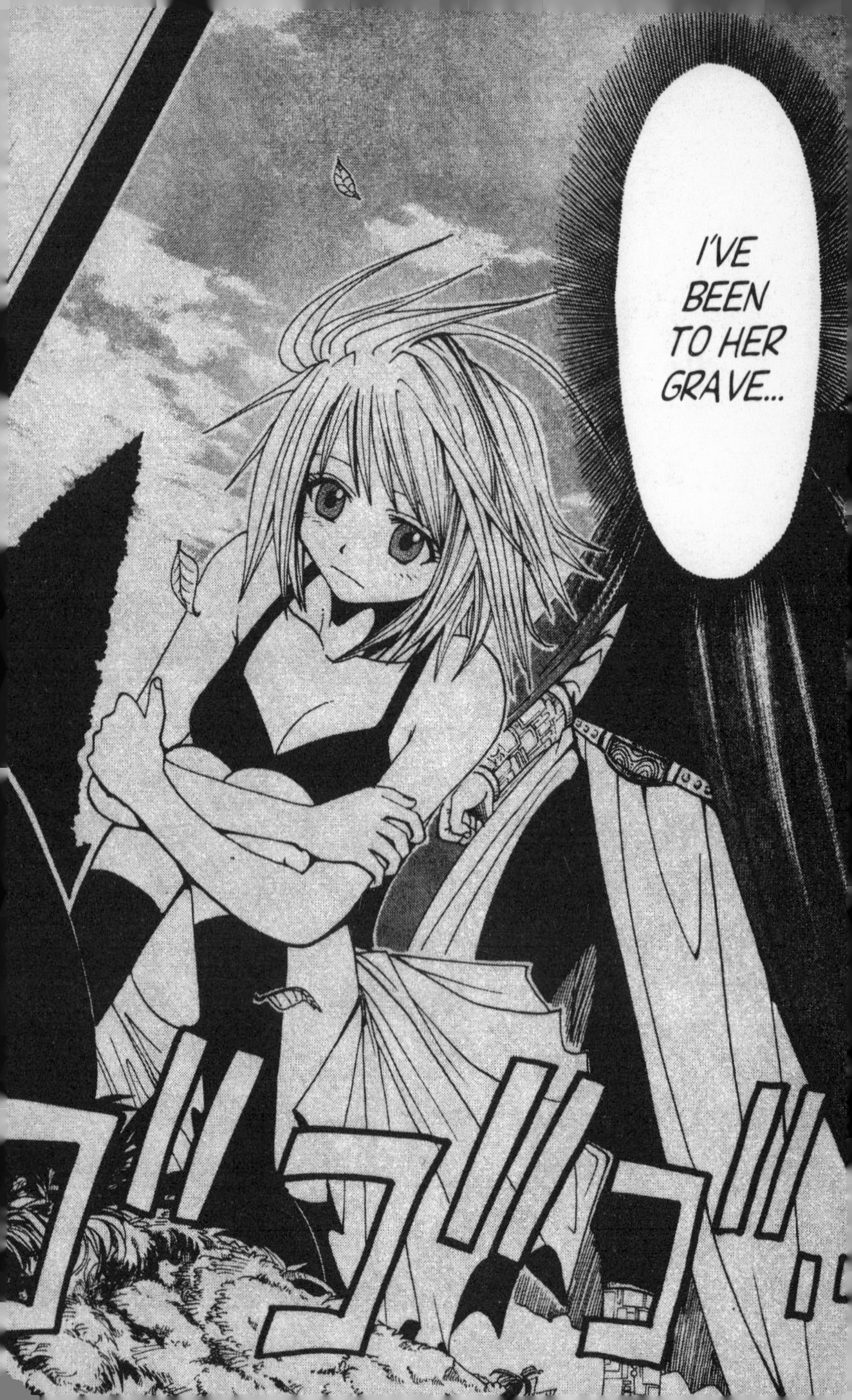
I'VE BEEN TO HER GRAVE...

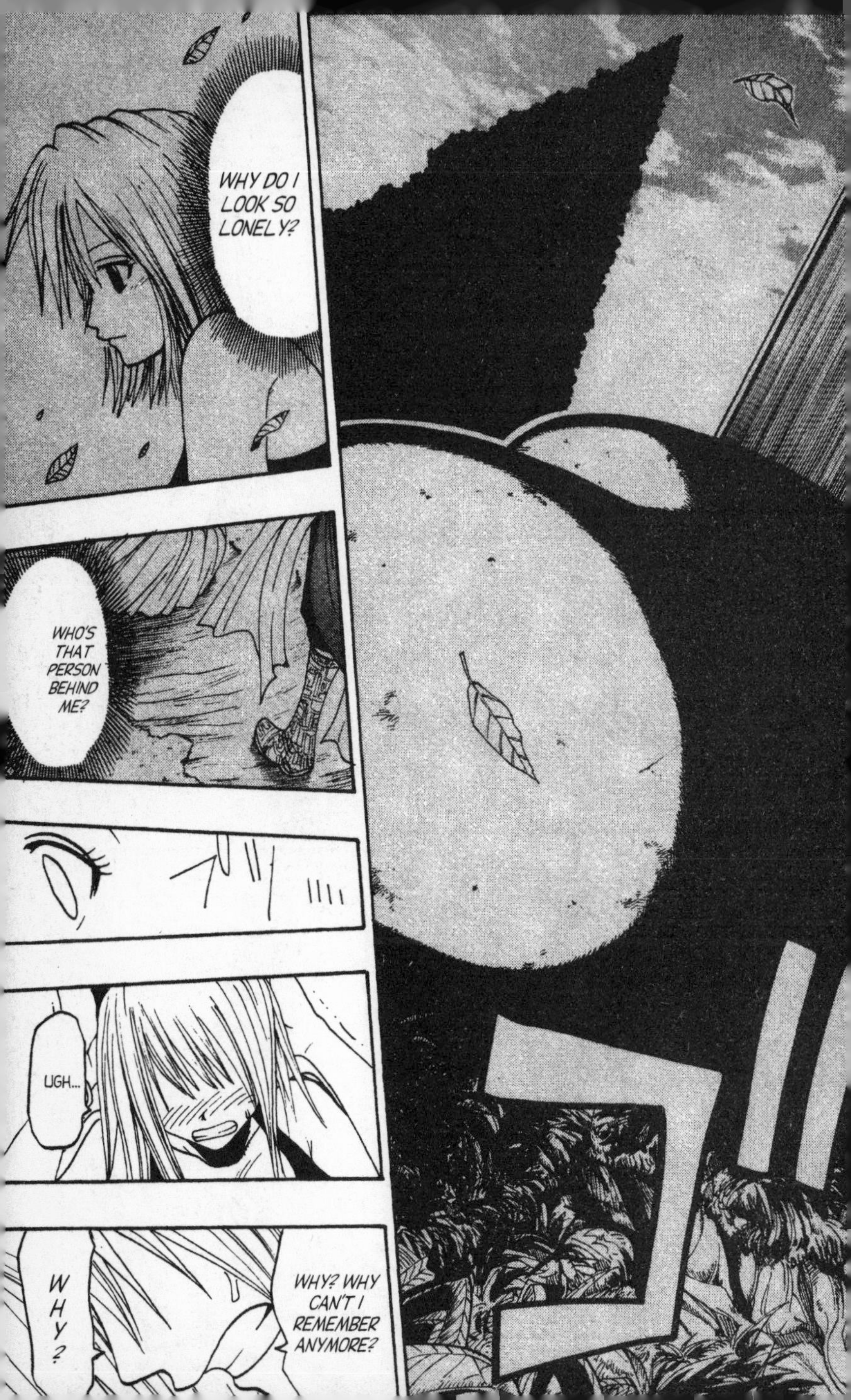
WHY DO I LOOK SO LONELY?
WHO'S THAT PERSON BEHIND ME?
UGH...
WHY? WHY CAN'T I REMEMBER ANYMORE?
WHY?

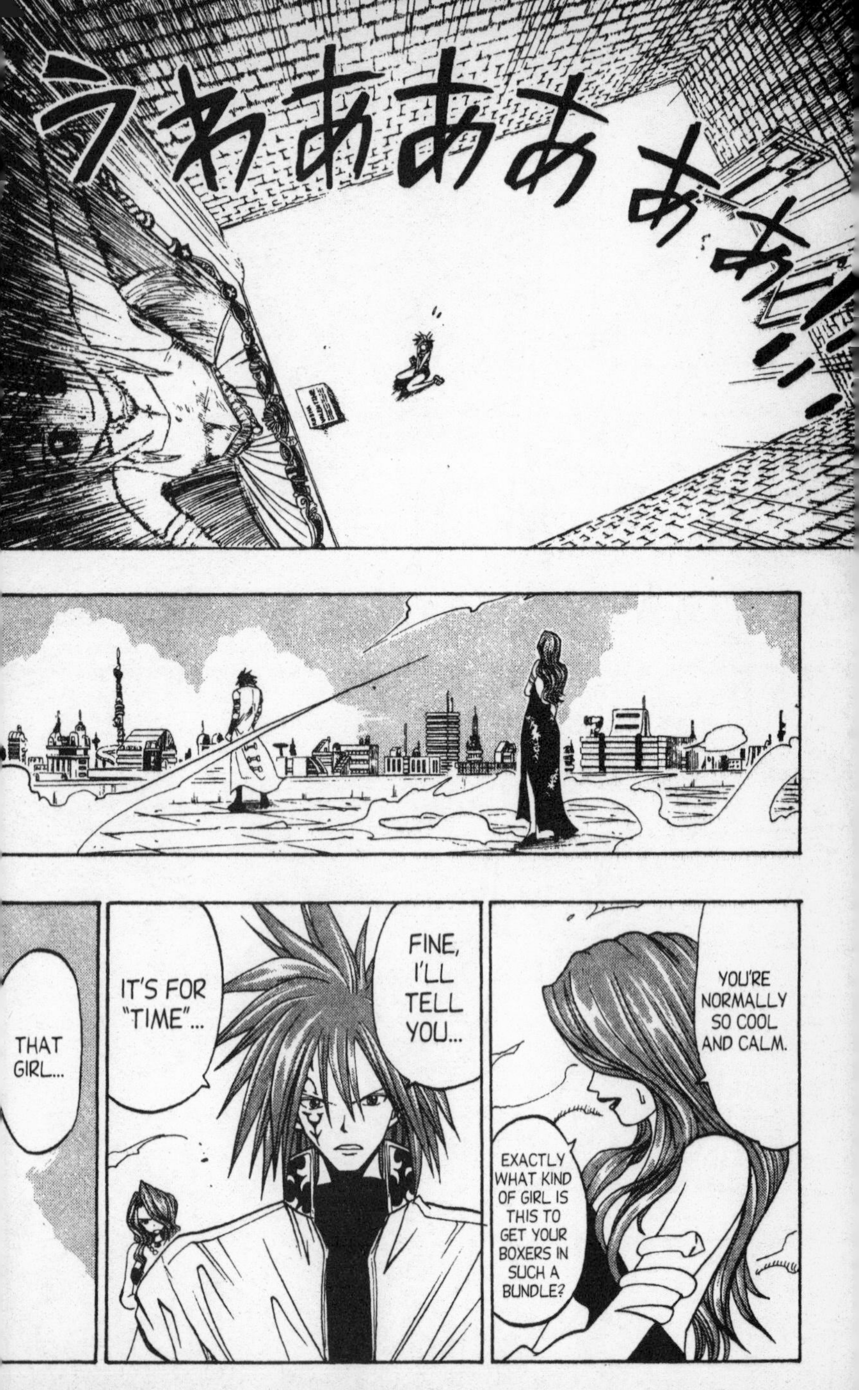
うわあああああ!!!
YOU'RE NORMALLY SO COOL AND CALM.
EXACTLY WHAT KIND OF GIRL IS THIS TO GET YOUR BOXERS IN SUCH A BUNDLE?
FINE, I'LL TELL YOU...
IT'S FOR "TIME"...
THAT GIRL...

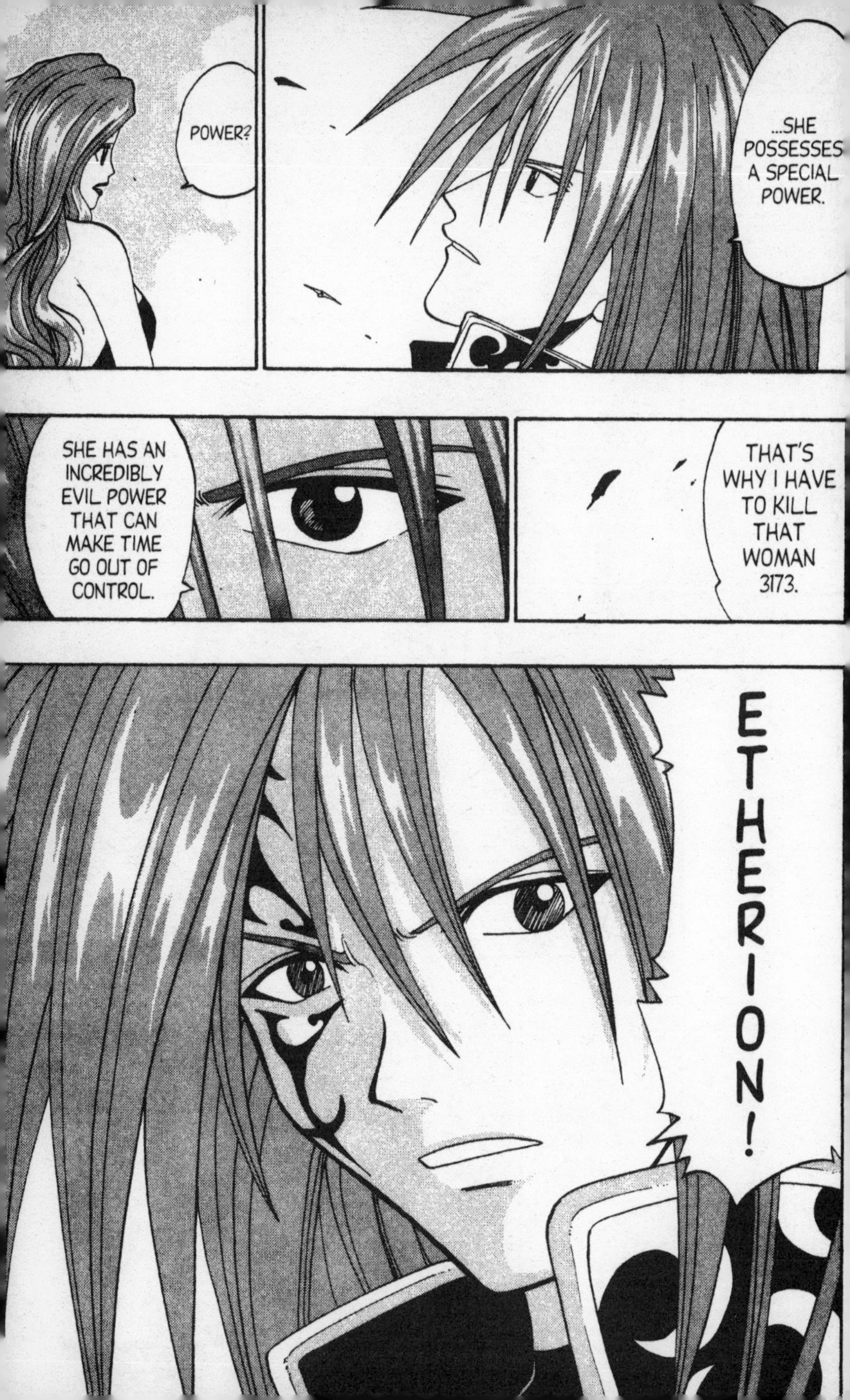

...SHE POSSESSES A SPECIAL POWER.
POWER?
THAT'S WHY I HAVE TO KILL THAT WOMAN 3173.
SHE HAS AN INCREDIBLY EVIL POWER THAT CAN MAKE TIME GO OUT OF CONTROL.
ETHERION!

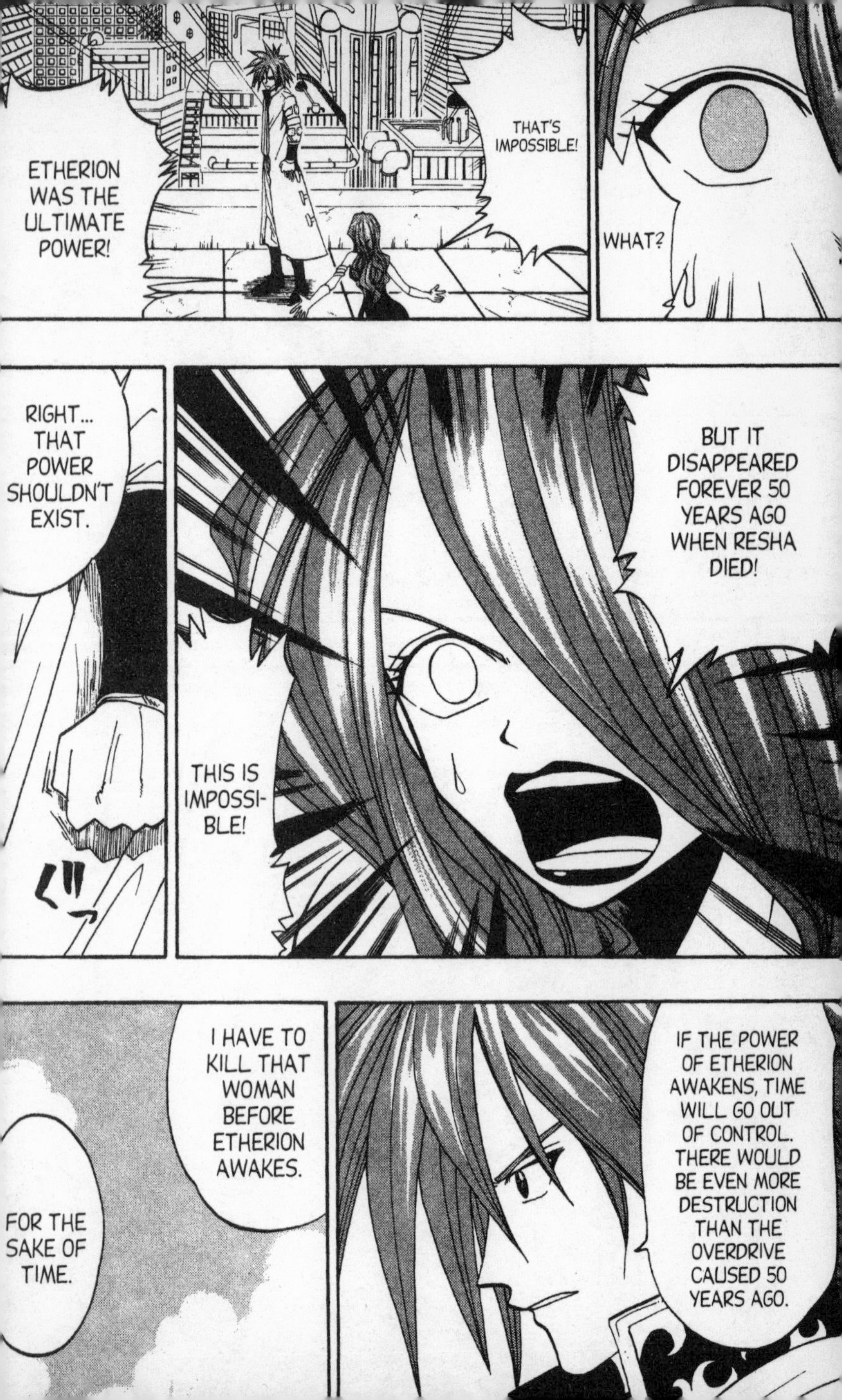
WHAT?
THAT'S IMPOSSIBLE!
ETHERION WAS THE ULTIMATE POWER!
BUT IT DISAPPEARED FOREVER 50 YEARS AGO WHEN RESHA DIED!
THIS IS IMPOSSI-BLE!
RIGHT... THAT POWER SHOULDN'T EXIST.
IF THE POWER OF ETHERION AWAKENS, TIME WILL GO OUT OF CONTROL. THERE WOULD BE EVEN MORE DESTRUCTION THAN THE OVERDRIVE CAUSED 50 YEARS AGO.
I HAVE TO KILL THAT WOMAN BEFORE ETHERION AWAKES.
FOR THE SAKE OF TIME.

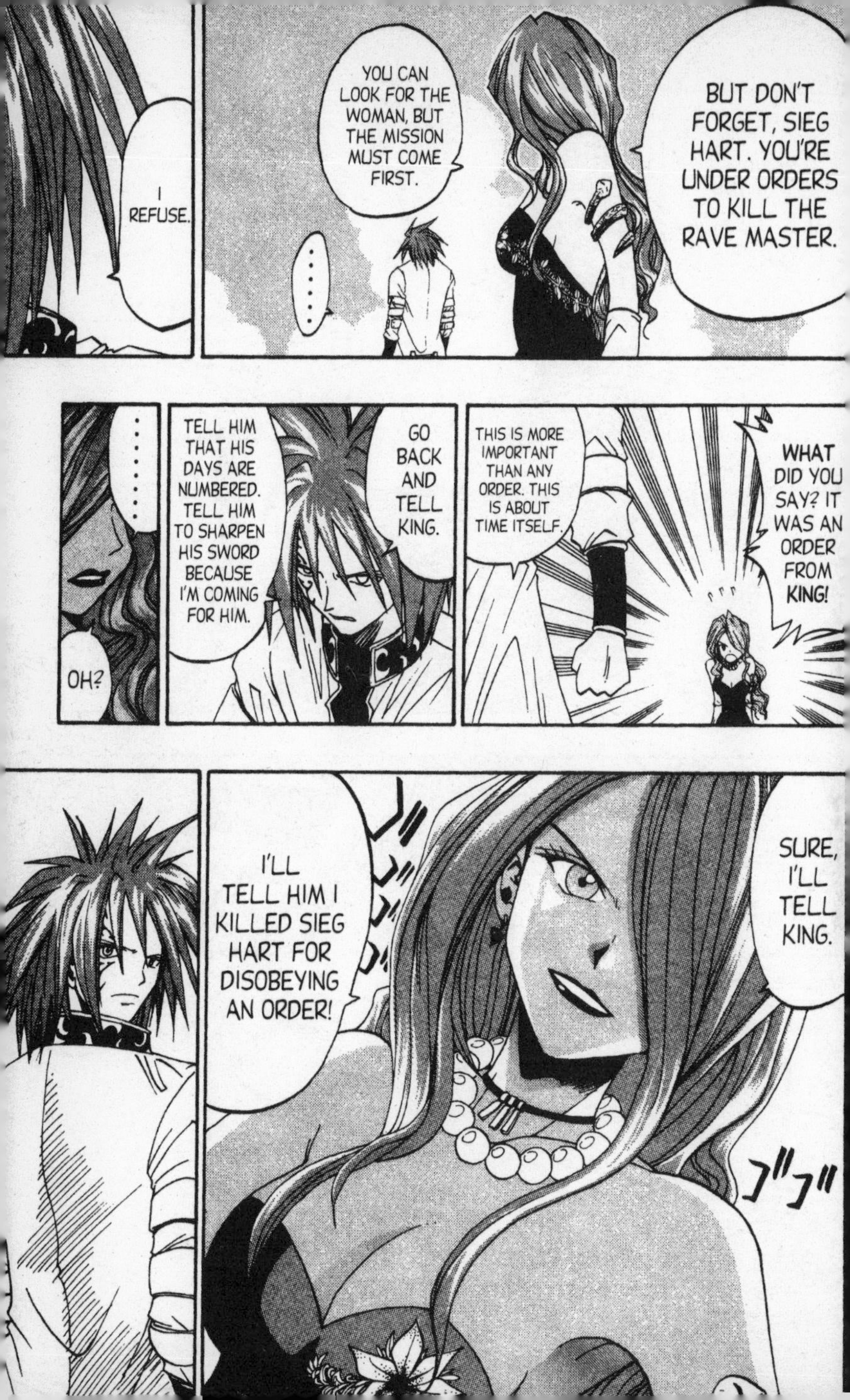
BUT DON'T FORGET, SIEG HART. YOU'RE UNDER ORDERS TO KILL THE RAVE MASTER.
YOU CAN LOOK FOR THE WOMAN, BUT THE MISSION MUST COME FIRST.
......
I REFUSE.
WHAT DID YOU SAY? IT WAS AN ORDER FROM KING!
THIS IS MORE IMPORTANT THAN ANY ORDER. THIS IS ABOUT TIME ITSELF.
GO BACK AND TELL KING.
TELL HIM THAT HIS DAYS ARE NUMBERED. TELL HIM TO SHARPEN HIS SWORD BECAUSE I'M COMING FOR HIM.
....
OH?
SURE, I'LL TELL KING.
ゴゴ
I'LL TELL HIM I KILLED SIEG HART FOR DISOBEYING AN ORDER!

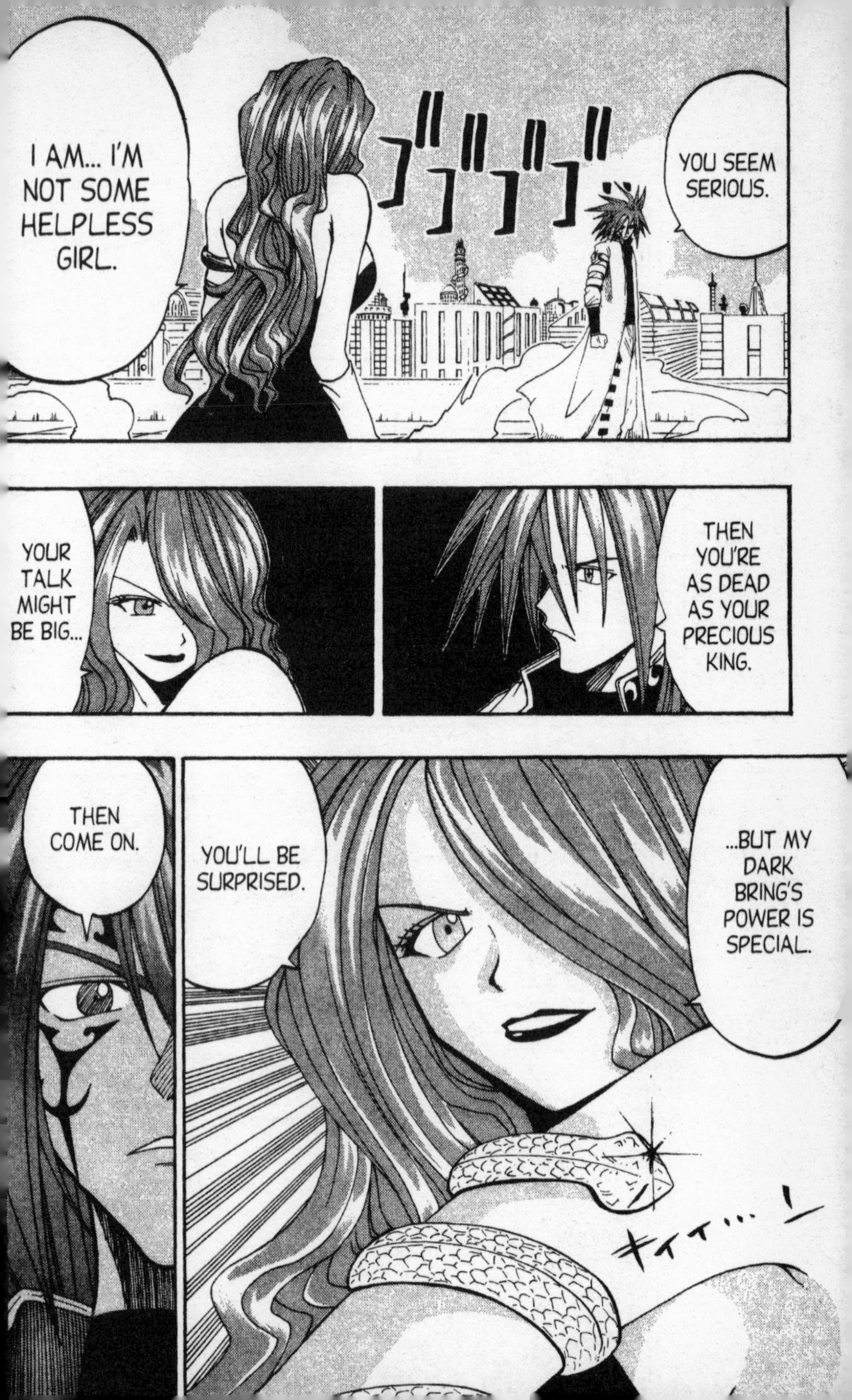
YOU SEEM SERIOUS.
I AM... I'M NOT SOME HELPLESS GIRL.
THEN YOU'RE AS DEAD AS YOUR PRECIOUS KING.
YOUR TALK MIGHT BE BIG...
...BUT MY DARK BRING'S POWER IS SPECIAL.
YOU'LL BE SURPRISED.
THEN COME ON.

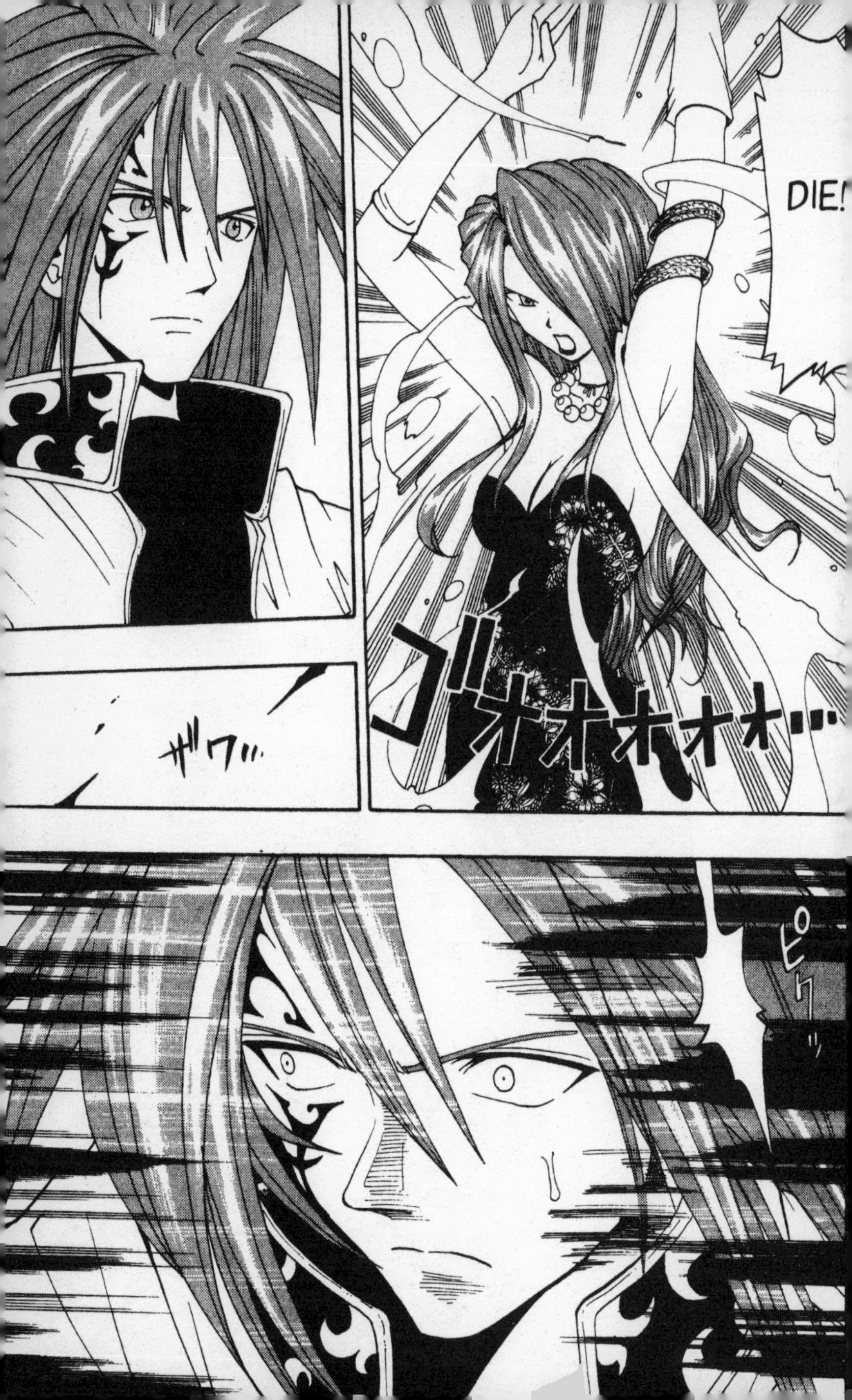
DIE!
ゴオオオオオ…
ザワ
ピクッ

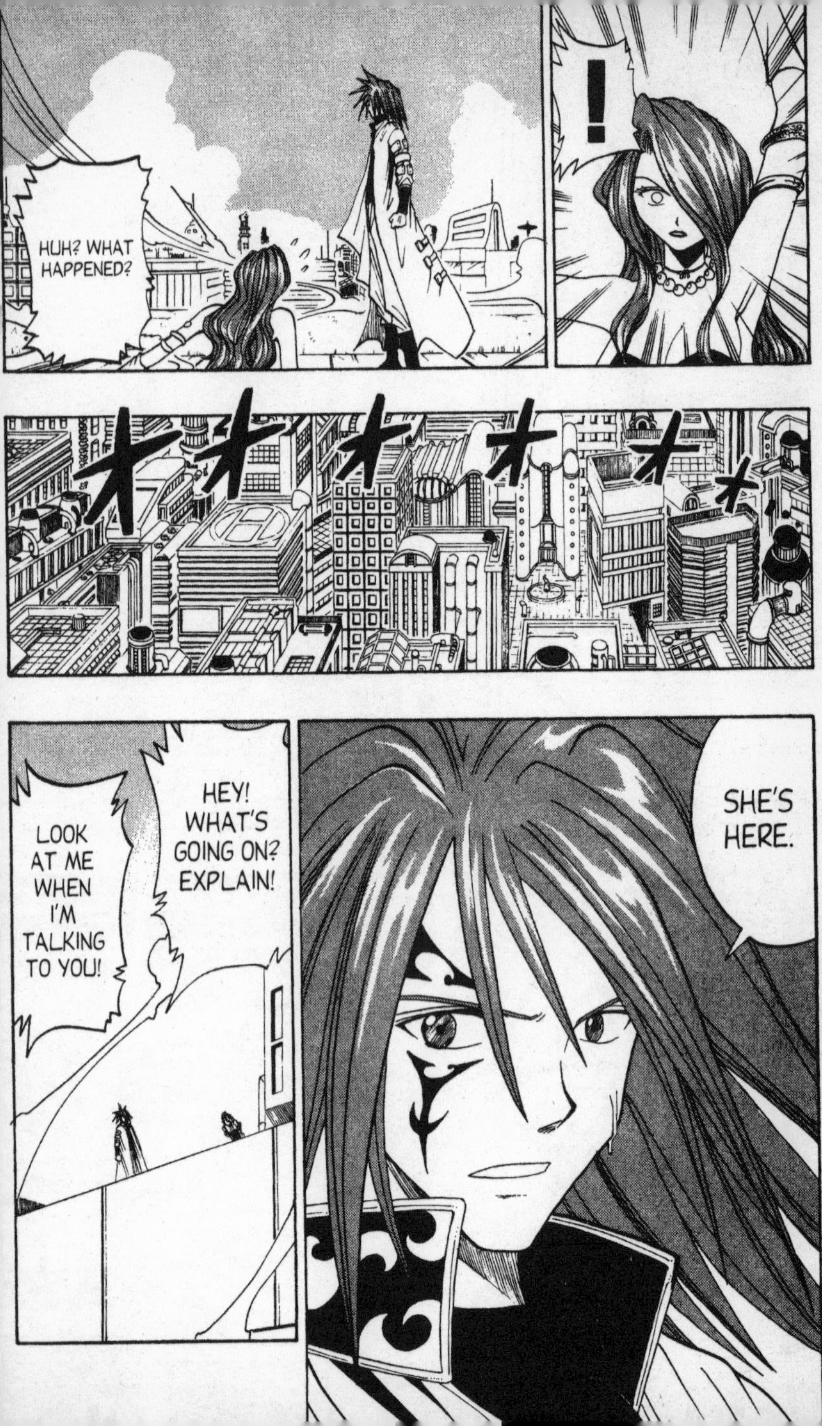
!
HUH? WHAT HAPPENED?
SHE'S HERE.
HEY! WHAT'S GOING ON? EXPLAIN!
LOOK AT ME WHEN I'M TALKING TO YOU!

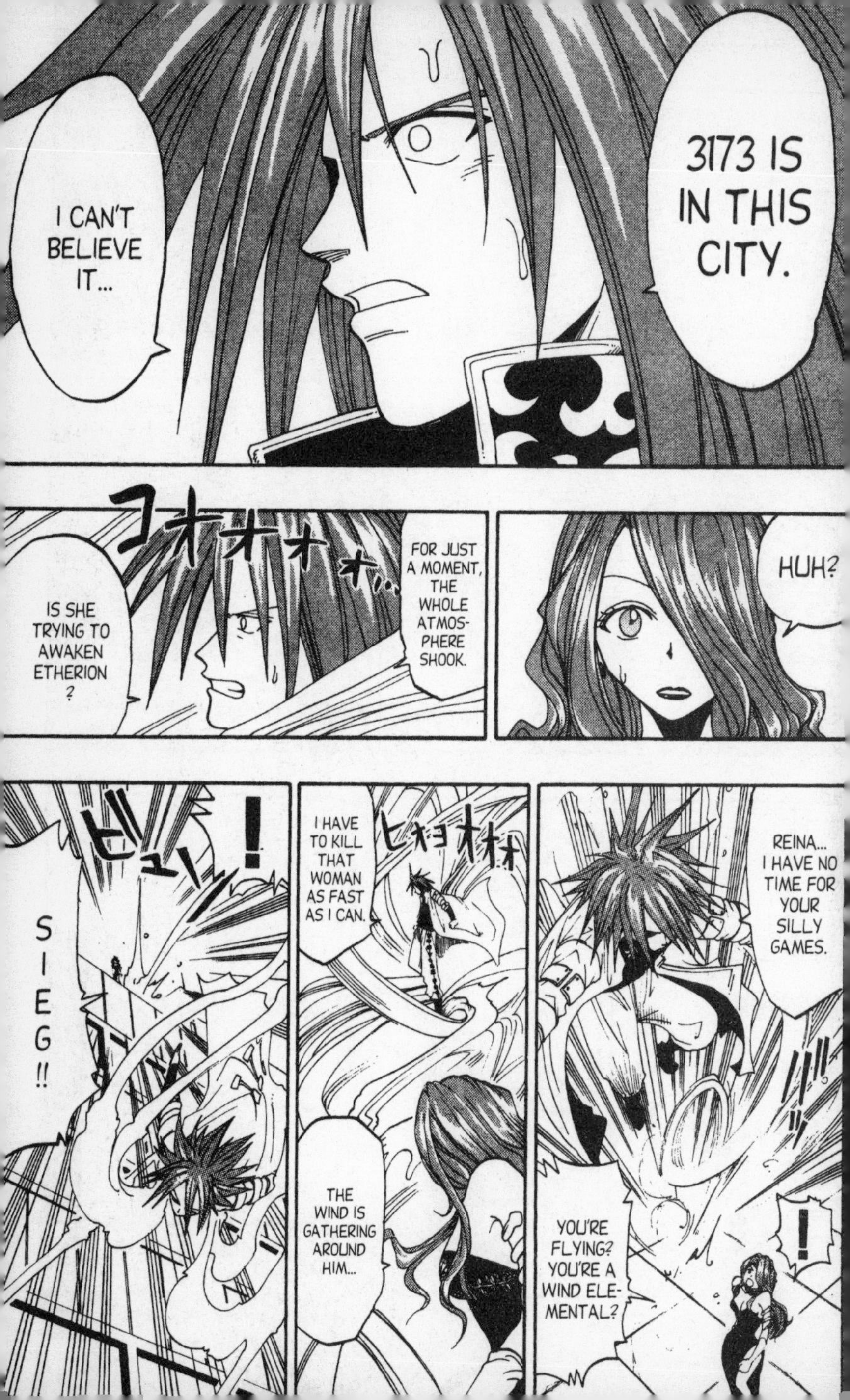

3173 IS IN THIS CITY.
I CAN'T BELIEVE IT...
HUH?
FOR JUST A MOMENT, THE WHOLE ATMOSPHERE SHOOK.
IS SHE TRYING TO AWAKEN ETHERION?
REINA... I HAVE NO TIME FOR YOUR SILLY GAMES.
!
YOU'RE FLYING? YOU'RE A WIND ELEMENTAL?
I HAVE TO KILL THAT WOMAN AS FAST AS I CAN.
THE WIND IS GATHERING AROUND HIM...
!
SIEG!!

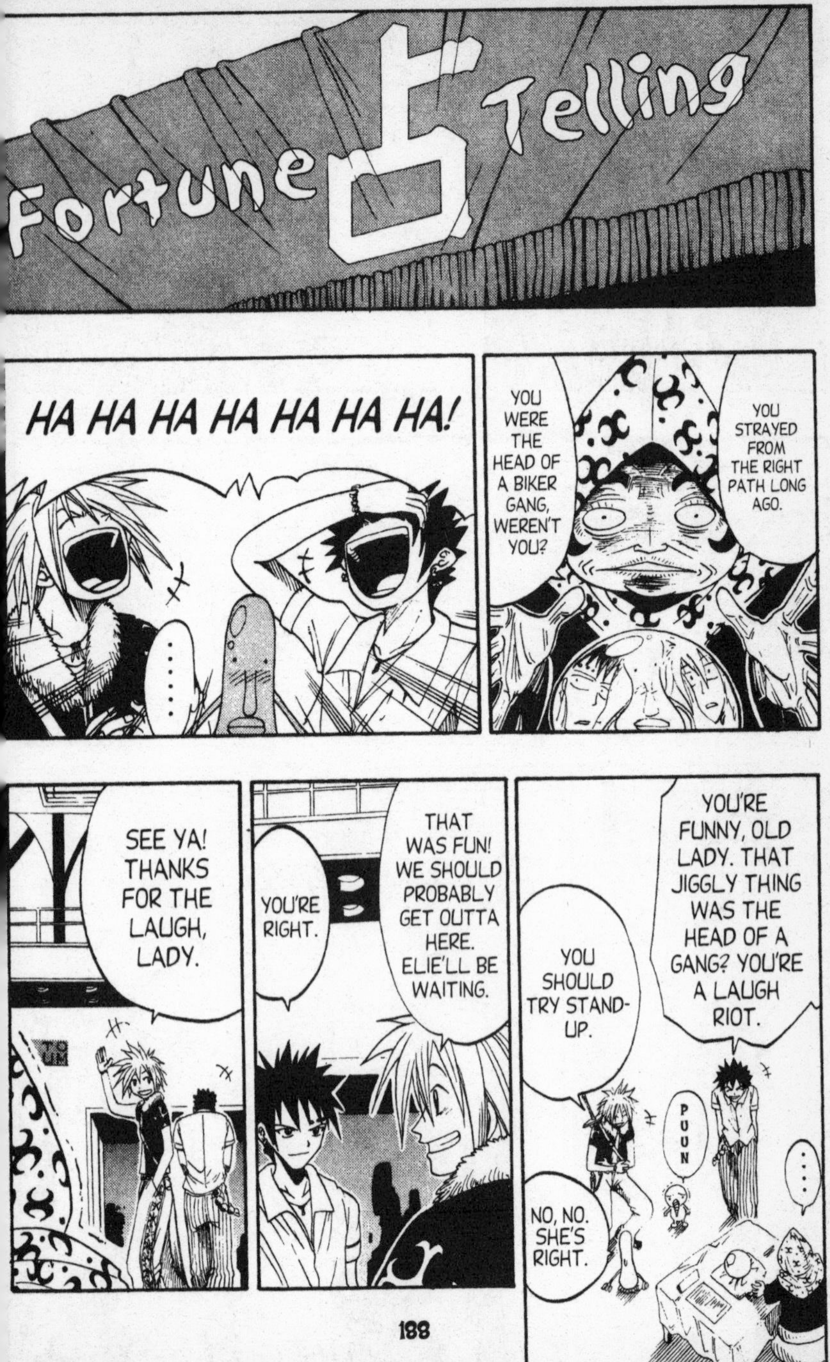

Fortune 占 Telling
YOU STRAYED FROM THE RIGHT PATH LONG AGO.
YOU WERE THE HEAD OF A BIKER GANG, WEREN'T YOU?
HA HA HA HA HA HA HA!
......
YOU'RE FUNNY, OLD LADY. THAT JIGGLY THING WAS THE HEAD OF A GANG? YOU'RE A LAUGH RIOT.
YOU SHOULD TRY STAND-UP.
PUUN
....
NO, NO. SHE'S RIGHT.
THAT WAS FUN! WE SHOULD PROBABLY GET OUTTA HERE. ELIE'LL BE WAITING.
YOU'RE RIGHT.
SEE YA! THANKS FOR THE LAUGH, LADY.

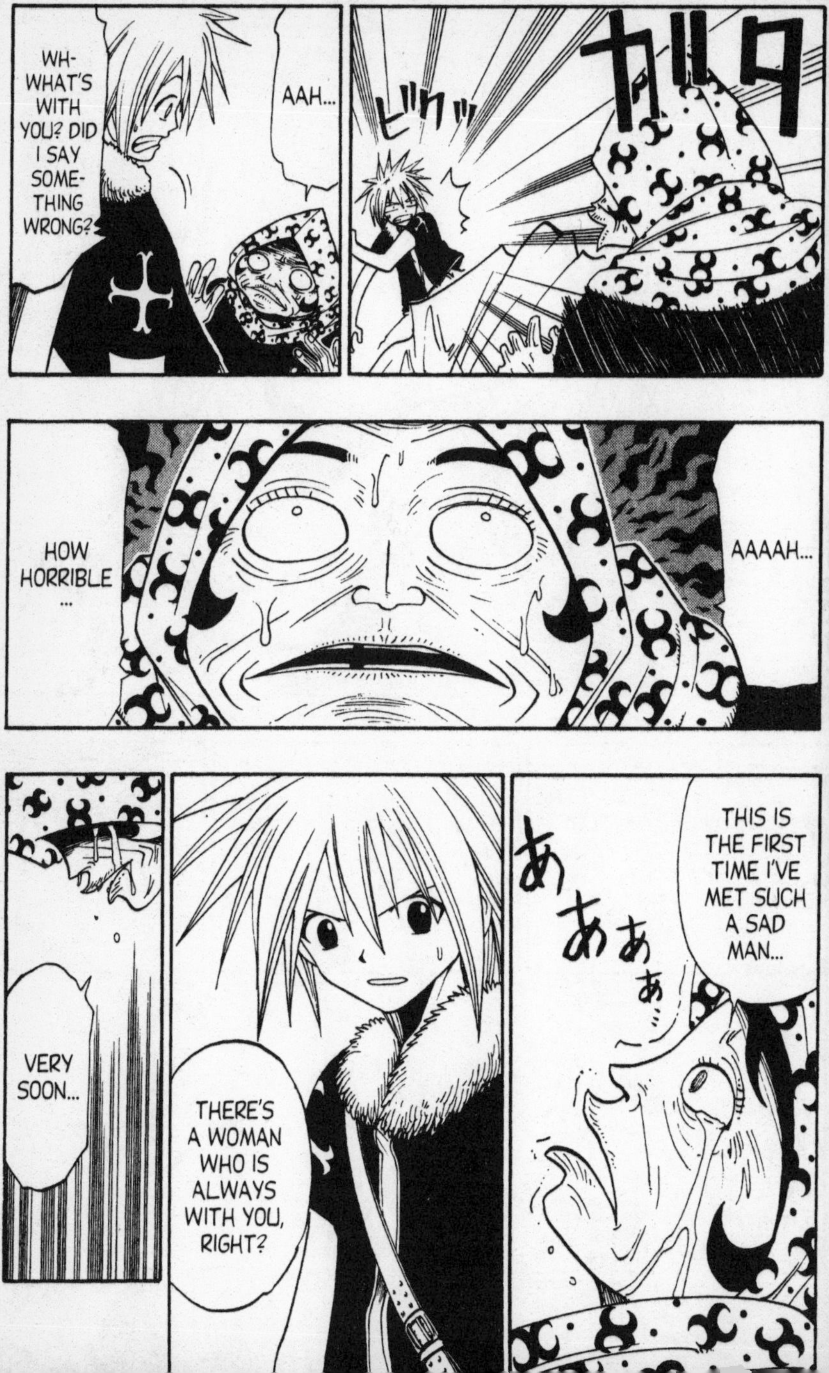
ビクッ
AAH...
WH- WHAT'S WITH YOU? DID I SAY SOME-THING WRONG?
AAAAH...
HOW HORRIBLE ...
あああぁ
THIS IS THE FIRST TIME I'VE MET SUCH A SAD MAN...
THERE'S A WOMAN WHO IS ALWAYS WITH YOU, RIGHT?
VERY SOON...

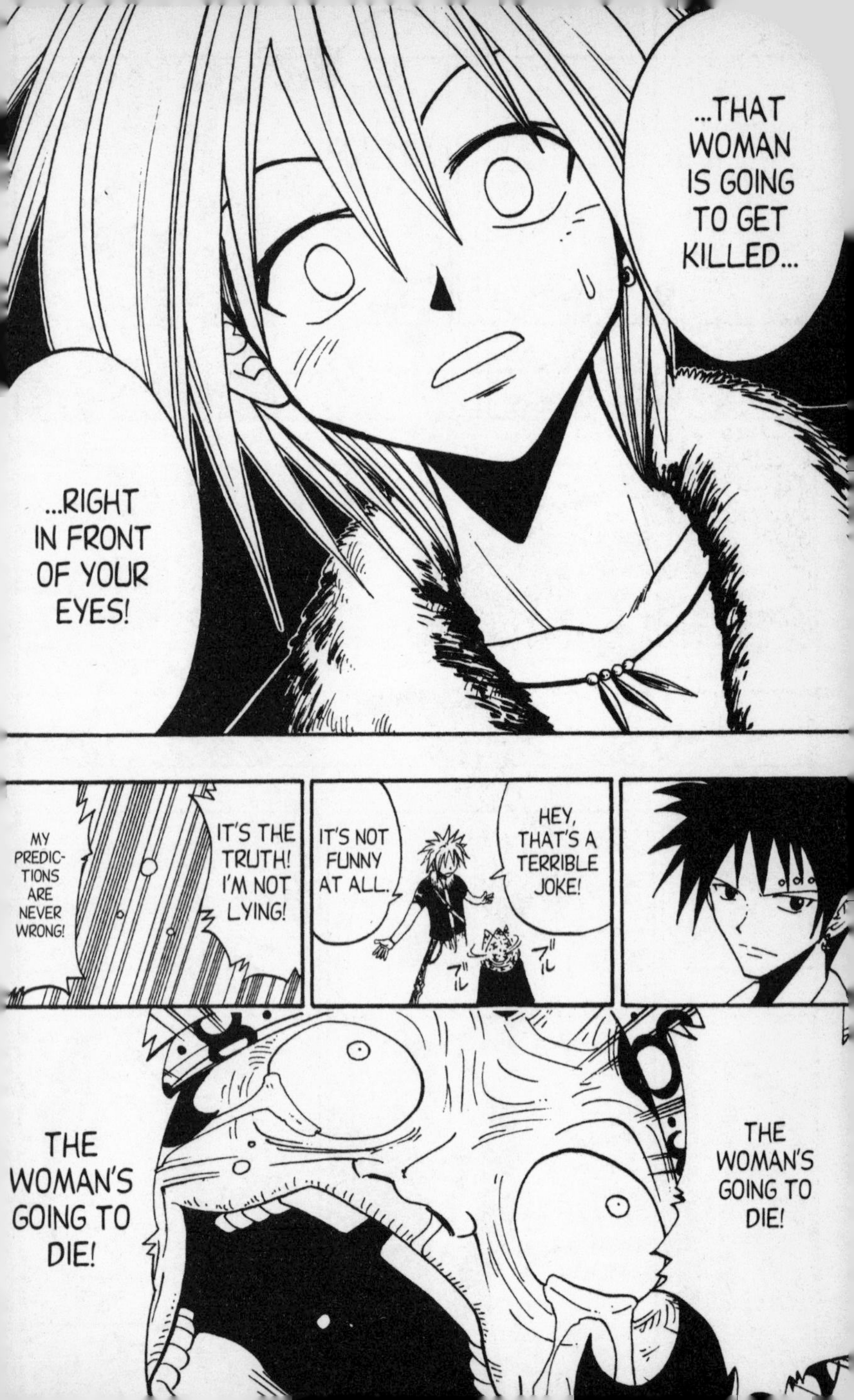
...THAT WOMAN IS GOING TO GET KILLED...
...RIGHT IN FRONT OF YOUR EYES!
HEY, THAT'S A TERRIBLE JOKE!
IT'S NOT FUNNY AT ALL.
ブル
ブル
IT'S THE TRUTH! I'M NOT LYING!
MY PREDIC-TIONS ARE NEVER WRONG!
THE WOMAN'S GOING TO DIE!
THE WOMAN'S GOING TO DIE!

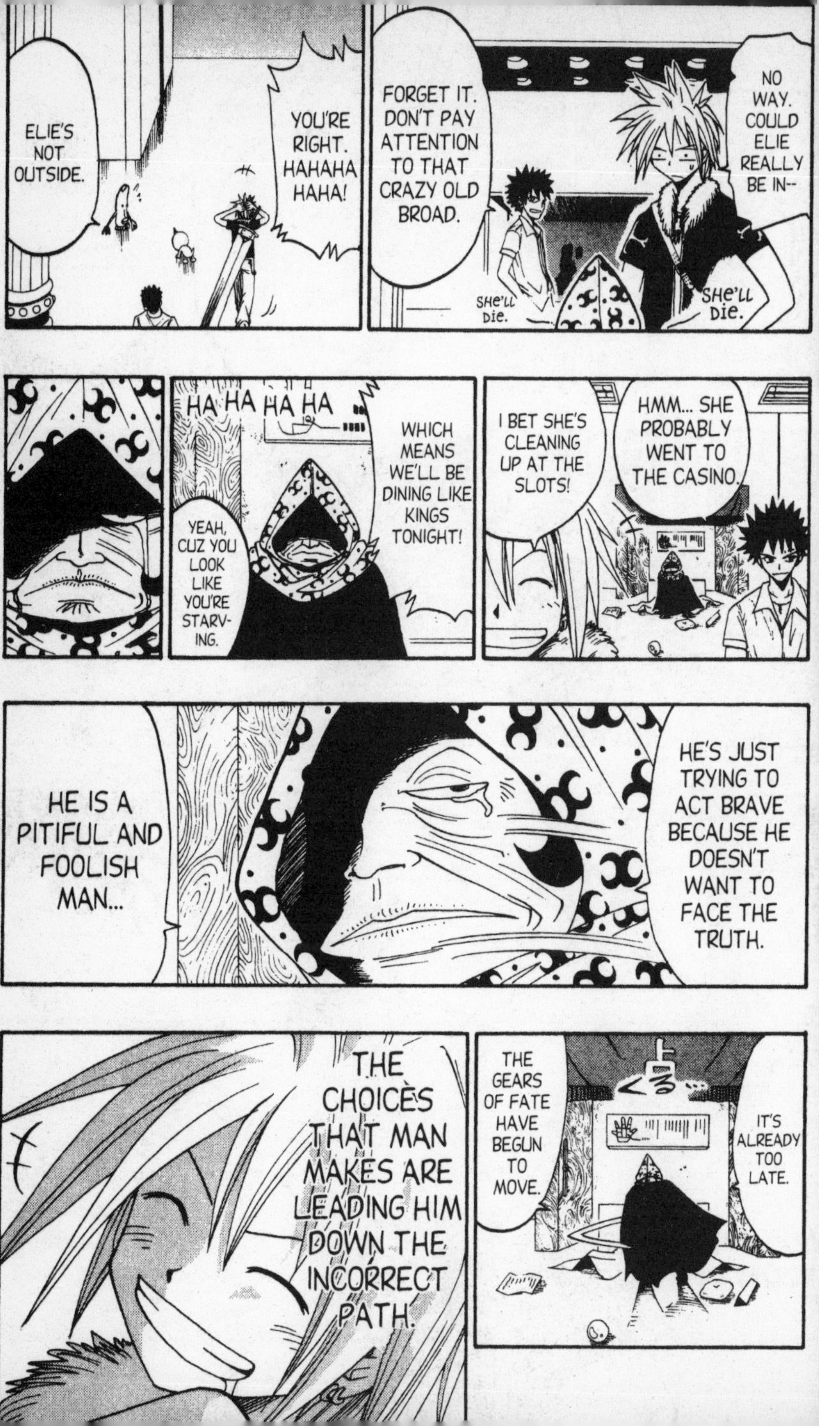
NO WAY. COULD ELIE REALLY BE IN--
SHE'LL DIE.
SHE'LL DIE.
FORGET IT. DON'T PAY ATTENTION TO THAT CRAZY OLD BROAD.
YOU'RE RIGHT. HAHAHA HAHA!
ELIE'S NOT OUTSIDE.
HMM... SHE PROBABLY WENT TO THE CASINO.
I BET SHE'S CLEANING UP AT THE SLOTS!
HA HA HA HA
WHICH MEANS WE'LL BE DINING LIKE KINGS TONIGHT!
YEAH, CUZ YOU LOOK LIKE YOU'RE STARV-ING.
HE'S JUST TRYING TO ACT BRAVE BECAUSE HE DOESN'T WANT TO FACE THE TRUTH.
HE IS A PITIFUL AND FOOLISH MAN...
IT'S ALREADY TOO LATE.
くる
THE GEARS OF FATE HAVE BEGUN TO MOVE.
THE CHOICES THAT MAN MAKES ARE LEADING HIM DOWN THE INCORRECT PATH.

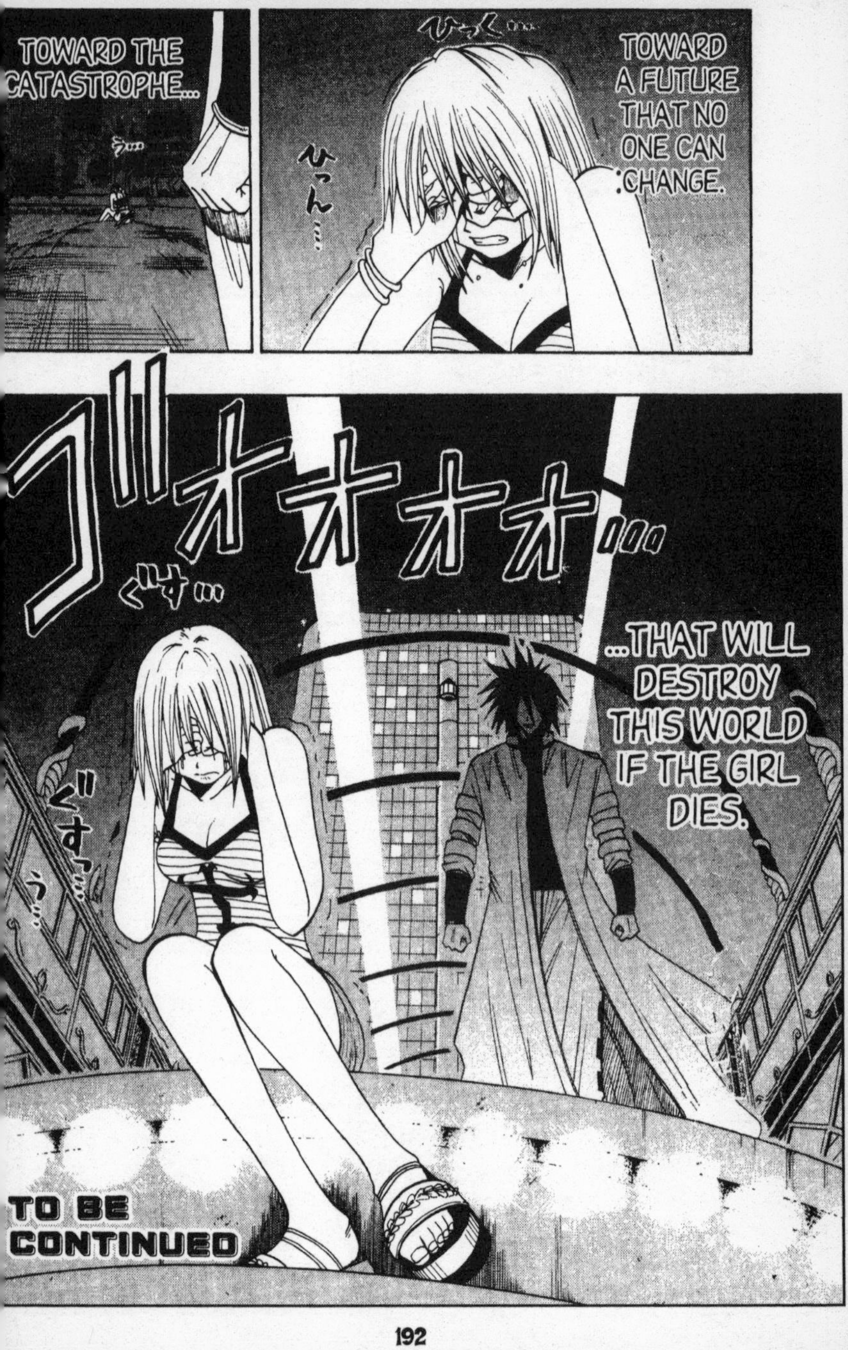
ひっく…
TOWARD A FUTURE THAT NO ONE CAN CHANGE.
ひっん…
TOWARD THE CATASTROPHE...
う…
ゴオオオオ…
ぐす…
...THAT WILL DESTROY THIS WORLD IF THE GIRL DIES.
ぐすっ…
う…
TO BE CONTINUED

THE GLUE MAN: POOSYA

WEAPONS: DARK BRING (GLUE TEAR)
BIRTHDAY / AGE: JANUARY 9, 0041 / 25
HEIGHT / WEIGHT / BLOOD TYPE: 147 CM / 71 KG / B
BIRTHPLACE: HIP HOP TOWN
HOBBIES: READING FUNNY BOOKS
SPECIAL SKILLS: PLASTIC MODELS
LIKES: REINA
TREASURE: HIS COLLECTION OF THINGS HE STOLE FROM REINA'S ROOM
HATES: ALL MEN

DESCRIPTION

THIS GUY IS THE ENEMY OF ALL WOMEN. I THOUGHT IT MIGHT BE INTERESTING TO FACE HIM OFF AGAINST GRIFF (ANOTHER PERVERT), BUT I ENDED UP KILLING THAT IDEA.

BY THE WAY, DID YOU REALIZE THAT HE SHOWED UP IN CHAPTER 3 (VOLUME 1) TOO?

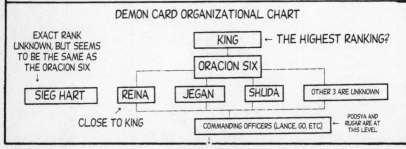

DEMON CARD ORGANIZATIONAL CHART
KING
← THE HIGHEST RANKING?
ORACION SIX
EXACT RANK UNKNOWN, BUT SEEMS TO BE THE SAME AS THE ORACION SIX
SIEG HART
REINA
JEGAN
SHUDA
OTHER 3 ARE UNKNOWN
CLOSE TO KING
COMMANDING OFFICERS (LANCE, GO, ETC)
← POOSYA AND RUGAR ARE AT THIS LEVEL
SMALL FRIES (GEORCO, ETC)

RAVE0077

Levin Minds the House 4: Let's Go Have Some Fun!

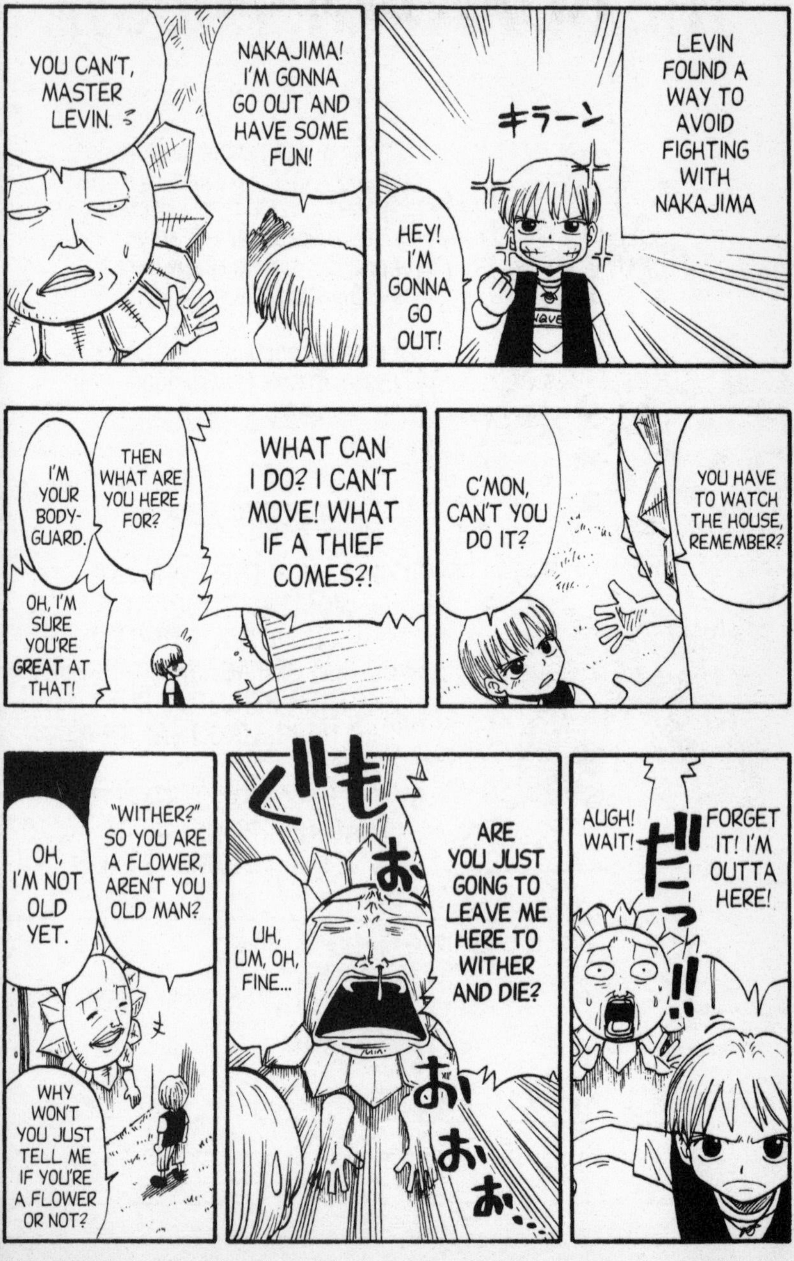
LEVIN FOUND A WAY TO AVOID FIGHTING WITH NAKAJIMA
キラーン
HEY! I'M GONNA GO OUT!
NAKAJIMA! I'M GONNA GO OUT AND HAVE SOME FUN!
YOU CAN'T, MASTER LEVIN.
YOU HAVE TO WATCH THE HOUSE, REMEMBER?
C'MON, CAN'T YOU DO IT?
WHAT CAN I DO? I CAN'T MOVE! WHAT IF A THIEF COMES?!
THEN WHAT ARE YOU HERE FOR?
I'M YOUR BODY-GUARD.
OH, I'M SURE YOU'RE GREAT AT THAT!
FORGET IT! I'M OUTTA HERE!
だっ!!
AUGH! WAIT!
ぐもおおおお…
ARE YOU JUST GOING TO LEAVE ME HERE TO WITHER AND DIE?
UH, UM, OH, FINE...
"WITHER?" SO YOU ARE A FLOWER, AREN'T YOU OLD MAN?
OH, I'M NOT OLD YET.
WHY WON'T YOU JUST TELL ME IF YOU'RE A FLOWER OR NOT?

"Afterwords"

IT'S BEEN A YEAR SINCE RAVE STARTED.
I THINK IT'S DONE WELL SO FAR... I'VE
NEVER WORKED ON THE SAME JOB FOR
MORE THAN A YEAR BEFORE.

IN SCHOOL, I WORKED MANY DIFFERENT PART TIME
JOBS. IN OTHER WORDS, I LOSE INTEREST
VERY QUICKLY.

I DIDN'T EVEN HAVE THE PATIENCE TO BE AN
ASSISTANT FIRST. I JUMPED RIGHT INTO BEING AN
ACTUAL MANGA ARTIST.

A YEAR AGO, I NEVER THOUGHT THAT RAVE WOULD
CONTINUE ON FOR SO LONG. AND IT'S ALL THANKS TO
YOU! YOU, THE ONES READING THIS BOOK RIGHT NOW.
THANK YOU SO MUCH FOR ALL OF YOUR
ENCOURAGEMENT!

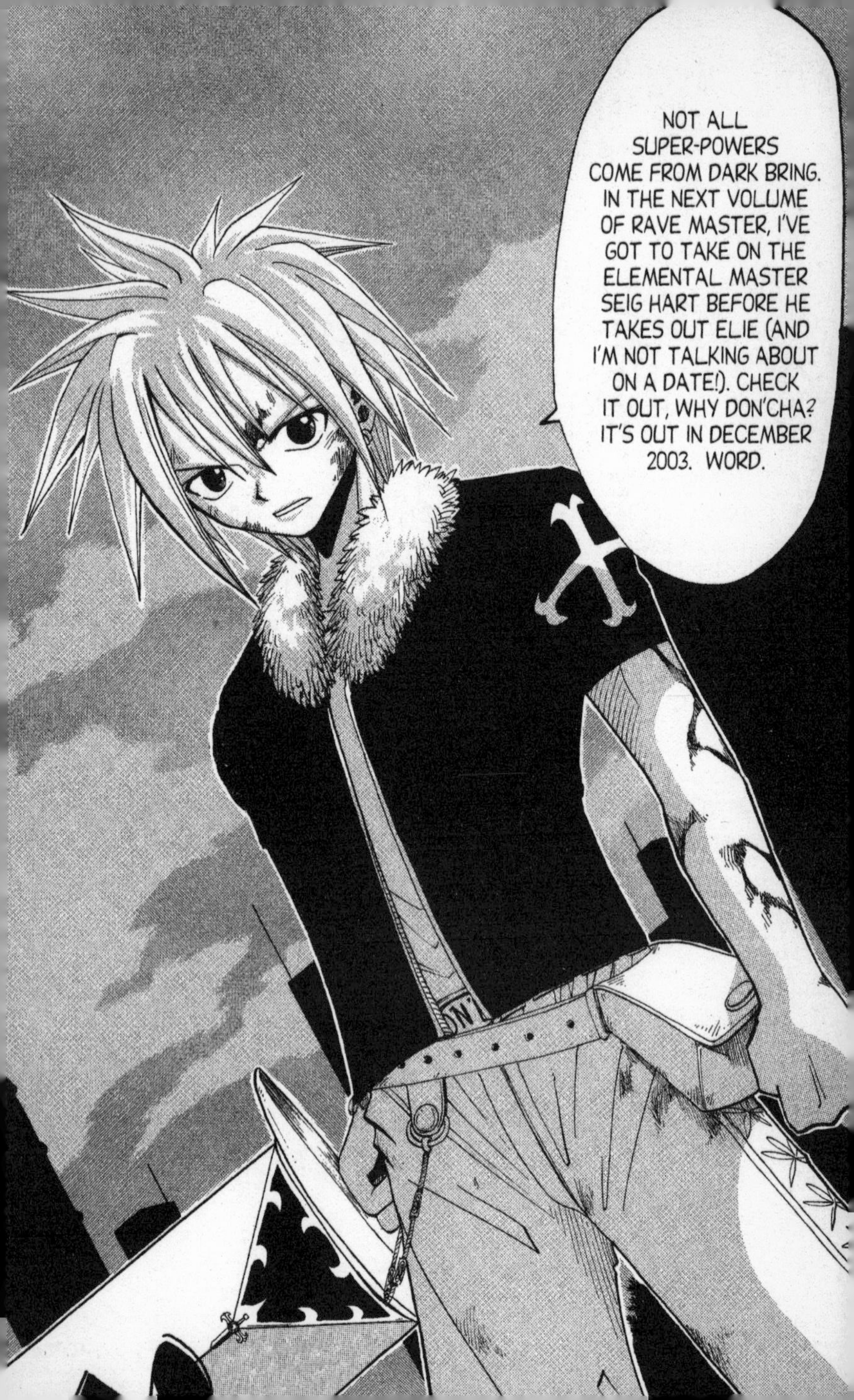
NOT ALL SUPER-POWERS COME FROM DARK BRING. IN THE NEXT VOLUME OF RAVE MASTER, I'VE GOT TO TAKE ON THE ELEMENTAL MASTER SEIG HART BEFORE HE TAKES OUT ELIE (AND I'M NOT TALKING ABOUT ON A DATE!). CHECK IT OUT, WHY DON'CHA? IT'S OUT IN DECEMBER 2003. WORD.

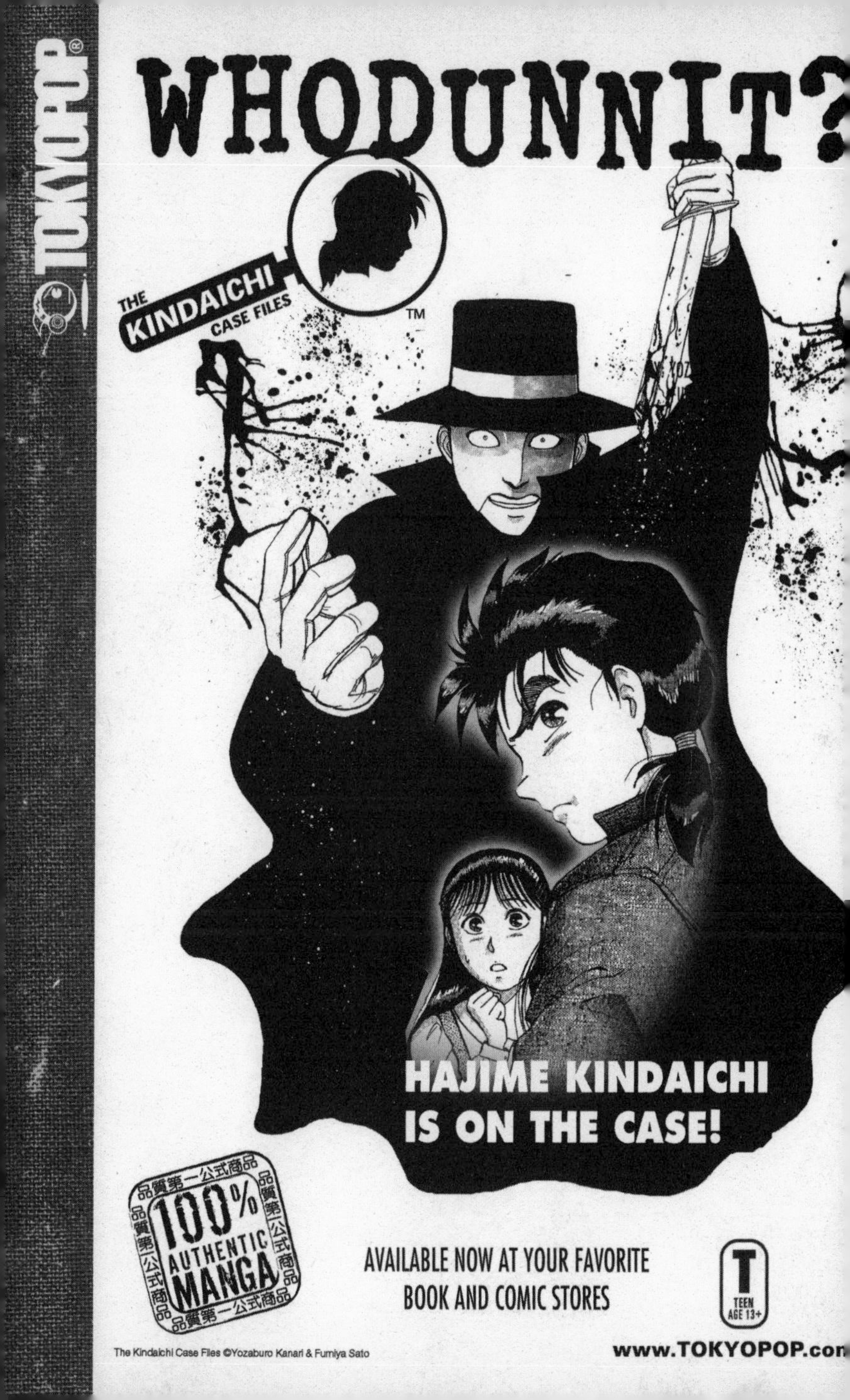

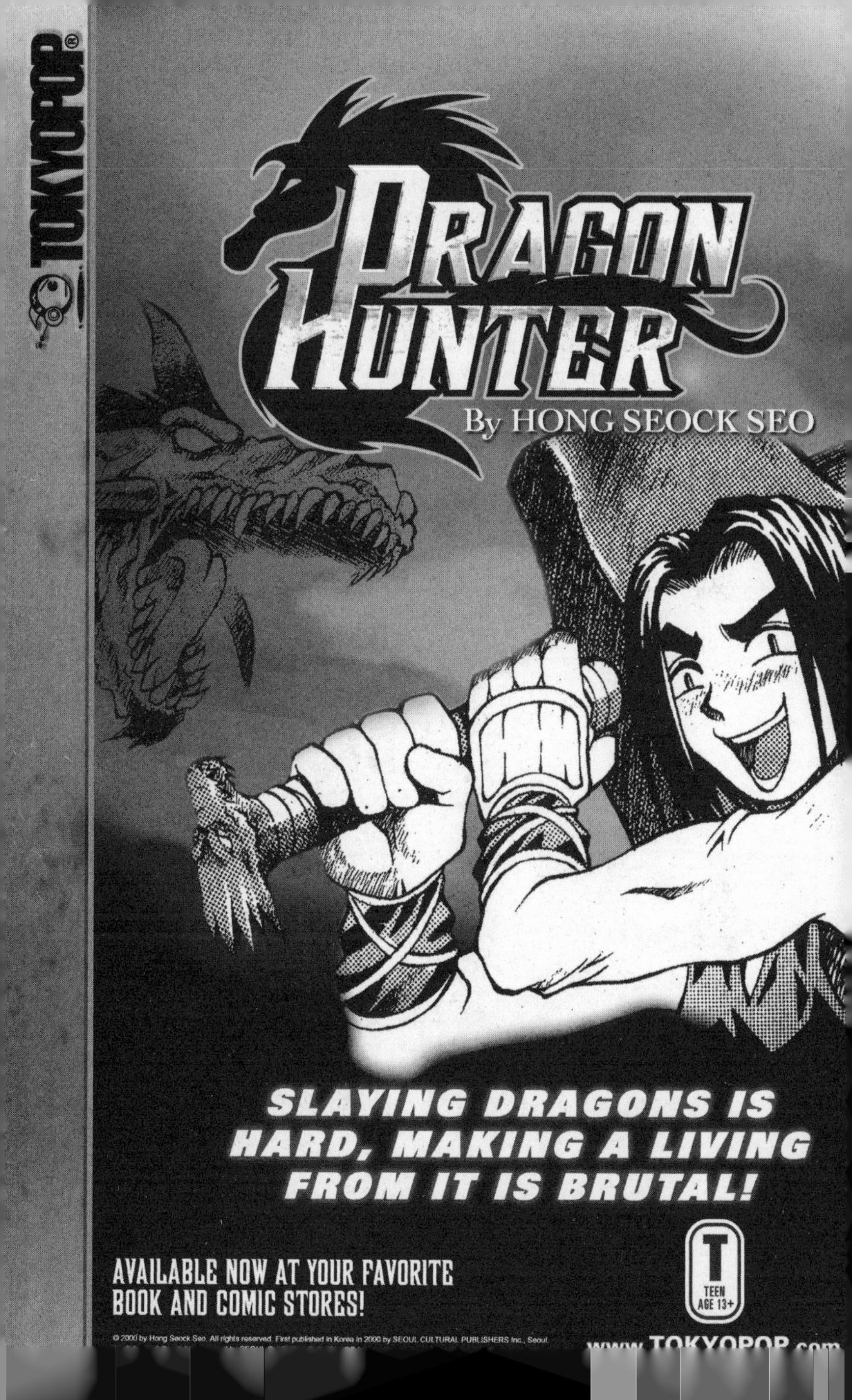
TOKYOPOP
DRAGON HUNTER
By HONG SEOCK SEO
SLAYING DRAGONS IS HARD, MAKING A LIVING FROM IT IS BRUTAL!
AVAILABLE NOW AT YOUR FAVORITE BOOK AND COMIC STORES!
T
TEEN AGE 13+
© 2000 by Hong Seock Seo. All rights reserved. First published in Korea in 2000 by SEOUL CULTURAL PUBLISHERS Inc., Seoul.
www.TOKYOPOP.com

STOP!

This is the back of the book.
You wouldn't want to spoil a great ending!

This book is printed "manga-style," in the authentic Japanese right-to-left format. Since none of the artwork has been flipped or altered, readers get to experience the story just as the creator intended. You've been asking for it, so TOKYOPOP® delivered: authentic, hot-off-the-press, and far more fun!

DIRECTIONS

If this is your first time reading manga-style, here's a quick guide to help you understand how it works.

It's easy… just start in the top right panel and follow the numbers. Have fun, and look for more 100% authentic manga from TOKYOPOP®!